909.04
B43t

126215

DATE DUE			

TRIAL AND ACHIEVEMENT

Currents in Jewish History

LIBRARY OF JEWISH KNOWLEDGE
Geoffrey Wigoder, General Editor of the Series

The Bible and Civilization
Biblical Archaeology
The Jews of the United States
Kabbalah
What Does Judaism Say About. . . ?
Trial and Achievement—Currents in Jewish History
Economic History of the Jews
Great Conflicts in Judaism
Jewish Thinkers
Jewish Concepts and Values

Library of Jewish Knowledge

TRIAL AND ACHIEVEMENT
Currents in Jewish History
(from 313)

H. H. BEN-SASSON

CARL A. RUDISILL LIBRARY
LENOIR RHYNE COLLEGE

KETER PUBLISHING HOUSE JERUSALEM LTD.

909.04
B43π
126215
Sept 1983

Copyright © 1974 by Keter Publishing House Jerusalem Ltd.
P. O. Box 7145, Jerusalem, Israel
All rights reserved, including the right to reproduce
this book or portions thereof in any form.

Cat. No. 51071
SBN 7065 1420 3

Designed by Amnon Ken-Dror
Printed in Israel

CONTENTS

INTRODUCTION

The starting point of this book is approximately midway through the course of Jewish history. "The first half" of Jewish history started about the 14th century B.C.E. (the wanderings of the families of the Patriarchs), and its broad area of influence was the Fertile Crescent of the Near East, including Egypt. The more specific arena in which the nation developed was Erez Israel — the Land of Israel (since Roman domination known also as Palestine). The penetration of Hellenism into the region extended the horizons of Jewish experience, bringing the Jews into contact with almost all Mediterranean lands and even further, in all directions. From the third century B.C.E. Jewish history and creativity were in contact with almost the entire Hellenistic (and from the second century B.C.E., with the Hellenistic-Roman) sphere of influence.

The Jewish Diaspora grew steadily and became the periphery of national development. While the center in Erez Israel and the huge concentration of Jews in the land of Mesopotamia and its neighboring regions remained predominantly agricultural up to the midpoint mentioned, the Diaspora of the Roman-Hellenistic world became progressively urban in its distribution and its occupational structure.

From the third century B.C.E., the Diaspora recruited from the Jewish population in the Land of Israel was augmented by the proselytization of masses of gentiles, who flocked to the Jewish faith, allegiance, and nationhood. Under these circumstances the spread was seen as a national gain, a function of the nation's dynamic strength. The first century Alexandrian philosopher, Philo, wrote: "For no single country can contain the Jews because of their multitude, and for this reason they inhabit the most extensive and wealthiest districts in Europe and Asia . . . , and while they regard the Holy City as their mother-city, in which is founded and consecrated the temple of the most high God, yet they severally hold that land as their fatherland which they have obtained by inheritance from fathers and grandfathers and great-grandfathers and still more remote ancestors for their portion to dwell in, in which they are born and reared. Into some of these they came at the very moment of their foundation, sending a colony to do a favor to the founders" (*In Flaccum,* edited and translated by H. Box (1939), paras. 45–46, p. 17). This conception of the Jewish dispersion became unacceptable in the circumstances created by the destruction of Jerusalem and of the Temple in 70 C.E., especially since, after the Bar Kokhba revolt (132–135), the exile was a polemical "asset" in Christian campaigns against Jewry.

Almost from the outset, Jewish existence was distinguished by its strong, well-articulated, and particular historical consciousness, initially transmitted only in oral tradition, but committed to writing at a very early stage of Jewish creativity. As a result of the impact of this historical consciousness on European culture, European ideas on ancient Egypt and Mesopotamia were dominated by Jewish traditions until the late 18th century when they were transformed by archaeological discoveries.

Monotheism and the attitude it engenders to humanity under the transcendent God, to time and the cosmos, to forms and modes of life and its scale of values have molded the Jewish spirit in all its various manifestations as transmitted in the Bible and, since Hellenistic times, also in other forms of Jewish literary activity. The stamp of monotheism and of associated conceptions and images is deeply engraved in biblical historiography, in the apodictic law, and, somewhat later in the development of forms — in the teaching and vision of prophesy.

Securely anchored in the relationship of Covenant that God made with Israel, Jewish national and religious sense is proud of the election of a tiny people to be God's lot and of being chosen by Him to carry the burden of His will as expressed in human activity. In its primary message, the Covenant-election structure knows little of material ascendancy; nor does it glorify earthly greatness. Jewish tradition, nourished in this structure, remembers that its people were not native to the land that became the land of its fathers. It tells at length of the humble comings and goings of the Patriarchs as strangers in this land. It stresses the sojourn in the "House of Bondage" in Egypt, and the "forty years" wanderings in the wilderness as the origins and the circumstance of the molding of the collective identity of the people and of its collective meeting with the one and only God, and acceptance of His Torah.

The elected people presents its fate and achievements as the work of human choice, endeavor, and daring, under and thanks to divine guidance. Alien status, serfdom, and the desert were given to it from the outset, and by external forces — by accident of birth and birthplace, and by the might of Pharaoh to whose serfdom they were driven by hunger. Pride of their own land, freedom, and town dwelling were attained and enjoyed by exercise of will, initially by the uprooting of the patriarch Abraham from his native soil and family circle to go to his destination. Freedom came after bondage, snatched from it. Jewish tradition sees the sojourn in the desert as a kind of long vacation from ordinary economic and even political life. It was devoted by God to the preparation of His chosen people to face a sown land and normal economic and political activity.

The triumph of sovereign human will was formulated by this tiny people through centuries of life in a small country lying on the highway of the politics, armies, culture systems, and art forms of the mighty and competing empires of Egypt, Assyria, the Hittites, Babylonia, as well as scores of smaller nations and principalities — all polytheistic. In this environment Jewish society and culture took up a stance of conscious and unequivocal opposition. "When we read in Psalm 19 that 'the heavens declare the glory of God; and the firmament showeth His handiwork' we hear a voice which mocks the beliefs of Egyptians and Babylonians. The heavens which were to the psalmist but a witness of God's greatness, were to the Mesopotamians the very majesty of godhead . . . To the Egyptians the heavens signified the mystery of the divine mother . . . In Egypt and Mesopotamia the divine was comprehended as immanent; the gods were in nature . . . The God of the psalmist and the prophets was not in nature. He transcended nature and transcended, likewise, the realm of mythopoeic thought. It would seem that the Hebrews, no less than the Greeks, broke with the mode of speculation which had prevailed up to their time" (H. & H.A. Frankfort, "The Emancipation of Thought from Myth," in: *Before Philosophy* (1949), 237).

Whatever one thinks about the very concept of "the realm of mythopoeic thought," one has to admit that Jewish thought indeed dared to oppose its world of the divine and of nature to that of polytheism (including that of the Greeks), in all the aspects that Frankfort listed, and more. Jewish opposition touched the domain of creative imagination. "It needs an effort of the imagination to realize the shattering boldness of a contempt for imagery, at the time and in the particular historical setting, of the Hebrews. Everywhere religious fervor not only inspired verse and rite but also sought plastic and pictorial expression. The Hebrews, however, denied the relevancy of the 'graven image'; the boundless could not be given form, the unqualified could not be offended by a representation, whatever the skill and devotion that went into its making" (*ibid.,* 242).

In another field of human endeavor, where the sacral and divine merged with the political and social, Jewish tradition again "heretically" and fearlessly broke the ancient and hallowed nexus, shaping its own mode of culture, radically different from the engulfing environment. The king of Egypt was a living god; in the towns of Mesopotamia an earlier "democracy" had given way, long before the appearance of the Jewish body-politic, to the rule of kings who were sacred stewards of the gods. Jewish tradition stood united on the human character of both the royal office and the royal person. There was a pronounced current of opinion that opposed the very idea of kingship. It was undoubtedly nourished by tribal traditions and by the memory of the sporadic and charismatic leadership of the "Judges" who had risen to deliver the people when oppressed. Yet, the bitter diatribe against kingship as essentially rapacious and tyrannical contained in "the law of the king" (II Samuel, ch. 8), is not only a horrified reaction of free men to the practice and spirit of sacral, polytheistic kingship, but expresses, in its intensity, the fear of having to worship living "graven images" on the throne. This fear and abhorrence go far to explain the revolts led by prophets against kings and dynasties in the northern kingdom of Israel. In southern Judea kingship was invested with divine sanction and reverence given to it as a sacral institution, which was evidenced in particular in the psalms and in many prophetic tales and utterances, but without giving up the insistence on its humanity. Biblical historiography depicts kings "warts and all"; their human weaknesses and failures are not hidden. It is almost "secular," and certainly irreverent, in its search for all too human passions and mistakes in judgment as motivations and explanations of events and personalities (on the basic assumption of prophecy about the good and the bad in the eyes of the Lord). This historiography appears both very searching, viewed from the modern angle, and utterly blasphemous and libelous, viewed from the angle of the fulsome royal inscriptions of Egypt or of the Babylonian royal chronicles, which never mention defeat or mistake. Jews have always insisted on a human savior, destined to be a ruler and leader of men.

The exiles from Jerusalem and Judah, with some elements of those exiled earlier from Israel, held on to their religious, cultural, and national identity in captivity, on Babylonian soil in the sixth century B.C.E. This was largely due to the anti-material vein in Jewish religion and culture. The exiles were also constantly fortified by the historical tradition about the origins of Israel − a tradition asserting that a house of bondage in an alien land may be formative and purifying in the long run. This was linked with a political view that saw not kingship, but people, as the be-all of social existence. Thus, a new structure of human allegiance was forged − to God, without sacrifice and temple; to nation, without land and state. This was at first only a short interlude. Cyrus the Persian became the redeemer who returned to their soil the group that was yearning to leave "the waters of Babylon" to return to their ravaged land and the ruins of their city. The exiles who returned to Jerusalem first reconstructed not the shattered kingdom, but an autonomous province, linked with its diaspora as a spiritual and ritual center to an increasingly dispersed, yet united, nation.

Insofar as we have knowledge of events and creativity under Persian domination from the sixth century B.C.E. (and indeed this is extremely scanty to the extent that some consider these centuries to have been a happy period devoid of history), a gradual and peaceful interpenetration of concepts and ways of life took place between the Jews and surrounding nations and cultures. When Hellenism came to rule, this trend at first continued, under the Ptolemies of Egypt, coupled with an even more intensive interpenetration of life mores and culture, as evidenced in the papyri concerning Judea, in the wisdom preached by Ben Sira, and in the semi-legendary traditions on the Septuagint translation of the Bible into Greek.

The Seleucid ruler Antiochus Epiphanes (reigned 175–163 B.C.E.) put to severe test the social entity of Judea, when he attempted, in conjunction with a group of hellenized priests at Jerusalem, to impose Hellenism, as life-style and worship pattern, on Judea and reconstituted Judaism. The challenge brought forth the response of the successful Maccabean revolt which gave independence to Judea. The success of Hellenism led to the breakup of most ancient societies of the Fertile Crescent. This could take place in such long-established structures only because in the society and culture that were nurtured under Persian overlordship there began the disintegration of the bond of unity between the vast majority of the people and their elite leadership circles which continued at a vastly accelerated rate under the Ptolemies and even more under the Seleucids. Around Judea the lower strata were abandoned by their leading circles. Ancient tradition became degraded to low-class "folklore." Hellenism stamped all higher, official, cult and culture with its character. This was forestalled in the Maccabean revolt by those social and cultural forces that brought forth martyrdom, guerilla warfare, and eventually the state, society, and problems of the Hasmoneans. The Jews too had their fair share of hellenization; there were social unrest, political revolts, religious splits, and the reassertion of the ancient anti-royalist spirit. But all this turmoil, creative in many fields in its own way, now occurred within the matrix of respected and prevalent Jewish tradition.

When Rome became the conqueror and upholder of Hellenism in the east (its armies conquered Judea in 63 B.C.E.), it clashed with this united nation and steadfast culture. The Jews were to become the only people in the east that frequently revolted against Roman might. The great revolt of the Jews (66–70 C.E.) was preceded and prepared by a messianic ferment, out of which early Christianity was also formed. The revolt can be properly seen, in the grandeur and carnage of its uncompromising fight unto death and suicide of its warriors, only as an ardent messianic movement.

From the Exile to Babylon and the return to Zion, through quiet penetration of culture and mores and through the fire and storm of the early Maccabean days and later in resistance to Rome and rising messianic vision, Jewish faith, culture, and society went through many transformations. Prophecy gave way to the modes of legal and moral discourse. At first sight this seems to be a sudden transformation, unheralded by precedents, but if the view (expressed by Albright) is accepted that the great prophets of First Temple days derived their rhetoric and poetic fervor for the sake of justice and peace for the weak and downtrodden from their function as pleaders at the courts, in a role somewhat similar to that of the ancient philosophers of Greece, then there was a seed of change for the new mood within the old field of activity. Historiography was rewritten from a priestly point of view in the "work of the Chronicler." Social justice was demanded, discussed, and achieved on much more prosaic and less utopian terms from the days of Nehemiah. Later came historiography on a hellenistic model, whether practised by Jews of the Diaspora or in Judea (e.g., the Books of the Maccabees, the works of Josephus). As the society and court of late Hasmonean days did not come up to idealistic expectancies, groups of Jews sought models of exemplary life built on the voluntary association of elite moralistic and religious groups. They tended to leave the cities and go to the Judean desert; they organized their economy on communal lines; many of them tended to celibacy. Documents discovered lately have shed new light on the life of such groups, known as Essenes. Apocalypse took over with phantasy where prophecy vacated. Legal thought and schools became more and more central and prolific. In sum, while politically and messianically "storm and enthusiasm" prevailed, religious and legal thought, (even apart from historiography or the great Jewish-hellenistic system of exegesis and philosophy developed by Philo of Alexandria) takes on more rational tones of feeling and discourse; the sage begins to dominate leadership and expression.

The Jews came to the period of "the second 17 centuries of Jewish history" dealt with in the following essays after a long series of trials and errors in leadership — charismatic and sporadic "Judges" (resembling the leadership under the first Maccabees and under the messianic figures of the days of response to the Roman challenge) inspired prophesy, often revolutionary; sacral priesthood, in particular in the High Priests under Persian, Hellenistic, and Roman overlordship; institutionalized charisma of royal dynasties, the Davidic and Hasmonean in particular. Last but not least, they learned to rely more and more on a leadership that came from intellectual ability, study, and learning joined to exemplary life.

From "the first half of their history" they also brought the memory of being a nation that "dwells lonely" amidst the nations. Isolated opposition to a polytheistic world became intensified to the point of defiant revolt with the challenge of the imposition of Hellenism by Antiochus Epiphanes in the second century B.C.E. Facing Roman might two centuries later, Jewish revolt took on the glow of messianic fervor. This hope for a better world in "the Kingdom of God" animated Jewish uprising not only in the Judean center. In the second century C.E., under Trajan, it burst out in the revolt of the Diaspora of Cyrenaica, Egypt, and Cyprus. In 132–135 Jews fought to the death under the messianic leadership of Bar Kokhba at Bethar, near Jerusalem. This people cleaving to its ancient identity and traditions continued to oppose idolatry, in which they included belief in an incarnated God-Messiah. Out of their radical conception of the absolute transcendence of the Divine and of the corresponding total response of man to it both as a nation and as individuals, Jews refused to believe in a suffering individual as the saving God. They rejected the concomitant concept of the contamination by "original sin" that renders man incapable of saving himself, but for the grace of the sacrifice of an incarnated and suffering God-Messiah.

The essays in this book, which are derived from my contributions to the *Encyclopaedia Judaica,* deal with Jewish history as affected by the rise of secularism, and with Jewish solutions and reaction to these challenges as well as with internal developments. Other essays deal with segments of Jewish thought and institutions. In several it has been considered advisable to trace in greater detail roots and antecedents in "the first 17 centuries." Most remain within the limits of "the second half of Jewish history," still in vigorous progress.

GLOSSARY

Aggadah, name given to those sections of Talmud and Midrash containing homilectic expositions of the Bible, stories, legends, folklore, anecdotes or maxims. In contradistinction to *halakhah*.

Agudat Israel, political party seeking to preserve Orthodoxy by adherence to *halakhah* as the principle governing Jewish life and society.

Aliyah, immigration to Erez Israel.

Anusim, persons compelled by pressure to abjure Judaism and adopt a different faith.

Ashkenaz, name applied generally in medieval rabbinic literature to N.W. Europe (initially to Rhine area).

Ashkenazi(m), German or West-, Central-, or East European Jews and their descendants.

Av bet din, title given to communal rabbis as heads of the religious courts.

Baraita, statement of *tanna* not found in the Mishnah.

Bet din, rabbinic court of law.

Bet midrash, place for higher rabbinic learning.

Bund, Jewish socialist non-Zionist party founded in Russia.

Cantonists, Jewish adolescents conscripted under harsh circumstances to czarist army.

Converso(s), term applied in Spain and Portugal to converted Jews, and sometimes more loosely to their descendants.

Dayyan, member of rabbinic court.

Dunam, unit of land area (1,000 sq. m., c. ¼ acre), used in Israel.

Exempla, legends or anecdotes from the lives of the sages to suggest emulation as instruction.

Frankists, followers of 18th-century pseudo-messiah Jacob Frank.

Galut, "exile," the condition of the Jewish people in dispersion.

Gaon (pl. *geonim*), head of academy in post-talmudic period, especially in Babylonia.

Habad, hasidic movement with intellectual attraction founded by Shneur Zalman of Lyady.

Haganah, clandestine Jewish organization for armed self-defense in Erez Israel under the British Mandate, which eventually became the basis for the Israel army.

Hakham, title of rabbi of Sephardi congregation.

Halakhah, an accepted decision in rabbinic law; parts of the Talmud concerned with legal matters.

Halukkah, system of financing the maintenance of Jewish communities in Erez Israel by collections made abroad.

Hasidei Ashkenaz, medieval pietist movement among the Jews of Germany.

Haskalah, "Enlightenment"; movement for spreading modern European culture among Jews, c. 1750–1880.

Herem, rabbinic ban of excommunication.

Huppah, marriage canopy.

Irgun Zevai Le'ummi (I.Z.L.), underground Jewish organization in Erez Israel founded in 1931.

Jewish Agency, international, non-governmental body whose aims are to assist and encourage Jews throughout the world to help in the development and settlement of Erez Israel.

Jizya, poll tax levied on unbelievers in the Muslim world as the price of the free exercise of their religion.

Kabbalah, the Jewish mystical tradition.

Kahal, autonomous Jewish community board.

Kallah, the months of Elul and Adar when large gatherings assembled to study in the Babylonian academies.

Kashrut, Jewish dietary laws.

Kazyonny ravvin, title of officials elected by the Jewish communities of Russia between 1857 and 1917, in accordance with the instructions of the government.

Kevuzah, small commune of pioneers constituting an agricultural settlement in Erez Israel (evolved later into kibbutz).

Kharāj, land tax in lieu of military service imposed on Jews in Moslem world.

Kibbutz, larger-size commune constituting a settlement in Erez Israel, based mainly on agriculture but engaging also in industry.

Kiddush ha-Shem, martyrdom in act of strict integrity in support of Judaic principles.

Kinot, lamentation dirges for fast days.

Kohen, Jews of priestly (Aaronide) descent.

Kolel, (1) community in Erez Israel of persons from a particular country or locality, often supported by their fellow countrymen in the Diaspora; (2) institution for higher Torah study.

Kristallnacht, organized destruction of synagogues, Jewish homes, and shops, accompanied by mass arrests of Jews, which took place in Germany and Austria under the Nazis in the night of Nov. 9–10, 1938.

Landsmannschaften, immigrant benevolent associations formed and named after its members' birthplace or East European residence, for mutual aid, hometown aid, and social purposes.

Lohamei Herut Israel (Lehi), anti-British armed underground organization in Palestine, founded in 1940.

Magen David, the six-pointed star, which became a widespread Jewish symbol.

Maggid, popular preacher.

Marranos, descendants of Jews in Spain and Portugal whose ancestors had been converted to Christianity under pressure but who secretly observed Jewish rituals.

Mashgi'ah, spiritual master and supervisor in a *yeshivah*.

Maskil, adherent of the *Haskalah* movement.

Mishnah, earliest codification of Jewish Oral Law (third century).

Mitnaggedim, opponents of Ḥasidism in Eastern Europe.

Mitzvah, biblical or rabbinic injunction.

Mizrachi, religious Zionist movement founded in 1902.

Moshav, smallholders' cooperative agricultural settlement in Israel.

Musar, traditional ethical literature.

Nagid, head of the Jewish community in Muslim countries in the Middle Ages.

Nasi, president of the Sanhedrin; he was also the spiritual head and, later, political representative of the Jewish people; later, the patriarch of the Jews.

Nili, pro-British spying organization that operated in Palestine, 1915–17.

Ostjuden, Jews from Eastern Europe, especially those who came from there to Germany.

Parnas, chief synagogue functionary, subsequently an elected lay leader.

Piyyut, Hebrew liturgical poetry.

Rebbe, teacher or ḥasidic rabbi.

Rosh Yeshivah, head of talmudic academy.

Rosh Ha-Shanah, the Jewish New Year.

Savoraim, Jewish scholars in Babylonia; c 500–700.

Seliḥot, penitential prayers.

Semikhah, rabbinic ordination conferring authority to render decisions in matters of ritual and law.

Sephardi(m), Jews of Spain and Portugal and their descendants.

Servi camerae regis, "servants of the king's chamber," definition of the status of the Jews in Christian Europe in the Middle Ages.

Shabbateans, adherents of the 17th-century pseudo-messiah Shabbetai Ẓevi.

Sheḥitah, ritual slaughtering of animals.

Shekel, the fee and card of Zionist membership.

Shtetl, Jewish small-town community in Eastern Europe.

Shulḥan Arukh, the definitive code of Jewish law.

Takkanah, regulations supplementing the law of the Torah; regulations governing the internal life of communities and congregations.

Talmid ḥakham, scholar of Jewish teachings, sage.

Talmud, compendium of discussions in the Mishnah by generations of scholars and jurists in many academies over several centuries.

Tannaim, rabbinic teachers of mishnaic period.

Tefillin, phylacteries.

Torah, the Pentateuch; entire body of traditional Jewish teaching and literature.

Wissenschaft des Judentums, movement in Europe beginning in the 19th century for scientific study of Jewish history, religion, and literature.

Yeshivah, talmudical academy.

Yevsektsiya, Jewish section of the propaganda department of the Russian Communist Party, 1918–30.

Yishuv, the Jewish community in Erez Israel.

Ẓaddik, ḥasidic leader.

Zohar, mystical commentary on the Pentateuch; main textbook of Kabbalah.

Part One

THE COURSE OF
JEWISH HISTORY

1

The Reshaping of Forces and Circumstances (4th to 7th Centuries)

At the beginning of the fourth century the vast majority of the Jewish people was dispersed in Mediterranean countries, a distribution which continued for many centuries afterward. Throughout their dispersion Jews were not only attached spiritually and emotionally to Erez Israel, but that country still harbored an important concentration of Jewish population. The great concentration of Jews in the "Persian" empire (Babylonia in Jewish historical-geographical nomenclature) flourished under the leadership of the exilarch,[1] increasing in numbers and with a prosperous economy which had a broad agricultural stratum and some involvement in commerce and crafts. In the Roman Empire the vast Jewish Diaspora was concentrated in great numbers in important cities, occupied as traders and craftsmen. The centers of the empire, Alexandria, Antioch, and Rome, were also essential to Jewish life as they were central to the empire. The so-called Edict of Milan, issued in June 313, was couched in terms expressing general tolerance and coexistence of religions; in reality it was the first step toward establishing the dominance of Christianity. Its declared intention was to grant *et Christianis et omnibus* freedom of religion to each person according to his choice. The definitions there of divinity fit monotheistic religions as well as an enlightened paganism. Deity is described as *Summa Divinitas* ("the Supreme Divinity") or *Divinitas in sede caelesti* ("Divinity in the heavenly throne"). The decree declares expressly that it was not designed to injure any person either in status or in religion. The sentiments to a large extent express a diplomatic softening for pagans and, for Jews, a gilding of the bitter pill of the beginning of Christian domination. However, they also reflect an existing mood in the relationship between the religions at that time that could have augured a future of real coexistence but in the event was destroyed by the pact between the Christian Church and the Roman Empire.

The interpenetration of modes of existence and conceptual patterns of the

---

[1]   Lay head of Jewry in Babylonia (i.e., Persian and Parthian empire) from 2nd cent. C.E.: in the ninth to 12th centuries head of Jewry in the Moslem lands; accepted as Davidic prince by all Jews of the time.

3

environment is evident in Jewish life in the fourth to sixth centuries. The decoration of synagogues, in both Erez Israel and in the Diaspora, shows readiness to use pictorial art, and even representation of human and animal figures, for synagogue murals and mosaics. It also demonstrates that pagan symbols had lost their idolatrous implications for the Jews, who took them over almost without change to adorn their own houses of worship. Thus a trend, evident notably at the synagogue of Dura Europos in Syria (see illustration) developed and became increasingly reflected in Jewish life at this time. The symbolic pictography and inscriptions on Jewish funerary reliefs also show, in both Erez Israel and the Diaspora, the same assimilation of pagan elements. The other side of this process, and parallel to it, was a continuing movement of proselytes to Judaism, the presence of Jewish elements in pagan magic papyri, and above all, the entry of many central Jewish elements into the pagan world, which made possible its Christianization. Without the strong appeal of specific Jewish images, concepts,

Representation of a human figure on the walls of the synagogue at Dura Europos, accepted as representing leadership and teaching in Israel: Moses or Ezra, wrapped in a *tallit*, reading the Law to the people.

and ways of life to many pagans, it is impossible to understand the sweeping success of Christianity.

This interpenetration, however, was not destined to become the framework of a social and political coexistence. The intense hatred generated during centuries of missionary propaganda and the fierce persecution to which it had been subjected caused the victorious Church in turn to adopt toward paganism the Jewish monotheistic stance at its harshest, and to employ in regard to Jews and Judaism the old popular pagan anti-Jewish animus, which developed into a tenet of dogmatic absolutism at its cruelest. The Church triumphant was suffering from the trauma of its treatment at the hand of the pagan empire. Both victorious and under shock, the *tertium gens* ("third party") formed by Christianity declined to confront Judaism on a basis of equality, and once achieving dominance took over all the potentialities and actualities of power with which to intensify division and persecution. This challenge, although the cause of much suffering, elicited a vital Jewish response in concentration on inner values and a refusal to continue the process of interpenetration. From the sixth century on, pagan decorative motifs are no longer to be found in synagogues, while painting of live figures for synagogue murals was abandoned for many centuries after that time.

During the fourth and fifth centuries the Jews in the Roman Empire both recognized and felt the effects of a sustained Christian effort to redefine their legal status, to blacken their image in the eyes of gentiles, and to reduce their standing in society. This policy was pursued with a curious combination of acute love-hatred toward the Jewish people and its history, and an even more acute fearfulness of Jewish competition for the spiritual allegiance of the disintegrating pagan world. Internal Christian dissensions in the fourth century added fuel to hatred of the Jews in a Church that was already divided on its conception of the Trinity, quarreling about theological definitions, even to the extent of hairsplitting, and unaccustomed to the use of force to impose its authority. It now began to turn to imperial powers of coercion on the one hand and to interference in state affairs on the other to provide the combined means and formula for working out the divine will in history. Striving to retain its newly acquired power, it regarded Arianism and other heresies that emerged in this early period as Judaizing attempts to undermine its precarious position. Jews were faced with an amalgam of denigratory propaganda and hostile legislation. This combination was to endure until the 18th century at least.

Christian Pressure and Propaganda

Already under the emperor Constantine I (306–337) laws were published forbidding the persecution of Jewish apostates to Christianity. In 339 Constantius II prohibited marriage between Jews and Christians, and the possession of Christian slaves by Jews. This last prohibition went far to undermine the economic structure of Jewish society, in agriculture in particular. At this period it was inconceivable to maintain any fair-sized agricultural unit without employing slaves, who were rapidly becoming Christianized.

A flicker of the old-type coexistence, this time with an anti-Christian emphasis and a pro-Jewish tendency, reemerged during the brief rule of Emperor Julian (361–363), regarded by Christians as "the apostate." His attempt to rebuild the Temple in Jerusalem, his respectful language in reference to Jews, and the rights he granted them were not only motivated by a wish to disprove the Christian contention that Judea had been obliterated with the rejection of Jesus, but were also actuated by esteem for a great Jewish past and for steadfastness in adhering to a religious historical course.

The Church and the Christian empire, alarmed but not sobered by the reemergence of paganism and its bid for an alliance with the Jews, crystallized the policy of obtaining laws against Jews and heretics. These were subsequently promulgated: " . . . in order that these dangerous sects which are unmindful of our times may not spread into life the more freely, in indiscriminate confusion. We ordain this law to be valid for all time . . . " (*Novella* 3 of Theodosius II, Jan. 31, 438). On this basis Jews were denied all civic offices and dignities because "we believe it is wrong that the enemies of the heavenly Majesty and of the Roman laws should become the executors of our laws, and that they, fortified by the authority of the acquired rank, should have the power to judge or sentence Christians, . . . as if they insult our faith . . . For the same reason we prohibit that any synagogue should rise as a new building" *(ibid.)*.

Hence, at this early stage, the foundations were laid for the conception that the holding of public office by a Jew constituted both an insult to Christianity and a danger to Christians. Of the two reasons cited, the first was prompted by the competition between religions still actual in the fifth century and the pride of victory. The second stemmed from suspicion of the character of the Jew who was seen as activated by base motives in dealing with other people. Thus a motivation was advanced for the principle that only if the Jews were humiliated and rendered powerless would Christianity and Christians be safe; on this principle Jews were barred from honors and public office in Christian states (and later in Muslim states) from the fifth until the 18th centuries. Although there were to be many exceptions to, and breaches of, this rule, these only proved its wide acceptance as amply evidenced down the centuries in the bitter opposition by the Church leadership to Jews holding positions of authority and in the consensus of popular opinion in Christian and Muslim society.

The change in legal status gained popular acceptance because of the consistency and virulence with which Church leaders preached hatred of the Jew. The eight anti-Jewish sermons delivered by John Chrysostom the Church Father in Antioch in 387 both reveal the existence of continuing good relationship at this time between parts of the general population and the Jews and instance the type of propaganda used by the Church Fathers to disrupt it. The sermons vilify the Jews, their synagogues, their way of life, and their motives of behavior at length and in scathing terms. St. Augustine had a deep historic sense of the vital force displayed by the Jewish people. Several times in his writings he returns to the mystery presented by the non-assimilation of a small people, separated from the rest of the population not only by its specific beliefs, but also by a detailed way of life, developing an individual culture, in an empire that was moving to increasing uniformity in all these respects. His conception of what the Jewish people might have been, and what under Christian dispensation it had become, emerges from his musings about the likely destiny of the Jews had they not constantly revolted against God, and finally rejected Jesus, and about the reason for their continued existence in the world:

"And if they had not sinned against Him, led astray by unholy curiosity as by some magic arts, falling away to worship idols and finally murdering the Christ, *they would have remained in the same kingdom, and if it did not grow in size, it would have grown in happiness.* As for their present dispersion through almost all the lands and peoples, it is by the providence of the true God, to the end that when the images, altars, groves, and temples of the false gods are everywhere overthrown, and the sacrifices forbidden, it may be demonstrated by the Jewish scriptures how this was prophesied long ago. Thus the possibility is avoided that, if read only in our books, the prophecy might be taken for our invention" (*City of God*, edited and translated by W.C. Greene, Book 4, 34 (1963), 129).

Augustine's assertion that a redeemed Jewish people would have remained happy and living as a separate nation in Ereẓ Israel was later remembered by few Christians. Both his assumptions, that the Jewish dispersion proved the truth of Christianity through the Holy Writ that is in Jewish possession, and that it was necessary to provide proof of the correctness of the biblical passages quoted by Christians from the text in Jewish hands to doubting infidels — neither Jewish nor Christian, but pagan — clearly indicate a situation of a triangle in which Judaism, Christianity, and paganism are confronted. Later on, his premises provided the theoretical formulation for Christian readiness to suffer Jews in their midst. Augustine's understanding of Psalms 59:12 (Vulgate 58:12) as relating to sufferance of the Jews, on the condition that they be visibly dispersed and humiliated, was widely quoted and applied in the Middle Ages.

At the same time that the church was preaching to its converted the dictum that the Jews continue to exist for the sake of Christianity as despiritualized guardians of a spiritual "Old Testament," the Jewish people were developing a great and fruitful new life of intellectual and social creativity. In about 359 a constant calendar was determined and formulated, thus basing sacred attitudes to time, its division, and purpose, on mathematical principles, and consummating a long process of Hellenistic cultural influence. The leadership provided by the patriarchate[2] and patriarchs through these difficult times, although frequently criticized, was on the whole successful and there was a productive period in both the Jewish and general cultural spheres. The patriarch Gamaliel b. Hillel maintained a regular correspondence with the great Antiochian rhetor Libanius over the last four decades of the fourth century showing points of contact between the great Jewish jurists and those of the Roman world.

Jewish creative and cultural activity was continuing at a time when a mob led by monks in 388 burned down the synagogue at Callinicum in Mesopotamia. Bishop Ambrose of Milan thereupon asserted the authority of the Church and overruled Emperor Theodosius I by insisting that the culprits should go unpunished. Also in this period Emperor Theodosius II and his ecclesiastical advisers attempted to deter Jews from worship by forbidding the erection of new synagogues. Jews reacted to this situation by recourse to both traditional and new solutions. The patriarchate was extinguished by imperial decree in 429. However Jewish leadership of the communities in the Roman empire continued in a less centralized but more successful form.

In Erez Israel the Jewish population held on to its soil and maintained its spirit of resistance by every means available, from the revolt in Galilee against Gallus in 351 up to the revolt in the reign of Emperor Heraclius and their alliance with the invading Persian armies in 614. In Babylonia the exilarchs were able to exercise their hegemony under more relaxed and stable conditions than those prevailing in the Roman and Christian sphere. But when a series of persecutions overtook the community in the second half of the fifth and the sixth centuries the exilarchs had the foresight to withdraw with their institutions to inaccessible regions and there to continue cultural activities and social leadership. In 495–502 the exilarch Mar Zutra II led a revolt, created a small Jewish state, and paid with his life for this attempt.

At the time of these events Jewish intellectual activity added a new dimension and prototype to the national literature. The academies of Erez Israel and Babylonia constituted a living forum for discussion of the tenets and implications of Jewish morals and Jewish law, continuing despite external humiliations and harassments. The redaction of the so-called Jerusalem Talmud

2   Head of the Jewish diaspora in the Roman Empire until fifth century; sacral authority within the frame of Jewish self-government.

took place in the second half of the fourth century. During the second half of the fourth century and throughout the fifth the redaction of the Babylonian Talmud was completed. Both Talmuds represent whole libraries of legal discussion and formulation — *halakhah* — and record fragments of moral and exegetical sermons — *aggadah*. The thoughts and efforts of numerous scholars are reticulated in them to form a protocol of the discussions, thus setting down a rich legacy for posterity and providing the exemplar for a specific mode of learning, of living, and of moral decision. The Talmuds became canonized in Jewish esteem alongside the Bible and the Mishnah — theoretically in a diminishing scale of sanctity. In practice, interpretation of the Talmud and the talmudic mode of discussion eventually dominated Jewish scholarship and set the pattern for Jewish modes of thought until modern times. After a short transitional period of creative activity by the *savora'im*,[3] the Talmuds were regarded as closed and canonized entities. Beside the Talmuds, there were in this period the amoraic *midrashim*[4]. These in technique bear close affinity to the writings of the Church Fathers, while in content and aims they represent a system of Jewish culture, its values and aspirations, and its defense against Christian attacks.

Redaction of the Talmuds

The degree and scale of Jewish influence on Muhammad and early Islam are much in dispute, but there is no denial of its existence and considerable significance. In the region of present-day Yemen, Semitic tribes became converted to Judaism and maintained a Jewish principality in Himyar that had close ties with the *nasi* at Tiberias. It was crushed by a coalition of Christian Byzantium and Ethiopia after a battle to preserve Judaism and with the death of the king Yūsuf dhu Nuwās in 525. These conversions were only part of Jewish creativity and cultural influence within early Arab society before Muhammad. There were also Jewish groups that exerted considerable influence on the Arab scene, partly through distinctly Arab modes of organization and life-style. Muhammad was greatly influenced by all these Jewish elements in Arabia. From early attempts at alliance with Jewish groups in Arabia — the so-called Jewish "tribes" — Muhammad turned savagely against them, and in a series of brutal wars and battles in the years 624 to 628 succeeded in either extirpating them or expelling them from Arabia. Awareness of these influences and of the alliances and wars of the past was important later in determining the attitude of Islam toward Jews.

3 Scholars who were considered as the link between the authority and mode of creativity of the *amoraim* (i.e., the sages whose teaching makes up the Babylonian Talmud) and that of the *geonim* (i.e., the heads of the academies under Moslem rule), c. sixth-seventh centuries.

4 Homiletic works that are composed mainly of exegesis on the Bible, legal discussions, and moral exhortation.

By the end of the sixth century two approaches toward the Jews were tried in
the Christian sphere. Emperor Justinian attempted to influence Judaism in a
missionary spirit, to interfere in the conduct of Jewish worship, and to direct the
Jews as to what they should retain or relinquish in their scriptures and beliefs. In
the preamble to his Novella 146 (Feb. 8, 553) he states expressly: "Necessity
dictates that when the Hebrews listen to their sacred texts they should not
confine themselves to the meaning of the letter, but should also devote their
attention to those sacred prophecies which are hidden from them, and which
announce the mighty Lord and Savior Jesus Christ." The post-biblical strata of
Jewish literature are to be excised: "The Mishnah, or as they call it the second
tradition [Deuterosis], we prohibit entirely . . . it is . . . but the handiwork of
man, speaking only of earthly things, and having nothing of the divine in it. But
let them read the holy words themselves, rejecting the commentaries" (as
translated by J. Parkes, *The Conflict of the Church and the Synagogue* (1961),
392–3).

Justinian's argumentation   against Deuterosis has a fundamentalist ring,
but the stress is on negation instead of a positive evaluation of the Bible. This
argumentative law is indeed the outcome of the perplexity of the Church in face
of the categoric rejections by the Jews of its message, in spite of centuries of
incitement against them, ·their humiliation and persecution. The emperor
supposed that only by the forcible removal of the layers of Jewish creativity
since the origin of Christianity – for that is intended by the forbidden
Deuterosis – which could not have come into being in a barren Judaism, would
Christianity penetrate by means of a "Biblicist" Judaism. The emperor failed in
his object – not only as many of his other strong-handed attempts had failed
because of the weakness of the empire in the late sixth century, but essentially
because the Jews remained consistently attached to the whole of their corpus of
scriptures and refused to become Jews according to Christian concepts. Not until
the 13th century was a similar approach again attempted, when a campaign was
launched against the Talmud, which also failed (see below).

At the end of the sixth century another attempt to eradicate the Jews in a
Christian country was begun in Visigothic Spain. With the changeover from
Arianism and the attempt to unite the country under Catholicism by King
Reccared I, compulsory conversion of Jews to Christianity became an integral
part of the policy of the Visigothic state. However, barehanded force proved no
more successful than Justinian's attempt at dictation.

Pope Gregory I at the end of the sixth century developed a different and
more enduring line of approach. In his many letters concerning Jews he
proposed to tempt them to Christianity even by offering fiscal alleviations in the
belief that if the first generation did not become fully fledged Christians the

second would become so. He thus authorized the use of economic pressure and reward to bring about Jewish apostasy. However, while insisting on strict maintenance of the status quo in respect of Jewish existence, he was vigilant in ensuring that Jews should not acquire any new rights or opportunities. He thus developed a practice which was in part based on application of the theory of Augustine and in part on a dogmatization of the various anti-Jewish laws of the later Roman emperors as incorporated in the Codes of Theodosius and Justinian. In his theoretical writings, Gregory views the Jewish way of life and Jewish identity as the arch-enemy of Christianity. Jacob here represents the gentiles, and Esau the Jews.

The sixth century also saw the reemergence of Jews in Western Europe north of the Pyrenees. The existence of a Jewish community at Cologne in 321 is already attested in an edict of Emperor Constantine. Discoveries of coins, and in the opinion of some scholars, also terra cotta figurines found at Treves (Trier), prove the presence of Jews — or at least of passing merchants — in several places in Western and Central Europe in the fourth century. However, there is no evidence of the continuance of these Jewish groups, or of the movement of individual Jewish merchants, in the disordered times of the barbarian invasions and the creation of the Germanic states in the late fourth and fifth centuries. South of the Pyrenees, in Arian Visigothic Spain and in the kingdom of Theodoric in Italy, Jews were to be found, living in relatively favorable conditions. The Arians did not simply adopt the attitude of the Catholic Church toward Jews; since individuals in these Arian Germanic states were regarded as subject either to the existing Roman law or the Germanic law of the conquerors, Jews were classified, under this definition, with the Romans. Procopius recounts (*De Bello Gothico,* 1, 5, 10.25) that the Jews of Naples courageously and stubbornly defended this city for Theodoric against the Byzantines in 536.

Western Europe

Though migration from a warmer southern climate to a colder northern one, and from an ancient and familiar cultural milieu to a new and uncivilized region is not usual, this was the direction taken by relatively many Jews during the sixth century when they appeared in the Catholic kingdom of the Franks in what is now France. They were attracted by the rare opportunities for enterprising merchants in the newly developing countries. Seen through the writings of Bishop Gregory of Tours, Jews were able to tempt bishops and princes with the spices and costly cloths they brought with them. In the second half of the sixth century there is mention of sizable communities, as at Clermont-Ferrand, Paris, and Marseilles, which had their own synagogue buildings — certainly not constructed in accordance with the requirements imposed by the Church — and stubbornly defended, sometimes to the death, their right to live as professing Jews. The figure of the Jew Priscus exemplifies the best in these groups: learned in the Bible, he disputed as an equal, and unafraid, with Bishop Gregory in the presence of King Chilperic about Judaism and Christianity. He died a martyr's death at Paris, having dispatched his son to safety in Marseilles. The Jewry of the kingdom is one of "mute Jewries" of Western Europe until the end of the tenth century, that have left no literary record; their culture and steadfastness under persecution are known only from Latin non-Jewish sources, and from enactments against them.

The Jewish Revolt in Erez Israel

On the eve of the appearance of Islam as a world power and third great monotheistic religion — the last throes of the disappearance of the old order of the classical world — Jews in Erez Israel again raised the standard of revolt in an attempt to reestablish Jewish rule in Erez Israel. Desperate through persecutions under Emperor Heraclius they rose in 614, joined the Persian armies then invading the country, and between 614 and 617 established Jewish rule in Jerusalem. Their failure and cruel suppression add to the character of this event in Jewish history as representing a last gleam of the classical constellations and one of the many harbingers of the new medieval situation.

2
Formative Times
(7th to 11th Centuries)

The conquest of the Persian empire by the Muslim forces obliterated polytheism as a political force within the entire horizon of Jewish existence. Jews had to accustom themselves to the situation that throughout "the whole world" monotheistic religions claiming the mantle of the Jewish faith were pursuing a consistent policy of derogation and humiliation toward the Jews. To the Christian clergy as a carrier of inculcation of hatred of the Jews in the masses was now added the Muslim clergy. On the other hand, the conquests of Islam reunified the vast majority of the Jewish people. By 712 Islam ruled from the borders of India to south of the Pyrenees, thus uniting under its sway more than 90% of the existing Jewish population. The success of the Muslims was seen by Jews as divine retribution for the evil and perfidy of Byzantium and Persia. The sudden change in the political order revived hopes for even greater changes that would bring about Redemption and the Messiah. It was not by accident that several militant Jewish messianic movements followed shortly on Islamic successes. Jerusalem was taken by the Arabs in 638. The Christian prohibitions on the entry of Jews to the Holy City were soon lifted. The attitude of the Muslims to the "People of the Book" was more favorable toward the Jews than had been that of the Christian rulers. The Muslims had much to learn from the Christian and Jewish infidels, while the existence of many religious groups other than Islam in the Muslim realm saved Jews living within its borders from the onus of being the main, frequently the sole, representatives of nonconformists there as they became in Christendom.

Under Islam

The Muslim conquest had far-reaching consequences for the Jewish economic and social structure. The first generation of Arab rulers knew little about agriculture, nor cared about it. They imposed a heavy burden on infidel farmers, not being concerned with the disastrous results. On the other hand, they respected trade and regarded the city as a favorable milieu for leading the good Muslim life. The military camps of the conquerors soon developed into cities. All this combined to draw Jews away from the villages and agriculture toward the developing towns and an appreciated occupation in trade. Their links with other Jews along the commercial routes in the vast empire worked in the same

13

direction, as did also the opportunities offered by the connections of Jews in Muslim countries for trading with their brethren in the Christian countries. In the lands taken from Byzantium, the new circumstances only completed a process of squeezing out Jews from agriculture that had been begun by the Christian denial of slave manpower to Jewish agricultural undertakings. In the former lands of the Persian Empire this was a relatively new process. By the end of the eighth century it had been more or less accomplished everywhere in the Muslim empire: although some Jewish individuals and groups remained attached to the soil despite unfavorable circumstances, the vast majority of the Jews became townspeople, and have retained this structure until the present.

Wherever a new city arose or an old one developed, Jews formed large and enterprising merchant and craftsmen communities, as in Kufa, Basra, and Baghdad in Iraq; in Cairo-Fostat and Alexandria, in Egypt; in Kairouan and Fez in North Africa; and in Córdoba and Toledo in Muslim Spain. Their occupations covered all the varieties found in the towns. Thus the foundation was laid for the variegated structure of Jewish economy and society in the Muslim city, which existed — with spatial and temporal modifications — up to the almost total liquidation of the Jewish communities in Muslim lands after the creation of the State of Israel.

In various regions of the Muslim Empire the lower strata of Jewish society were occupied in every kind of craft. An anti-Jewish writer in the ninth century, in what was certainly a tendentious one-sided view, could even regard certain of the coarser crafts as the main occupation of the Jews in Egypt. The upper stratum of Jewish society in the caliphate engaged in large-scale trade and in money-lending, sometimes even supplying organized and regular loans to the state. In the tenth century certain rich Jewish families were known as the court financiers, their security of tenure deriving to a large degree from the fact, well known to the caliph and his officials, that the huge loans advanced came not only out of the personal fortune of the Jewish banker, but out of amounts lent him by Jewish merchants of lesser means.

In Muslim Spain, as early as under the united Umayad caliphate (660–750), the position achieved by Ḥisdai ibn Shaprut demonstrates the rise of a Jewish official and merchant to political eminence mainly on the basis of his personal abilities and culture. This is even more strikingly exhibited in the 11th century in the person, culture, and career of Samuel ha-Nagid (Ibn Nagrela; 99–1056), a commander of Muslim armies in Spain, vizier of a Muslim king, great Hebrew poet, eminent talmudist, master of a fine Arabic style, mathematician, philosopher, and statesman — both as a theoretician and in practice — in an absolute state. Muslim Spain gave rise to many similar personalities and families, wholeheartedly Jewish, blending both Jewish and Greek-Arabic culture, and aristocratic in behavior and feeling. Grouped around them, and relying heavily on their munificence, were galaxies of poor poets and scholars devoted to their art and the pursuit of philosophy, often highly creative, like the famous Solomon ibn Gabirol. In Kairouan, North Africa, there flourished also under Fatimid rule (969–1171) a circle of physicians and scholars influential at court and leaders of their communities. In the Mediterranean seaports in the 10th to 12th centuries there was well organized Jewish trade, relying basically on written communications between merchants as well as the maintenance of well ordered books of trade and accounts and a well regulated merchant organization relying on Jewish law.

The successes of these high dignitaries and influential courtiers naturally ran counter to the basic Islamic attitude toward the Jews, to the legal status it was ready to grant them, and, above all, to popular sentiment. Samuel ha-Nagid, for example, was not only bitterly attacked by his political enemies – as he testifies abundantly in his poems – and vilified by scurrilous popular songwriters, but was also sharply assailed by the eminent Muslim philosopher and poet Ibn Hazm (Samuel's son Jehoseph fell victim (1066) to the pent-up hatred of the mob).

The basic Muslim attitude to infidels is set out in the so-called Covenant of Omar[5] formally ascribed to the year 637 but almost certainly formulated much later. The concept of the *ahl al-dhimma,* "the people of protection" – which comprised both Jews and Christians as deserving of the right to exist under Muslim rule as the *ahl al-Kitāb,* the "People of the Book" – provides for security of person and property, and permission to pursue religious worship and codes of behavior according to the law of the faith concerned, on condition of payment of fixed taxes to the caliph's treasury (one such tax taken automatically from the field area, did much to drive out Jews from agriculture) and under a set of rules ensuring the constant humiliation and isolation of the infidels by believers. Many of its humiliating conditions are taken over from old anti-Jewish laws of Christian origin, but they also contain certain detailed provisions stemming from conceptions and symbols of social prestige found in Muslim society. Sunni[6] rulers usually tended to apply these rules strictly to the majority of the Jews (and Christians). Shi'ite[7] rulers tended to be more capricious and offensive in their attitude. The Fatimid caliph of Egypt, al-Ḥakim bi-Amr Allah (996–1021),

---

5   The basic set of terms and conditions for the status and life of infidels and the People of the Scripture (i.e., the Jews and Christians); it is ascribed to the Caliph and represents the conditions and mentality of mid-eighth century.

6   The majority of the Moslems that followed the teaching and accepted the authority and legitimacy of the first Caliphs.

7   The minority opposition that accepted the authority and teaching of 'Ali, the son-in-law of the prophet, and of his descendants.

embarked on a systematic policy of humiliation of the Jews and Christians in the second half of his reign. Among his inventions can be included the badge of shame, later taken over by the Church in the fourth Lateran Council of 1215, for he compelled Jews to wear only black robes in public and to carry a wooden image of a calf (in memory of the calf which the Jews had worshiped in the desert). The constancy of the Muslim system of humiliation, coupled with freedom to exercise autonomy and opportunity to engage in most economic activities in the cities, is illustrated by both the relatively few exceptions made in favor of gifted infidels as well as by the relatively few sharp outbreaks of extreme governmental persecution or mob fury.

Intensifica-
tion of
Christian
Attitudes

Meanwhile, Christian society continued to develop, under the guidance of the Church, its pernicious hatred of the Jews. Though the upper ranks of the Church hierarchy accepted, both in theory and in practice, the relatively "mild" attitude toward the Jews of Augustine and Pope Gregory I, the lower ranks tended to be more consistent than their superiors and inclined to question in their sermons the compromise implicit in the Jewish denial of Christianity under Christian rule, thus veering toward the attitude suggested by the legislation of Justinian and Reccared I. Various factors – both general and relating in particular to Jews – helped to shape attitudes toward the Jews in various Christian countries in various times and circumstances. The unifying and directing overall Christian influence was the divided attitude displayed by the Church – less hostile at the top, and increasingly hostile in the lower ranks. Royalty, the nobility, and the townspeople added elements colored by their own interests to the prevailing temper but always merging with one of the two aspects of the Church attitude.

Seventh-century Visigothic Spain waged a continuous struggle against Jewish existence. A series of laws was promulgated throughout the century to punish Jews for adhering to their faith, to ensure supervision of their behavior as good Christians by local Christian priests, and to take away their children from them in order to educate them in true Christian homes as good Christians. Cruel punishments were threatened to those who would not obey; "the Jews" alluded to in these enactments were evidently forced converts to Christianity who persisted in adhering to the faith of their fathers. The enactment of these measures over the course of a century goes far to show the strength of the devotion to Judaism of communities of Jewish merchants who have left no trace in Jewish literature and culture other than the testimony of persecutory laws to their steadfastness in face of danger. It was a tragic prelude to the tragedy of the Marranos of Spain in the 15th and 16th centuries. Both in the seventh and the 15th centuries, the Jewish tragedy was the result of a Catholic drive for unification and the uniformization of belief and thought in Spain.

In the Carolingian Empire of the eighth and ninth centuries, trade and

mercantile connections were at a much higher premium than in the declining
Visigothic kingdom, hence the treatment of Jews was much better, though
always within the framework of the general attitude set by the Church. Emperor
Louis the Pious (778–840) and his advisers in particular were favorably disposed
to Jewish trade, and under him court society treated the Jews well. The charters
he granted to Jewish merchants show that these traders engaged in large-scale
trade and were well regarded by the court. Further details are embedded in
Archbishop Agobard of Lyons' criticism of the Jews and of the court attitude to
them. There we find that they were in social contact with society; that they
were important at fairs; and that Jewish merchants were protected by a
high-ranking noble, the *magister Judaeorum*. Agobard bitterly criticized Jewish
influence, Jewish culture at Lyons, and the anti-Christian disputations in which
the Jews engaged. In particular Agobard opposed the protection accorded to
Jewish slave trading. The south Italian 11th-century chronicle of Ahimaaz
registers the impression made by persecutions instigated by Emperor Basil I
(867–86). The chronicle conceives a Jewish leader, R. Shephatiah, as the
opponent of the emperor, on earth and in heaven.

The 10th and 11th centuries saw the continuing Christianization of the
minds, and in particular the emotions and the imaginations, of the peoples in
Western Europe. The importance of Jews as international merchants, and
gradually as local merchants too, continued to be appreciated. Jews were also
valued as a colonizing element in the reemerging town life in these countries, as
the charter of Bishop Ruediger of Speyer (1084) offering them attractive
concessions clearly shows. A Hebrew fragment relates that the Jews set the
granting of a fortified quarter as a condition for their agreement to move from
Mainz to Speyer. The bishop thus met the request of desirable colonists for
defendable quarters. Only six years before the First Crusade, in 1190, Emperor
Henry IV granted the Jews of Speyer and Worms charters giving them extensive
rights of trade and self-government.

By this time the social and religious ferment in Western Europe was nearing
its peak. Jews were expelled from Mainz in 1012. The investiture conflict
between the papacy and the emperor and the propaganda for a Crusade in the
11th century both resulted from the deepening and intensification of Christian
political theory and emotions inflamed to a high pitch of duty to take revenge
for Jesus' passion and death. With the growth of the influence of monks, the
feelings of the lower clergy found a potent and articulate vehicle of expression.
All this combined to bring about widespread massacres of the Jews during the
First Crusade (1096), in particular of the communities of the Rhine, as well as
the Jewish response to this challenge by the acts and the ideology of martyrdom
(kiddush ha-Shem).

*First
Crusade*

The seventh to eleventh centuries were a formative period for a redisposition of Jewish leadership and its social ratification. In the pattern of leadership formed by the institutions of the exilarchate, the *geonim* (academy heads), and their academies, there emerged an aristocratic hereditary hierarchy consisting of many families of scholars, traditionally devoted to study and assuming leadership in a fixed system of precedence and gradation; another more limited circle was constituted of families of *geonim,* entitled to succeed to the autocratic leadership of the academies; finally there was the leadership exercised by the Davidic dynasty of the exilarchic house. Over the course of centuries this system tried to combine the principles and practice of intellectual attainment, sanctity of life, hereditary succession, and hierarchic promotion. Despite the tensions and contradictions inherent in this combination, it worked successfully for a remarkably long time. The system, based on centralization, and by example from above, induced throughout Jewish society appreciation of aristocratic descent combined with learning and leadership. This structure and set of social values began to break up, not under the attacks of the tenth-century Karaites,[8] although these were directed expressly and sharply against it, but through the disintegration of the supporting framework of the caliphate, and the appearance of local Jewish leadership which, while remaining aristocratic in attitude and values, was no longer connected with the center at Baghdad and with the hierarchy of the academies. Individualistic tendencies were also at work here.

This structure, with its extreme claims to authority, sanctity, and aristocracy, has remained an isolated chapter in the pattern of Jewish institutions of scholarship and leadership. Flourishing from the 8th to 11th centuries, and in decline up to the 13th century, it represented for Jewish history a singular experiment of centralistic leadership based on aristocratic stratification combined with individualist intellectual values. The concept *"yeshivah"* still remains, but beyond the borders of the caliphate and after the 13th century there was no attempt to organize it on the lines of family units and as an hierarchic ladder. The term *gaon* became understood in Europe to designate "genius," and its original hierarchical meaning was lost, to be rediscovered by modern research. The system was gradually replaced by local leadership, such as that of the *nagid.*[9] Alongside there began to emerge, even in Muslim countries,

8   Sect that originated in the eighth century, originally as the strict adherents to the *halakhah* (law) of their founder Anan (therefore named later in this initial stage as Ananites); characterized in the tenth century by religious radicalism, extreme individualism, and strict rationalism; from c. the 12th century marked mainly by literal biblicism and opposition to the talmudic tradition.

9   Since end of tenth century title accorded to heads of Jewries in the several Islamic principalities.

the local community unit, based on cohesion of its members and the needs specific to Jews living together and feeling a common responsibility in a certain locality.

North of the Pyrenees, Jewish community leadership around the beginning of the 11th century shows the influence of the individual predominating, based on personal charisma and learning alone. It is exemplified in the figure of Gershom b. Judah, "the Light of the Exile,"[10] and in the ideals set out by Simeon b. Isaac of Mainz,[11] reaching its consummation in the personality and leadership of Rashi[12] and the figures who by their personal qualities and example led their communities to sacrifice themselves in the spirit of *kiddush ha-Shem* (see below, chap. 8) during the persecutions of the First Crusade. The regular organs of local community leadership and the synods of local community leaders, which convened at the fairs and in central commercial towns like Cologne, served in this milieu to support leadership by the individual or by the isolated community or as an alternative to it.

The Jewish leadership used various methods of influence and systems of instruction to exercise authority. The Babylonian *geonim* and their academies have received a somewhat distorted image in the view of later generations because the main source of information on them and their activities derives from the responsa[13] they sent, on the authority of the academy, to legal questions submitted to them by communities or individuals. In reality, they achieved their goal of establishing the Talmud as the criterion for the normative Jewish way of life and thought, not only or even mainly, through this legal and exegetical correspondence. Although the responsa literature of the *geonim* is highly diversified, and has been regarded with high esteem down through the generations, it was only part, and in their estimation only a substitute, for direct methods of exercising centralistic moral and social control of Jewish society. Wherever and whenever possible, they preferred direct instruction given to assemblies of scholars either by the *gaon* and the collegium of his academy (which served both as a supreme judicial court as well as a high academy of

---

10 Lived c. 960–1028; of the founding layers of Jewish society leadership and culture in Northwestern Europe; liturgical poet, talmudic authority, to whom weighty social reforms are ascribed.

11 Born c. 950; one of the first liturgical poets of Northwestern European Jewry.

12 Lived 1040–1105; the most authoritative Bible and Talmud commentator for traditional Judaism.

13 Term used for both the answers as well as the questions exchanged by individuals and communities with Rabbis considered either because of their office (as in the ninth-12th centuries the heads of the academies in Baghdad) or because of their scholarship as the authorities on Jewish *halakhah*.

learning) in the *kallah* months[14] or by sending out an emissary or a representative of the *gaon* to the communities.

The *geonim* also sent out letters when assuming office, called by Saadiah Gaon[15] the "letter on assuming lordship" *(Iggeret Tesurah)*. Several letters of such purport of the 10th and 11th centuries[16] evidence an aim to impart instruction to the people in simple and rational language, appealing to their emotions and needs. In his letter Saadiah Gaon repeatedly stresses that it is the duty of his office to teach Jews, to lead and to admonish them. He invites questions and appeals. This high conception of geonic office justifies the assumption that many more such pastoral letters were sent out but have been lost in later centuries and in places where geonic institutional and moral authority was no longer binding. The *geonim* extended their influence also by instilling in the people a deeply mystical conception of the sacredness of the academies and their heads. They especially emphasized the value of their blessing and the danger of incurring their ban *(ḥerem)*.

The productive Jewish cultural and religious life which continued in these centuries was frequently stormy. Almost at the outset of the geonic campaign to establish the Talmud as the book of life for the Jewish people it encountered the revolt of Anan b. David,[17] and the early Karaites. These represent in the eighth to ninth centuries an archaistic and rigoristic trend, turning away from talmudic and geonic "modernization" toward a biblical primitive conception of the Jewish way of life, ideals, and duties. The concept of all-pervading holiness, a demand for the reinstatement of harsh old prescriptions, an insistence on adherence to detailed local custom, and a program of self-isolation for the camp of true believers made this movement a throwback to various ancient sectarian tendencies of the Second Temple period. Even in this opposition the strength of talmudic modes of thought is evident, for Anan employs talmudic dialectics frequently and with skill in his writings; what he opposed was reliance on law based on talmudic collective discussion and the alleviations it introduced.

---

14   The two mass gatherings of Jews to study at the academies, one in the month of Elul, before the High Holy Days, and one in the month of Adar, before Passover.

15   Lived 882–942; Egypt-born *gaon* of Sura academy, great talmudic scholar and philosopher.

16   e.g., Saadiah Gaon in *Dvir,* 1 (1923), 183–8; and in: *Ginzei Kedem,* 2 (1923), 34–35; Nehemiah Gaon in: J. Mann, *Texts and Studies,* 1 (1931), 78–83; Israel, son of Samuel b. Hophni, *ibid.,* 167–77; Sherira Gaon, *ibid.,* 95–105; Hai Gaon in *Ginzei Kedem,* 4 (1930), 51–56.

17   Lived in the eighth century; son of the exilarchic family and failed aspirant to the office of exilarch; scholar and ascetic; formulated his own *halakhah;* his followers, the Ananites became the core of later-day Karaites.

The change in cultural temper and religious mood among the Jews in Muslim countries in these centuries — to a large degree due to the influence of Islamic society and culture, and to the penetration of Greek philosophical ideas to both Muslims and Jews — is evident in the development of Karaism as well as in the fight against it. Whereas Anan was authoritarian to the core and the *geonim* who opposed him at first rejected his views in the name of the sanctity of tradition and on the basis of the authority of their academies, both Karaite and Rabbanite conceptions and argumentations had changed very much in the same direction by the tenth century. Both sides were now mainly contending within the framework of religious rationalism, that worked a transformation in the conception their own stand and that of the opponents.

The Karaites of tenth-century Jerusalem called themselves *Avelei Zion,* the Mourners for Zion. This appellation stressed the basis and aim of their lifestyle. Their theory was founded in a religious rationalism individualistic to the point of religious anarchy. Their leaders and theoreticians stress, each in his own manner, in their exegesis, polemics, and chronography, that strict adherence to the Bible should stem from a deep sense of individual responsibility that cannot and should not rely on any external authority but only on the individual's reasoning powers. This is to them the sole legitimate means of understanding the sacred Scriptures, the Jewish way of life, God's will in history, and the cosmic order. They preached intensively this theoretical approach to their opponents: "Know, O our brethren the children of Israel, that each one of us is responsible for his own soul . . . O house of Israel have mercy upon your own souls and have pity upon your children. For behold, the light is burning and the sun is shining. Choose for yourselves the good way . . . The Karaites do not say that they are the leaders . . . they say to their brethren, the children of Jacob: Study, and search, and seek, and investigate, and do that which occurs to you by way of solid proof and that which seems reasonable to you" (as translated L. Nemoy, *Karaite Anthology* (1952), 118–9).

The writings of the *geonim* of the 10th and early 11th centuries show a similar application of rationalism. Saadiah Gaon wrote his "Book of Beliefs and Opinions" in the early tenth century to explain Jewish Rabbanite theory and practice on systematic rationalistic philosophical grounds and to defend it against opponents through rationalist argumentation. He opposed the Karaites in the name of religious rationalism, which demands that men should rely on accumulated tradition and binds them to obey the guidance of national collective leadership. Rationalism afforded Saadiah — and, in an even more extreme approach, the *gaon* Samuel b. Hophni (d. 1013) — the incentive and the means to combat anthropomorphic interpretations and uphold radical rationalist exegesis of the Bible. On the other hand, to Karaites it furnished weapons for

Cultural and Spiritu- al Life

destructive criticism of the Talmud. Although the theoretical and practical consequences were to be widely divergent, they stemmed from a common point of departure based on a rationalist approach.

The divergences and conflicts often divided the Rabbanite and Karaite camps more deeply among themselves than the controversy between the two sides. By its nature Karaite individualist rationalism gave rise to innumerable divisions. The much larger Rabbanite section, united formally, became increasingly diversified with the development of local custom and local culture which became more important as the centralizing framework of the caliphate and the authority of the exilarchate and Babylonian academies began to decline. Even more decisive was the difference between communities within the Muslim environment and influence and those in the Christian sphere.

The difference is thrown into sharp relief when the world of thought and religion of the Babylonian academies is confronted with that of the Jews of southern Italy. This Jewry was important in its time and for later generations from many aspects. The Jewry of Ashkenaz[18] was conscious of its cultural roots in southern Italy. The Ashkenazi rite of prayer originated there. In the 12th century Jacob b. Meir Tam[19] formulated the cultural debt of Ashkenaz to southern Italy by his paraphrase of Isaiah 11:13; "For out of Bari shall go forth the Law and the word of the Lord from Otranto." Mystic circles of the Ḥasidei Ashkenaz[20] (see below, chap. 9) traced nebulous origins of their traditions to semilegendary figures active in southern Italy. The wealth of Jewish traditions and culture there is revealed in the Josippon chronicle,[21] completed in 953. The liturgical poems *(piyyutim)* composed by Jews of this region during the period are the products of a considerable Hebrew liturgic and poetic activity. In the Ahimaaz chronicle, completed in Capua (southern Italy) in 1054, the traditions, the venerated figures, and the ideals of the upper circles of this important Jewry emerge in striking contrast to the rationalist world of Babylonian Jewry. The chronicle abounds with miraculous elements. Use of the Divine Name frequently appear as a magic formula with powers over death, for supplying miraculous

18   Term used (on the basis of identification of biblical lists of peoples with European regions) first for the Jewish settlement in present-day Germany and the Jewish culture evolved there; later came to denote the Jewry of Eastern Europe too and the Jewish culture of all these areas, as juxtaposed to the Jewish culture that emanated from Spain and in exile, Sepharad.

19   Rabbenu Tam; lived c. 1100–1171; great talmudic scholar of the northern French school of the tosafists; social leader.

20   An elite group in central and western Germany mainly in 12th and 13th centuries. Its teachings influenced many outside their circle.

21   Since the author of this work was not known, it was frequently attributed to Josephus. It was very popular in the Middle Ages.

defense, and as a device for speedy transportation. Vampire-like women are reported to snatch, in the dark of night, children who in turn are snatched away and kept alive by holy sages. In religious outlook this world reveals all the elements that Hai Gaon[22] despised and warned against in the 11th century (see: *Oẓar ha-Geonim* ed. by B.M. Levin, 4 (1931), 6, 10–12, 13–27, nos. 7, 16, 20–21 responsa to *Ḥagigah*).

In Muslim Spain, at the courts of Jewish grandees, a different cultural trend developed in the 10th and 11th centuries. The clash that occurred between Ḥisdai ibn Shaprut (see above, p. 14) and his court poet and grammarian, Menahem ibn Saruq, demonstrates on the one hand the lordly attitude of the maecenas and on the other the proud individuality of the poor intellectual. In the 11th century Samuel ha-Nagid and his son Jehoseph (see above, p. 14) lived in ostentatious luxury and prided themselves on it. According to many opinions, they were among the main builders of the Alhambra palace in Granada. The writings of Samuel ha-Nagid display a rational, highly individualistic and somewhat sensual temper. The responsa of Isaac b. Jacob Alfasi[23] provide evidence of the trends in Torah learning and communal culture characterizing the middle strata in Jewish society in Muslim Spain.

Archbishop Agobard describes the culture of the Jewish community at Lyons and the literature it possessed as both mystic and talmudic in its conceptions. The Jews in the lands of the Franks in the 10th to 11th centuries are also known from their own works and expressions of opinion. The Jews of Provence described themselves to Ḥisdai Ibn Shaprut in the tenth century as "Your servants, the communities of France." They were in close contact with the Muslim Spanish Jewish courtier and tried to persuade him to influence the authorities at Toulouse to stop the practice of a local custom harming and insulting the Jews. Their letter is written in flowery Hebrew (Mann, *ibid.,* 1 (1931), 27–30). The community of Arles had specific ordinances for trade regulation about this time. The Anjou community recorded, in rich Hebrew, an event that proves Jewish contact with and influence in the Christian environment in the south. It relates of a woman proselyte who "has left her father's house, great riches, in a far land, and has come for the sake of the name of our God to nestle under the wings of the Divine Presence. She has left her brethren and the grandees of her family; she settled in Narbonne. The late rabbi David married her . . . as he heard that they were looking for her he fled with her to our place." A new place of refuge was now being sought for the noble proselyte

---

22 Lived 939–1038; head of the academy of Pumbedita; considered traditionally the last of the *geonim*.

23 Lived 1013–1103; community leader and teacher in northern Africa and Moslem Spain, composed epitome of the Babylonian Talmud.

widow and her baby child (*ibid.*, 32–33). This type of Jewish culture flourishing in close contact with its environment was to continue in Provence and bear many fruits.

A distinct and productive Jewish culture developed in the 10th and 11th centuries in northern France and on the eastern bank of the Rhine. The mystic traditions of southern Italy were not forgotten here but toned down. This culture flourished in a patrician merchant society regulated according to Jewish law *(halakhah)*, and was based on Torah study, on the whole of the Jewish heritage as a living integrated force. In the liturgical poems of Simeon b. Isaac, ideals are set forth and behavior described which were to be typical of the early Jewry of Ashkenaz for many generations. This culture produced the first almost complete commentary on the Bible and the Babylonian Talmud, the work of Rashi which has remained the basis of traditional Jewish Bible and Talmud study. Through this it also influenced to a considerable extent Christian understanding of the Bible, in particular through the impact on Nicholas of Lyre[24].

It was in this northern, Christian environment that Jewish family structure underwent a revolutionary reformulation. Monogamy became the pattern of the Ashkenazi Jewish family by force of the so-called "Decrees *(Takkanot)* of Rabbenu Gershom b. Judah, the Light of the Exile." This change was reinforced by a complementary one: a *herem* ascribed to the same authority invalidated a bill of divorce made for a woman without her prior consent.

These formative centuries also saw the conversion of a Mongol society to Judaism. The Khazars[25] — the royal family and court, and their warrior class in particular — accepted Judaism in the eighth century. This created a state ruled by a Jewish aristocracy in the strategically important region between the Volga and the Caspian Sea in the eighth to tenth centuries. The report of this conversion influenced contemporary and later Jewish thought. In modern times its memory was to play a certain role in discussions about the origins of the Jews in Poland-Lithuania and Russia. The Khazar state practiced full tolerance toward merchants of various denominations, both those living in it as well as those passing through. It controlled important trade routes and fulfilled a critical function in the history of Christianity in Eastern Europe as it served as a buffer state between dynamic Islam and the Slav peoples in what is now Russia — by which the Khazar state was later destroyed.

On the threshold of the 12th century Jewish history stood at the end of the successful period of the experiment to combine a hierarchical and hereditary

---

24   Lived 1270–1349; his Bible exegesis took much from Jewish exegesis; it was very influential on Christian exegesis after him.

25   The story of the Khazars was utilized as the literary setting of one of the best-known apologetics of Judaism — Judah Halevi's *Kuzari*.

social structure with individualist criteria of learning and intellectual attainment; the former experience in leadership and economic development had shown both the importance and dangers in the existence of a gigantic political framework like the caliphate and of its breakup; the latter was expressed in the Jewish sphere in cultural diversification and the emergence of various systems of leadership. Rationalism was the dominating influence — at least among the upper circles and intellectuals — among the Jews in Muslim countries. Mystical and even magical leanings were found among those in Christian countries. Great individual leaders were merging; individualism and local particularism began to assert themselves in the leadership. In regions of cultural and social contacts and transit, like North Africa, southern Italy, and Provence, Jewish cultural creativity was due in no small part to these circumstances. The latecomer to the Jewish scene, the budding culture of Ashkenaz, produced great achievements almost at the start and a capacity for expressing revolutionary halakhic and social changes. The upper circles of Jewish society had a fluent command of Hebrew though in everyday life they used the languages of the countries they lived in; in Muslim countries Arabic was used for literary expression, in particular for legal decisions and philosophic deliberations. Rashi found it necessary to intersperse his commentaries with many Old-French terms in order to be understood by his readers. Jews continued along the path that was to lead them from the use of Greek and Latin, as a cultural medium, through adaptation of alien languages to the development of Yiddish [26] and, later, Ladino.[27] Hence a trend apparently leading to assimilation became a valuable means of attaining an individual culture and cohesion. Judaism was still attracting individuals in the west of Europe, like the French deacon Bodo, who adopted Judaism in the ninth century, while in the east of Europe it attracted the leading sector of a Mongol nation, the Khazars, ruling its state for over two centuries. The hatred and massacres engendered by the Crusades produced in response the spirit of *kiddush ha-Shem,* which was described and taught in the early 12th century as representing the Jewish holy war against the enemies of the Lord.

[26] The language of most Jews of Ashkenazi culture.
[27] The language developed out of Castilian by the Sephardi diaspora after the expulsion from Spain.

The Crystallization of Jewish Medieval Culture (12th to 15th Centuries)

Effects of Crusades

The 12th century continued the series of shocks for Jewish society in Europe and for the Jewish spirit everywhere initiated by the movement and spirit of the Crusades. The Second Crusade (1146–47) and the Third (1189–90) brought massacre, plunder, and terror in their wake to Jews in Western Europe. The tenth-century French churchman Bernard of Clairvaux gave strong popular expression to the old-established conception of the higher Church echelons of combining a policy toward the Jews of humiliation and isolation with defense of their life and property. In his letter to "the English People" sent also to "the Archbishops, Bishops, and all the clergy of eastern France and Bavaria," he states:

> "The Jews are not to be persecuted, killed, or even put to flight . . . The Jews are for us the living words of Scripture, for they remind us always of what our Lord suffered. They are dispersed all over the world so that by expiating their crime they may be everywhere the living witness of our redemption . . . Under Christian princes they endure a hard captivity, but 'they only wait for the time of their deliverance' . . . I will not mention those Christian moneylenders, if they can be called Christian, who where there are no Jews, act, I grieve to say, in a manner worse than any Jew . . . "

That his missionary hopes and expectations serve as a main argument in his defense of the Jews is even more evident in another letter to the archbishop of Mainz opposing the incitement to massacre preached by the monk, Raoul. Bernard argues:

> "Is it not a far better triumph for the Church to convince and convert the Jews than to put them all to the sword? Has that prayer which the Church offers for the Jews, from the rising up of the sun to the going down thereof, that the veil may be taken from their hearts so that they may be led from the darkness of error into the light of truth, been instituted in vain? . . . " (*The Letters of St. Bernard of Clairvaux.* transl. by Bruno Scott James (1953), nos. 391, 393).

This was the most that a great Christian mystic and ascetic could say against shedding the blood of Jews to the Western European populace in 1146. These letters were reprinted by anti-Nazi Church circles in Germany immediately after the Holocaust!

Left to their own resources the Jews protected themselves by leaving the towns and moving to castles of the nobility — paying money for the Christians to leave the castle so as to defend it themselves. This policy, successful in most cases, had tragic consequences for the community of York, England (1190). True to the ideal of *kiddush ha-Shem,* when the Jews were surrounded in the tower they killed themselves.

Jewish steadfastness to the faith in itself served to forestall some attacks. Those who adopted Christianity when threatened with death in 1096 were permitted by Emperor Henry IV to return to Judaism despite a sharp protest by the pope. Though the religious-fanatical motive for Jew-killing remained among Christians throughout the Middle Ages, it was now becoming interwoven with economic, social, and emotional elements. Bernard of Clairvaux had hinted at hatred for the Jewish usurer as a motive for attacking Jews. The blood libel from the 12th century onward (see below, chap. 10) and the libel of desecration of the Host[28] from the 13th century created a vicious circle around the Jew. Each accusation presupposes the Jew as treacherous, blood-lusting, sadistic, God-hating, and devil-worshiping. Each libel added darker shades to this conception of the Jew. Dramas on the passion of Christ combined with imagery in Romanesque and Gothic church sculpture, stained glass, and paintings to imbue deep in the thought and imagination of the Christian populace, through the greatest expression of Christian art, the image of the Jew as a horrible and horrifying fiend.

As Christianity encompassed the mental horizon of all Western Europeans in this era, the Jew remained the main — often the only — representative of nonconformity in a conforming society. As in the fourth century, so in the 12th and early 13th century, as well as in the early 15th, an upsurge of heretical movements and social tensions within Christianity (e.g., Hussites) intensified the fear of the Jew and hatred of him. In the struggle between papacy and empire, the leaders of the Church became used to demagogic formulas and the deployment of popular forces and violence to serve their own purposes. The attitude and legislation of Pope Innocent III express clearly this interpenetration of policy and vulgar enmity of the Church attitutde toward Jews, even in papal

[28]   The spurious belief that the Jews on the one hand considered that the Wafer of the Host was transubstantiated into the blood and body, and, on the other hand, still desired to desecrate it.

formulations. Mercilessness in enforcing servitude of the Jews, extreme hostility, and debased rhetoric and menaces appear there in a potent and vicious combination. The Augustinian-Gregorian conception of sufferance of the Jews amid Christian society — restated in a missionary vein by Bernard of Clairvaux in the middle of the 12th century — assumes with Innocent III in a letter to the king of France of Jan. 16, 1205, the following shape:

" . . . Though it does not displease God, but is even acceptable to Him that the Jewish Dispersion should live and serve under Catholic Kings and Christian princes until such time as their remnant shall be saved . . . nevertheless such [princes] are exceedingly offensive to the sight of the Divine Majesty who prefer the sons of the crucifiers, against whom to this day the blood cries to the Father's ears, to the heirs of the Crucified Christ, and who prefer the Jewish slavery to the freedom of those whom the Son freed, as though the son of a servant could and ought to be an heir along with the son of the free woman . . . "(S. Grayzel, *Church and the Jews in the 13th Century* (1933), 104—6, no. 14).

This great lawyer relies on and quotes the information that "it has recently been reported that a certain poor scholar had been found murdered in their [the Jews'] latrine" (*ibid.,* 110). He does not hesitate to quote at the beginning of a detailed anti-Jewish letter that the Jews are to be considered "in accordance with the common proverb: 'like the mouse in a pocket, like the snake around one's loins, like the fire in one's bosom' " (*ibid.,* 115, no. 18).

Innocent III tried to deflect to the Jews his anti-imperialist policy of exploiting popular force and sentiment. In 1198, at the very beginning of his pontificate, he wrote:

"To the Archbiship of Narbonne and to his suffragans, and also to the Abbots Priors, and other prelates of the Church, as well as to the Counts and Barons, and all the people of the Province of Narbonne . . . We order that the Jews shall be forced by you, my sons the princes, and by the secular powers, to remit the usury to them; and until they remit it, we order that all intercourse with faithful Christians, whether through commerce or other ways, shall be denied the Jews by means of a sentence of excommunication . . . "(*ibid.,* 87, no. 1).

Consistent in his attitude, he carried through this policy as the program of the Church in the Fourth Lateran Council of 1215. There the representatives of the Catholic Church ordered:

"By a decree of this Synod, that when in the future a Jew, under any pretext, extort heavy and immoderate usury from a Christian, all relationship with Christians shall therefore be denied him until he shall have made sufficient amends for his exorbitant exactions. The Christians, moreover, if need be, shall be compelled by ecclesiastical punishment without appeal, to abstain from such commerce. We also impose this upon the princes, not to be aroused against the Christians because of this, but rather to try to keep the Jews from this practice " (*ibid.*, 307).

These measures failed, mainly thanks to the opposition of the secular rulers, yet they encouraged anti-Jewish propaganda by the mendicant orders against Jewish usury, in particular by the Franciscans, especially in Italy of the 15th century.

The Jews in Muslim Spain were profoundly shaken in the 12th century by the successful Christian *Reconquista* from the north and by the Muslim response in the waves of the fanatical Almohads erupting from North Africa to infuse a new fighting spirit into the Muslim ranks. Many communities were dispersed; many Jews fled to the south, to other Muslim countries. Many Jews, both in North Africa and in the territories in Spain under Muslim rule, were forced to adopt Islam. Others flew northward to the Christian principalities of Spain. At first the Jews experienced a general feeling of crisis and loss. Gradually, Jewish refugees in the Christian principalities found new functions and a new importance within the general society, in the colonizing and economic sphere as well as in the cultural and scientific. The Jewish element was entrusted with the colonization of fortified parts of the town taken by the Christians; they were given many administrative posts especially in the financial field. *Christian Spain*

Papal protests against the honors and powers conferred on Jews did not prevail in Spain during the 12th to 14th centuries against the needs of the state for the expertise and initiative of the Jews. Jews also became the transmitters of Muslim-Greek philosophy and science to Christians — a role entrusted to them, and to apostates from Judaism, in many other Christian courts and Church circles of the 12th and 13th centuries, as translators of Arabic and Greek texts into Latin. Many Jews served as mathematicians, astrologers, field surveyors, and, above all, physicians, at the Christian courts. They thus created the courtier circles of Jewish society in the kingdoms of Christian Spain. This paradox of crusading Christian states granting to Jews a major role in colonization, administration, economy, and science was the basis of the normal Jewish town economy and society there, Jews being found in almost every walk of urban social life and economic activity. This situation continued up to the expulsion from Spain in 1492, though it deteriorated from 1391 onward.

Ich bitt euch (vñ leihe mir zu hand/   Was euch gebürt gebt mir verstand/
Bar gelt auff bürgen oder pfand/

The Jewish moneylender as seen by a German, Augsburg, 1531. His function is expressed in the words of the borrower above: "Please, Jew, give me now cash as seems reasonable to you against guarantees or security."

North of the Pyrenees

In countries north of the Pyrenees, there developed gradually, after the massacres of the First Crusade, a specific Jewish economic and social pattern, more and more Jews being forced by circumstances to engage in one occupation only, mainly in usury. This trend never penetrated Jewish life in Christian Spain or Muslim countries where moneylending was one of many Jewish livelihoods. It was also not continued as the main Jewish occupation in Poland-Lithuania from the 16th century onward. With the 15th century, Jews began to turn increasingly to other occupations in the countries where moneylending had been formerly predominant in Jewish life. In the Middle Ages this function of the Jews was mainly the supply of consumption loans (for commercial loans were supplied by Christian moneylenders despite Church prohibition). It was necessary for the needs of the town population and nobility (a necessity proved by the fact that when Jews were expelled from German towns, as happened in the 14th and 15th centuries, they were returned quickly because the need for loans was felt).

However the high interest rate stemming from the scarcity of ready money and precious metals in the Middle Ages and the method of taking pawns to ensure repayment — as well as the fact that taking interest was considered immoral and unreasonable in medieval Christian moral and economic theory — added Jewish usury to the score of other evil Jewish practices and trades. The image of the cruel Jew extortionist and crafty financial trickster was merged with the Christ killer and child murderer. Shakespeare created the figure of Shylock, on the basis of Italian influences, more than 300 years after the last Jew had been expelled from England. To the present day, anti-Semites and apologetic Jews are obsessed by the notion that the "usurious spirit" of the Jews is a trait to be reprehended or explained.

The attitude of Jews toward moneylending on interest in the Middle Ages was governed by the rationale of merchants and townspeople who were out of tune with the agrarian spirit of the biblical, mishnaic, talmudic, and Church prohibitions. There does not appear in the writings of Jewish commentators on the Bible and decisors of the Middle Ages the philosophic argumentation as to the barrenness of money and the insensibility to the concept of economic enjoyment from the passage of time which constantly recurs among Christian writers. Except for the few influenced by Christian attitudes, Jewish lawyers and moralists consider the biblical prohibition on lending on interest as "a decree of divine majesty" to be carried out according to the letter, even if not understood in spirit. The Bible forbade lending to "your brother," and the Jews in the medieval cities, who certainly could not perceive any demonstration of brotherly attitude toward them by their Christian neighbors, interpreted the prohibition at this minimum and saw no reason, either logical or moral, to extend this unreasonable decree toward non-Jews. In fact, Jewish legal authorities tried to find legal formulas allowing the taking of interest by Jew from Jew — as Christians did also, despite their theoretical moralistic objections, with regard to the interest by Christian from Christian. Among Jews this was formally achieved in 1607 by the Councils of the Lands of Poland-Lithuania (see below, chap. 4). In 1500 Abraham Farissol expressed the attitude toward the taking of interest through a theory which assumed the existence of a different social and conceptual order in biblical times and in accord with the Greek philosophers who justified the prohibition on taking of interest. However, as of now, human society was structured on other principles:

"A new nature, different obligation, and another order pertains, inherently different from the first. This is: to help your fellow for payment coming from the one who is in need of something. Nothing should be given to another free of charge if he is not a charity case deserving pity."

He lists payment for work, rent for accommodation, and hire of work-animals as cases to prove this point. He considers it a logical consequence to pay for the use of the capital of another man:

"For a money loan is sometimes much more important than the loaning of an animal or a house, hence it is natural, logical and legal to give some payment to the owner of the money who gives a loan in the same way as people pay rent for houses and cattle, which come to one through money ... the first natural order has been abolished and no one helps another person for nothing, but everything is done for payment" (from his *Magen Avraham*, in: *Ha-Zofeh le-Hokhmat Yisrael*, 12 (1928), 292–3).

This foreshadowing of modern theorists about capital and gain is the end result of the Jewish attitude toward money and interest throughout the Middle Ages.

Black Death   The catastrophe of the Black Death persecutions and massacres of 1348–49 was both the culmination of the suspicion and distrust of the Jew which made it conceivable to see him as the natural perpetrator of the crime of well-poisoning, and, in Germany, the culmination of over 50 years of almost uninterrupted anti-Jewish attacks, libels, and massacres. Yet Jewish society showed its great resilience in reconstructing its communities and rebuilding its economic activity and ties several years only after these persecutions in the very places where they had been killed as dangerous beasts. Even in Christian Spain and Poland-Lithuania this catastrophe had its impact, though it was not to be so destructive as in Central Europe.

Expulsions   The Jews were expelled from England in 1290 to return there only in the 17th century. They were expelled almost totally from most of France in 1306. After these expulsions, in 1348, there remained the shocked and reorganized cluster of Jewish communities in the German lands; the Jewish center in Christian Spain was still intact, though signs of danger were not lacking. In Muslim lands, the Mongolian incursions brought devastation of population and cultural difficulties for Muslims and Jews alike, but the status, economy, and demography of the Jews remained relatively the same as before, for better or worse. The new Jewish center in Poland recovered speedily after 1348, and continued to develop economically, moving out of moneylending activity toward trade and crafts; demographically and socially, there were already signs of the future dynamism and expansion of this Jewish center.

The legal status of the Jews and their security remained unstable as the result of the First Crusade. The old system of granting charters and imperial episcopal protection and defense was found totally wanting in the face of popular incitement and attack. The state, as well as the Jews, were searching for a new formula and new guarantees for safety. This search went on in a situation in which even the would-be protectors were liable to be the deadly enemies of the Jews, as for example, Louis IX of France, who considered that the right way to speak to a Jew was with a sword in his belly. The Holy Roman Empire tried at first to include Jews in the *Landfrieden* ("public peace") protection (1103) along with other defenseless Christian people. This did not work out well because of the very nature of the concept *Treuga Dei* ("Truce of God") which was intended as a Christian measure for the protection of Christian folk. Gradually, there began to crystallize, during the 12th and 13th centuries, a new conception of the status of the Jew. The complex of ideas underlying this new attitude toward the Jew in the Christian body politic came from two different, though parallel, sources – from imperial legalistic conceptions of the rights of ownership of the sovereign over certain elements of the population and his obligations toward such chattels on the one hand, and on the other out of papal and ecclesiastical conceptions of the sovereignty of the vicar of Christ over those who crucified him and the right and duty of the pontiff to instruct Christian rulers how to behave in a Christian way. Legendary influences, legal notions, and fiscal hopes of the chance to exact maximum extortion in taxes and contributions from Jews merged with old imperial conceptions of the duty to give protection and the safeguarding of ordered life to embrace all the inhabitants of the realm. From early formulations that the Jews "belong to our chamber" (*attineant ad cameram nostram,* Emperor Frederick Barbarossa, in 1182), through the final legal conception of Emperor Frederick II expressed in 1237, that "imperial authority has from ancient times condemned the Jews to eternal servitude for their sins" *(cum imperialis auctoritas a priscis temporibus ad perpetrati iudaici sceleris ultionem eisdem Iudeis indixerit perpetuam servitutem)* in his charter granted to the city of Vienna, there arrived the term given currency by the same emperor that the Jews were *"servi camerae nostrae, sub imperiali protectione"* – "serfs of our chamber, under imperial protection."

Serfs of the Chamber

King Henry III of England formulated with Christian candor in 1253, "that no Jew remain in England unless he do the King service, and that from the hour of birth every Jew, whether male or female, serve Us in some way" (in his *Mandatum Regis; Select Pleas, Starrs . . . of the Exchequer of the Jews,* edited by J.M. Rigg (1902), xlviii). This legal conception served in many cases as a license for the capricious extortion of money from Jews. Duke Albert Achill of Brandenburg declared in 1463 that each new Holy Roman emperor had the right to burn the Jews on his accession, to expel them, or to take a third of their property; the last he was actually going to do as the emissary of the emperor.

"The servitude of the Jews" did not always work to their detriment. Considered as royal chattels they usually enjoyed royal protection. Neither the emperor nor other rulers derived from this concept of Jewish servitude the practice of stripping from Jews their right of free movement, nor were they barred from inheriting the property of their fathers. Jews expressly appreciated the implications of these positive and negative aspects to their servitude. On the basis of this concept of servitude very different legal structures and practices could be and were sanctioned. Up to 1391 Christian Spain derived very few consequences that operated to the detriment of the Jews. But, on the pattern of an Austrian charter issued in 1244, a system that gave rise to many such consequences was constructed in Central and Eastern Europe.

Jews in the Middle Ages often expressed their attitude to the legal and political framework in which they were living in their discussions of the conception that "the law of the government is law" *(dina de-malkhuta dina),* as applying to Jews. Their deliberations on these themes show their estimate of, and preference for, differing political systems and legal structures. On the whole they are shown to be pro-royalist and against disruptive forces. They are for "the old," "the customary and hallowed law," and against arbitrary innovation.

Deteriora-
tion in
Christian
Spain
At the end of the 14th century, as the Christian reconquest of Spain was almost completed, when Christian society in Spain no longer felt the need for Jewish tutelage in colonization, administration, or culture, the paradox of a favorable Jewish existence within a fanatical Christian society began to disintegrate. Preceded by inimical propaganda, in 1391, many communities there were attacked. Thousands of Jews accepted Christianity under compulsion, thus creating in Christian Spain, as well as in Jewish society, the phenomenon and problem of the Marranos, and later on, the creation of the Spanish Inquisition (1480).

A century of pressure exercised by forcing the Jews to listen to missionary sermons, the holding of religious disputations, and constant social and mental stress followed. In the end, the Jews were expelled from Spain in 1492. They were again cruelly compelled to apostasy, their children being taken away from them, in Portugal in 1497. As the Jews in large tracts of southern Italy were compelled to apostasy or expelled by 1492, and were expelled from Sicily in 1492–93, there were almost no Jews left in Western Europe by 1500, from the north of the British isles to the tip of Sicily, except for isolated communities in France and for the remnant of the Jews in central and northern Italy. At the time that Columbus discovered the new continent and made the Atlantic a highway for transport and trade, the Jews were not permitted to cross the Atlantic, though not for long. Many of those expelled from Spain went directly to the Muslim countries of northern Africa or to the territories of the Ottoman Empire, which received them favorably; others arrived in these lands via Portugal and Italy, and many remained in Italy. There also began a movement away from Spain into the Spanish Netherlands, which formed the nucleus of the later Jewish return to the shores of the Atlantic.

Disappear-
ance of
Geonic
Hierarchy
The leadership of Jewish autonomy and communal life had been developing during these centuries toward the complete disappearance of the old geonic hierarchy, which vanished by the end of the 13th century. Maimonides and Samuel b. Ali Gaon[29] clashed sharply about this in the late 12th century. Samuel was sure that the *gaon* and his academy were the only feasible leaders for the Jewish people and the custodians of Orthodoxy. Maimonides considered that the system of a publicly supported hierarchic structure of scholars was wrongful

---

29   Head of the Baghdad academy; died 1194.

and sinful; he asserted that the hereditary office of the *gaon* was corrupting by its very nature. This was a confrontation between the claim to leadership by the nascent individualist charisma and old-established hierarchy and institution. Maimonides did not oppose the exilarchate; his descendants, and possibly he himself, carried the title and office of *nagid* in Egypt. His "Letter to Yemen" as well as many of his responsa are in the great tradition of the epistles of instruction and legal leadership of the *geonim*. There were signs of a resurgence of local communal leadership among Jews throughout the Muslim lands during these centuries.

In the kingdoms of Christian Spain, communal life had been much more involved, tense, and diverse than in the countries to the north and south. Tension between the various social classes to which the variegated economic structure and relatively large numbers in these communities gave rise was aggravated by disputes over the mode of election to, and composition of, the community institutions as well as by acute differences of opinion over the mode of tax assessment, the composition of the assessory bodies of the community, and actual justice or injustice in distribution of the tax burden. These causes of social friction operated with particular intensity in the 13th and 14th centuries, as in the community of Barcelona. They sometimes gave rise to "political parties" along lines of division between the rich and poor members of the Jewish community, like those in Saragossa about 1264. Such divisions and parties became intertwined with, and often focused on, ideological and social controversies; the latter mainly reflected the disparities between the leanings of the well-to-do and courtiers in Jewish society toward rationalism — and, as their enemies accused them, often also toward hedonism — and the inclinations of the lower middle classes, the poor, and a minority of the upper classes toward Kabbalah mysticism, and moral reform of an ascetic type. These elements were central in particular during the great storms aroused in Jewry by the Maimonidean controversy[30] (in the 1230s and around the end of the 13th and beginning of the 14th century). These theoretical and practical conflicts also related to questions of the study of general culture and of the correct attitude toward mixing in gentile society. The vortices of social, economic, political, and religious problems complicated as well as enriched the social and communal life and thought of the Jewry of Christian Spain. The phenomenon of the Marranos further aggravated as well as deepened the problems of division and unity among Jews and influenced their fate and nation.

The actual leadership of Jewish society and the communities was generally in the hands of the great courtier aristocratic families which claimed it as their

Communal Life in Christian Spain

30   See below, chap. 9.

birthright — like the families of Benveniste, Perfet, Alconstantini, Ibn Ezra, Ibn Waqar, and Ibn Shoshan. All were families who for generations numbered among their members financiers and financial administrators and advisors to the court and nobility, physicians, great merchants, and cultural leaders. There were, of course, varying combinations of men active in these professions in each family. From the end of the 12th century their claims were challenged frequently and vigorously, and often with success, by the supporters and leaders of anti-aristocratic and anti-rationalist trends. These leaders often came from the great families and were a product of their type of culture. The Jewish leadership in Christian Spain defended the communities they represented and the legal and social status of the Jews not only through their contacts and influence at court, but also through their intimate acquaintance with the cultural and legal complex of Christian social and judicial attitudes toward the Jews — both of the Church as well as of the state rulers — as the ideas expressed by the general council of the Aragon communities held in Barcelona in 1354 show (Y. Baer, *Die Juden im christlichen Spanien*, 1 (1929), 348—58, no. 253). Despite its political sagacity, this council failed in its attempt to create a central body for the Jewry of Aragon where local particularism was strong. Castile Jewry, on the other hand, had a centralizing institution in the office of the *rab de la corte* ("court rabbi"), which helped to promote cohesion among the Jewish communities in the kingdom. This enabled the Castile communities to hold the great synod of Valladolid in 1432 with its comprehensive program of reform and restoration (*ibid.*, 2 (1936), 280—97, no. 217).

The personal charisma of the individual scholar, in conjunction with local particularized community organization, continued to dominate Jewish leadership north of the Pyrenees, and with the emigration of Jews to western Slavic countries was transplanted to Poland-Lithuania. Attempts to achieve a centralized leadership by synods in the first part of this period (up to 1348) in the West were essentially linked either with the great figures of revered scholars, like Jacob b. Meir Tam for the area of present-day France, in the 12th century, or with the authority of old and important communities like Rome in Italy or Troyes in Champagne. These councils exerted authority through a system whereby their original decisions were sent for approval and support to the main communities and important scholars and leaders who did not attend the synod. The center of gravity of Jewish leadership would thus tend to move from place to place or from scholar to scholar, though for most of the time Rome held a central position, in curious parallel to its position in the Catholic world. Individual leaders and single communities, as well as the synods and their written missives, dealt with variegated problems arising out of Jewish religious, economic, and social life, and the opposition by the outside world. An extreme example of the devotion of the leader to his people attained in those tense centuries is that of Meir b. Baruch of Rothenburg in Germany at the end of the 13th century who refused to permit the Jewish communities to ransom him from the dungeon to which he had been arbitrarily confined, in case this set a precedent for exacting similar extortion through the persons of other leaders.

The trend to elevate the position of the woman in Jewish society, expressed in these regions by the imposition of monogamy, continued. It is proposed by the French scholar Perez b. Elijah of Corbeil at the end of the 13th century;

> "Who has given a husband the authority to beat his wife? Is he not rather
> forbidden to strike any person in Israel? Moreover Rabbi Isaac has written
> in a responsum that he has it on the authority of three great sages that one
> who beats his wife is in the same category as one who beats a
> stranger . . . We have therefore decreed that any Jew may be compelled, on
> application of his wife or one of her near relatives, by a *herem* to
> undertake not to beat his wife in anger or cruelty or so as to disgrace
> her . . . If they, our masters, the great sages of the land agree to this
> ordinance it shall be established" (L. Finkelstein, *Jewish Self-Government in
> the Middle Ages* (1924) 216–7; and G.G. Coulton, *Medieval Panorama*
> (1955), 614–5).

This is also an example of how an individual scholar would turn his personal decision into synodal *takkanah*.

From a legal demand for unanimity in communal decisions voiced in France in the 12th century, Jewish leadership in these countries came to accept the binding force of the vote of the majority against the minority, as formulated in the 13th century in Germany. This marks a changeover from Germanic and primitive notions of decision-making to Roman and more developed systems, again parallel to developments in gentile society. Thus, for the first time elements of democratic decision-making entered Jewish social leadership. The Jewish communities used their prerogative to decide on ordinances — *takkanot* in Hebrew — designed to meet the challenge of changing times and conditions with responses fashioned out of the arising needs, though within the framework of the *halakhah*. Among these ordinances we find the granting of absolute competence within the community area to the local court (the ordinance of the *herem bet din*). They also sometimes closed the community to new permanent settlers, without prior permission (the *herem ha-yishuv*). Jewish society participated in the general trend prevailing in the cities where they were living to regard the city within its walls as an independent separate entity that took everything it could under its own authority. On the other hand, dissatisfaction with these innovations, and the opposition of many prominent rabbis to the new self-sufficiency of the city community represented an inherently opposing trend which was to be found within the Jewish community. According to this immanent trend, the Jewish community regarded itself as a cell in a living and united, though dispersed, body politic and nation. These aspects of Jewish social policy found their clear-cut expression in the community of Ashkenaz owing to the absence of the other diversifying problems and causes of tension found in the communities of Christian Spain.

After the catastrophe of the Black Death persecutions the need for a single guiding and comforting hand made the position of the influential scholar in the Ashkenaz community much more formalized and institutionalized than previously or as it continued in the communities of Spain. Concomitantly with the local community organs and the sporadic councils and synods, there is evidence in the regions of Ashkenaz, in particular in the southeast, of the emergence of a salaried and officially accepted single rabbi of the community. In Austria there is first clear mention of the conception of *semikhah* as a rabbinical diploma. Such accepted rabbis constantly used the title *manhig* ("leader") which fell into disuse in the 16th century. Demands were made, and are still being put forward to the present day, claiming the exclusive right of the *"mara de-atra"* ("the lord of the locality") to the jurisdiction and control of religious functions in his locality. Both the growing authority of the institutionalized rabbi and the wish of the secular powers to exploit this authority for fiscal purposes led to the appointment (from the 13th century) of a *Hochmeister,* or *Judenmeister,* for the whole of the German empire, or for large parts of it. This practice was transposed at the end of the 15th and beginning of the 16th century to Poland-Lithuania, in the appointment of *seniores* and chief rabbis to lead the Jews and help in the collection of taxes.

Cultural Creativity   To turn to cultural creativity for the period, the 12th century had been a very creative period in the history of Jewish culture. A series of great personalities and literary works expressed and countered the trauma of the Crusades and Almohad disturbances. They responded to this challenge of suffering and deterioration by adding new spiritual layers, by shaping new patterns of culture, and by forming new theories about the nature of the Jewish people, the meaning of its history and fate, and its place in the Divine purpose and general history, by framing different legal and moral formulations to meet the social and religious needs of the suffering people. The chronicles of the First Crusade and *kiddush ha-Shem,* as well as the general chronicles of Abraham ibn Daud in Spain of the 12th century, affirm — though expressed in different ways and on different subjects — a basic conviction envisaging the Jewish people as God's militia on earth that has to carry His banner proudly, courageously, and defiantly, whether in open knightly encounter, or in the bitter choice of suicide rather than surrender of its principles. This merges with the Maimonidean depiction of the history of the Jewish people as that of the beleaguered camp of truth, which withstands all the attacks and stratagems of its enemies. This was the opinion of the majority of Jewish thinkers at this time.

In contrast to this general opinion, the Spanish poet-philosopher Judah Halevi gave expression to the different view that humiliation and suffering are the direct road to fulfilling the Divine Will; that all that was lacking in Jewish humiliation and suffering was the full and willing acceptance of this position by Jews, though they have accepted it "midway between compulsion and willing submission," for they could join Christianity or Islam by making a verbal declaration of faith. Opinions also differed in the nature of the election of the Jewish people. Judah Halevi considered this an election of the natural Israel continuing lineally through the generations. Blood will tell; if a Jew is bad in one generation, the good is only latent in him and will come out in his descendants: "Israel among the nations is like the heart among the members of the body." As the central life-gifing force, it therefore suffers from and is contaminated by everything that is found in the subsidiary members. Gentiles may join the Jewish faith but proselytes will never attain to the prophecy reserved for deserving pure-blooded Jews.

The view of Maimonides represents a diametrically opposed school on these matters. For him the criterion for Jewish election rests on joining the Jewish faith and on acceptance of Jewish cohesion out of conviction. In a letter to a Norman proselyte he summed up this view that is inherent in many of his other writings. To the proselyte's question if he may pray in the first person plural when speaking about the fate of the Jewish people and the miracles performed for it. Maimonides gave a categorical "yes":

"The core of this matter is that it was our father Abraham who taught the whole people, educated them, and let them know true faith and divine unity. He rebelled against idolatry and made away with its worship; he brought in many under the wings of the Divine presence; he taught and instructed them and he commanded his children and his family after him to follow the Divine path ... therefore, everyone who becomes a proselyte to the end of all generations and everyone who worships the name of God only according to what is written in the Torah is a pupil of Abraham, they all are members of his family ... hence Abraham is the father of the righteous ones of his descendants who follow his ways and a father to his pupils and to each and every one of the proselytes ... There is no difference at all between you and us in any aspect .... Know, that the majority of our fathers who left Egypt were idolaters in Egypt, they

mixed with the gentiles and were influenced by their deeds, until God sent
Moses . . . separated us from the gentiles and brought us under the wings
of the Divine presence – for us and for all proselytes – and gave us all one
law. Do not make light of your descent. If we relate ourselves to Abraham,
Isaac, and Jacob, you are related to the Creator of the world . . . Abraham
is your father and ours and of all the righteous who follow his ways" (see
his responsa, ed. J. Blau (1960), 548–50, no. 293).

Maimonides thus considers that all Israel are elected twice as "a nation of
proselytes," once through Abraham, and secondly, through Moses. This is in
tune with his theory that Christianity and Islam are devices to educate the
gentiles toward eventually accepting Jewish law. They now occupy themselves
with the law – as either a figurative pattern, according to Christianity, or an
earlier dispensation only according to Islam – and will be acquainted with it and
ready to accept it fully when the truth dawns on them with the coming of the
Messiah (his *Yad ha-Hazakah, Hilkhot Melakhim,* Constantinople version,
chapter 11).

The 12th century also produced a flowering of biblical exegesis both in
France (such as Joseph Kara; Menahem b. Helbo; Eliezer of Beaugency; Samuel
b. Meir (Rashbam); this school influenced the Christian St. Victorine school of
Bible exegesis in France), and in Christian Spain (such as Abraham ibn Ezra;
Joseph Kimhi). The 12th century also inaugurated the school of the talmudic
commentators, tosafists, in France, which continued its activity well into the
14th century and whose influence spread first to Germany and later to Jewish
scholarship everywhere. From a formal and structural aspect they studied and
taught the Babylonian Talmud, recording their comments as additions – *tosafot*
in Hebrew – to the commentary of Rashi. Their system of incisive analysis and
subtle dialectics make the work of this long line of scholars in reality a new
"Talmud of France."

Maimonides attempted in the 12th century to codify talmudic law and views
in a systematic presentation according to Greek principles of structure and
division, leaving out all talmudic dialectics and discussion (in his code *Yad
ha-Hazakah*). He also attempted the synthesis of Jewish revealed faith and creed
with Aristotelian Arabic philosophy (in his *Guide of the Perplexed*). These
attempts, as well as his opposition to institutionalized leadership, were at the
heart of the Maimonidean controversy which raged at varying pitch throughout
this period.

The Jewry of Christian Spain continued both the tradition of biblical exegesis
(for example, David Kimhi), of philosophic thought (for example, Shem-Tov
Falaquera; Abraham Bibago), and of talmudic learning, expressed both in

novellae as well as in responsa, and in codification (for example, Solomon b. Abraham Adret; Nahmanides; Asher b. Jehiel (originally from Germany); Jacob b. Asher; Isaac b. Sheshet Perfet). Valuable poetry based on Arabic models was written in most of these centuries there (by Abraham ibn Ezra, Moses ibn Ezra, Judah Halevi, Meshullam Da Piera, etc.).

Provence formed a separate Jewish cultural province up to the expulsions of 1306. Its great communities were most active in the Maimonidean controversy. The writings of the Ibn Tibbon family, of Jacob Anatoli, of Menahem Meiri, of Abraham of Béziers, show throughout the high level of Jewish culture, much creativity in many fields, as well as a high level of general culture. Provence was to a certain degree a meeting place, and therefore also a battleground, for the influences of Jewish culture in Spain from the south and of Ashkenazi culture in France from the north, though many specific ingredients gave it an additional individual tinge of its own.

It was in Provence and Christian Spain that the influential circles of the Kabbalah and its variegated literature gave a new lease of life to mysticism and had a growing influence in this direction among Jews and on Judaism. The 13th-century esoteric Zohar literature, as well as the 14th-century *Sefer ha-Kanah,* express much social criticism and opposition to rationalism and the aristocratic circles. In particular the *Ra'aya Meheimna,* a later stratum of the Zohar, contains many images of ideas related in symbolism, tendency, and character to those of the Franciscan Fraticelli. The 14th-century works contain skillful satirical sketches of situations, modes of behavior, and types of leaders and leadership, which had incurred the odium of the extreme mystic opposition. In Germany — around Regensburg and Worms — there arose the elite Hasidei Ashkenaz movement of the 12th and 13th centuries (see below, chap. 7).

In Poland-Lithuania there are many indications that the 15th and early 16th century saw not only the transposition of the characteristic Ashkenazi culture there but also the expression of considerable rationalist elements, that were in the main suppressed by the end of the 16th century. There also appeared popular elements reflecting the life of the masses and expressing a more vulgar trend with less respect for learning. This reached quite extreme proportions, in particular in the southeastern districts of this realm, and developed and spread among later generations.

The level of general education was relatively very high in all the communities of this period. It was typical of Jewish life in 12th-century Egypt that a lady on her deathbed should write to her sister:

Ideals in Education and Scholarship

"My lady, if God, exalted by He, ordains my death, my greatest last wish to you is that you should take care of my little daughter and make an effort that she should learn. I am very well aware that I am putting a heavy burden on you, for we have not even what is necessary for her upkeep, let alone for the expenses of teaching, but we have before us the example of our mother, the servant of God" (S.D. Goitein, *Sidrei Ḥinnukh* (1962), 66).

Blind teachers were at a premium in those regions, for girls could sit before them without problems. A responsum of Maimonides (ed. J. Blau (1960), 71–73, no. 45) mentions a woman teacher of boys in 12th-century Egypt, who made her living from this profession. Various references show the widespread extent of learning and knowledge among almost all Jewish men and many Jewish women in Europe. A late-12th-century monk contrasts the education usual among the Jews with the ignorance among the Christians, of his own acquaintance:

"But the Jews, out of zeal for God and love of the law, put as many sons as they have to letters, that each may understand God's law ... A Jew, however poor, if he had ten sons would put them all to letters, not for gain, as the Christians do, but for the understanding of God's law, and not only his sons, but his daughters" (in B. Smalley, *Study of the Bible in the Middle Ages* (1952), 78).

In the upper circles of Jewish society, learning and scripture took on the additional value of esthetic enjoyment. Judah ibn Tibbon — physician, merchant, and translator in 12th-century Provence — enjoined his son Samuel, the future translator of Maimonides from Arabic into Hebrew: "My son! Make thy books thy companions; let thy cases and shelves be thy pleasure-grounds and gardens. Bask in their flowerbeds, pluck their roses ... If thy soul be satiate and weary, change from garden to garden, from furrow to furrow, from prospect to prospect. Then will thy desire renew itself and thy soul will be filled with delight" (I. Abrahams, *Hebrew Ethical Wills,* 1, (1948), 63). This father also admonished: "See to it that the penmanship and handwriting is as beautiful as thy style" (*ibid.,* 69). The cardinal social value of learning in all strata of Jewish society has been succinctly put by a father defending the teacher against his wife, who considered the teacher too exacting with their sons: "We are esteemed by people on account of knowledge ... Without knowledge a man is not worth a farthing with people even if he is from a worthy family" (S.D. Goitein, *op. cit.,* 35).

Certainly, times of trouble, expulsions, and the difficulties of colonization in distant regions and places must have led to some diminution of knowledge and education among Jews, but in the main, this testimony is a reliable indicator of the general level of Jewish culture everywhere in this period.

Throughout the Jewish Diaspora of this time the scholar and student was the ideal of individual perfection, and learning the greatest social asset among Jews. Freed from the fetters of the hereditary family structure of the gaonate, while based on the same conception of the supreme sacredness and values attached to it, the position and image of the student and sage again attained the stature they had in late Second Temple days and talmudic times. In Spain as in Germany, in Persia as in Poland, the more learned a Jew, the higher the esteem in which he was held. This attitude emerges sharply in a bitterly critical homily of the leader of the *Ḥasidei Ashkenaz,* Eleazar b. Judah of Worms, on the subject of learning and merits:

"For in life there may exist one who is not God-fearing but is more proficient in dialectics, more keen-witted and more skillful to explain problems than one who is God-fearing. For in this world it is customary to honor one man above his fellow; like one who is rich and has everything that he wants, but he does not do the will of God in accordance with his riches, for it has been decreed that he should enjoy this world through the honor of his riches so that the grandchildren of the great scholars shall intermarry with him. So is it the same with Torah study — one who does not deserve it is honored with it because they so desire in heaven. And as riches were given to the one who does not deserve it, in order to cast him into hell, so the same applies to a scholar who is not deserving, who causes others to sin, who judges falsely, despising the good ones, enjoying and hating them; and he has superiority over them — for the righteous one falls before the evil-doer; and he is successful, for his pronouncements are obeyed, and he has pupils who help him; time is favorable to him and he is victorious over his enemies who are superior to him. But in the world of the souls, the righteous one shall be given abundant wisdom. As he [the righteous one] is profound and God-fearing, in the same measure in that world of the souls, they will give the righteous one abundant wisdom to be victorious, and also ability in dialectics to ask and answer, and his pronouncements shall give law to this world" (*Ḥokhmat ha-Nefesh,* 1876, folio 20a, repr. 1968).

Both social tension and a cultural tradition are expressed here, through appreciation of intellectual achievement as the supreme ideal of human attainment, while, at the same time, perceiving its mundane aspects as an economic and social asset given by God to undeserving men to serve as a temporary reward and a pitfall. The elements in Jewish society of social preferment of the rich as well as of the learned, the custom of intermarrying, and the social authority they enjoyed are stressed. In bitter opposition, R. Eleazar envisages an other-worldly, spiritualized, image of the sage and Torah study. Dialectics in argument, and victory in achievement are part of his spiritual attributes too. The sage is the ideal for all, for the established leadership as well as for its determined critics, whether accepted as he is in life or viewed as an embodiment of supreme virtues.

Christian at-
tacks on
Talmud

The Church, during the 13th century, made a sustained effort to belittle and, ultimately, to eliminate, the main Jewish intellectual preoccupation of that time, the Talmud. Pope Gregory IX was suddenly amazed, at the quite late date in Jewish-Christian relations of June 9, 1239, at what had come to his attention. He wrote:

"To the archbishops throughout the Kingdom of France, whom these letters may reach: ... If what is said about the Jews of France and of the other lands is true, no punishment would be sufficiently great or sufficiently worthy of their crime. For they, so we have heard, are not content with the old Law which God gave to Moses in writing: they even ignore it completely, and affirm that God gave another law which is called 'Talmud' ... " (in S. Grayzel, *Church and the Jews in the 13th Century* (1933), 241, no. 96).

He therefore initiated the confiscation and burning of the Talmud. This policy was continued at first — though successful initially only in some of the Christian countries — by Pope Innocent IV, who discovered on May 9, 1244, that Jews "rear and nurture their children" on the Talmud, which "is a big book among them, exceeding in size the texts of the Bible. In it are found blasphemies against God and His Christ, and obviously entangled fables about the Blessed Virgin, and abusive errors, and unheard-of follies ... " (*ibid.,* 251, no. 104). All these endeavors had no effect. Jewish learning continued to flourish. The Talmud remained its basic book. Pope Innocent IV himself was convinced in the end that the Jews would not live as Jews without the Talmud. Thus this attempt to change for Jews the content of their own culture failed in the 13th century as it had failed in the sixth. In Christian Spain, where the meeting of culture and minds was much closer, the main attempt against the Talmud aimed on the one hand to discredit it, and on the other to use its aggadic elements for christological purposes. This trend is expressed in the *Pugio Fidei Adversus Mauros Et Judaeos,* completed c. 1280 by the Dominican Raymond Martini, as well as by the efforts of the apostate Pablo Christiani in his disputation with the Spanish rabbi and communal leader Naḥmanides in 1263 at Barcelona, where he

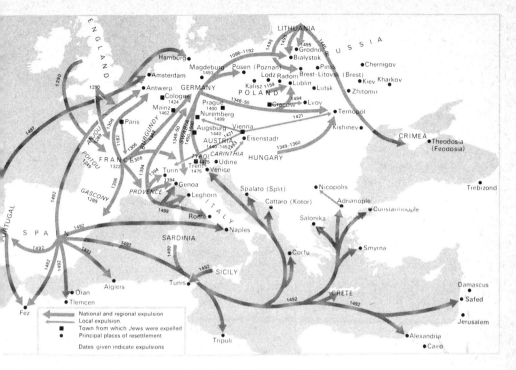

Some of the expulsions of Jews between 1000 and 1500 C.E.

tried to prove from the *aggadah* that Jesus was the Messiah. These, as well as subsequent polemical works and disputations, did not eliminate the Talmud from Jewish education and influenced only certain Jews in Christian Spain in the late 14th and 15th century who were already driven toward Christianity by the combined pressures of terror and the sight of Christian successes in life.

The end of the 15th century appeared a time of final liquidation of Jewry not only in Christian Spain and Portugal but also throughout Europe. The blood libel of Trent, Italy, in 1475, subsequent libels, litigations, and expulsions in and from German cities and principalities that began then and continued well into the 16th century, the expulsion of Jews from Cracow in 1495, as well as from Lithuania, seemed to presage that sooner or later all Christian principalities would follow in the steps of Spain. Yet the expulsions in Germany remained piecemeal because of the fragmentation of the empire. In many cases Jews attained through the expulsions a wider dispersion around or near the cities from which they had been expelled, and new and better means of livelihood. In Poland-Lithuania the trend to expulsion was reversed.

By the time of the great expulsions the Ashkenazi culture of the communities of France, Germany, Bohemia-Moravia, and Poland-Lithuania on the one hand and the Sephardi culture of those of Spain (to be developed and diversified in

Wave of Expulsions

the new places of settlement) on the other had already crystallized in individual forms of prayer rite, in customs, in content of education and creativity, and in social composition, and in differing modes of contact with, and attitudes to, the gentile environment. There were meetings of minds and persons, and crosscurrents of cultural influence and exchange between the Jews of Ashkenaz and Sepharad before the expulsions. Naḥmanides esteemed Ashkenazi Jewish culture and prayed that it would strike roots in Spain. The legal codifier Asher b. Jehiel and his sons brought this influence with them from Germany to Spain. The works of Rashi and the tosafists, written in France, were diligently studied in Spain. Moses b. Jacob of Coucy in France went to preach in Spain and according to his own testimony was influential there. On the other hand, the influence of Maimonides, of the rationalist biblical exegesis typical of Abraham ibn Ezra's work, and the influence of Kabbalah were strongly felt in Ashkenaz.

Yet, in sum, these remained random encounters and influences at book level only. When the link with Provence was broken in 1306, contacts between Ashkenaz and Sepharad became even fewer. The exodus of about 300,000 Spanish Jews to the Mediterranean lands in North Africa and Asia, but also to Italy, to the Balkans, and gradually to the Netherlands (still under Spanish rule), and from there to northwestern Germany, brought the gradual, and in some cases even swift, breakdown of the old partitions. Ashkenazim and Sephardim met in the context of actual social and cultural life. They did not always like what they saw. But the result strengthened mutual acquaintance and influence, while creating much more clearly defined and specific contours in Ashkenazi and Sephardi culture. The Sephardi Jews considered that they had been uprooted by expulsion from their beloved fatherland in Spain and from a culture which they considered superior to all other gentile cultures. They were also wholeheartedly devoted to their specific form of Jewish culture. This was the reason for the remarkable cultural takeover by the Sephardi refugees of many of the communities to which they came.

4

Transition to Modern Times
(16th — 17th Centuries)

Five main processes may be considered as causing the break up of medieval configurations and bringing about the changeover to modern ones.

The expulsion from Spain ultimately created a much larger and better equipped, economically and culturally, Jewish society in the cities of the Ottoman Empire. It renovated and invigorated the Jewish settlement in Erez Israel and Jewish messianic hopes. By making possible the emergence of a community of openly professing Jews in the Protestant Netherlands, as well as by the movement to northwestern Germany, and to England, it gave rise to a whole network of Jewish "capitalist" occupations and activities, in close and fruitful contact with the new Christian churches and sects, and with the colonial activity of the Dutch and the English. It sent Jews across the oceans: the first Jewish settlements in the New World came under Dutch rule as also the first settlement in present-day New York (then New Amsterdam) in 1654.

The second main process took place in Poland-Lithuania. The colonizing and economic activities of Jews there until the Chmielnicki massacres of 1648 created a Jewry that formed, to all intents and purposes, the predominating element of "the third estate" in this kingdom. Demographically and ecologically this community underwent a great expansion that created the nucleus of the mass Ashkenazi Jewish population of modern times. Close touch with village life and economy improved the conditions of Jewish life and changed habits. In the cities owned by the Polish nobles the predominantly Jewish townships of Eastern Europe grew up which later produced the *shtetl* of the Pale of Settlement in czarist Russia and of Galicia in Austria. As a result of these population movements by the end of the 17th century, out of approximately a million Jews in the world, about half were Sephardi and half Ashkenazi, mainly concentrated in the Ottoman Empire and Poland-Lithuania, respectively.

The Reformation in Christianity from 1517 broke up the unitary and constricted frame of Catholic uniformity surrounding the Jew in most of Europe. He was now no longer the only nonconformist in a culture of total agreement. The failure of both the Reformation camp and the Catholic to achieve decisive victory in their common bid to reestablish Christian uniformity created the first hesitant appearance of tolerance. Jews were as yet not thought of in this connection, but the very notion was to create, later on, modern conditions for their existence. On the other hand, the Reformation – in particular, in the style set by the German Martin Luther – unleashed popular furies and made mass passion and violence the main instrument of religious innovation. This raised the problem of the status of the Jews, not only for change toward betterment of their lot, as Luther intended in his missionary zeal and hopes in 1523; it also opened roads toward exacerbating the lot of Jews and radical vulgar propaganda to extirpate their existence, as the disappointed rancorous ex-monk Luther proposed in 1543:

> "What then shall we Christians do with this damned, rejected race of Jews? Since they live among us and we know about their lying and blasphemy and cursing, we cannot tolerate them if we do not wish to share in their lies, curses, and blasphemy ... We must prayerfully and reverentially practice a merciful severity ... Let me give you my honest advice ... "

There follows a detailed seven-point program of arson, expropriation, abject humiliation of, and hard physical labor for, the Jews.

> "If, however, we are afraid that they might harm us personally ... then let us apply ... [expulsion] ... and settle with them for that which they have extorted usurously from us, and after having divided it up fairly, let us drive them out of the country for all time" (from his *Von den Juden und Iren Luegen,* 1543).

Short of the Auschwitz oven and extermination, the whole Nazi Holocaust is pre-outlined here. The Reformation had unleashed situations and attitudes with regard to the Jews as well as many other matters, open in all directions and for all comers, toward human relations with and better treatment of the Jews, as well as toward increased enmity and destruction. This openness and struggle between extremes were to become later one of the hallmarks of "the Jewish question" in modern history.

In Jewry, the great messianic movement of 1665–66, like the Reformation, was medieval in aspect while pointing toward ultra-modernism at the same time. The pseudo-messiah Shabbetai Zevi and his enthusiastic followers put to test the belief in a miraculous redeemer, although arriving in the end at apostasy to Islam. They felt during this great upsurge of faith and ecstasy inwardly liberated and on the threshold of political glory. Within the space of three years, all of them lost any hope of soon reaching the splendor and most of them lost the last shreds of any sense of liberation. The movement reflected the unconscious crisis of medievalism, which burned out in the flame of miraculously borne messianism. Its prophet, Nathan of Gaza, deemed that God was now free from exile but His people was not. From this it was but a step — even if a gigantic and revolutionary one — toward a program of secularization: the people must seek its freedom and redemption through its own, human, powers, employing the ways and means of the world.

The last, but not least, of these processes occurred in the great community of Marrano origin at Amsterdam. People who had been brought up in the traditions of the Jewish underground in Spain found that the Jewish community with which they now came in contact, its strict regulations and exacting authorities, were not at all the antithesis of the Church and its dogmatics that they had been formerly taught to see in Judaism. The atmosphere of sectarianism and religious discussion in the Netherlands, of comfortable burgher life and its easy theology, of friendly contact between cultured gentiles and individual Jews added to the disappointment which the Marranos experienced with actual Jewish society and led to revulsion and revolt. From this aspect, Baruch Spinoza is both the end result of a line of development of Maimonidean trends in Sephardi Jewry as well as the first representative of a type of modern non-Orthodox Jew. The life and tragedy of Uriel da Costa[31] expressed this in a different way. The activities of Hamburg Sephardi Jews, who helped to engineer a revolt in Portugal in the 17th century, and served as consuls and financial representatives of the country in which they were not allowed to set foot on pain of death, represented yet another component in the same mosaic of modernization. Figures like Leone Modena[32] and Simone Luzzatto[33] in Italy, each in his own way, were an articulate expression of the unformulated change toward modernization and alleviation of the Orthodox way of life. The historiography and historiosophy of Azariah dei Rossi[34] express, in a less extreme but more thorough way, the readiness for questioning and change that began to appear at this time.

Most of the results of the last three processes described above still lay in the near or distant future by the end of the 17th century; while the first two were at work and wielding an influence throughout the 16th and 17th centuries.

---

31   Lived 1585—1640; philosopher and freethinker; twice excommunicated; committed suicide.
32   Lived 1571—1648 in Italy; rabbi whose interests were many, often conflicting; his writings show a lively and open mind.
33   Lived 1583—1663; rabbi with much knowledge of and interest in political theory and philosophy.
34   Lived c. 1511—1571 in Italy.

The refugees from Spain organized themselves almost everywhere they arrived, and as soon as they could, into separate "synagogue-communities," mainly formed by groups coming from the same community, district, or domain. In this way they broke up the framework of the existing local community, rejecting the cohesion it represented through settlement in the same place. Such a situation was a reversion to a time in the 10th to 12th centuries when many places in the Near East had both a synagogue "of Erez Israelites" and one "of the Babylonians." They set a pattern for similar organizational behavior in other Jewish immigrant groups, sentimentally attached to each other and to the memory of their place of origin, and yet without ties to their new place of settlement. It was to emerge in modern times in the behavior and organization of the *Landsmannschaften* and of synagogues named after places of origin as in the United States and other countries.

Within a relatively short time the Spanish refugees achieved the feat of becoming the tone-setters and social leaders of the native Jews in territories

Traditional dress of Jewesses in Morocco showing the combination of local style with elements brought over by exiles from Spain.

Left: Leone Modena (1571−1648). The fact that he included a portrait of himself in his book *Riti Hebraici* (Paris, 1637) stems from a lifestyle that was both Jewish medieval and Jewish modern.

Right: Baruch Benedict Spinoza (1632−1677), key European thinker, rebel, excommunicated from the Jewish community of Amsterdam.

embracing the Balkans and large parts of the Ottoman Empire and North Africa. Economically, too, the refugees achieved great progress. In the Ottoman Empire some of them became courtiers of the sultan, physicians (Joseph and Moses Hamon, his son; Abraham ibn Megas), bankers, and diplomats (Don Joseph Nasi; Solomon Abenaes). In these surroundings, where the harem played an influential role, Jewish women also became prominent (like Dona Gracia Nasi). Sometimes there arose a combination of Jewish physician and diplomat (Solomon Ashkenazi). All these Jews were active in the customary Spanish manner in their new and strange settings. The mass of the refugees turned to commerce and crafts with considerable success. The economy of Safed in the 17th century was based on a broad and stable occupational structure of clothweaving, shopkeeping, and peddling. Many engaged in international trade. Some used the land routes, through the southeastern parts of Poland-Lithuania to the center and west of Europe; some traded by sea routes, in the Mediterranean and on the European shores of the Atlantic, linking up in this way with the northeastern wing of the Sephardi dispersion in the Netherlands and northwest Germany, and toward the end of the period, with Jews in England too. In this manner, economic activity brought association and cooperation to the three great

Economic Activities

Gracia Hannah Mendes Nasi, a leader in Jewish life and struggle for self-respect, portrayed as a 16th-century *"Grand-Dame,"* on a medal by Pastorino de Pastorini, 1553.

dynamic centers of Jewish social and economic life — the Ottoman Empire, Poland-Lithuania, and the northwest of Europe. The Jews of Poland-Lithuania, on their part, carried on a large-scale export and import trade both with Central and northwestern Europe, and with the Ottoman Empire, in particular its Black Sea shore and Balkan districts. Jews in the Netherlands and northwestern Germany dealt on a considerable scale, frequently in colonial goods and diamonds, with Central European Jews (who bought these luxury goods mainly for the local upper nobility or for export to the east). They similarly traded with the Jews of Poland-Lithuania, buying agricultural produce on a large scale and selling them luxury goods, cloths, and printed books. Thus this vast configuration of Jewish economic activity created an extensive network of commercial traffic on the threshold of modern times.

The Jews of Central Europe were the weakest link, demographically and economically, in this chain of Jewish activity. Yet they were to profit greatly from it. The combination of connections and supplies created by the export trade of luxury goods and diamonds from northwest Europe and the Ottoman east, and the import of vast quantities of agricultural produce, cattle fodder, cattle, and horses from Poland-Lithuania, enabled the Jews of the German Empire, few and weak at this time and therefore pliable and reliable tools of the princes, to become, at the end of the 17th century in increasing numbers, the agents and *Hofjuden* to royal courts and royal armies.

Apart from the fragmentation of local cohesion through synagogue membership, the whole trend of communal organization outside the Ottoman Empire lay toward centralization and strong leadership. This was the time when the Councils of the Lands[35] of Poland-Lithuania and of Bohemia-Moravia showed their greatest achievements. An attempt was made, unsuccessfully, to set up a similar organization in fragmented Germany at Frankfort on the Main in 1603. Numerous similar attempts were made among the Italian Jewish communities. The Mahamad[36] of northwestern Sephardi Jewry aroused opposition by its strict Orthodoxy and authoritarianism. An attempt in 1538 to reinstitute the ancient sacred authority of rabbinic ordination *(semikhah)* as a preparation and precondition for the creation of a Sanhedrin was another expression of the tendency toward overall leadership and centralization. The great and successful legal codification activity of Joseph Caro in Safed, and Mordecai Jaffe, Solomon Luria, and above all Moses Isserles in Poland, again expresses — by literary extension of the possibilities inherent in *semikhah* — the trend toward central and authoritative instruction and leadership.

Safed Mysticism

Jewish cultural and religious life showed considerable activity in these centuries. Safed became a short-lived but very important center of Jewish mysticism and learning in the 16th and early 17th century. It formed a dynamic community of great mystics (like Isaac Luria; Moses Cordovero; Hayyim Vital; and a galaxy of others), and of talmudic scholars (foremost were Jacob Berab and Joseph Caro). Their societies and groups developed customs that later were to be widely accepted in Jewish communities. Kabbalah spread from Safed throughout the Jewish world. This was not only mystic and aesthetic in mood, but also bore the stamp of highly developed, proud, and self-conscious individual personalities. The movement of Shabbetai Zevi expresses both the power and the fragility of this mood and of such individuals. Safed also witnessed the birth, in the 16th century, of the *Shulhan Arukh,* the standard Jewish legal code, and of halakhic activity of many other types.

In this period there occurred also the first sharp and systematic criticism of Ashkenazi Jewish education. Judah Loew b. Bezalel of Prague, and the circle around him, which had adherents not only in Bohemia-Moravia, but in Germany and Poland-Lithuania as well, strongly criticized the lack of didactic methods, the exaggeration in the teaching and use of dialectics, in particular with young students, and the unsystematic and unequal teaching of various components of Jewish traditional culture. They demanded a return to plain logic, to the Mishnah as the core for talmudic study, to proper attention to Torah, and to didactic progression from the easy to the difficult portions and subjects. With some of them, this criticism assumed a note of demand to return to the Bible. The criticism was heard, and failed in its aim. Jewish society in Central and

Approaches to Education

---

35   See below, Part 2, chap. 4.
36   The appellation of the community leadership in Sephardi diaspora communities.

Eastern Europe was unwilling to take up either the new curriculum or the new methods. These pedagogues and critics had to wait for modern times to achieve a positive appreciation.

Traditional Torah study and the central position of the student in Jewish society continued throughout this period. Although encountering tensions and dangers in the materially successful societies of the Ottoman Empire, Poland-Lithuania, and northwestern Europe, the importance of learning remained undiminished in Jewish life. Jewish communities everywhere had numerous yeshivot and scholars, naturally of unequal stature. The *takkanot* issued by communities and synods provide instruction and advice on the spreading of learning. Even if much of this reflects more of the ideal than the reality, it still expresses the scale of values of Jewish society of the 16th and 17th centuries.

Political and ideological thought was alive in particular in the 16th century. Chronicle writing received a new impetus under the impact of the expulsion from Spain and the needs for reappraisal in the constantly changing situation (resettlement in the Ottoman Empire and other countries) and developed in light of the changes in Jewish outlook brought about by the Reformation. Solomon ibn Verga in his *Shevet Yehudah* refers to the problems of relations between Jews and gentiles, and of the Jewish fate, out of a feeling of danger and weakness. In his chronicle the Christian view of the problem as Ibn Verga understood it is given prominence alongside the Jewish view. The weakness of the Jews in history is explained by the Christian "Thomas" to the Spanish king as:

> "That originally while the Jews found favor in the eyes of God, he would fight their wars, as it is known to all . . . . Therefore they did not learn the ways of war for they did not need them . . . and when they sinned God turned away his face from them and they thus remained losers on all counts — they were ignorant of weapons of war and its invention, and the will of God was not with them; they remained naked and fell like sheep without a shepherd" (*Shevet Yehudah*, ed. by A. Schochet (1947), 44).

Samuel Usque in his *Consolaçam as Tribulaçoens de Israel* (English edition: *Consolation for the Tribulations of Israel* (1965)) regards the tribulations and hopes of the exiles within a broad view of world history and divine providence. Another 16th-century historian, Joseph ha-Kohen, describes Jewish history in his various volumes and also gives separately the history of the Ottoman Empire and of the French. His stand is consistently pro-Reformation, vehemently anti-papal, and throughout imbued with the spirit of the late

Renaissance world view and appreciation of history. He hopes that the wars of religion will result in the birth of toleration for all. David Gans provides in his *Zemah David* (1592) a separate treatment of Jewish and general history, quoting *in extenso* from German chronicles and citing the name of author and page, thus revealing an assumption that his Jewish readers might refer back to his sources. Throughout he is revealed as a patriot of Bohemia, an admirer of Prague and of Bohemian achievements in the past. His is the first systematic expression of attachment by Ashkenazi Jews to the land on which they are living and to the past of their environment. Many lesser chroniclers, mainly in Italy, relate themselves to Jewish troubles in the 16th century generally, taking into account the views of the host society. The Cretan rabbi and historian Elijah Capsali in his extensive chronicles (the greater part at present in manuscript) shows an absorption with the ways of governments and the ideas of the reigning circles both in the Ottoman Empire and in Venice. His description of the fate of the exiles from Spain and their welcome in the Ottoman Empire has additional value as an expression of the attitude of the native Jewish communities where the exiles were received and as evidence of the spell that Sephardi culture rapidly cast over them.

Political and historiosophic thought finds deep if sometimes involved expression in the ideas of Judah Loew b. Bezalel of Prague [37]. In his *Be'er ha-Golah,* in the part entitled the "seventh well," he antedates by 50 years at least the protest of John Milton against the censorship of printed books. Most of the arguments of these two thinkers run in parallel, of course each expressing the writer's own mood. The rabbi of Prague, unlike the poet of England, also stresses the knightly concept that one has to regard discussion in printed books as a kind of duel where an honorable opponent must ensure that his adversary is armed in the best way possible, so that victory will be an act of valor and not an overwhelming by brute force. Throughout his many works, didactics and the methodology of preaching and learning are a main concern of Judah Loew. He devoted much thought to problems of the organismic character of national cohesion, seeing a divine guarantee through the nature of nationality that Jewish exile and humiliation cannot be eternal.

Political and Ideological Thought

His writings, like the writings of many other scholars of Poland-Lithuania, Bohemia-Moravia, and Germany in this period, contain many allusions to and proposed solutions for social problems. The tension that existed between the lay leaders of the communities and the rabbis arose largely because both came from the same families, were usually related by marriage, and, above all, received the

---

37   Lived 1525–1609. A great scholar and teacher who became a semi-legendary figure.

same education in *yeshivot*. Hence, there was an inclination among community leaders to assume rabbinical authority and functions and among rabbinical authority and functions and among rabbis to see themselves as leaders. The claims were not mutually exclusive. In most communities and periods an unstable harmony was worked out, but the tension was part of the arrangement.

In prospering Poland-Lithuania much thought was also given to the economic effort, to the correct attitude of rich to poor, and to the proper structure for Jewish society. At one extreme, the great legal authority Moses Isserles[38] asserted that riches and material success are given by God to the deserving Jew. Poverty proves either that the poor man is undeserving, or if his merits are evident, that there is some hidden blemish in his character which would have been revealed with riches: he is not given riches so that he may remain unblemished. At the other extreme stood the great preacher Ephraim Solomon of Luntschitz. In his ideology riches are usually evil. Drawing a kind of dual comparison he tells rich Jews that they cannot prove their merits from their worldly state for then they would also have to admit the righteousness of the gentiles from their success. Similarly, he considers that the gentiles cannot bring arguments against the Jews from their worldly success, for they would also then have to admit the righteousness of patently evil persons among Christians who have been materially successful. Riches in his metaphor are spoiled meat desired unwisely by the foolish child but thrown by a prudent father to the dogs. This preacher was also much concerned about religious and moral sincerity in a society which admired devotion, study, and charity and thus made these moral values also preeminently social assets. In his opinion social reward for and recognition of good deeds endangered the foundations of spiritual worship and Torah study in what seemed to him a society that tended to materialism, in particular among the upper strata.

In the emerging centers of Jewish life, tension resulted from the meeting of divergent traditions and the encounter between the old-established society and ways of life and the force and vitality of new and inviting circumstances. The type of thought and hegemony provided by men like Elijah and Moses Capsali (Turkish rabbi and communal leader), the rabbinic authority Elijah Mizraḥi, and other representatives of the leadership structure of the old communities clashed with the attitudes and aims of new leaders of the Sephardi types, like Gracia and Joseph Nasi or the great Sephardi rabbis of the Balkan peninsula, such as the

---

38   Moses Isserles (1525–1569), also known as the Rema. One of his best known achievements is the version of the *Shulḥan Arukh* that he produced, in which he added glosses that made the work acceptable to Ashkenazi Jewry.

Salonikan talmudist, Bible scholar, and kabbalist Joseph Taitazak. This conflict fructified each side in the 16th and 17th centuries. This process of confrontation and mutual influence took place in a Jewish culture and society which combined the old Romaniot[39] customs and ways of life of the Byzantine environment in the Balkans and Asia Minor, of the Muslim environment, elements of the old Babylonian Jewish culture, and the social and cultural traditions of the great centers of Jewish life in Egypt, Kairouan, Fez, and other communities in North Africa. It encountered representatives of the Sephardi Jewish culture which had developed in close contact with Christian culture in Spain and who were conscious of the value in and greatness of their historical experience and mode of leadership. Within a relatively short space of time, both the Romaniot and North African were either put aside or submerged by the Sephardi influence. To a scholar of the stature of Samuel b. Moses de Medina, the Salonikan halakhic authority and communal leader, it was self-evident that the Sephardi prayer rites and order of worship should be preferred in Balkan communities because of their intrinsic superiority.

The tribulations of the exiles and refugees gave new impetus to the ancient reality of Jewish brotherhood. Abraham ibn Mega, who was physician to Sultan Suleiman the Magnificent, gave evidence in the second half of the 16th century, that "The Jewish people − whether one be great or small, rich or poor, endeavor to rescue [a fellow Jew] in [danger of] life or property . . . They also tithe their money for the ransoming of captives, strangers, and outsiders, without knowing from where they come, if only they are called Jews. This is done every day, as I have seen and heard myself. Such is their excellent custom in all holy communities. Jews living in small towns do this even more devotedly, with all the means available to them, even if they are few in number" (*Kevod Elohim*, (1585), III, Chap. 3, fol. 126a). Thus communities on the Mediterranean littoral for generations rendered assistance to poor arrivals and to hostages of sea pirates.

Attempts at Political Action

On occasion the travail of readjustment took the shape of a clear-cut issue of Jewish foreign policy. A dispute over this arose within Jewry in the 16th century, when an attempt was made to use Jewish economic activity as a defensive punitive weapon in extreme cases of insult and injury to Jews. It was opposed by considerations of caution and the hope that part of the aims could be achieved by less dangerous means. (The same dilemma was to return much later, in deliberations over initiating a boycott of Nazi Germany.) When Pope Paul IV ordered that a number of Marranos who had escaped to Ancona from Spain

---

39   In this context the culture and prayer-rite of the Jews of the Byzantine, and later Ottoman, empires until their contact with the exiles from Spain in the 16th century.

should be burned at the stake, the circle around Dona Gracia Nasi and other Sephardi groups in the Ottoman Empire attempted to use Jewish commercial power in the Mediterranean both to put pressure on the pope and to reward the duke of Pesaro, who had given asylum to those who had escaped from Ancona. As Joseph ibn Lev, a contemporary Sephardi rabbi, described it:

"Several people arose who wanted a great revenge for the holocaust of these just men . . . they demanded from the sages and the holy [Jewish] communities that they should assent to and put in force a valid agreement that no Jew among those living in the Ottoman Empire shall be permitted to trade in Ancona, since the Divine Name has been defiled by this pope, the lord of this place. Moreover, some of those who lived in Ancona have escaped the mortal danger of this destruction, and have come to the city of Pesaro where they have been welcomed by the duke, the ruler of this land, who thought that the Jews of the Ottoman Empire would come to trade there and would boycott the city of the pope who did evil to their brethren as well as actions that have never been done before, viz, to burn the Talmud in contempt. The above-mentioned duke will also spend much money to improve the seaport of this city, so that ships may lie there in safety. Now, if he sees that the Jews will pay him evil for good, it is almost certain that he will extradite the men, women and children who escaped from Ancona . . . to the pope, who demands them in order to put them to death" (*Responsa*, 1 (Constantinople, 1556, 1959[2]) 140a).

This closely reasoned argumentation, that combined feelings of national pride, perception of the political use of trade opportunities, and an open-eyed appreciation of the motives of the Christian rulers, was opposed by what may be called the Italian Jewish party. These did not deny the strength and possibilities attaching to Jewish trade in the Mediterranean in the 16th century but argued against the boycott because it would endanger the Jews living in the Papal States. They also considered that "even if this agreement is not made, the duke of Urbino will not cause any harm to those he has accepted; for he is a considerate and sagacious man who knows that this miserable people cannot obligate all the Jews. Moreover, he is overjoyed at their settling in his land because they, of necessity, cannot trade in Ancona, and will trade in his city." The Italian party also put forward the arguments that the Marranos from Spain could have been more careful and should have avoided settling under the rule of the head of the Catholic Church (Joshua Soncino, *Naḥalah li-Yhoshu'a*, no. 39).

In Poland-Lithuania also there arose a question of overall Jewish policy with economic implications. The question of contracting for the customs duties and customs stations by Jews was differently decided in the late 16th and early 17th century by the councils of Poland and Lithuania. The first decided to direct Jews to avoid these lucrative posts because of the enmity they provoked in the Polish middle and lesser nobility; the Lithuanian council expressly decided later to assist Jews to lease and retain them out of a clearly stated policy that despite the dangers to the community they involved, if the customs were managed by Jews this would benefit the whole of Jewish trade and improve the Jewish position in general.

Jewish policy and aims were being put forward after the invention of printing and the spread of printed books not only in memoranda to rulers and Church leaders, but also in works published to bring Jewish views before the Christian public. Simone Luzzatto published his *Discorso circa il stato degl' Hebrei* . . . in Italian in 1638. This work of a rabbi and leader of a Jewish community is addressed to the Venetians as an apologetical argument for the existence of the Jews in Venice. In it Luzzatto stresses the economic and social usefulness to the civic society of Venice of a commercially and financially active minority which had no other focus for its loyalty, or a better place to look to, than the city of which they were inhabitants. He even explains at some length that there are "Catholic" trends in the Jewish faith and behavior, which are inherently opposed to the "Protestant" ones. Luzzatto emphasizes the basic honesty of the Jews and their obedience to law. After listing some of the faults which are to be found among Jews, he enumerates traits:

"Worthy of some consideration: steadfastness, and unimaginable consistency in their faith and in the keeping of their law; unity in the dogmas of their faith although they have been dispersed throughout the world for 1,550 years; admirable courage, if not in going to meet dangers, then at least, in the strength to suffer troubles; a unique knowledge of their holy Scriptures and of their commentaries; charity and good will toward all as well as help to each and every one of their nation, even if he is a stranger and an alien. A Persian Jew cares about the problems of an Italian Jew and tries to help him; distance of place does not cause separation among them, for their religion is one. In matters of sexual passion, they behave with considerable abstinence; they are loyal and careful about the purity of the race, that it should be without admixture; many of them show considerable sagacity and know how to carry through the most complicated business; they behave with submission and respect toward any man who is not of their religion; their transgressions and sins have in them almost always more of the lowly and ugly than of cruelty and evil" (*ibid.*, Consideration 11).

This work was to have much influence in mercantilist centers and among Christians who were beginning to advocate better behavior toward Jews. The Dutch scholar Manasseh Ben Israel continued this line of argument, though in a very different and more upstanding manner, in his various writings and, in particular, in his efforts to obtain the readmission of Jews into England. He stressed the advantages that had accrued to the Netherlands by the admission of Jews into that country and by their active participation in colonial trade there, and compared this position with the decline of Spain and the disadvantages it had encountered after the expulsion of the Jews. He formulated a petition for the readmission of the Jews to England. In common with many English sectarians who supported his case, he regarded the settlement of Jews at "the end of the earth [i.e., Angleterre]" as a necessary precondition to the coming of the Messiah.

Stirrings of Religious Toleration

The 16th and 17th centuries brought the first stirrings of a change in attitudes toward the Jews. The Jewish chronicler Joseph ha-Kohen discerned in the wars of religion in France a hope for an emerging permissiveness enabling each man to live according to his own religion. In the Calvinist Netherlands an attitude of toleration of Jews, and even respect for them and their way of life, developed without granting them political rights or formulating a fully expressed theory for their toleration. This came about not only through day-to-day peaceful contacts with the highly cultured Jewish circles in Amsterdam and other cities of this country, but also through the respect of the Calvinists for the Law and their efforts to create a Christian society partly on biblical foundations. Some sectarians expressed "the desire . . . to raise the Old Testament to the position of natural law" which the Dutch Christian jurist Hugo Grotius opposed in his *De Jure Belli ac Pacis* (1735, Prolegomena, para. 48). Against this position, he stresses that many of the laws of the Old Testament had been abolished by the New, but he does so in a respectful tone. When asked about the proper behavior to adopt toward the Jews, he advised in his *Remonstrantie* (of 1615), that the canon law relating to Jews should be kept in principle, but that in practical economic terms they should be allowed "liberty to trade, do business and manufacture, and enjoy in freedom exemptions and privileges in the same way as the other burghers and citizens." In France, Jean Bodin, in his *Heptaplomeres,* was so emphatic in affirming the superiority of the Judaic trend of religion over the Christian that it is arguable whether he was Jewish or Christian at heart. Extreme sects and leaders of the Reformation, like Andreas Osiander and Sebastian Franck in Germany, through the spiritualization of the Christian teaching and their almost anarchistic attitude to authority, arrived at an individualistic approach to each man which was favorable even to the toleration of Jews and Muslims.

Gradually there began to emerge the conception of separation of Church and State, which was to be the main road to toleration, even of Jews. Roger Williams, of New England, advocated this attitude from a Christian point of departure in *The Bloudy Tenet of Persecution for Cause of Conscience Disgust* (1644). He asserted that "true civility and Christianity may both flourish in a state or kingdom, notwithstanding the permission of the diverse and contrary conscience either of Jew or of Gentile" (*ibid.,* 2). John Locke was to make this conception the mainspring of change and revolution in his *Letter Concerning Toleration* (1689), published in Latin, and immediately translated into Dutch, French, and English. Locke differentiates sharply between Church and State, considering that civil rights should be granted to all. Limitations and humiliations do not change either the character or the standing of a religion. He wrote concerning the Jews: "is their doctrine more false, their worship more abominable, or is the civil peace more endangered by their meeting in public than in their private houses?" (J. Locke, *A Letter Concerning Toleration,* ed. by M. Montuori (1963), 103). Various lawyers – the foremost being John Selden in England and Johannes Buxtorf in Germany – developed interest in Jewish law as a basic element in the European legal system. A man like Johann Christoph Wagenseil, though drawing attention to Jewish attacks on Christianity in his *Tela Ignea Satanae* (1681), still supported a limited toleration of the Jews, mainly out of missionary zeal. In this atmosphere, even the English economist, Sir William Petty, showed considerable interest in various trades of the Jews and their characteristics. His opposition to them, and the even sharper opposition of Johann Becher in Germany, was largely based on a different interpretation of the data given by Luzzatto and Manasseh Ben Israel.

By the end of the 17th century much of the old medieval structure had gone. The distribution of the Jews in the world was totally different from that at the end of the 15th century. Spain had vanished from the Jewish horizon, as well as its dependencies overseas. France was also almost in the same category. On the other hand, England again had a flourishing and well connected Jewish community from 1655. The Jews of the Netherlands were already an integral and respected element of the economic life of this country in the cities; to some extent also they were attached to it socially, though they did not enter its political structure. The Jews of Poland-Lithuania, despite the sufferings and deprivations they underwent between approximately 1648 and 1660, had become economically, and to a considerable degree socially, an integral and predominant part of the third estate in this realm. In the Ottoman Empire members of an invigorated Jewish society occupied important positions in economic and social life, though the old conceptions of political and social humiliation of the Jew still predominated.

5
Up to the Completion of Emancipation
(to 1880)

Several changes in political and social theories in Christian society, as well in the political structure of Europe, combined to usher in modern times for Jews, though they were not concerned primarily with these developments. The centralization of the state that began in the France of Richelieu and Mazarin spread gradually, both in fact and in theory, to most states of Europe. In its progress the new disposition of relations between the state and those living on its territory caused many changes, for both good and evil, in the position of the Jews and their legal status. The centralist state created, by its very nature, an aversion to particularism in any shape, whether organizational, legal, or cultural. It opposed, above all, the corporations as the essence of the old feudal, uncentralized, state, Everything standing between the sovereign and the individual was now considered not only a barrier, but a sin. Whereas, in medieval kingdoms, the Jewish community was but one in a network of autonomous and semi-autonomous bodies, that were then considered the skeleton of the body politic, it now appeared one of the most obnoxious, because persistent, manifestations of egoistic group-will against the all-inclusive rights of the state. As the centralist state also opposed local dialects and customs, the Jewish community was doubly obnoxious, for it was a corporation devoted to a separate culture, way of life, language, and religion. Many of the clashes between state and Jews in modern times, many of the misunderstandings between Jews and some of their best friends, were the result of this basic antagonism between iron centralism and the unflinching Jewish will for autonomy.

Centralization demanded one law for all in the state and by its very nature opposed the existence of different legal statuses for different groups living in one state. When centralization was later combined with egalitarian trends, this added political philosophy, to a *raison d'état* and thus made legal equality for the Jews a logical as well as a political necessity for a centralist, egalitarian state.

The disfavor into which corporations had fallen, and their rapid disintegration, was also hastened by economic developments. It meant, for the Jews in the cities, the weakening and disappearance of social and economic bodies fundamentally inimical to Jews because of their Christian foundations, their long tradition of excluding Jews from trade and crafts, and of hatred toward them. The forces working against the corporations also opposed on ethical and ideational grounds the corporative medieval spirit that abhorred competition and innovation. The break-up of the corporations unstopped the dam that had long held up individual energies; Jews benefited from this moral revolution as did other restricted individuals.

As with many other changes to be encountered in modern times, the change in status of the corporation had ambivalent effects for Jews. It bettered their economic and social opportunities, and weakened the social elements that were the main carriers of hostility toward them. On the other hand, it made Jewish national semi-independence, and social and cultural creativity, antiquated and offensive. Centralization meant, on the whole, abolition of inequalities, but it also meant suppression of particularities. Jewish society found itself in the new modern state facing the break-up of its national, religious, and social cohesion in exchange for the benefit of material and individual gains. At this time it seemed — to those Christians who because of general social trends interested themselves in the lot of the Jews — that the dissolution of a separate Jewish framework and absorption into the general body of the state was a matter of time, and of a short time only. In countries where the centralist trends were strongest, in continental Western and Central Europe (apart from the Netherlands and England), the Jews numbered several thousand at the most in one state. As general cultural and spiritual currents were moving in the same direction, only "people fighting the trend of history" seemed to be making the foolish attempt to oppose them.

The 18th century also witnessed the dawn of the great ahistorical school of the Enlightenment. This saw men in the abstract, as disembodied individuals only; national culture and religious separateness were so many "coats of paint." The past had no compelling force; only the present mattered, and this could be improved and perfected by the use of reason. In the application of this theory, writers and ideologists of the cast of Voltaire did not dream of abandoning French as a vehicle of expression or the basic French values of life. They were more anti-Christian than anti-national. Many of them developed a hatred of Judaism as the matrix of Christianity. Though extremely individualistic in theory, many of them searched for another parentage or anchorage than the Jewish for their culture. This prompted the 18th-century flirtation with the Far East, and the latter-day anti-Jewish tinge to their admiration for the Greek past. Many criticized the Old Testament with the old anti-Jewish odium to which was now added the goal of discrediting Christianity. In the Enlightenment, as in the trend toward centralization and against corporation, Jewish society met an attitude that was favorably inclined toward the individual Jew while inimical toward his traditions and social cohesion. The demand for disavowal of nationality on rationalist grounds meant in practice for the Jew acceptance of French or German or some other national culture instead of his own. This groping between extreme individualism in theory and national assimilation in practice had already become, by the end of the 18th century, the source of some of the greatest individual successes as well as of the most distressing tragedies in Jewish existence in modern times.

New economic views, in particular mercantilism, combined with even greater and more radical expression of the centralist state — first absolutism and, later on in the 18th century, enlightened absolutism — to create differing approaches to Jewish legal status and Jewish economic activity. The mercantilist and absolutist ruler of the early 18th century looked at every increase in population as desirable, so long as, and on the condition that, it served economic progress. This progress was no longer measured by agrarian standards. The growth of industry and trade, the increment of precious metals, and coin circulation in the state were now valuable goals.

The type of economic activity practiced by Jews had thus, by the 18th century and even earlier, begun to exert an influence on social economic theory and practice. At the same time political theory with regard to Jews had not changed in ruling circles, where they were hated and despised as before. As this combination of economic innovation and political conservatism with regard to Jews existed mainly in countries of Central and Western Europe, where the Jewish population was relatively small, it created a new approach for the treatment of the Jews.

This approach aimed mainly at having as many "useful" Jews in the state as possible — "useful" in this connotation meaning a rich Jew who could help the industrial and commercial development of the country through his activity. Such a Jew must be made to contribute the maximum possible to the state treasury; this exortion sometimes took curious turns of invention, as in the case of the *Judenporzellan* in Prussia, so called because Jews were obliged to buy a certain quantity of porcelain wares on the occasion of their weddings in order to promote directly the development of this industry.

At the same time it was the policy of the absolutist ruler to ensure that the economic opportunities and well-being afforded to the useful Jew for the sake of the state should not result in the calamity of an increasing Jewish population. Jews therefore had to register officially, and their weddings were supervised. A "protected" or "privileged" Jew on these principles could not transfer his rights to all his children but only to one of them. The others had to apply for rights for themselves, granted for a proper payment only if they were considered useful in their own right. Otherwise they were demoted to the status of the unprivileged, unprotected Jew who always faced the threat of expulsion and had usually to pay piecemeal for continuing his existence in the state. The 1750 Prussian regulation for Jews embodies systematically and in detail the execution of these principles.

This situation contributed to accelerate the fragmentation of Jewish society. The privileged Jew became richer, the unprivileged one, poorer. The first went into trade and finance operations on a large scale, with the state's blessing. The unprivileged had either to earn his livelihood as an official or servant of a privileged Jew or to eke out his living precariously as a peddler or a moneylender on pawn in the old style. As this situation became a rule in many principalities of Germany in particular, it put for the Jew a premium on enrichment and economic initiative as the only means of bettering his lot and obtaining some type of broader acceptance by the state. Combined with the former structure of the Court Jews, it led during the 18th century to unprecedented variegation in economic Jewish activity, in particular among the richer strata, hand in hand with an unprecedented social and cultural differentiation in Jewish society. As most of the communities thus affected lacked strong continuous traditions, this being the result of the multiple expulsions in the German Empire from the 16th century onward, disintegration proceeded unchecked by cultural strength. With the development of the *Landjudenschaften* type of communal leadership, the influence of the Court Jew and of the rich Jew grew, while estrangement between him and poorer Jews also became proportionately greater.

In the Netherlands and southern France (e.g., Bordeaux, Nantes) there was another line of cleavage — between the more prosperous Sephardi Jew who was more acculturated to the host society, and the less well-to-do and less acculturated Ashkenazi Jews in these countries, in particular in France, where the line of division had also a regional character, most of the Ashkenazi Jews being concentrated in Alsace and Lorraine.

Enlightened absolutism added another element to the former attitude of mercantilist absolutism toward Jews. This aimed at "betterment of the Jews" so as to make them less "harmful" to general society — for whose weal the enlightened absolutist ruler felt himself responsible — as well as to prepare them gradually for increased rights and better conditions if and when they might deserve them. The tolerance edict of Emperor Joseph II issued in Austria in 1782 embodies the most systematic attempt to carry out this policy in relation to Jews. It continued the attempts to hold down their numbers, though granting them a few alleviations in the field of economic activity, while setting out a whole system of measures aimed at their "education" through their linguistic and social assimilation and curtailment of their unproductive economy.

At the same time, several circles of intellectuals and sectarian divines of the

16th to 18th centuries developed more intensely and more consequentially the approach to real toleration and a different appreciation of the Jew and his status. Jewish apologetics of this period found a more appreciative reception in these circles. Typical and most systematic of such innovators was John Toland of England. In his *Reasons for Naturalizing the Jews in Great Britain and Ireland, On the same foot with all other Nations, Containing also, A Defence of the Jews against All Vulgar Prejudices in all Countries* (1714), he relies expressly on the work of Simone Luzzatto which he promises to translate into English. He uses many mercantilist arguments in favor of the Jews. Toland is ironic toward the anti-Jewish Christian hierarchy, applying a new twist to an old Reformation accusation against the Christian hierarchy that it derived its hieratic and hierarchical spirit from the precedents of Jewish priesthood. In the spirit of upholding the "betterment of the Jews" he promises that they will achieve productivization after they had been granted rights. Even Toland was not ready to permit them to hold state office, though he was prepared to see them as officials in the municipaltiy and the bourse. He adduces

Arguments for Tolera- tion

> "those whole streets of magnificent buildings, that the Jews have erected at Amsterdam and The Hague: but there are other Jews enow in the World to adorn London or Bristol with the like, the fifth part of the People in Poland (to name no other country) being of this Nation . . . " (*op. cit.*, 17),

as an argument for encouraging Jewish settlement, in which mercantilist considerations are combined with a novel appreciation of the masses of the Jewish population.

New, and presaging a different attitude toward Jewish culture and the Jewish fate, are his words:

> "'Tis true, that in Turkey they enjoy immoveable property, and exercise mechanic arts: they have likewise numerous Academies in Poland, where they study in the Civil and Canon Laws of their nation, being privileg'd to determine even certain criminal Causes among themselves: yet they are treated little better than Dogs in the first place, and often expos'd in the last to unspeakable Calamities" (*ibid.*, 43).

This acceptance of Jewish learning and a Jewish autonomous judiciary as positive factors still had long to wait before they were appreciated even among friends of the Jews in the 19th century. Toland was representative in this connection of the positive religious attitudes held by small Christian sects in

Western Europe toward Jews and Judaism which is often overlooked in the
general picture of the change of attitude to Jews. Typical of this approach and
its innovatory, almost prophetic, view of Jewish potentialities are his words in a
letter to a friend in 1709:

"Now if you'll suppose with me this pre-eminence and immortality of the
MOSAIC REPUBLIC[40] in its original purity, it will follow; that, as the Jews
known at this day, and who are dispers'd over Europe, Asia, and Africa,
with some few in America, are found by good calculation to be more
numerous than either the Spaniards (for example) or the French[41] : So if
they ever happen to be resettl'd in Palestine upon their original
foundation, which is not at all impossible; they will then, by reason of
their excellent constitution, be much more populous, rich, and powerful
than any other nation now in the world. I wou'd have you consider,
whether it be not both the interest and duty of Christians to assist them in
regaining their country . . . " (Appendix 1, to his *Nazarenus* (1718), 8).

Pro-Jewish argumentation proceeded along the main line of enlightenment
reasoning in Germany. Its principal and most influential spokesmen were
Christian Wilhelm von Dohm[42] and Gotthold Ephraim Lessing. In a series of
literary works — his drama *Die Juden,* his *Die Erziehung des Menschengeschlechts,*
and most influential and celebrated of all, his drama *Nathan der Weise* —
Lessing put the case for treatment of Jews as equals in humanity on the
basis of deistic conceptions of religion and enlightenment conceptions of
nationality and mankind. His parable of the "Three Rings" became famous as
expressing the basic similarity of all monotheistic religions. Lessing did not
defend Jewish separate existence, he defended the right of the individual Jew to
be treated like a human being, despite his religion and outward appearance.
Lessing was influenced in this, like Dohm later, by the personality and views of
Moses Mendelssohn. Dohm in his work proposed achieving the betterment of
the Jews with a clearly defined aim toward improvement of their condition.
The impact of Moses Mendelssohn represented an old-new type of Jewish
encounter with the host society, unfamiliar in Germany. As a scholar in the

*Moses
Mendels-
sohn*

[40]   This term is in itself an expression of respect and esteem towards the Jewish body politic
      (emphasis in original).
[41]   The number of Jews is exaggerated beyond measure, showing the profound impression
      made on both friend and enemy by their vitality and movement in the Diaspora.
[42]   End of 18th–early 19th century; German historian, economist, and diplomat, one of
      the earliest defenders of the Jews in print in modern times.

employment of a rich Jew, his position was very similar to that of the scholars in the retinue of the Jewish courtiers in Spain. Mendelssohn met intellectuals as an intellectual, men of enlightenment as a leader in the enlightenment philosophy. He put the case not of the material "usefulness" of a Jew but of his cultural usefulness. Defending the separation of Church and State, and defining Torah as a social constitution or Jewish national law, he presented a Jewish approach toward "Enlightenment." There were several families in his Berlin circle who were more radical in their efforts to achieve practical assimilation. Some of them despised the Jewish faith and culture. The readiness of Christians of high social and cultural standing to meet individual Jews as equals, and the refusal of the enlightened absolutist state to grant rights even to "enlightened" Jews, created conditions of social temptation and psychological pressure to leave the faith and become apostates. This was the beginning of the considerable trend toward apostasy, which at the end of the 18th century and during the 19th was to take away more than 200,000 Jews from Judaism in Europe.

Egalitarianism and Emancipation in U.S.   The United States of America opened a totally different line of approach to the Jews. In the new land, uncontaminated by traditions of oppressive practice toward Jews, where many sectarians appreciated the model of the "Mosaic republic" for their own society, emancipation of the Jews came as part of the independence and liberation of the American states. Despite former partial limitations included in constitutions of the former colonies, the new states accepted equality of peoples of all religions as a matter of principle and of fact. The views of the founder of Rhode Island, Roger Williams, in the 17th century were thus fulfilled. Some social discrimination and several remaining legal disabilities were quickly removed during the end of the 18th and beginning of the 19th century. Thus 1776 is a date not only in United States history but also in Jewish history marking the first emancipation as a matter of general policy.

With the growing of revolutionary sentiment after the American Revolution, many people were prepared to regard the equality of the Jews as a test case for the application of egalitarianism as a guideline for political and social life. Yet the French Revolution did not grant immediately or as a self-understood matter equality of rights to Jews. Despite the preparatory work accomplished by the historiography of Jacques Basnage and the works of Abbé Grégoire, the hostile tradition of public opinion toward Jews was still very strong in France. In the long and complicated discussions and legal enactments that took place between 1789 and 1791 an important role was played by the fact that many in France were ready to grant — and indeed granted — rights to the "good" Sephardi Jews of the south, while they were reluctant to grant similar grants to the "uncivilized" Jews of Alsace-Lorraine. Jewish emancipation met here — not for the first time in history, but for the first time in the course of emancipation in

"Grand Sanhedrin des Israélites de France," lithograph by Emile Vernier depicting the meeting of 45 rabbis and 26 lay leaders convened by Napoleon on February 4, 1807, to confirm the decisions taken by the Assembly of Jewish Notables.

modern times — with the fact that the egalitarian principle is dependent upon popular sentiment, and often these do not coincide in regard to the attitude toward Jews.

French Revolution

Final emancipation was carried through in the end as a matter of revolutionary logic by Robespierre and his followers in 1791. The same logic demanded that emancipation be granted only to Jews as individuals — which, spelled out in practice, meant only to Jews ready and willing to leave their own culture and identify and to assimilate into the French — and not to Jews as members of a separate nation.

The tensions and complexities underlying emancipation in a country of old anti-Jewish tradition were brought into sharp relief under Napoleon Bonaparte. On the one hand, he carried on the tradition of the French republican revolutionary armies. which had brought equality to Jews in the Netherlands, in Italy, and in German cities and principalities. On the other hand, Napoleon sensed the historic unity and character of the Jews and disliked their independent spirit. He was also sensitive to the disturbing problem of Jewish moneylending as it had emerged in Alsace-Lorraine. He therefore turned to ancient notions of creating a semi-representative type of leadership for Jews as an instrument for carrying out his objectives concerning them. In 1806 he convened an Assembly of Jewish Notables and later on created a Sanhedrin to give religious sanction to the answers of the Assembly to the questions put to it by his emissaries. The two institutions, constituted of Ashkenazi and Sephardi members from France, Italy, and Germany, accepted the main demands of the centralist empire while striving to keep as far as possible within the framework of Jewish law and tradition. The Sanhedrin's decisions of 1807 to a large extent provide an explanation of Jewish customs and morals in terms understandable to French Bonapartist society. They cover much legal ground, and, without explicitly departing from the basis of messianic hope and Jewish national cohesion, make patriotism to the present-day state "the religious duty of all Jews who were born or settled in a state, or who are so considered according to the laws and conditions of the state to regard this state as their fatherland" (["... de regarder le dit Etat comme sa patrie"] from *Decisions Doctrinales du Grand Sanhédrin qui s'est tenu à Paris au mois d'Adar Premier, l'an de la Création 5567 (Fevrier 1807), Sous les Auspices de Napoléon-Le-Grand, Avec la traduction littérale du texte Français en Hébreu* (1812), 42).

While exacting this declaration of French patriotism from the Jewish notables and rabbis. Napoleon prepared a series of laws which in practice limited the equality of Jews before the law. Demanding from the Jews the full consequence of emancipation, he denied them part of its content. It is a historical irony that Napoleon's decrees against the Jews lapsed through their non-renewal by the Restoration Bourbon regime.

In the west of Europe the Jewish status did not deteriorate after the downfall of Napoleon: the struggle for full emancipation of the Jews in England went on in a relatively tranquil atmosphere; the Netherlands, and Belgium separated from it in 1830, retained Jewish emancipation. In France, after the lapse of the Napoleonic decrees in 1818, the condition of the Jews continued to improve. In 1831 the state began to pay salaries to rabbis; in 1846 the last minor legal disabilities for Jews were abolished through the influence of Adolphe Crémieux, a French Jewish statesman who obtained in 1870 the decree conferring equality on the Jews of Algeria.

Germany   In Germany there were different developments. The Romantic reaction against revolutionary rationalism reasserted in modern terms the validity of old Christian assumptions against equality of the Jews. The Congress of Vienna refused to ratify the rights of the Jews acquired under the Napoleonic conquest: the implications of the proposal concerning their rights "in" German cities and states was changed by substituting ratification of laws granted "by" German cities and states. Even worse was the reaction of public sentiment. Respectable philosophers deliberated on the impossibility of Jews being citizens of a historic Christian state. Vulgar publicists like Hartwig Hundt-Radowsky advised expulsion of the Jews, vilified their character, and hinted that their murder would be no more than a transgression. The so-called Hep! Hep! disturbances against Jews that occurred in Germany in 1819 were but a violent expression of this reactionary movement. The equality of Jews in German society was certainly hindered by the deep-rooted popular prejudice against them. Their legal equality was much delayed and complicated by the fact that even their friends were divided into the school of those who demanded, as in the 18th century, their assimilation and "betterment of character" as a precondition to the equality of individual Jews, and those who saw emancipation as a precondition to assimilation and "betterment of character."

Typical of the modern German was the attitude of radicals there to *"Die Judenfrage"* ("the Jewish question"). Feuerbach and his disciples carried over the 18th-century enmity to Jews on the grounds of their religion and prejudices. The Protestant theologian Bruno Bauer actually demanded their Christianization before any acceptance of Jews into society. Karl Marx considered Judaism evil, and Mammon the Jewish God. He differs from Bauer in considering that Jews could be emancipated legally while remaining as themselves in society because, as he formulated it, capitalist society is becoming "Judaized." Social emancipation would come only in a revolutionary society where there is neither Judaism nor Christianity and the historical trend of "capitalist Judaization" is stopped and reversed. Until then Marx considered it axiomatic that the Jewish religion includes contempt of theory, of art, of history, and of man as a goal in himself: "The social emancipation of the Jew means the emancipation of society from Judaism." This scion of the Jewish people thus despised past Jewish creativity and tradition, declaiming in a prophetic tone against the culture of the Jews.

Jewish emancipation was achieved in German states as a result of various legal enactments, their retraction, and reenactment throughout most of the 19th century while German society, in particular its higher echelons, did not accept Jews during this period. In England Jewish emancipation was completed through a struggle for the abolition of Christian formulas in the oath upon taking a seat in parliament or entering public office. Radical opinion in England was much more prepared for the grant of full religious equality than in France. The Welsh philosopher Richard Price criticized paragraph 10 of the French "Declaration of the Rights of Man and of the Citizen" of 1789 because of its rider to religious equality — "provided his avowal of them does not disturb the public order established by the law." In his view this was mistaken: "For it is obvious that in Turkey, writing against Mahomet; in Spain, against the Inquisition; and in every country, against its established doctrines, is a disturbance of public order established by law; and therefore, according to this article, punishable." He would have enacted the right of man "also to discuss freely by speaking, writing, and publishing all speculative points, provided he does not by any overt act or direct invasion of the rights of others . . . " (from his appendix to "A Discourse on the Love of Our Country," 1789). This historical tradition of the recognition of separate entities as equal, and not of individuals only, was to find expression in the whole approach to the "Jewish Question" in England as well as in the United States.

When the English historian Macaulay rose in 1833 to support the proposal to abolish Jewish disabilities he based his case not only on actual situations and abstract principles but also to a large degree on the glorious Jewish past which guarantees a great future for the Jews as emancipated citizens in any state. "There is nothing in their national character which unfits them for the highest duties of citizens . . . In the infancy of civilization, when our island was as savage as New Guinea, when letters and arts were still unknown to Athens, when scarcely a thatched hut stood on what was afterwards the site of Rome, this condemned people had their fenced cities and cedar palaces, their splendid Temple, their fleets of merchant ships, their schools of sacred learning, their great statesmen and soldiers, their natural philosophers, their historians, and their poets. What nation ever contended more manfully against overwhelming odds for its independence and religion? What nation ever in its last agonies gave such signal proofs of what may be accomplished by a brave despair. And if, in the course of many centuries, the oppressed descendants of warriors and sages have degenerated from the qualities of their fathers, if, while excluded from the blessings of law, and bowed down under the yoke of slavery, they have contracted some of the vices of outlaws and of slaves, shall we consider this as a matter of reproach to them? Shall we not rather consider it as matter of shame and remorse to us? Let us do justice to them . . . Let us open to them every career in which ability and energy can be displayed. Till we have done this, let us not presume to say that there is no genius among the countrymen of Isaiah, no heroism among the descendants of the Maccabees." (*Selected English Speeches,* Ed. E.R. Jones, 1960. 275—6.) He did not demand of Jews that they should give up their messianic belief. He equated it with the Christian millennarian belief in the coming redemption. When at last Lionel Nathan Rothschild was enabled to take his seat in Parliament in 1858 as a professing Jew, the struggle for Jewish emancipation in England closed in accordance with principles laid down much earlier.

The changes in Jewish life, culture, and status in Western and Central Europe that had resulted through the impact of economic and cultural processes at work in general society with implications for the Jews, and the entry of Jews supported by the interests and aims of the host societies into various economic and social functions, influenced relatively small numbers of Jews. In Eastern Europe the changes resulted from political and social upheavals that influenced masses of Jews, mainly in the direction of evolving new systems and developments of their old culture and society. The partitions of Poland-Lithuania (1772, 1793, 1795) among Austria, Russia, and Prussia, broke up the greatest Jewish concentration of Europe into three parts, disconnecting old lines of communication and severing long-established relations between communities in towns and regions. The political and spiritual turmoil into which Polish society was thrown preceding the partitions, and the revolt led by Kościuszko against the partitions and its failure, raised, among a host of other problems, the Jewish question too.

Polish Partitions

The growing importance of the Christian third estate at the time of the death throes of Poland-Lithuania was an adverse factor for the Jews. On the other hand the economic importance of the Jews there and the egalitarian principles penetrating from the West began to work for Jewish equality. How to achieve the "betterment" of the Jews and their "productivization" became themes of some importance about this time in some circles of both Polish and Jewish society. Their effects on relations between Jews and Poles for the time being were doomed to remain theoretical considerations only. The status of the Jewish masses of former Poland-Lithuania was to be determined from now on by powers influenced by totally alien traditions of treatment and attitude toward Jews.

Russia, which obtained the lion's share of the Jewish population, had had no Jews under its rule since the 15th century, when the "Judaizing" movement caused such a scare that Jews had been totally excluded from the country. In campaigns before 1772 the Russian armies would drown Jews or kill them in other ways in cities they had taken. This could not be done with the vast masses of Jews she now acquired. Of the other powers, both Prussia and Austria were already dedicated to the mercantilist-absolutist system of discriminating between individual Jews and controlling their population. Both were now confronted by large numbers of Jews, the majority of whom were poor, and uncontrollable in their demographic growth.

Empress Catherine II was prepared to see the Jews as an integral part of the town population in the newly acquired districts, and she defined their legal status as such, granting them even the right to vote for municipalities. This almost immediately created difficulties: the Russian autocratic government did not permit townsmen to settle in villages; yet, many Jews were living in them. To this was added the aim of the now politically dispossessed Polish nobility to take over the place the Jews had filled in the economy of the villages. The Russian government on its side was troubled by the situation, in which it found itself socially allied to the Polish Catholic nobility, while from a religious and national point of view it felt obliged to promote the interests of the Belorussian and west Ukrainian Greek-Orthodox peasantry. Jewish merchants began to enter eastern, originally Russian, districts, and to compete with local merchants. The government therefore began to consider ways and means of dealing with this new Jewish aggregate and the problems it raised.

Czar Alexander I met, in the committee he created for clarifying this problem, with two opposed opinions similar to those currently debating this question in the West. Some members of the commission considered that Jews had first to be granted rights so as to improve them and "make them harmless." Others considered that the Jews had first to be rendered harmless and to be "improved" before they could be granted new rights. The statute for the Jews promulgated in Russia in 1804 was largely based on the second view. One of the main measures to prevent their causing harm to the peasants, by inducing them to buy alcoholic drinks and damaging them in other ways, was the demand that Jews should leave all the villages within four years. Another result of this trend was the unique invention of drawing a second borderline within the border of the state: Jews were not permitted to settle or live in the territory east of this line. The permitted area included regions taken over from Poland with an addition of several more in the southeast of the state. Thus the Pale of Settlement of the Jews was created in Russia (in a process of line drawing and area redistributions that went on well into the 1830s), to remain in existence until the Revolution of 1917.

The Pale of Settlement, from its creation, was doubly constricting. Jews could not go beyond its borders, while within them they were driven from the villages to the townships and cities. As the Jews were an integral part of the village economy, and village occupations constituted the livelihood of a considerable number of Jews, their expulsion from the villages was not easy to implement; many decrees and counter-decrees were issued through the greater part of the 19th century, and still it was not accomplished in full. Jews also left the villages for other reasons. The Polish uprisings of 1830 and 1863 caused much impoverishment among the Polish nobility; many of its most enterprising members emigrated from the country, and the Jewish village economy was thus much impaired. In the 1840s Jews tried to carry on their former business in alcoholic beverages through leasing the vodka monopoly from the government. From the 1860s, however, they left even this branch.

Western and Central Europe after Emancipation

Economic and social developments in West and Central Europe were different from those in Eastern Europe. The upper strata of Jews in Central and Western Euope became wealthier with emancipation or semi-emancipation. The banking house of the Rothschilds developed from its relatively modest origins at Frankfort on the Main to become the arbiter of international loans and monetary transactions in Europe in the first decades of the 19th century. Byron could exclaim:

"Who hold the balance of the world?
Who reign O'er congress, whether royalist or liberal?
Who rouse the shirtless patriots of Spain?
(That make old Europe's journals squeak and gibber all).
Who keep the world, both old and new in pain
Or pleasure?
Who make politics run glibber all?
Jew Rothschild, and his fellow-Christian, Baring . . . " (*Don Juan,* Canto
12, V).

In France, the brothers Pereire dealt in international banking on a smaller
scale. Gerson von Bleichroeder was not only a banker of first magnitude in the
third quarter of the 19th century, but also the financial adviser of Bismarck.
These banking houses participated to a large degree in the financing of railroad
construction too, as did also Baron Maurice de Hirsch. The importance and
function of these international rival banks was already declining by the 1880s,
when national banks and limited liability share banks took over much of the
finance and financial activity in many countries. Many of these Jewish bankers
and largescale contractors and merchants were ennobled, and thus moved even
farther away from common Jews.

In Western and Central Europe, Jews also entered the free professions. In
medicine, they continued a long and much respected Jewish tradition. In other
professions they were newcomers. In the legal profession they were new in the
sense that Jews did not participate in general, state-regulated law practice until
the emancipation, but they brought with them an old tradition of Jewish legal
deliberation and practice. Jews entered newspaper publishing, editing, writing,
and reporting. The great news agencies of Reuter in England and Bernhard Wolff
in Germany were founded and directed by Jews. Though university chairs were
still withheld from Jews, they entered many of the lower ranks of the academic
world. Many Jews contributed to literature; some apostates like Heinrich Heine
and Ludwig Boerne were notable. Among apostates who gained prominence in
politics and social thought were Benjamin Disraeli, Julius Stahl, and Karl Marx.
Jews also entered politics, some gaining prominence, like Lionel Nathan
Rothschild and David Salomons in England, Adolphe Crémieux in France, and
Gabriel Riesser in Germany. Jews were active in the leadership of revolutionary
movements, as Hermann Jellinek and Adolf Fischhof in the 1848 revolution of
Austria. Many Jewish intellectuals were active in the 1848 revolution in
Germany. The names of Ferdinand Lassalle and Moses Hess were prominent
among revolutionary leaders. Many Jewesses of the upper circles were famous
for their salons and cultivated mode of life, both in Berlin and in Vienna at the

time of the Vienna Congress. Later on, Jewish patrician social life became well known in Central and West European cities. At the same time, small merchants and peddlers, horse and cattle dealers, smallscale moneylenders, and representatives of other lesser occupations were common among Jews in Bavaria, Alsace-Lorraine. and above all, among immigrants coming from the eastern districts of Germany and Austria to the central districts.

Migration Trends from End of 18th

Jewish migration in Europe had changed direction by the end of the 18th century — or even somewhat earlier — and up to the 1890s. It now went from east to west, but occurred mainly within the borders of states. In Russia, it moved from the densely populated parts of Lithuania and Belorussia to the more thinly populated districts of the Ukraine. In Germany, it moved from the Posen districts to the center and west of the country, filling gaps created by the apostasy of the Jewish upper strata and veteran families. In Austria, it went from Galicia to the regions of Vienna and Hungary; in France, from Alsace-Lorraine to the center and west of the country. Jews from Bavaria, as well as other districts of Germany, in particular up to the unification of Germany in 1870, emigrated to the United States and some to England. All these immigrants in their new places of settlement met with the manifestations and results of the

A Jewish street in Hungary — drawing of the Jewish quarter of Sighet, from J. Pennell, *The Jews at Home,* London, 1892.

industrial and commercial revolution in Europe. They also gradually absorbed, in layer after layer of immigration, the new trends of cultural adaptation and assimilation already at work among the older communities there. The Sephardi communities of England and the United States were pioneering in this process. Their members became the upper layer of Jewish society in these countries.

In Eastern Europe, Jewish occupations remained at the end of the 18th and beginning of the 19th century within their former framework. The *shtetl* not only developed an economic structure of its own during the first half of the 19th century under the impact of the expulsions from the villages, and through the development of a new chain of economic and social relations with the villages from the *shtetl* centers, but also created an ecological pattern of its own. The *shtetl* economy of small shopkeepers, craftsmen, peddlers, and peddling craftsmen established itself to become the typical economic set-up for the majority of Jews in the Pale of Settlement. In its midst, and at the heart of *shtetl* life, was the central market place, around which there stood the main shops and taverns for tea and alcoholic beverages. Market day was the time of earning and activity, when the villagers arrived to buy and sell. For many *shtetl* Jews their township was actually their home from Friday through Sunday only, since the rest of the week they spent peddling or working as itinerant craftsmen — cobblers, tailors, smiths — in the villages. Social differentiation was much slower in developing, and up to the 1840s only a sprinkling of Jews had entered the newly opened free professions. A few Jews enriched themselves in Russia as large-scale traders and bankers, or somewhat later, as railroad-building contractors, such as Samuel Poliakoff or the Guenzburg family. By the 1880s, master craftsmen and journeymen in the Pale together numbered approximately half a million. In the incipient industries, as of cloth manufacture in Lodz, a Jewish proletariat was beginning to emerge.

East European Shtetl

In West and Central Europe developments in Jewish society took their direction from the upper circles connected with the centralist state structure. Jews contributed to its economy in loans and banking, industrial enterprise, and largescale international trading, in particular in the extreme west and northwest of Europe, at the end of the 18th and beginning of the 19th century. Up to the 1880s there was a progression toward banking and commercial undertakings on an increasingly greater scale, toward entry in considerable numbers into the free professions and general society, and toward political and social leadership. In the East, while the typical *shtetl* economy and society was developing, the social distance was widening between the increasingly impoverished strata of shopkeepers, peddlers, and craftsmen, and toward the end of this period, some industrial proletariat, and the relatively narrow group of wealthy bankers, constructors, and largescale merchants.

Despite these differences between East and West, which gradually became even greater in Europe, and were at their most prominent between the Jews of the West and those of the Ottoman Empire and Islamic countries who had suffered from the general cultural and economic backwardness of their host society, the consciousness of unity and contacts between different elements of the Jewish populations did not diminish. Even where demographic and economic developments differed, cultural forces and traditions common to all were strong unifying factors.

Population Growth   This is evinced in the process of the remarkable population growth among Jews during most of the 19th century, accelerated in the 1890s. At the beginning of the 19th century there were approximately three-and-a-quarter million Jews in the world, of whom two and three-quarter million were in Europe, mostly Ashkenazim, and about half a million were outside Europe, mostly Sephardim. At the beginning of the 1880s there were seven-and-a-half million Jews, of whom about seven million were in Europe, mostly Ashkenazim. The rate of growth of the Jewish population was almost everywhere twice that of the general population, even in backward countries. This was at a time of a great growth of population everywhere. The Jewish population naturally benefited from its concentration in Europe, where the gains of medicine and preventive hygiene first made their mark, as well as from their concentration in towns, where again these cultural advances first had their effects. However the specifically high Jewish rate of growth was mainly due to two factors: to a much lower infant mortality and to the good care taken of the ill and aged. Here old cultural-religious traditions gave an advantage to the Jewish population. As a result of the developments in population growth and migration the distribution of Jews in the world at the beginning of the 1880s was approximately four million in czarist Russia, one-and-a-half million in Austria-Hungary, 550,000 in united Germany, approximately 300,000 in the Ottoman Empire, and approximately 200,000 in the United States.

Several developments in Eastern Europe between the 1860s and 1880s led to a considerable radicalization in the ideology of the youth and a marked cleavage within Jewish society; on the other hand, through the selfsame developments, they led to greater similarity in social structure and the problems facing Western Jewry. The demand of the Russian government (1827) requiring the Jewish community in most of the Pale of Settlement to supply youngsters as Cantonists for prolonged Russian army service[43] gave rise to much bitterness

---

43   The conditions of service of these adolescents – and the very long periods for which they were mobilized–were intended to create a gulf between the Cantonists and their families and thus to induce them to convert to Christianity.

within the communities between the leading circles, who were responsible for mustering the quota, and the lower strata, who suspected the former of evading this onerous duty in the case of their own children and putting it on the children of the poor. Jewish society as a whole was embittered toward the tyrannical government of Russia that used army service as a means of bringing about the assimilation of young boys.

The government of Czar Nicholas I again put forward a constitution for the Jews in 1835. Apart from exclusion of the paragraph concerning expulsion from the villages, this constitution was a summary of former disabilities, including a prohibition on Jewish residence within 50 versts (33 miles) of the western border. The constitution promised various alleviations for Jews turning to Russian culture, again a continuation of former policies. Thousands of Jewish families applied for agricultural settlement, and many were settled in the south. In 1840 a new commission for research into the Jewish legal status and existence was set up. Both the premises it worked on and the decisions arrived at had a markedly anti-Jewish bias. Czar Nicholas I also attempted to enforce changes in Jewish education and dress; he abolished Jewish *kahal* (autonomous community board) autonomy in 1844, and planned to classify the Jewish population into five classes, according to their "usefulness." This project, as well as his cruel policy toward the Jews, was abandoned after his death in 1855.

Czar Alexander II attempted the solution of the Jewish problem, again on the basis of discrimination between Jews but in this case through showing favor toward small professionally educated groups of Jews, with the aim of bringing by their example the general Jewish population — to which no alleviation was granted — to the main road of general culture and productivization. During the 1860s various groups of such Jews were granted various exemptions from anti-Jewish discriminatory legislation, the main prize being the permission to live outside the Pale of Settlement. This right was granted to Jewish merchants who paid the highest scale of tax, to Jews who had academic diplomas, and, in 1865, to Jewish craftsmen. This trend was not continued in the 1870s, while public opinion as well as state policy turned against minorities in Russia in general, and Jews in particular. Only in Rumania was the Jewish status and Jewish existence even worse than in czarist Russia. The intervention of the Congress of Berlin in 1878 in favor of Jews in the Balkan states, and chiefly of those in Rumania, helped them only formally, but not in actual practice.

Jewish autonomy all this time was being attacked, both from without and from within, not only in its form as a corporation, but also as a bastion of religious and social separatism. The early Jewish enlightenment circles regarded the community establishment as an institution for enforcement of Orthodoxy and meddling in their personal lives which they did not intend to suffer. To

Communal Organization

intellectual dilettantes of means, of the type of Isaac D'Israeli, the father of Benjamin, community service was a nuisance. As he declared in 1813 to those who had elected him *parnas* of the Sephardi community in London:

"A person who has always lived out of the sphere of your observation, of retired habits of life, who can never unite in your public worship, because as now conducted it disturbs instead of exciting religious emotions, a circumstance of general acknowledgment, who has only tolerated some part of your ritual, willing to concede all he can in those matters which he holds to be indifferent; such as a man, with but a moderate portion of honour and understanding, never can accept the solemn functions of an Elder in your congregation, and involve his life and distract his business pursuits not in temporary but permanent duties always repulsive to his feelings" (in: C. Roth, *Anglo-Jewish Letters* (1938), 238, no. 115).

This is an expression not only of D'Israeli's personal taste and indolence, but also of the trend toward assimilation and a renunciation of Jewish social cohesion and cultural tradition. With increased assimilation, such tendencies against autonomy became sharper and more meaningful. For people who appreciated the way of life and habits of the society of their environment, the forms of Jewish prayer, burial, and marriage customs even looked ludicrous.

Despite these forces undermining the organized Jewish community, it not only continued to exist in the West but even gained new strength and an articulate structure there through the system of consistories imposed by Napoleon, who was interested in utilizing the community organs as functionaries of the state. This situation continued with some changes in most of continental Western Europe. In England the Board of Deputies of British Jews began to act on behalf of the whole of the British Empire from the time of the chairmanship of Moses Montefiore (1838). The Jewish organizational framework in England — and, patterned on it, in many of the dominions — acquired an even more authoritative position in the second half of the 19th century with the establishment of the authority of the chief rabbi and with the organization of the rigid United Synagogue.

Communal organization in the United States proceeded along different lines. Divisions between the first layer of Jewish immigration there, the Sephardi, the second, mainly German Jews, and the beginnings of the third, of Eastern European Jews, in conjunction with the size of the country and the huge size of the cities in which the Jews tended to concentrate, combined to create the type of synagogue community which had been established by the exiles from Spain. This was later to develop, with the mass immigration of Eastern European

Jews after 1881, into the *Landsmannschaften* form of community, which still retained many of the religious aspects of community leadership and life. The same factors also led to the creation of secular ideological associations, such as the Arbeter Farband and Workmen's Circle. By the mid-19th century attempts toward centralization were made in the United States also, though in the main these were ephemeral. About this time there also developed a type of organization suited to the upper-middle-class elements of U.S. Jewry, introducing orders on the Masonic pattern devoted to Jewish problems. One of the first, and still the most influential, was the B'nai B'rith order.

In Central Europe, religious and social fragmentation led to many breaches within the Jewish community, mainly brought about by the Orthodox wing which felt itself threatened by the growing predomination of Reform elements in Jewish society. By the 1880s the Orthodox sector achieved in both Hungary and Germany — ironically with the help of liberals in Parliament — the right for every individual Jew to leave his local community. It resulted in the institution and ideology of the *Austrittsgemeinde*[44]. These religious and cultural orientations led to new forms of association within the state of the Reform and Orthodox sectors, and, in Hungary, also of the Neolog[45] trends. They convened their own conferences and synods of rabbis.

Religious and Cultural Differentiation

In Eastern Europe Jews in general retained a strong attachment to the ancient community structure. Ḥasidism on the one hand and the emergence of secular Jewish political and social organizations on the other produced new elements of leadership, which mostly cooperated with the community organization, while trying to use it for their own purposes and according to the ideals guiding them. Thus in regions where Ḥasidism predominated the local rabbi became very much subordinated to the authority of the ḥasidic *ẓaddik*,[46] whose follower he was, or to the authority of the *ẓaddik* who had the largest following in the community.

From about the beginning of the 1880s the aims and weight of secular political parties began to influence the policies and composition of the community leadership. The abolition of the *kahal* by the Russian government in 1844 did not greatly restrict actual community work. The Jews continued with their own leadership structure even if having to use different names for it in reference to the state authorities.

---

44   German for "secessionist community," the term used in 19th and 20th centuries for the Orthodox groups in Germany that considered it their duty to secede from local communities in which the non-Orthodox had gained the majority.

45   Informal appellation of Reform communities in Hungary.

46   Literally, the righteous one; in the ḥasidic movement of modern times it is the appellation of the charismatic (and, from the third generation of the movement, hereditary) leader of the community.

The adherence of Jews to their own conception of the personality and type of education required for religious leaders was strongly in evidence in their reaction to the requirement of the czarist government that rabbis be educated in Russian culture and enlightenment trends. Seminaries for such rabbis were opened by the state at Jewish centers such as Vilna and Zhitomir but were boycotted by traditional scholars, and the graduates were considered *ipso facto* unfit for the rabbinate. The government therefore deputed its own state-appointed rabbis in many places, the so-called *kazyonny ravvin;* however the Jews continued to acknowledge their own rabbis, generally looking upon the *kazyonny ravvin* as an insult or joke.

Religious and cultural life between approximately the middle of the 18th century and the 1880s underwent a continuous process of differentiation, enrichment, and involuntary pluralism. Hasidism introduced the charismatic personality as a regular element of leadership, which was later on institutionalized in the dynasties of hasidic *zaddikim.* At first Hasidism was bitterly opposed both for its tenets and the temper and way of life of hasidic groups, in particular at the courts of the *zaddikim.* The opposition failed, although it was led by the greatest rabbinical authorities (like Elijah the Gaon of Vilna) who made lavish use of their powers of excommunication as well as by the lay community leadership which strongly attacked it. As a result the opposition itself created a new school of Lithuanian *yeshivot* expressive of its own ideals and attitudes and gradually formed a new Lithuanian Mitnaggedic[47] pattern of Jewish subculture. Due to the basic conservatism of Hasidism, despite the suspicions cast on it by its opponents, and since the main attention of its opponents was concentrated on giving direction to their own pattern of culture, there emerged (more or less by the 1830s) an uneasy coexistence between these two groups.

As the *Haskalah* movement and the *maskilim* also remained within the framework of Jewish society, despite the sharp disagreement and suspicion between them and the conservative elements, Jews began, by about this time too, to accustom themselves to the existence of various trends within Jewry. Both the tension between them and the reluctant partial recognition reciprocally accorded by each side now resulted, for the first time since the period of the Second Temple, in the existence of clearly defined groups — differing in many aspects, cultural, religious, and social — but all regarding each other as within Jewry and partaking of Judaism, considering its own brand of Jewishness to be superior. Even Reform and assimilated Jews were defined publicly as Jews. This

---

47   From *Mitnaggedim,* the opponents; since end of the 18th century the appellation of the opponents of Hasidism.

situation led to a heightening of intolerance on the formal level but to mutual toleration in practice. Jewish life was much enriched by the competing cultural streams, variety in modes of life, and diverse types of leadership existing within Judaism side by side in disharmony but with a tacit agreement to disagree.

The great personalities of the founders of these trends became the ideal prototypes for future generations — both through the history of their own lives and by means of the legends and semi-legends woven around them. In Ḥasidism, Israel Ba'al Shem Tov (founder of the ḥasidic movement) and the circle of his pupils, among the *Mitnaggedim*, Elijah Gaon of Vilna and his circle of pupils, and, in *Haskalah*, Moses Mendelssohn and his disciples, served both to fructify and influence cultural trends and individual behavior, as well as to accentuate differences.

Elements in Ḥasidism such as the ḥasidic dance and song, the camaraderie of ḥasidic groups and courts, ḥasidic tales and accounts of wonders, not only colored the culture of the majority of East European Jewry but later, in the 20th century, influenced semi-secular and secular teachings and movements, like those of Martin Buber[48] and Ha-Shomer ha-Ẓa'ir[49] in its early stages, as well as the patterns of behavior of many other Jewish youth groups in the late 19th and the first half of the 20th century, and much of secular Hebrew and Yiddish literature.

The Mitnaggedic Jewish culture both created representatives of a scholarly lay elite in the Lithuanian towns and townships, and did much to give new stature and dimensions to the *talmid ḥakham*. The influence of *Mitnaggedim* ideals and attitudes is reflected in the teachings of men like Simon Dubnow[50] and in much of the secular and non-ecstatic trends of Jewish life in Erez Israel, the United States, and in South Africa.

Haskalah led in many cases to extreme assimilation, but on the other hand it continued, in particular in Eastern Europe, its original cultivation of Hebrew, and its creation of a secular Jewish literature, in philosophy, historiography, and above all, in belles lettres. In Central and Western Europe its influence bifurcated in the often convergent directions of the Wissenschaft des Judentums on the one hand, and of Reform Judaism on the other. In Eastern Europe *Haskalah* often provoked the opposition of the Jewish masses through the collaboration of its enthusiasts with oppressive governments in attempts to impose on them secular education and changes of language, dress, and custom. Yet it was mainly on the foundations laid by *Haskalah* thinking, methods, and achievements that secular

48   Late 19th and 20th century philosopher and Zionist theoretician.
49   Zionist-Socialist pioneering youth movement.
50   Lived 1860–1941; Russian historian and political ideologist.

Hebrew culture and literature could develop within the framework of Zionism in the 20th century.

Western and Central European Jews were thoroughly emancipated by the end of the 1860s. While increasingly involved with the culture and society of their environment, they could not remain unmoved by the plight of their unemancipated brethren in Eastern Europe, in the Balkan states, and in the Ottoman Empire. The rebuffs met with by many of the assimilationists in gentile society, and their own emotional and intellectual inability to adhere strictly to the rationalist (ahistorical) dogmas of the enlightenment, caused Jewish assimilation to remain paradoxically a specific phenomenon, in both Jewish and Christian societies. Cumulatively, these factors led in 1860 to the creation in Paris of the Alliance Israélite Universelle, an international organization of assimilated Jews. These united their efforts, for the sake of religious brotherhood, to help their oppressed and inarticulate coreligionists, despite national differences. The activities of this organization included diplomatic action and the establishment of schools and welfare institutions in the countries of "backward" Jews, thus subconsciously expressing Jewish solidarity. Its many successes in part provided a challenge that led anti-Semites to readapt ancient libels about Jewish strivings for world domination into a malignant and influential myth through the forgery of the Protocols of the Learned Elders of Zion.[51] In a relatively short time the international structure of the Alliance began to weaken under the strain of national solidarities. English Jewry created its own Anglo-Jewish Association, and German Jews eventually established their own Hilfsverein der deutschen Juden.

Cultural differentiation also led to many innovations and changes in Jewish life. Exponents of the Reform trend admitted explicitly that it was proposed to break down halakhic barriers — which were considered latter-day increments on the core of pure Jewish faith — between Jew and gentile. These included *kashrut,* the prohibition on mixed marriages, and many of the Sabbath laws; there was also a move to abolish mention of the hope for a Messiah and for the return to Zion, and the use of the Hebrew language in prayer. On the last points Zacharias Frankel[52] seceded from the radical majority of the Reform and demanded a more conservative and historical approach. This created yet a new facet of Jewish religious and cultural activity in Central Europe and later in the United States.

---

51 This work has been rightly termed by a modern scholar "a warrant for genocide."

52 Lived 1801–1875; rabbi and scholar; founder of the "positivist-historical" school which later influenced the Conservative movement in the United States.

With the aim of throwing light on, as well as learning about, their own past, in order to present the case for emancipation and proposals for assimilation on a more respectful and firmer basis, the leading scholars of the Wissenschaft des Judentums[53] gradually developed a broader and increasingly secularized approach to their research into the Jewish past. The historical work of I. M. Jost (1793–1860) is the first sustained modern attempt of this type by a Jew.

Jewish ideals underwent a reformation with the aim of serving and reorientating Jewish religious consciousness. Reform circles tended to regard the Messiah not as a person who would come to redeem Israel but as a universalist process to redeem humanity. On the basis of this conception Leopold Zunz, the pioneer of the Wissenschaft, called the European revolution of 1848 "the Messiah." A latter development of this conception was the theory of Jewish "mission": Israel had to see itself as the guardians and carriers of pure monotheism for all mankind; in modern circumstances assimilation would only help to fulfill this duty. Pointing to the social, religious, and political failings of Christianity, such theorists considered their "purified" Judaism the destined vehicle for making monotheism paramount. "The spring of nations" of the 1848 revolution introduced a new complication and an added tinge to the trends of assimilation and acculturation. Jews in Prague for example found themselves caught between the crosscurrents of German and Czech nationalism. In Budapest they were caught in the triangle of German, Magyar, and Slav national demands, and in Galicia in the triangle of German, Polish, and, later on, Ukrainian demands. The upsurge of national consciousness give rise to animosity against Jews. The Czechs resented the assimilation of Jews into the German sector, while many Slav nationalities contended their assimilation into the Magyar group. Hence from now on the question whether to assimilate or not to assimilate was joined with the problem into which nationality to assimilate.

With the growing democratization of political processes in various European states to the west of the Russian border, and the emergence to political influence of the mass of elementary school graduates, Jews were to encounter in most of the countries of their emancipation mounting popular prejudice and a new phenomenon in the influence of the stereotype, whereby the press, and popular art and literature destined for the masses, presented various social manifestations through the medium of clichés and images. The stereotype image of the Jew in modern times was based on and bore the imprint of the baleful image of the Middle Ages, but its representation by various groups was fashioned by their own fears. To conservative and right-wing groups the Jew had become by the

53   Early 19th-century movement aimed at a scientific knowledge of Judaism by subjecting it to criticism and modern methods or research.

Sir Moses Montefiore and Adolphe Crémieux on their diplomatic mission for those accused in the blood libel of Damascus, 1840; a commemorative medal reflecting the impression made by the intervention of Jewish notables from the West on behalf of their brethren in the East.

1860s the prototype of the wicked arch-innovator, and Jews were stigmatized as the destructive bacteria of the social body. To the left-wing radical he appeared the evil representative of the capitalist spirit, the arch-schemer and arch-exploiter. The common bond of the medieval anti-Jewish legacy let these opposed stereotypes coexist with and even complement each other.

The blood libel case in Damascus in 1840 shocked Jews everywhere, not only because of the cruelties inflicted on the victims and absurdity of the charge but also and mainly because they saw a recrudescence of an extreme medieval-type expression of Jew hatred. It led Moses Hess in his *Rom und Jerusalem* (1862) to reject his own assimilationist and revolutionary past. His sense of isolation and humiliation caused by the anti-Jewish attitude of the left-wing Marxist radicals brought him back to a deep feeling of the historic continuity of the Jewish nation and to place great hopes for its future on its land. Hess had a much greater impact than commonly accorded him: his response fitted the challenge felt by many Jews in West and Central Europe.

The historian Heinrich Graetz was deeply moved and influenced by this work. In 1863 he wrote to Hess: "I am now in a state to let you know something that will interest you. The plan of settlement in Erez Israel — or *Yemot ha-Mashi'ah* [i.e., "days of the Messiah," Hebrew in the original] — is beginning to crystallize." In 1870 he communicated to Hess an idea of "a very cultured Englishman, a Christian"; Graetz was not permitted to communicate the whole idea, but could only ask "whether in France, in which Jews already have military training, and there are men of courage among them, there may be found about 50 that could become a kind of gendarmerie. They will find excellent

Awakening Nationalism

employment but they must bring with them a certain measure of Jewish patriotism. . . . Please look into this matter and tell me your opinion" (published in: Zevi (Heinrich) Graetz, *Darkhei ha-Historyah ha-Yehudit,* ed. by S. Ettinger (1969), 268, 272).

The state of mind of Jews, in particular those who from alienation returned wholly or partially to Judaism, was influenced in the 1860s to 1890s both by their hostile reception in Christian society and the spectacle of awakening nationalism among suppressed peoples. When Italy united in the 1860s a new geographical term became a political reality. Germany united to become a mighty empire through its victory of 1870–71. Slav peoples were demanding independence and fighting for their cultural identity against German or Magyar demands for their assimilation. Other Slav nations had revolted against the Ottoman Empire and established their independence. Ancient Greece had been resurrected relatively long previously (at the end of the 1820s), and Philhellenism had become a long-enduring fashion and ideological trend among cultured people in Europe. The whole meaning of Jewish assimilation was questioned in the light of these developments. Was Jewish continuity and culture less cogent and valuable than that of Serbs? Were Jews better received by the dominant nations than the Slavs and the Magyars? Inevitiably the question was asked, Why give up?

From the 1840s gentile circles in England expressed hopes and formulated plans for "Jewish restoration to the Holy Land." These projects were supported not only by sectarians without political power but also by political leaders like the Earl of Shaftesbury. Pamphlets were published. Some activists like Laurence Oliphant went to Erez Israel to try to work them out. These projects and ideas were in a large degree prompted by the rapid and visible weakening of the Ottoman Empire and the anarchy within it. The Ottoman Empire was considered at that time "the sick man of Europe." The Crimean War was fought in the 1850s over the settlement of its fate. Though subsequently kept alive, this empire appeared to offer good opportunities for obtaining concessions and charters, in particular as the system of capitulations[54] made interference in its affairs possible and even easy.

This combination of external circumstances and the examples of national struggle and national resurrection was noted inside Jewish society by people who were either disappointed in their contacts with the environment or who, rooted in Jewish culture and society, reacted to the ravages brought about by

---

[54]   Treaties signed between Ottoman sultans and the Christian states of Europe concerning the extraterritorial rights which the subjects of one would enjoy in the state of the other.

assimilation. It was no accident that the pioneers of the idea of combining the reawakening of Jewish national consciousness with the return to Erez Israel came either from the cultural borderline of assimilation like Moses Hess and his followers, or from the social borderline of the eastern districts of Germany where Jews living their own traditional life saw destructive influences advancing upon them; such were Elijah Guttmacher and Zevi Hirsch Kalischer, or Judah Alkalai from the heartland of the Slav struggle for independence against the Ottoman Empire in Serbia (Yugoslavia). In the United States of America Mordecai Manuel Noah proposed (1825) the creation of the Jewish state "Ararat," first in the United States, while later on his attention shifted to Erez Israel.

Jewish Life in Erez Israel   Jewish society and settlement in Erez Israel were then in a stagnant phase, following earlier development. A certain renaissance of Jewish life in the land began with the groups who went there under the leadership of Judah Hasid [55] (1700) from Europe and Hayyim b. Moses Attar [56] from the Maghreb (1742). Social and religious activity in Eastern Europe brought over groups of both *Hasidim* (1777) and *Mitnaggedim* (1808–10). By the mid-19th century all these groups, and additional immigrants, mostly elderly, had coalesced into a fixed pattern of settlement and society. Jerusalem, Hebron, Tiberias, and Safed were "the four lands of holiness" in which Jews customarily settled. The income of over half of them, according to some estimates even up to 80% of the community, came from *halukkah*. [57] At this time *halukkah* was a much respected institution for rendering financial assistance and homage by those remaining in the Diaspora, with its comforts and opportunities, to those who went to Erez Israel to represent the nation in prayer and Torah study at the holy places.

Jewish culture reached high standards in this society. Most Jews there devoted their lives to divine worship in one way or another. The *halukkah* distribution also imposed a pattern of social organization since the *kolel* unit was formed according to the source of *halukkah* income and perpetuated the settlers' ties with their towns and regions of origin. The Sephardi element in this society tended to engage more frequently in ordinary business and crafts than the Ashkenazi. This element was thus more congenial to the early Hovevei Zion ("Lovers of Zion," early Zionist movement) and Zionist comers in the 19th and early 20th centuries. It was also the background for the choice of the Sephardi

55   17th-century Shabbatean preacher.
56   Lived 1696–1793; rabbi and kabbalist.
57   The term later came to denote, in a derogatory sense, their way of life and scale of values.

pronunciation for modern Hebrew by its pioneer Eliezer Ben-Yehuda. The capitulations system helped to keep the settlers in touch with the consuls of their lands of origin. While abroad the *meshullaḥim* (emissaries) not only collected money for the *ḥalukkah* but also brought the message of Ereẓ Israel to the Diaspora, and kept Jews everywhere in living contact with Ereẓ Israel through the sermons they delivered and accounts of conditions there. One of the main grounds of division between the Orthodox and Reform sectors in Jewry derived from differences in attitude toward messianic hopes, Ereẓ Israel, and the use of the Hebrew language in prayer, with the former emphasizing in minds and emotions the centrality of these factors to Jewish life and thought.

The position of the Jews at the end of the foregoing period can be briefly summarized. By the end of the 1870s the Jewish population was in the process of constant and unprecedented growth, due largely to the persistence of old traditions of family cohesion and philanthropy. In the West both economic and social developments were moving in an upward direction, the old Sephardi families leading the way in these achievements, whereas in Eastern Europe conditions were growing worse, with a greater proportion of Jews deriving their livelihood from small businesses and workshops, and some growth of a working proletariat. The *shtetl* economy and society had crystallized. Migration was still largely taking place within the borders of states, in the general direction from east to west. Apostasy and assimilation, and to a certain extent also mixed marriages, had made considerable inroads into the upper strata of Jewish society in the great cities of Central and Western Europe, which were largely replaced by the human and cultural reservoir of Eastern European Jewry. In Central and Western Europe Jews had entered almost all professions, though their appointment to state and university posts was very slow. Although Jewish emancipation was complete almost everywhere in Europe except for czarist Russia, the equality granted to Jews in Rumania and other Balkan states by the intervention of the powers and international conferences, like the Berlin Congress in 1878, remained on paper only. Growing achievements, acculturation, and emancipation had taught that the attainment of equality was as much a social and psychological problem as one of legal status. The first two aspects could not be legislated. The stereotype of public expression and propaganda, and the attainment of the masses to political and social power, did not permit the slow and delicate processes of social and cultural adjustment to equality to develop naturally. Jews were active and had achieved positions in science, in law, in the press and journalism, in medicine, in the arts, and in trade and banking. Some occupied important places in politics, yet their Jewish origin always remained recognizable to others as well as to themselves, even in the case of apostates like Benjamin Disraeli or Karl Marx. Their reactions to this situation differed from denigration of the Jewish character and culture (Marx) to pride in Jewish descent and even a claim to racial superiority (Disraeli). Most Jews active in public life preferred not to help fellow Jews or to become involved in Jewish matters. In this attitude there was little difference between the conservative Achille Fould in France and the liberals Eduard Lasker and Ludwig Bamberger in the German parliament or the revolutionaries Ferdinand Lassalle and Johann Jacoby. Jewry had become much diversified as a result of over a century of intense differences in opinion and changes in mood. Yet it remained united in consciousness though divided emotionally and in ways of life. Toward the end of this time the example as well as the antagonism of awakening nationalism had combined with the beginnings of a renaissance of Jewish national and cultural consciousness and creativity to influence in various ways — some starting originally as paths to assimilation like the Wissenschaft des Judentums — to renewed striving for cohesion, to internalized cultural creation, and to a vaguely felt need for independence in the land of their fathers.

6

To Modern Times
(1880 to the Present)

The absolute growth of the Jewish population was constant and impressive up to the Holocaust. There were approximately 14 million Jews in the world around 1918 and 16 million Jews around 1937. Even the terrible loss of about six million Jews through the horrors of the Holocaust still left at the end of World War II a nation of approximately 11 to 12 million. According to estimates, the number of Jews in the world by 1970 was higher than immediately after World War I.

The rate of growth slowed down continuously. The use of contraception and the ideal of a one-child or two-child family, which became increasingly prevalent among town populations in general, were felt among Jews in most of Europe and other continents, in particular from the middle of the 1920s. The effects — social as well as emotional — of the Holocaust caused, according to some estimates, a slight reversal of this trend and of the diminution in the Jewish birth rate. Mixed marriages up to the rise of Hitler to power became a continuous drain on the Jewish population. Their proportion in some countries and cities grew to more than one quarter of the total of Jewish marriages. Over three-quarters of the children of such marriages were brought up as non-Jews. The above-mentioned phenomena were evident in the European Jewish family; communities in the Mediterranean lands and particularly in Muslim countries were almost not affected by them until quite recently. In Europe again racist anti-Semitism and the revulsion felt by Jews at its appearance led to both a decrease in the number of such marriages from the late 1930s and a much higher proportion of affiliation among the offspring of such marriages to Jewish identity.

From the end of World War II mixed marriages multiplied, in particular in Western Europe and the United States, while the degree of attachment of such couples and their children to the Jewish nation remained very much in the balance. As a result of the combination of these phenomena the rate of growth of the Jewish population decreased from 2% annually before World War I to 1.1% in the 1920s, and to 0.8% in the 1930s. Although East European Jewry (except in Soviet Russia) was relatively little affected by the phenomena of the

While Russians visit the Holy Land, the Jews themselves take good care not to stay there. Our illustration shows Jewish emigrants on an Atlantic liner going to the "land of the free" to blossom out in time as twisters of the Lion's tail

Jewish emigrant families huddled in the ship hold on their way to the land of freedom — print by Frederick Villiers, 1901.

small family and mixed marriages, other factors, such as the persecutions, the years of hunger and of massacres between 1918 and 1923, the economic crisis of 1929, and the anti-Jewish economic and social policies in most of the "successor states" to Austria-Hungary and Russia between the two world wars, combined to produce the same effects on the Jewish population as in the West.

Two processes changed the dispersion and ecology of the Jews in the world throughout this period. Emigration, from 1881, transferred masses of Jews from Eastern Europe overseas (largely to the United States), and shifted the center of gravity for Jews in terms of environment and cultural influence. Societies and cultures which had been molded predominantly by English tradition, and by the pluralist pattern created by the "melting pot" of multinational immigration, increasingly became the hosts for Jews. These were now the matrix of the challenge and response of Diaspora life, instead of the Germanic or Slav environment and the homogeneous, predominantly intolerant, cultures by which the Jews had been surrounded before the great wave of emigration. In its own macabre way the Holocaust led in the same direction, for extermination overwhelmingly affected the communities of Central and Eastern Europe.

Secondly, in the whole of this period the Jews in the world underwent a constant and accelerating process of urbanization and even megalopolitization. Even while the *shtetl* society and economy were still almost intact in Eastern Europe though much changed by the effects of emigration and economic and social nutrients, in 1914 there were already over 100,000 Jews living in each of 11 cities in the world. In the old area of Jewish settlement Warsaw numbered approximately 350,000 Jews, Lodz more than 150,000, Budapest approximately a quarter of a million, and Vienna more than 150,000. In the new area of Jewish settlement created by the pace of emigration London numbered more than 150,000 Jews, Philadelphia in the United States more than 175,000, Chicago about 350,000, and New York 1,350,000. The trend has continued, both in absolute numbers as well as in the proportion of Jews in metropolitan cities relative to the general Jewish population in a country. On the eve of World War II over one-third of the Jews in the world were concentrated in 19 cities which each numbered more than 100,000 Jews. New York alone numbered about two million Jews, somewhat less than half of the total of Jews in the United States. After Jewish emancipation in Russia in 1917 and the abolition of the Pale of Settlement and in particular after the industralization of Soviet Russia from the

The harsh reality of the sweatshop – drawing by Jacob Epstein c. 1902.

A SWEAT-SHOP GIRL MOVES HIS FANCY DEEPLY

1930s, Russian Jewry also tended to become increasingly concentrated in the big industrial and administrative centers. This development is in line with the general trend in the world toward urbanization, but far outpaces it. In the 1970s, Jews outside the State of Israel were concentrated in the largest and most complex urban settlements in the world, New York having the largest single concentration of Jews in any place and at any time. The mass exodus of Jews from Arab states under pressure after the creation of the State of Israel again assisted this trend. Many of the small Jewish communities in backward towns were liquidated and their members resettled in large urban concentrations, mostly in the State of Israel or in France.

By 1937 the dispersion of the 16 million Jews in the world and their proportion among the general population was as follows:

Country	Number	Percentage of Jews in General Population
Erez Israel	384,000[1]	over 20
Poland	3,000,000[1]	10.4[1]
Lithuania	160,000	7.6
Rumania	1,130,000	6.2
Hungary	485,000	5.9
Latvia	94,388	5.0
Turkey (Europe)	58,000	4.7
Austria	285,000	4.6
The Maghreb (present Libya, Algeria, Morocco and Tunis)	310,000	from 5.6 to 1.3
U.S.	4,350,000	3.6
Iraq	100,000	3.1
Czechoslovakia	375,000	2.6
Soviet Russia (in Europe)	2,700,000	1.9
Greece	120,000	2.2
The Netherlands	120,000	1.7
Argentine	250,000	1.4
Canada	170,000	1.4
England	300,000	0.7
France	250,000	0.7

[1] Estimate.

After the Holocaust about 50% of the Jews were living on the American continent, while only one-third remained in Europe and the Soviet Union. From 1945 Erez Israel became the main haven of refuge; France also absorbed many

Jews from North Africa. Among approximately 14 million Jews in the world in the 1970s, about 6 million were living in North America, predominantly in the United States. About 2½ million were living in the State of Israel. There were about three-quarters of a million in Southern and Central America, and about 200,000 in South Africa and Australia. The majority of Jews living in France in the 1970s arrived there through very recent emigration, mainly from North Africa, and the majority of Jews in England and Switzerland were the result of immigrations from 1880. The distribution and concentration of Jews in various parts of the Soviet Union was the result both of movements toward the east after 1917 and of movements even farther east during World War II.

The emerging pattern therefore reveals that the vast majority of Jews live in new surroundings, though for a considerable number this change was ardently wished by them (in the State of Israel for historical and ideological reasons. and in the United States because of its attitude toward them). Western Europe in the 1970s numbered more than one million Jews, of whom about half a million were living in France and about 450,000 in Great Britain. The Soviet Union numbered approximately three million Jews; the number of Jews in other communist countries was contracting steadily; they had reached a vanishing point in Poland, because of its current virulent anti-Semitism. Jews had also left most Arab and Muslim states. The history of the Jewish population between 1880 and 1970 shows great vitality in movement, in adjustment to new environments and patterns of living, and in the creation of a state. Its present ecology makes the problems of Western urban civilization paramount in Jewish life. Their location and numbers have changed through their own dynamics as well as through the forces of human cruelty, of racism, and anti-Semitism.

The evil of stereotypes and vulgarization increasingly made itself felt in its impact on Jewish life from the 1880s. The ruling circles of the czarist state and society adopted a policy of open anti-Semitism in order to divert the resentment of the masses to the Jews. These circles were considerably disturbed and angered by a phenomenon of their own creation that had appeared in Jewish society. In the 1860s and 1870s Jews had been promised alleviations and rewards as a prize for acquiring secular education and skills in line with the government policy of remolding them into satisfactory citizens. The Russian government, however, had no conception of the strength of the cultural traditions of veneration of study and respect for the student among Jews. Jewish society in Russia, by the criteria of its own culture, was considerably more educated and intellectualized than Russian society. When the aspirations of Jewish youths now turned toward secular learning and Russian culture, the ruling circles were dismayed by the "flood" of Jews that was threatening their high schools, universities, and consequently, the composition of the Russian intelligentsia. They turned

Racism and Anti-Semitism

increasingly to the policy of severely restricting the numbers of Jewish students by imposition of the numerus clausus (quota). They also applied higher standards to Jewish pupils in Russian high schools and made more exacting demands on them.

Frustration and anger swept the youth who were eager to learn outside the sphere of their own traditions, who had been ready at first for assimilation and service to the Russian state, and who were now being punished for revealing the high cultural level of their society and their own individual abilities. The trend toward academic education and free entry to the professions could not be halted among the Jews of the Pale of Settlement. Thousands who were not accepted at Russian universities went westward for their education, mainly to Germany and Switzerland. In university cities in these countries Jews formed a large part of the "Russian student colonies." They knew that, having obtained a degree, back in Russia they would still be discriminated against because of their Jewishness.

The state thus fostered the radicalization among Jewish students and a Jewish intelligentsia, who identified themselves with the revolutionary struggle for freedom and a better society in Russia. Hence the proportion of Jewish intellectuals among the leading cadres of the various Russian revolutionary parties grew increasingly larger, and was much greater than their proportion to the general population and at total variance with the social background of their homes. The czarist authorities and their supporters were quick to clutch at the stereotype of the "Jewish subversive spirit" in opposing the Jews, and pointed out to them — by discriminatory measures as well as by massacres — that the western border was open to Jews to emigrate (while the eastern border of the Pale of Settlement remained closed). The government thus hoped both to solve "the Jewish question" and to weaken the revolutionary movement at one stroke.

In 1881 a wave of massacres swept over southern Russia, hitting about 100 communities. From then on massacres as well as arson in the Jewish townships, which were built of wood, became endemic in czarist Russia. In 1891 the the Jews were expelled from the city of Moscow, an event that alarmed Jews throughout the country for they saw it as a reaffirmation of the Pale of Settlement policy. In 1903 there occurred a massacre in Kishinev that set off a wave of anti-Jewish violence. The ruling circles also made great efforts to involve the Poles in these outbreaks. They were successful at Bialystok. In 1912 an anti-Jewish boycott was organized in Warsaw. Thus Russian Jews were faced by the menace of pogroms, i.e., constant physical assault and robbery; these were certainly abetted by the authorities, and — as the official archives showed, when opened after the revolution of 1917 — in many cases organized by police functionaries and financed by societies close to the government. Jews reacted against this situation by the creation of self-defense organizations, a pattern of behavior which continued until the period of the pogroms under Petlyura, Makhno, and Denikin during the civil war after the Revolution of 1917.

The Jews of the Pale of Settlement and Galicia and Austria reacted to the straitened economic circumstances, even more strongly than to the waves of unprecedented hatred and violence in Russia, by mass emigration. Between 1881 and 1914 over 2½ million emigrated from Eastern Europe (c. 80,000 anually), over two million of them to the United States, creating the great Jewish center there. Over 350,000 settled in Western Europe; centers of Jewish tailoring and trade in England and in other countries were created by this emigration, since a large proportion of the Jews were tailors and many who formerly had no profession joined their ranks. Many others turned to peddling. The "greenhorns" were unacquainted with the language and culture of the new country and dependent to a large degree on economic help and spiritual help from earlier arrivals. They clustered together, thus creating "ghettos" in the great cities of the east coast of the United States and in Western Europe. These were at first islands of Eastern European Jewish culture and way of life, where Yiddish was spoken and Yiddish literature, newspapers, theaters, and journalism burgeoned amidst the surrounding cultures.

For the second generation, the traditions of learning and respect for intellectual activities and the free professions pointed to intensive study and the acquirement of a profession as the way to social betterment. This naturally entailed deep acculturation. The dynamics of traditional Jewish culture in an open and more or less tolerant society created the present broad strata in Jewry of those occupied in the free professions, of the intelligentsia, writers, artists, and newspapermen in the United States and other Western countries. The children and grandchildren of the poor and hard-working immigrant parents, who at first labored in the grueling atmosphere of the sweat shops "pulled themselves up by their own boot straps" thanks to a tradition that took the road of learning and social leadership and service wherever and whenever permitted.

The present situation, where the vast majority of Jewish youth enters the universities and other academic institutions, can be interpreted as being no less the result of an acceleration of immanent Jewish trends than a part of the present general trend toward academic education. The vestiges of occupations such as tailoring and peddling are rapidly disappearing. Productivization has taken a different and unexpected turn in modern Jewish society in the West.

Up to 1932 German Jewry was in the forefront of intellectual achievement and the acquirement of free professions, though it never achieved the type of social acceptance found in other Western societies. In Germany too the development was away from the crafts and petty trade to academic professions. medium and largescale business enterprises, and public service. German Jewish society experienced during this period a certain undercurrent of tension between its acculturated strata and the *"Ostjuden"* (Eastern European Jews) who, whether as immigrants or as transients, caused some offense by their culture and way of life, in particular through fear of the "bad impression" they could make on cultured good Germans.

However at the end of World War I there was a rise in anti-Semitism. The defeat of Germany in war was explained by the myth, propagated by extreme right-wing elements, that circulated after 1918 of the "stab in the back" that the victorious German army had received from revolutionaries, pacifists, and intellectuals under the influence of the cowardly "Jewish spirit," as opposed to the heroic and creative "German spirit"; such accusations, combined with resentment at Jewish commercial and financial activity in Germany during the great inflation of the early 1920s there, reinforced the old stereotype evil image of the Jews. Fuel was added to the old hatred by the preeminence of Jews in many scientific fields and, even more, their activity on the liberal and left-wing side of German politics (Walther Rathenau, minister for foreign affairs of the German republic, was assassinated in 1922; Kurt Eisner, head of the socialist republic of Bavaria in 1918, and Rosa Luxemburg, as the symbol of left-wing socialism, were murdered).

Racism was threatening to become from the second half of the 19th century the new buttress of quasi-scientific rationalizations of the hatred of the Jews when its older religious props were disintegrating. These ideas were influenced by successes in the organization and development of agriculture and cattle breeding along racial lines, by the stimulus of racist and semi-racist policies toward Negroes everywhere, and toward "natives" in many parts of the British Empire, and by the penetration of Darwinian biologistic concepts of the "war for survival" and "survival of the fittest," which led to a sociological Darwinism that was first used in conflicts between social circles in Christian society and in republican France.

There gradually emerged in Europe a racist theory which postulated the division of mankind into "higher" and "lower" races and into "good" and "bad" breeds. Carried over from the disciplines of nature and economics, where functionalism and teleology could flexibly suggest the breeding of a race for a specific purpose, this theory acquired cruelty and absurdity when applied to humanity and to the area of absolute imponderable values and goals. When combined with the stereotypes of the Jew and his character it acquired the ultimate horror of a racial scale, where the "Aryan," which stood in Nazi race parlance for Germanic, represented the best type of man, while the "Semite," which in the same parlance was actually intended to designate the Jew, came to represent an irreparably evil and harmful blood and race.

The growing influence of Adolf Hitler and the Nazis, the medieval-type poison disseminated by newspapers like *Der Stuermer,* the theories propounded by Alfred Rosenberg and expounded by Josef Goebbels, created a dangerous situation and oppressive attitude toward Jews even before the seizure of power in Germany by Hitler in 1933. The public vote, the adherence of the youth, and the increasing "respectability" of the Nazis and Nazi ideas among the right wing of German society, pointed the way to the Holocaust. The influence of this development in the heartland of Europe, in a country and nation famous for their culture, became threatening for Jews everywhere.

Anti-Semitic political parties and organizations had begun to appear in Germany and Austria-Hungary in the 1870s. These had from the first made in clear tones "socialist" claims against Jewish exploiters, "Christian" aims against subversive Judaism, and overt hatred of the blood and the irradicably evil character of the Jew. In 1882 a first international congress of anti-Semites convened in Dresden, marking the conception of an all-European war against the Jewish "international conspiracy." The anti-Jewish agitation of Edouard Drumont in France reached its peak and was defeated in the Dreyfus affair in the 1890s. Right-wing sentiment against the Jews lingered on actively in France after the decisive defeat of the anti-Dreyfusards, however: it attracted many embittered intellectuals, Catholic and radical.

Another type and tradition of anti-Semitism was active and virulent in the "successor states" of Russia and Austria-Hungary. These faced a large Jewish participation in the "third estate" (Poland and Lithuania) and in the intellectual elite of the country (Hungary). Memories of the war against Russia, when Jews were suspected of Russian leanings in the east of Poland (leading to the massacre in Pinsk), and memories of the communist revolt in Hungary led by the Jew Béla Kun intensified enmity against the Jews. Obliged by the minority treaties and by their internal economic and political situation to refrain from open action against Jews in the 1920s and early 1930s, these states developed, in particular Poland, Rumania, and Hungary, a systematic policy of anti-Jewish measures camouflaged as measures intended for the improvement of trade or crafts or for stricter sanitation. Taxation also served as a weapon against Jews. Public opinion and economic semi-official organizations served the same purpose, such as the Rozwój organization[58] and cooperatives in Poland. The numerus clausus was introduced openly or clandestinely. Jews did not obtain state employment, while the "general" measures mentioned above enabled closing down of Jewish shops and workshops and made economic activity difficult for them. Public opinion encouraged this policy and was in turn officially encouraged in hostility

[58]   Anti-Semitic Polish nationalist organization.

to Jews. Attacks against Jews by students and the youth were endemic in Rumania, where they were scarcely punished, and became more and more frequent in Poland.

Following the arrival of the Nazis to power between 1934 and 1939 all these various brands of anti-Semitism on the continent of Europe tended to merge, accepting to a greater or lesser degree the racist theory and cruel methods of the Nazis. On the other hand, this provoked growing revulsion from anti-Semitism in some conservative and Church circles, though expressed hesitantly and not generally leading to much activity against anti-Semitism.

The Nazis set the tone in introducing racism as a basic concept in law with the Nuremberg Laws (1935). They gradually tried out on European public opinion as well as "educated" German society the steps of open boycott, violence, and harsh isolation of the Jews and expropriation of their property, culminating in the *Kristallnacht* action of November 9–10, 1938. The badge of a yellow *"magen David"* served to mark the Jew outwardly. Jews were given a spurious autonomy appointed and closely supervised by specially trained "experts" of the SS and Gestapo. By the eve of World War II not only the non-communist states of Eastern Europe but also fascist Italy under Mussolini and pro-Nazi political parties in the West, like that of Oswald Mosley in England and the Croix de Feu in France, had accepted — some enthusiastically, some reluctantly — the Nazi line toward Jews, though not always all the details of Nazi behavior toward them. The civil war in Spain (1936–39), where thousands of left-wing Jews fought and died in the ranks of the international brigades of the republic against the armies of the Caudillo Franco, served in the case of the Jews as in other aspects, to rally the extreme right wing of Europe closer to Hitler and make his victims its enemies.

Jews everywhere were hard hit economically by the crisis of 1929, as were almost all sectors of the public in Europe and the United States. The New Deal of Franklin D. Roosevelt did much to help them in the United States, where they were again in the mainstream of development of the whole country. Yet the early 1930s were a difficult time not only economically but also socially for Jews there. The odium incurred by Roosevelt and his measures often related to Jews too. Public agitators like Father Coughlin used the new medium of radio to preach hatred against Jews.

Soviet Russia after 1917   In the Soviet Union there continued, up to 1928 approximately, a long period of the break-up of the *shtetl* economy and the penalization of many Jews as "bourgeois elements," in the legal, economic, and social aspects of existence. This policy was followed, even if they had been petty shopkeepers or smallscale artisans under the czarist regime, without taking into account the restrictions that had forced them into their petty bourgeois status. In this case also a "general line of policy" turned out to be destructive and unfair to Jewish society in particular. During the economic crisis the Soviet government was favorable to Jewish autonomy (there were many preponderantly Jewish municipalities and even several such regional administrative units even after the end of the 1920s). The industrialization program that began around 1928 gave new opportunities to Jews and began to compensate many of them for the former social havoc.

In the 1920s the Soviet state encouraged a change in Jewish economy and society through agriculture and settlement in compact groups, first in the Crimea and the south of the Ukraine — which had been traditional areas for Jewish agricultural settlement with governmental encouragement from the first half of the 19th century — and later in what was proclaimed to be the autonomous Jewish region of Birobidzhan. The projects proceeded rapidly with the help of Jews from abroad. In 1926, 150,400 Jews gained their livelihood from agriculture, approximately 6% of the total. By 1928 they numbered 220,000 (8.5%). A peak was reached in 1930 with 10.1% of Russian Jews in agriculture. Subsequently a steady decline both in absolute numbers, and even more proportionally, set in. During the collectivization of Soviet agriculture most Jewish settlements were practically de-Judaized by an "internationalization" process, i.e., the introduction of non-Jewish peasants. The Jewish settlements were finally obliterated during the Nazi occupation of World War II.

In Argentina, where the funds provided by Baron de Hirsch and vast tracts of available land seemed at the end of the 19th century to ensure prosperous Jewish settlement, this prospect withered away in the 20th century through the lure of the cities and lack of idealistic and national motivation. The failures of these attempts — state-supported in Communist Russia and supported lavishly by private means in the open economy of Argentina — proved, no less than the success of the similar attempts in Erez Israel, that only ideals could reverse the trend in Jewish society toward urbanization manifest from the eighth century.

The years between 1880 and the creation of the State of Israel in 1948 were also ones of creativity in Jewish social organization and forms. Where the old community structure continued to exist it was destined to acquire importance through the activities of Zionists, autonomists,[59] and other Jewish political party representatives, to revive and use it as an instrument for national, secular, social, and educational policy. It was further strengthened when the community organization became, under the minority treaties, a recognized cell of Jewish self-government as a minority in a number of states. International Jewish organizations patterned after the Alliance Israélite Universelle continued to appear with specific goals for diplomatic or philanthropic activity. To combat

59   See page 193.

CARL A. RUDISILL LIBRARY
LENOIR RHYNE COLLEGE

anti-Semitic propaganda the B'nai B'rith order set up its Anti-Defamation League in 1913, while in Germany the Central-Verein deutscher Staatsbuerger juedischen Glaubens carried on such activity until its prohibition by the Nazis. Various organizations for the aid and direction of emigration arose in this period, the most prominent being the HIAS and later the Palestine offices of the Zionist Organization; ORT, OSE, and above all the American Jewish Joint Distribution Committee (from World War I) served to provide training for professional skills, health needs, and massive charity wherever required. The Jews of the United States who were emotionally attached to *"di alte heym"* and still retained memories of the hardships they underwent while taking root in the "New Country" made charity not only a duty and function but also a social bond and an ideal in life, a factor of cohesion in itself, and in forging links with other Jews; this proceeded from the time of World War I, in particular in relation to Palestine and later on the State of Israel.

The year 1897 saw both the convention of the first Zionist Congress and the creation of the first state-wide Jewish socialist party, the Bund of Russia. The calling of the Zionist Congress and the method of ensuring its permanence through elected institutions acting in the interim between congresses, and, above all, through the institution of the shekel, created an international Jewish framework that saw itself the representative of its "voluntary citizens," and "a state in preparation." The Zionist Organization created the instruments of the Jewish National Fund and Keren Hayesod, which served as financial agencies of this extra-territorial state. Even Orthodox Jewry found itself compelled at the beginning of the 20th century to organize in this novel form of a political party, establishing the Agudat Israel. This form took root: the Folkspartei, the Jewish Socialist Workers' Party (Sejmists), and other Jewish groups organized as political parties to advance their aims, sometimes on a territorial and sometimes on an international basis.

In the Soviet Union the ruling Communist Party created its "Jewish section," the Yevsektsiya, in 1918, which served as an instrument of agitation and propaganda in opposing the Jewish religion and Hebrew national culture. In the Soviet Union also emerged Jewish units of local municipal and regional autonomy. The search for forms continued in the attempt to create a Jewish Agency to unite Zionists and non-Zionists in work for Erez Israel, and later in the method of raising bonds for Israel to assist an independent Jewish state. Cultural activity was also organized in the free countries through separate organizational frameworks, like the Central Yiddish School Organization (CYSHO) for Yiddish schools and culture, and Tarbut for Hebrew secular schools and culture. The various trends of Jewish religious thought and life developed organizations of their own, in particular flourishing in the pluralist

United States, in the shape of the three main groupings of Reform, Conservative, and Orthodox, with several splinter groups. Many organizations tended to link themselves in one way or another to the State of Israel, though there is also in the United States the American Council for Judaism, active mainly as anti-Zionist and anti-Israel. In the camp of the New Left, stirrings have been felt toward expression and organizational articulation on specific Jewish matters and issues, though in the main it is inimical toward, and destructive of, Jewish cohesion.

Jewish involvement in general culture and service to it became greater and more creative in this period. Henri Bergson, Hermann Cohen (who expressed himself not only as a general philosopher but also as a Jewish one), and Edmund Husserl are but a few of those who contributed to philosophy. Mathematics and physics increasingly attracted Jews who were very creative in these fields, like George Cantor, Albert Einstein, Hermann Minkowski, Robert Oppenheimer, Edward Teller, and Lev Landau. The work of Georg Simmel, Emile Durkheim, and later that of Claude Lévi-Strauss is central to sociology and anthropology. Many Jews have contributed to the literatures of various countries; most of them cannot avoid the Jewish problem, even when consumed by *Selbsthass* ("self-hate"). In art, the creations of Amedeo Modigliani, Chaim Soutine, and others are important in the modernist trend. Through the work of Marc Chagall the *shtetl* life and mythology, and motifs and images from the world of Midrash and Jewish legend have gloriously and colorfully entered European art. By granting the 1966 Nobel Prize for Literature to Shemuel Yosef Agnon, European society recognized the place of modern Hebrew literature and creativity in world literature, recognizing at the same time the Jewish acculturated contribution to European literature by granting it also to Nelly Sachs. In the State of Israel, which continued schools and trends of artistic creativity from mainly Eastern Europe and Germany, are found many varieties, forms, and schools of literary and artistic expression, increasingly rooted in the life of the state.

Contribution to General Culture

The Jewish specificity of this entrance to the' humanities and literature was expressed by the German historian Ernst Troeltsch, who combined appreciation of the Jewish contribution with recognition that it was new to European culture and somewhat alien. He states that for Hermann Cohen

> "history is concerned rather exclusively with the ideal future, and this is a systematics consisting purely of thought and ethics of the organized will of humanity. Through this the ideal Jewish approach to history finds its expression among the various approaches possible within the circle of our culture, for, since 1848, new conditions and new assumptions have been created through the entry of Judaism into literature and spiritual activity,

first and foremost in the field of history . . . This is given its most energetic expression by Cohen"(*Der Historismus und seine Probleme* (1922), 542).

André Gide reacted in a hostile fashion in 1914 to Jewish intrusion into French literature:

> "Why should I speak here of shortcomings? It is enough for me that the virtues of the Jewish race are not French virtues; and even if the French were less intelligent, less long-suffering, less virtuous in all regards than Jews, it is still true that what they have to say can be said only by them, and that the contribution of Jewish qualities to literature (where nothing matters but what is personal) is less likely to provide new elements (that is, an enrichment) than it is to interrupt the slow explanation of a race and to falsify seriously, intolerably even, its meaning. It is absurd, it is even dangerous to attempt to deny the good points of Jewish Literature; but it is important to recognize that there is today in France a Jewish literature that is not French literature, that has its own virtues, its own meanings, and its own tendencies" (*Journals of André Gide,* transl. by J. O'Brien, 2 (1948), 4).

This reflection on the essential difference between Jewish and French creativity is preceded here by the reaction of Gide, who later became for a while a left-winger and Communist fellow traveler, to the character of the young Léon Blum, the future Socialist premier of France, leader of the Front Populaire before World War II: "I cannot fail to recognize nobility, generosity, and chivalry, even though when applied to him these words must be considerably distorted from their usual meaning." Gide considered that these traits could not be applied in their usual meaning to Blum because of "his apparent resolve always to show a preference for the Jew, and to be interested always in him, that predisposition . . . comes first of all from the fact that a Jew is particularly sensitive to Jewish virtues." He suspects too that this completely assimilated young man "considers the Jewish race as superior, as called upon to dominate after having been long dominated, and thinks it his duty to work toward its triumph with all his strength . . . He always talks to you as a protector. At a dress rehearsal, when he meets you by chance . . . he . . . makes everyone think . . . that he is the most intimate friend you have in the world" (*ibid.,* 3–4).

Anti-Semitic insinuations and touches thus often entered even where Jews and non-Jews seemingly mixed on the most equal terms in the salons of literature and science.

The renaissance of Jewish solidarity and national thought that began in the 1860s continued and developed in the period under consideration. All the circumstances of the general growth of nationalism, the break-up of the Ottoman Empire, and above all, the feeling of Jews that they were not wanted in the social and cultural world around them with growing awareness that social and cultural understanding and acceptance mattered, led to a return to Judaism and to specific solutions for it. Leon (Judah Leib) Pinsker[60] suggested in his *Autoemancipation* (1882) that Jews could free both themselves and the world from the malaise of anti-Semitism if they would only make a sustained effort to return to the "state of nature" of a nation living in its own land and within its own social and economic framework, and ceased to frighten others by persisting in a ghost-like existence in exile. His ideas coincided to a considerable degree with ideas of other Jewish thinkers of different shades, like Nathan Birnbaum, Moses Leib Lilienblum, and Peretz Smolenskin.

A supreme example of the Jew shocked out of complacent assimilation was Theodor Herzl. Through his imaginative thought and charismatic leadership he rallied around his personality and ideas all those who wanted a Jewish effort for the creation of a home of their own. Herzl stood outside most of Jewish culture, and was indifferent even to Hebrew. He put his trust mainly in diplomacy and in the possibility of obtaining a charter from the Ottoman Empire and shaping out autonomous Jewish existence within it: methods and hopes that were destined to disappointment. Nevertheless, Herzl had the power to carry over his trauma, his consequent pride in being a Jew, and his political sense for symbols and forms of leadership, and to bequeath them to Zionism after him. His attempt in 1903 to lead Jews to a *"Nachtasyl"* in Uganda,[61] mainly for the sake of alleviating the sufferings of Russian Jews, failed in a large measure due to the opposition of those very Jews. The territorialists who later wanted to continue this trend of Herzl's thought were destined to fail in all their attempts, lacking the motive force of the historic attachment to Erez Israel. The various organizational and financial instruments created in Herzl's lifetime and soon after his death were to assist the ultimate achievement of the Jewish state by enlarging their methods and including "practical" settlement work.

From the days of the Bilu[62] pioneers in the late 19th century Jewish settlement activity in Erez Israel did not stop despite many problems and failures, and despite the political view that was reluctant to engage in settlement before achieving a proper charter. The French philanthropist Baron Edmond de Rothschild intervened to assist Jewish settlement from 1883. His

---

60   Lived 1821–1891; leader of the early "Lovers of Zion" (Hibbat Zion) movement.
61   The Uganda Scheme – the British government proposal for an autonomous Jewish colony in British East Africa.
62   An organized group of young Russian Jews who pioneered the modern return to Erez Israel.

methods were often bureaucratic. His officials lacked contact with the settlers, but the money poured in (1½ million pounds sterling over approximately 15 years) and the instructors he sent helped to save them from economic catastrophe and to embark on various agricultural and horticultural efforts.

The main problem of the Zionist settlers at the beginning of the 20th century was ideological and social. Tensions between them and the *halukkah* settlers created a gulf between the "old *yishuv*" (pre-Zionist community) and the "new *yishuv*," as the two sectors in Erez Israel came to be called. The settlers of the first villages soon accepted French culture, spread by the Alliance schools as well as by the officials of the Baron. The Zionist thinker, Ahad Ha-Am, was shocked at what he saw in both the cultural superficiality of Zionist leadership and the emptiness of purpose in the settlements. He suggested a new "spiritual" Zionism. His positivist thought contributed much to the ideological buttressing of secular Zionism.

In 1904 there began the Second Aliyah, which continued until 1914. Its pioneers brought with them high standards of Jewish and general culture, lofty ideals of socialist collectivism and productivization, and a deep conviction that ideals may be proved only through living according to them. Among the approximately 40,000 who came in this way, many of whom left after a relatively short time, were several leading personalities. Some were destined to lay the foundations and lead the State of Israel (David Ben-Gurion, Izhak Ben-Zvi, Berl Katznelson, Aharon David Gordon, among many others). Gordon stressed the revolutionary and creative character of physical work, the supreme value of the return to nature. These people considered that work by Jews in the fields and roads of the Jewish settlements was a precondition to national revival as well as the path to individual renewal. They aimed to form a Jewish peasantry and a Jewish agricultural proletariat, hence their struggle for work by Jewish labor and for Jewish land, a struggle that continued up to the establishment of the State of Israel. The followers of Gordon organized the Ha-Poel ha-Zair party in 1905. Some of them, more radical in outlook and adherents of Yiddish as the national language, organized in the Po'alei Zion. By their joint effort the pioneers created the organization of agricultural laborers in 1911.

The greatest achievement — and, as it would now seem, a lasting contribution to the social organization of mankind — was made by these pioneers with the help of funds of the Zionist Organization and instruction by some experts in creating the types of communal living and agricultural settlement in the cooperative moshav (cooperative smallholders' village) and in the collective communes of the kevuzah and kibbutz. The last two relate back as if instinctively to the old tradition of Jewish communes in the Second Temple period. They were fundamentally influenced by ideals of social justice and equality, and of national service. Both consciously and subconsciously, the kibbutz served, through its spirit of collective brotherhood, to maintain the high cultural level and intensive social life of the pioneers in conditions of hard physical effort and economic hardship.

Malaria, the hot climate, and despair of attaining their objectives were the enemies against which the Jewish idealist settlers had to battle from the first days of the Bilu'im. Despite many attempts and failures, and even a relatively high rate of suicide, and although the some 40 existing agricultural settlements contained only a minority of the approximately 80,000 Jews in Erez Israel by 1914, they formed a strong social and ideological core that remained ready to continue to expand as soon as the war ended in 1918.

Following the tradition of Jewish self-defense, and true to the conception that everything should be done by the Jews themselves, as well as through a romantic renaissance of the striving for physical valor, the pioneers of the Second Aliyah decided to take the defense of the Jewish settlements into their own hands. In 1909 they created the Ha-Shomer organization (Association of Jewish watchmen). Those who formed it intended to be more than mere watchmen, and took for their model of behavior that of the warrior bedouin. This organization lost several of its first members in defending the Jewish settlements. Some of them also through their way of life and the courage they displayed developed an ideal prototype for the role of the Jewish defender.

Before World War I Eliezer Ben-Yehuda had succeeded in bringing back Hebrew to life through its use by personal example, and propaganda for it as a living language. The wealth of its literary, legal, and philosophical strata considerably contributed to its revival. This became firmly established through the "language conflict" between the supporters of Hebrew as the only language to be used for every field and activity, and those who considered that German

Ha-Shomer in Galilee, c. 1910. Note the Bedouin style, dress, and array.

should be used for various subjects and spheres for which Hebrew was not considered ripe, in particular for teaching at the new Technion in Haifa. After pressure by the Hilfsverein der deutschen Juden to carry through German, the determined stand of teachers and public opinion decided the day for Hebrew in 1913.

World War I and its Aftermath   World War I tested Jewish nationality as a political concept in the international arena. Zionism was in disarray. Conceived as an international movement and organization for carrying out Jewish policies by modern political means, it found itself divided between the two warring camps. Its main offices were in Germany, while the main body of its supporters were in the lands of Germany's enemies or in neutral countries. From the days of Herzl, Zionist diplomacy had relied both on friendship with the Ottoman Empire, using the influence of Germany for this purpose, as well as on the friendship and support of England. Now these mainstays were in conflict. The Turks were gradually drawn into the war and when they entered it they had already become particularly suspicious of Jews and Zionists.

Jews everywhere found themselves in a similar predicament. Culturally they admired Germany; the Austro-Hungarian Emperor Francis Joseph was considered a friend and protector of Jews. Russia and the Russians were hated and feared, in particular by the great mass of the recent immigrants from Russia, who now formed the great centers of Jewish population in the United States and England. On the other hand, the Western democracies, and in particular England, were traditionally considered the states and societies most favorably inclined toward Jews. The Turks, who became the allies of Germany in 1914, were considered cruel and unreliable. When German successes in the East brought great areas of the Pale of Settlement under German rule, the attitude of the Austro-Hungarians toward the Jews compared favorably with that of the Russians. Jewish officers in the German and Austro-Hungarian army, in particular army chaplains, came in touch with the Jewish society in the conquered territories, and did much to assist it. This encounter also brought important results for the Jewish consciousness of the German Jews themselves. Many of these German Jews made the acquaintance of *"Ostjuden"* life and culture in its home and began to respect and even to admire it. Much of the later understanding between these two sections of Jewry in the period between the two world wars stemmed from this encounter. The Russians, on the other hand, often maltreated Jews during their retreat, and expelled many of them eastward, suspecting them of spying for the Germans. They thus broke up on their own initiative — as they thought temporarily — the structure of the Pale of Settlement. Jews in the West, in Germany, and Austria-Hungary, were well informed about the various aspects of the situation in the East. Left-wing radicals, both Jewish and non-Jewish, wished for the downfall of all autocratic rulers, but in particular prayed for the downfall of the arch-autocrat in Europe, the czar.

Most Jews served in the armies of their respective countries, and did not feel obliged to form a specific Jewish policy and attitude, but for scattered reflections and sentiments influenced by the considerations mentioned. Army service had an important result for Jewish society, as at least one million Jews received a sound military training under conditions of war. This served to good effect after the war, when Jewish ex-servicemen took over the self-defense of Jewish communities in many places in Eastern Europe.

A sector of the Zionist leadership and many of the rank and file thought and behaved on similar lines. Their main policy was to wait and see. They argued that it would endanger the Jewish population in Erez Israel if Zionism took a stand against the Turks and it would harm the Jews in Russia if Zionists entered into an agreement with the Turkish-German side. A small but very able and devoted minority thought otherwise. It included the veteran Zionist Max Nordau, Chaim Weizmann, Vladimir Jabotinsky, Pinhas Rutenberg, Joseph Trumpeldor, and Meir Grossman. They considered that Zionism should have an active policy. They estimated that a victory for a side which included the Turks would mean an end to the whole of Jewish development in Erez Israel. The phenomenon of the Polish legions who had served in the Napoleonic armies and the persistence of Polish national policy without a state of its own, the example of similar Italian units and policies before the attainment of Italian independence, and admiration for the symbolic figures of Garibaldi and Cavour influenced the thoughts of some of them.

They came to the conclusion that there could be no greater political asset than to create an activist, pro-Entente, Zionist-Jewish policy, and that there could be no finer expression of national behavior than to create Jewish units that would fight against the Turks, when, for the first time since the Jews had fought in alliance with the Persians and took Jerusalem from Emperor Heraclius in 614, Jewish blood would again be part of the price for the land. Basing themselves on these precedents, the Jews hoped that they would obtain a seat and a say with the victors, and they were sure these would be the Western democracies. For some of them there was also added the ideology of a renewal of the courage and warrior spirit of the nation through its formal and actual participation in the war. The hostile behavior of the Turks in the land further spurred Aaron Aaronsohn to form Nili, a spy group in Erez Israel, to serve the Allies.

The differences of opinion were decided by acts. Trumpeldor and his associates organized a group that was accepted as a unit of muleteers; this battalion served with distinction at Gallipoli. It was recruited mainly from Jewish refugees from Erez Israel in Egypt. Trumpeldor forged both through instruction and personal example a high morale and brave behavior among these soldiers. Jabotinsky in the meantime worked tirelessly in England for the formation of a Jewish Legion in the British army to fight for the liberation of Erez Israel. He seized on the fact that many of the Jewish immigrants were not due for army service in England; their exemption caused anti-Semitism, and from his point of view they were a ready reservoir for his intended unit. The British began to incline to his view as the war was prolonged and they saw that the opposition of the mass of the Jewish population in the United States to the Allied cause was a considerable hindrance to the U.S. entry to the war. One hundred and fifty of the Zion Mule Corps, as Trumpeldor's unit was eventually called, joined Jabotinsky in London. In August 1917 the 38th Battalion of the Royal Fusiliers, or as they were called from the end of 1919, the "First Judeans," composed almost entirely of Jews, mainly from London, was officially instituted. In 1918 this battalion fought in Erez Israel. Its commander was Colonel John Henry Patterson, formerly commander of the Zion Mule Corps. In the U.S. Pinhas Rutenberg, with the help of David Ben-Gurion, Izhak Ben-Zvi and Chaim Zhitlovsky, mobilized in 1917 approximately 6,500 men who were to form the 39th Battalion of the Royal Fusiliers. After the conquest of Erez Israel by the British, the 40th Battalion was formed out of Erez Israel volunteers, many of whom later became activists of the Haganah, like its leader Eliyahu Golomb.

Activist policy carried the day on the diplomatic and political fronts also, thanks to the actions of Chaim Weizmann and his supporters. Despite many obstacles put in the way by Jewish assimilationists the Balfour Declaration was issued (Nov. 2, 1917). Thus, at the end of World War I, clearly conceived Jewish policies were brought into effect through the importance of the new Jewish concentration in the United States, the ability and readiness for sacrifice among the intelligentsia circles of Russian origin, and the devotion and courage of the pioneers in Erez Israel. The latter also had not only kept the Jewish settlements intact under the hostile Turkish regime, but had undergone the ordeal of severe persecution after the discovery of the Nili spy group.

The years 1917 to 1921 were decisive from many aspects in Jewish history. In 1917 the Jews in Russia acquired full emancipation and the Pale of Settlement there was abolished by the democratic Provisional Government. Legal emancipation was eventually attained by Jews in all of Europe. Despite the sufferings and confusion caused by the civil war, and the Communist policies with regard to Jewish society and culture, this achievement still formally remains in force, though with the terrible interlude of the years of Nazi domination. The institution of minority rights and treaties seemed to ensure, in countries to which they applied, the right of Jewish self-government, cultural hegemony, and a means of maintaining Jewish identity and cohesion on the basis of international guarantees. No longer pertinent, they were important between the two world wars. The Balfour Declaration, and later on the Mandate for Palestine conferred on the British, opened the long and tortuous path to the State of Israel. At the time many saw the opportunity and did not estimate the difficulties. United States Jewry emerged as the great political force and financial mainstay for all Jewish activity. At the same time the massacres perpetrated by the Ukrainian and White Russian bands and armies on Jews in pogroms in the Russian civil war, the cruelty and hostility displayed toward them by many of the new national states in Europe, and the social and spiritual crisis in Germany presaged future dangers and complexities. Communist domination in Russia cut off one of the most devoted sectors of Zionist activity, Jewish cultural creativity, and pioneer spirit from the main body of Jews in the world and from participation in the settlement of Erez Israel.

The impetus of Zionist successes brought the quick reorganization of Jews in Erez Israel, under patterns suggested by Zionism, in the Knesset Yisrael[63] all-country structure, through the Va'ad Le'ummi[64] and the Chief Rabbinate, *The Yishuv in Erez Israel* which had as its first head the leading spiritual personality of Abraham Isaac Kook. Circles of the "old *yishuv*" opposed this development and refused to participate in the common organization, basing their argument partly on their opposition to voting rights for women. They appealed to the League of Nations and obtained the right of secession. They were supported by the Agudat Israel. Though unpleasant, their secession and opposition could not hinder Zionist and *yishuv* activity in Erez Israel.

Life and development in Erez Israel between the two world wars were influenced by and decided through a number of processes and events. Arab national opposition within the country to the Jews and their enterprise hardened with every success attained by other Arab countries to achieve independence or to approach it, and with every success attained by Jewish settlement and society in Erez Israel. In a series of violent and cruel outbursts in the years 1921, 1929, 1933, and 1936–38, the Arabs tried to break Jewish morale and enterprise. The 1921 excesses achieved for them the Churchill White Paper (1922), which gave a restrictive definition for the concept of the Jewish National Home, after the closure of Transjordan to Jewish settlement through the creation of a separate Arab emirate (later kingdom) there. Later outbursts brought in their wake commissions of inquiry, and diplomatic activity which in one way or another brought proposals of concessions to the Arab cause.

63 The official Jewish community in Palestine when it was organized as a corporate entity (1927).
64 The National Council of Jews of Palestine (1920–48).

The history of relationships in the triangle between the Jews, Arabs, and British authorities in Ereẓ Israel is a long succession of flat Arab no's to a series of compromises loaded heavily in their favor. It is also a chapter in the history of colonial British officials the majority of whom were drawn to the romantic Arab against the ordinary European Jew. Jewish immigration to Ereẓ Israel was limited by various criteria and formalities; Jewish land acquisition was hindered in many ways. Only a minority of the British officials, and only in a limited number of cases and actions, did fulfill the mandatory power's obligation of furthering the "Jewish National Home."

Jews were divided among themselves as to the best ways of furthering their enterprise. In the dispute between Weizmann and the U.S. jurist and Zionist leader Judge Louis D. Brandeis there came to the fore the question of preference for individual initiative on accepted economic lines or preference for national and collectivist enterprises, sound from a social and ideological viewpoint more than an economic one, which began to occupy Zionist attention from the time of this quarrel. Religious Mizrachi circles complained about the secular and often anti-religious character of many of the settlers and settlements. The educational system set up by the new *yishuv* was divided between two networks: a modern Orthodox one and a "general" one with secularist leanings. The ultra-Orthodox circles maintained a network of their own. The readiness of Jews to come to Ereẓ Israel was often dependent on the political climate in the Diaspora. Thus the great immigration of Jews from Poland in the mid-1920s was nicknamed the "Grabski *aliyah*" after the Polish finance minister who through his discriminatory taxation policy influenced many to undertake *aliyah*.

Despite these hindrances and vacillations, progress continued unbroken throughout the period. The number of Jews in Ereẓ Israel grew in the 1920s about threefold, reaching 160,000. At the end of this decade there were 110 agricultural settlements (against 50 in 1920), cultivating 700,000 dunams of land. The electrification project of Rutenberg progressed, and the Potash Company successfully exploited the resources of the Dead Sea. The Plain of Jezreel became Jewish; irrigation for Jewish agriculture was swiftly developed. The new forms of the kibbutz and moshav proved themselves viable and were much admired by Jewish and general public opinion. In 1925 the first secular Jewish university was founded, the Hebrew University of Jerusalem. This progress continued in the 1930s, accelerated by the needs and plight of German Jewry. In 1933 there were one quarter of a million Jews in Ereẓ Israel, and by 1939 half a million, 120,000 of whom lived in 252 agricultural settlements. These included 68 kibbutzim and 71 moshavim. Mixed agriculture became the main basis of the Jewish settlements' economy, freeing them from dependence

The prefabricated walls and watchtower go up at Kibbutz Massadah on its first day, March 22, 1937.

on one source of income only, though citrus plantations were very successful. The skills, abilities, and money of German Jews did much to develop industry and advance technology.

Even the Arab revolt and frequent attacks on Jewish settlements and traffic on the road did not succeed in halting progress. The method of "Stockade and Watchtower" *(ḥomah u-migdal)* was invented to erect, overnight, defensible settlements. Fifty-five new Jewish settlements were founded between 1936 and 1939. World War II found the Jewish settlement in Ereẓ Israel strong, active, and alert socially and economically. By 1939 many were embittered against the mandatory government which prevented Jews, then in mortal danger in Europe, from reaching haven in Ereẓ Israel. As other states had already raised barriers in the 1920s against immigration (e.g., the quota of 1924 in the United States whose terms prevented the entry of many Jews there), Ereẓ Israel was at that time the only society willing and eager to receive them, but for the refusal of the British. Jews developed a network of "illegal" immigration which smuggled tens of thousands of Jews into the country. Measures taken by the mandatory authorities to suppress this immigration caused further clashes.

The defense system, strategy, and tactics of the Jews in Erez Israel were based from 1921 on the underground mass organization of the Haganah. It had to develop its training and arms supplies clandestinely. Up to 1945 strategically always on the defensive against the Arabs, it had to develop under pressure of attack new tactics to respond to different challenges. In the meantime there were differences of opinion over the share of various social circles in the leadership of the Haganah, expressed mainly in terms of right-wing and left-wing, different policies as to the methods and timing of reaction to individual acts of terror, and from the late 1930s also differences over the question if and to what degree to oppose by armed force the British anti-Zionist legislation and measures. These led to splits in the Jewish forces. A group of the minority right wing advocating an activist response to Arab terrorization formed a separate armed underground, generally named the "Irgun Bet" in the 1930s. In 1937, after two splits, the Irgun Zeva'i Le'ummi (I.Z.L.) emerged and, in 1940, the Lohamei Herut Israel (Lehi). From many aspects these were more extreme developments of the former right-wing "Irgun Bet."

The Haganah attempted with considerable success to form legal Jewish militia and defense units in cooperation with the mandatory government. In the personality of Orde Charles Wingate it found a devoted British officer who identified himself with the Jewish cause. On the eve of World War II a large number of the Jewish youth in Erez Israel were organized one way or another for defense, and ready to serve. They supplied the volunteers for the various Jewish units, and later on the Jewish Brigade Group in the British army of World War II was formed. In this unit, in turn, many who were later to be commanders of the Israel Defense Forces gained experience of large-scale training and operations. In the Palmah, the Haganah created a striking force of youth trained in commando style who through close links with social life in the kibbutzim were emotionally and ideologically devoted to the new Jewish society. Consciously and subconsciously all these various military and para-military organizations and units drew their inspiration from the conviction, crystallized in Russia at the time of the pogroms, that human stature demanded active armed defense by the Jews of their honor and their life. They were also inspired by historical memories revived on the soil of Erez Israel: the acts of the Maccabees, the example of the great revolt against the Romans (66–70), and the deeply implanted readiness for *kiddush-ha-Shem,* which had already assumed a secularist form in sacrifice for an ideal in the activities of Jewish revolutionaries in Europe from the second half of the 19th century.

Between the world wars there was achieved at one and the same time the final transformation of Hebrew from a literary language into a full-scale living language and the formation of Yiddish as a language for literary and scientific expression from a spoken popular dialect. The attainments of Hebrew before World War I were now broadened and deepened by a rich literary creation — much of it begun before World War I but reaching a peak and social recognition between the two world wars (Ḥayyim Naḥman Bialik, Saul Tchernichowsky, Zalman Shneour, Nathan Alterman, Shemuel Yosef Agnon, among a galaxy of poets and writers). In the Hebrew University at Jerusalem, the Technion in Haifa, and in all aspects of everyday life, in the elementary school and kindergarten, in the units of the defense organizations as in professional work and writing, old mishnaic, talmudic, and midrashic terms were given new meanings and connotations to serve modern needs. Many new terms were coined. Many Jews in the Diaspora began to study and use Hebrew as a living language, considering it and forging it into a powerful bond and rich symbol of unity with the Jewish past and of participation in the emerging new Jewish spirit in Ereẓ Israel.

Hebrew and Yiddish

Yiddish also continued to evolve and diffuse literary works on a high level before World War I and after it (Mendele Mokher Seforim, who through his work and personality formed a link between Hebrew and Yiddish literature, Shalom Aleichem, Sholem Asch, Der Nister, Peretz Markish, David Bergelson, and many others). It was cultivated and perfected, and attained precision in expression and grammar, in academic institutes (e.g. YIVO), and school systems. For many Jews — mostly anti-Zionist or left-wing, but also some among the Orthodox — Yiddish became a symbol of the greatness of European Jewish culture of the Ashkenazi type, and of what they considered the abiding value of continued Jewish existence in the Diaspora. Nathan Birnbaum, an early pioneer of Zionism, served through his leadership and personality as a link between these various groups of "Yiddishists." In the Soviet Union, mainly through the ideology and activities of the Yevsektsiya circles, as well as among radical circles of the Yiddishist camp elsewhere, Yiddish became a symbol of the break with the religious "clerical" and the "bourgeois nationalist" past. It was used to work for and express total secularization as the basis for specifically Jewish life and creativity in the new society. This found technical expression by adopting changes of spelling and vocalization to wipe out the last traces of Hebrew and religious influence from the language.

Thus, on the eve of the Holocaust, Jews had two fully developed national languages, two competing conceptions as to the center of gravity of Jewish achievement and Jewish continuity, and two incipient conceptions of the relation to the past and the character of future culture. Two sets of literature were being developed and sustained at a high level; two paralled structures of

World War II and Holocaust

Cutting the Jew's beard: the confrontation of a martyr with the sadists.

scientific and educational effort were being activated successfully. Hebrew stood for a hope of the eventual unity of Jews throughout the world, on the basis of the common past rooted in biblical, mishnaic, and talmudic times, and striving for a renaissance in the land of Israel. Its secular tendencies were also directed toward the transformation of this past unity and those past treasures into new forms capable of containing the entire former complex. Yiddish expressed the feeling that what had happened in Europe from approximately the tenth century onward, and more or less north of the Pyrenees, was what mattered and should be handed on to be transformed and used. It stood for the belief in *"Doyigkeyt"* (the value of what is here and now in Jewish life, meaning Europe, and the European communities overseas, and the elements that were present and activating in their culture in the 20th century). It was intended to be the abiding vehicle of autonomous secular Jewish culture and life in the Diaspora based on a European Jewish Ashkenazi cultural pattern. The Holocaust cut the existential plane from under Yiddish. Its achievements, and goals, and the conceptions it expressed remain in this literature and in the progress it made in competition with established Hebrew in a relatively short time. In the Soviet Union Yiddish was helped by the prohibition of Hebrew and by state aid provided for Yiddish institutions and literature. This also vanished with the anti-Jewish stands adopted by Stalin and the "liquidation" of many Yiddish writers and artists after the end of World War II. Tension between the "Hebraists" and "Yiddishists" was considerable between the two world wars. After the Holocaust it became a matter of the past.

Unlike the outbreak of World War I, World War II found the Jews everywhere united in the cause of the war against Hitler. The Molotov-Ribbentrop pact of August 23, 1939, caused some fanatical Jewish communists to deviate for a short time from this natural course, to which they returned gladly in 1941 with Hitler's attack on Soviet Russia. Each German victory — a series unbroken up to the end of 1942 — spelled horror and doom for the Jews who came under their rule. As clearly evident now from documents captured and from the fragments of "Jewish museums" that Hitler began to erect, his clearly formulated plan and avowed intention was to exterminate first all the Jews in Europe and later all Jews in the world, so that future generations could see what Jews were only as museum exhibits. The Nazis saw and pointed to Jews as the vermin of humanity whose house had to be cleaned of them in order to be made fit for the future great culture under pure Aryan domination.

The Nazi methods in dealing with Jews were an unvarying compound of deception, human cruelty, and the use of both psychological pressure and technical harassment to break the spirit of the victims and dehumanize them before their final dispatch. In the ghettos, in the various *Aussiedlung* (transfer of population) actions, in the death camps, the same pattern of sadistic torture proceeded, creating a constant and worsening situation of hunger, epidemics, arbitrary executions and inhuman cruelty, and in the end death for the emaciated body, taking the maximum care to use every ounce and particle possible for the benefit of the great Aryan German culture. Under this pattern it was intended that the victims lose all sense of time and individuality; the humanly impossible was always possible in the organized chaos and nightmare surrounding the Jews. Degradation was as much the aim as killing. This system was applied in the full to Jews, though it was also applied to other enemies and opponents of the "thousand-year Reich."

Despite this satanic dehumanization by a mighty state machine, there were indeed Jewish uprisings, in the Warsaw Ghetto, and several other ghettos, and in the Treblinka death camp as well as several others. There were Jewish partisans wherever they could find shelter, which was often denied to them by non-Jewish partisans.

The Nazis were able to deceive their decent victims because no ordinary human being could conceive the existence of such depths of vileness in the human mind, even having read *Mein Kampf* and meeting with the Nazis. The Nazis used a series of cover names and cover conceptions to confuse the Jews. The terms "ghetto," or "elders of the Jews" *(Judenrat), Judenpolizei* (Jewish police), the slogan "labor makes free" at the entrance to death camps, the fiendish invention of sending Jews to a "bathroom" that was really a gas chamber, constituted a mixture of medieval concepts, that apparently ensured life with humiliation, and modern concepts of service and cleanliness, so that the Jews should not realize their fate.

The process of actual extermination frequently began with mass pogroms in the old czarist style. It continued in the nightmarish journeys in goods trains under horrible conditions to the ghettos in Poland. On Jan. 20, 1942, the details for the final mass extermination were settled by the so-called Wannsee Conference at Berlin. At this conference the liquidation of 11 million Jews was envisaged, and from the following year was largely implemented at Auschwitz and the other camps. The Warsaw Ghetto revolt of April–May 1943 was a last stand manifesting Jewish courage and belief in the future and the human spirit. By the time the Nazis had been defeated between four-and-a-half and six million Jews were already dead; the Holocaust was carried out in such a way that exact numbers are difficult to ascertain. When the gates of the death camps were opened at Buchenwald, Bergen-Belsen, Dachau, and elsewhere, hundreds of thousands of living skeletons were found in them. They had to be brought back to ordinary human life.

The Holocaust showed the inhumanity to which anti-Semitism and racism could bring, not only despite, but in the main through, mass culture, mass education, and the use of mass media for propaganda and indoctrination. The executioners were dehumanized beyond recovery in the process. The victims were intended to reach this state but the Jewish vitality and spirit, and the demonstration of Jewish brotherhood, quickly brought back most of the survivors to personal integration and proud human stature. The numbers that had been tattooed on their skins in the camps were not obliterated: most of those Jews learned to live with them, and gained a renewed belief in humanity.

The Holocaust was organized by the Germans. The German people knew of it. Such an operation could be carried out only be means of the technology at its disposal, and the victories achieved by its sons, but many other peoples of Europe, in particular of Eastern Europe, took part in the initial mass pogroms, and collaborated in the murders. It was not by accident that Hitler chose Poland in which to carry them out. Some nations — the Dutch, the Danes, the Swedes, the Bulgarians, and many Italians — showed courage in helping and hiding Jews, later to be esteemed by Jews and honored with the Hebrew appellation *Ḥasidei Umot ha-Olam,* meaning "The Just and Righteous among the Nations." Few came out openly on their side. A notable exception was the mass action of the Amsterdam port workers. The Western Allies were afraid of German propaganda and on many occasions took good care not to be trapped into specific and open actions of help to the Jews as Jews. The bombing of Auschwitz was considered impossible on technical grounds, while aid by air to the Polish insurgents in Warsaw was conceived and carried out despite Russian opposition. On general grounds of condemning torture and inhumanity the Allies included the account of the Jews also in their warnings to the Germans of the day of reckoning to come. But they refused to counter the singling out of Jews for destruction by the Nazis by singling Jews out themselves for help and protection.

It seemed after the Holocaust to many, friends and enemies alike, that with regard to Jews Hitler had achieved his purpose of breaking their spirit, though he had failed in achieving their total extermination. In looking at the physical wrecks in the camps, and in counting the scanty remnants of European Jewry, it seemed to the foreign secretary of the Labor government, Ernest Bevin, as well as to many other level-headed statesmen, that the time had come to liquidate the enterprise of European Jewry in Erez Israel after its virtual liquidation in Europe. Emancipation had again returned formally to Jews all over the world; the anti-Semitism of Stalin was yet to be seen. The pressure of the Jewish masses for immigration to Erez Israel seemed to be gone with annihilation of these masses. Economically rich countries were ready to receive the remnants; why imagine that they would insist on going to a poor, dangerous, and effort-demanding little country? The Jews of Erez Israel had witnessed the horror of the destruction of millions of Jews, of the conception of Jews as subhuman beings, and the passivity of the democratic and communist pro-Jewish world. It seemed that ensuring a guaranteed status of an autonomous and prosperous minority in an Arab state should satisfy the Jews of Erez Israel, while rehabilitation and immigration would help what remained of European Jewry.

This view and plan was upset by the spirit and readiness to undergo mortal risks and physical sufferings by three elements of the Jewish people. The greater part of the remnant in Europe refused to be lured by comfort in other Diasporas. Even the many who went to the countries of Western Europe and the United States, and even those who found it possible to return to live in German cities, conceived that they could see no other compensation for their humiliation, for the torture and death of their brethren — and no other surety or hope that a Jew could continue to live among men and be considered a fellowman — but the creation of an independent political and social existence in a Jewish state in Erez Israel. The Jews of Erez Israel showed themselves at this juncture ready to face both Arabs and ultimately British might and risk everything for the creation of a Jewish state. The cooperation of the soldiers of

Prelude to Independence

the Jewish Brigade in Europe was enlisted, paratroopers were dropped behind Nazi lines during the war, emissaries of the Haganah and the Irgun Ẓevai Le'ummi (Irgun) were sent to Europe, and they began again to organize "illegal" immigration.

The attempts to enter Ereẓ Israel were met by the British authorities by expulsions. The immigrant ship *Exodus* was intercepted and went from port to port in Europe. Later on the immigrants were concentrated at Cyprus, but the ships — congested and unseaworthy — continued to arrive off the shores of Ereẓ Israel at night. The story of their embarkation, journeyings, perilous disembarkation, and of running the cordon of British military and police in the country, lit a flame and became a legend, a record of devotion and heroism. The Irgun, and in particular the Leḥi, turned to acts of sabotage and individual terror against the British. Undeterred by the specter of mass anti-Semitism and the enmity of states and statesmen, and not heeding allegations of "dual loyalty" and "Jewish lobby," U.S. Jewry poured its enthusiasm, its money, its position as Americans, into the struggle to assert a proud Jewish identity to offset the image of the skeletons in the camps. They were joined by many non-Jews who felt that their

The refugee ship *Theodor Herzl* arriving at Haifa port, April 13, 1947.

support was not only a matter of justice to the Jews but even more of giving back trust in humanity to small peoples.

The Jews had been ready in 1937 to accept in principle the proposition of the British Peel Commission of Inquiry for the partition of Erez Israel, though not all the details of the plan. In 1942, at a conference in the United States, the Biltmore Program was accepted by the Zionist organization which set forth clearly the goal of the creation of a Jewish state. Now even the most pro-British elements among the Zionists began to waver in their loyalty to the mandatory power. Other commissions were sent to Erez Israel, searches for arms were made by the British in Jewish settlements, there were arrests, and hints were frequently thrown out that the British might leave the Jews to their fate, withdrawing their protection and leaving them on their own to face the Arabs. A mixed Anglo-American committee of inquiry proposed in April 1946 the immediate entry of 100,000 Jews mainly from the "displaced persons" camps in Europe to Erez Israel. The U.S. president, Harry S Truman, supported this recommendation; the British prime minister, Clement Attlee, refused it by attaching a condition requiring disbandment of the Jewish illegal armed organization and handing in of their weapons. The struggle continued. From the end of 1945 the Haganah also took part in actions against the British. When in 1946 the British arrested the leaders of the *yishuv,* the Irgun reacted by organizing the mining of the King David Hotel in Jerusalem where many government officials were killed.

The fate of the ship *Exodus* in 1947 aroused world opinion against the British government. The British then at first proposed the "Morrison Plan for Partition," which was rejected by both Jews and Arabs. In April 1947, Ernest Bevin carried out his threat and turned to the United Nations, withdrawing from the sole British responsibility for Erez Israel. The Jews refused to be frightened. To the surprise of many, the Soviet government joined that of the United States in supporting partition and the creation of a Jewish state in Palestine. On Nov. 29, 1947, the United Nations General Assembly adopted, by a majority of 33 votes against 13, a resolution on the partition of Palestine. The actual plan was very disadvantageous to the Jews, but the Arabs immediately proclaimed war against it. The Jews had to prepare for this war clandestinely; the Arabs had the support of their states and the sympathy of the British government to help them in their preparations.

When war broke out on May 15, 1948, with the proclamation of the establishment of the State of Israel, the armies of seven Arab states invaded the territory intended for the Jewish state. In a series of battles, during which they had to organize and improvise under fire, the Jews repelled these armies. They proved in the process the value of their underground organizations and of the

Establishment of State of Israel

approximately 24,000 trained men who had fought in one way or another in World War II, as well as the valor of thousands of volunteers who flocked from many Diaspora countries to fight for their nation. The War of Independence, in its two phases (interrupted by a short-lived cease-fire), not only enabled the State of Israel to exist; its course also changed the map of the proposed Jewish state in the latter's favor. The borders of the Rhodes armistice of 1949 were much more viable than those of the U.N. resolution of 1947. The war took a toll of thousands of lives. In besieged Jerusalem alone about 1,600 civilians were killed by the shellings of the Jordanian Arab Legion, then commanded by British officers.

Since then the State of Israel has been surrounded by the hostility of the Arab world, which considers itself at war with Israel and likes to think of Israel as being in a state of siege to be ended with Arab victory. The Arabs not only proclaim a *jihad* ("holy war") against Israel but also organize systematically, as a matter of declared policy, an anti-Israel economic boycott. The attitude of the Arabs was to see the State of Israel as a "non-state," destined ultimately for obliteration. This total and totalitarian hatred was given its deadly expression through the aggression of the combined armies of Egypt and Syria against the State of Israel, on the holiest day for Jewry and Judaism, the Day of Atonement (October 6) 1973.

This Arab hostility has brought about until now the consummation of the "Ingathering of the Exiles" from the Muslim countries, which had already begun well before World War I. The enthusiasm of Yemen Jews for *aliyah* had been manifested from ancient times, and began to be realized before World War I. After the war of Independence almost all went to Israel; for many of them their air flight was an abrupt transition from conditions of tenth-century Muslim technology and life to the 20th-century society of Israel. Their adjustment was miraculously rapid and successful. Yemen Jewry has enriched Israel culture with its traditions in song and dance, colorful dress and customs. The Jews of Syria and Iraq remained in continuous contact with Erez Israel. They made up a not inconsiderable part of the "illegal immigration" during the mandatory period — often experiencing danger and persecution in the countries of departure. After the establishment of the state they left for Israel "illegally," having to organize self-defense and underground movements in circumstances of mob hostility and brutal persecution by the state. Most of them had to abandon all their possessions to go to Israel. A large number of the Jews in Iran also left the country, though they did not face state enmity there. With the increase of hostility in North Africa many — though by no means all — of the Jews there went to Israel.

This ingathering has created, for the first time since the dispersion of the

Jews, a meeting of the diverse varieties of Jewish culture and social life that have crystallized over a period of at least 2,000 years in widely differing environments and circumstances. A vast, almost unprecedented, process of reacquaintance, and mutual acculturation has thus begun, and is, it seems, successfully under way. The Hebrew language, the educational system, and army service, serve as accelerating and cementing factors, though there remains still much tension and misunderstanding between the various elements.

To Jews everywhere the creation of the State of Israel was not only a reassertion of their humanity, but a fulfillment and obligation to strive for further human and Jewish perfection and service. This has been stated as follows:

"To sum up: the political rebirth of Israel is the very essence of Jewish history. She has absorbed into herself the experiences and activities of generations, the covenant of generations. She has renewed the covenant with the land out of a longing, through the creation of a new community, to develop the Covenant of Man into an Eternal Covenant" (B.Z. Dinur, *Israel and the Diaspora* (1969), 186).

In this period the State of Israel victoriously stood up to three wars (the 1956 Sinai Campaign; the 1967 Six-Day War; and the 1973 Day of Atonement War). It was subject to terror tactics and guerilla warfare almost continuously. At the same time it gathered in hundreds of thousands of Jews from the Arab States, and as the behavior of the population has shown during the Six-Day War of 1967, it succeeded within this short span in imbuing most of them with its ethos and with serviceable acquaintance of European technology and scientific methods in the conduct of affairs. This state has up to the present proved democratic in the full sense of the term, in its conduct of the political process and the freedom of press and discussion. Hebrew culture is continuously developing. In the Law of Return (1950) the state asserted its basic Jewishness in proclaiming that every Jew has the right to go there and become its citizen. The State of Israel is not only far from being besieged to all practical intents and purposes but has been one of the important advisers to developing countries in Africa and Asia. Basically secular, it does much toward maintaining links with Jewish law and tradition, though the extent of this application is at the center of heated public discussion.

All over the world emancipation is formally in force for Jews, with a few unimportant exceptions. In practice Jews are severely persecuted in most Arab countries, and suffer governmental harassment and total denial of rights to develop their own culture in all communist countries. There is proof, however, that the cultural activity and consciousness continues as always, even under persecution.

Soviet Jews have begun to fight for links with their brethren outside Russia and for *aliyah*. This struggle, after almost 40 years of silence and total assimilation, is essentially a rejection of individual emancipation granted on the assumption of the extirpation of Jewish identity and unity and of the willing assimilation of the Jewish individuals. It is of course also a reaction against the attitude and behavior of large sections of the Soviet population and the Soviet government toward the Jews during the Holocaust and in its aftermath. This struggle has become one of the focal phenomena in Jewish life the world over. The redemption of Soviet Jewry became a major challenge for the entire Jewish people. In many countries and in most sections of Jewish society this struggle forges anew the unity of the Jews, transcending even great differences in world view and life-attitude among Jewish individuals. Phenomena of self hatred and lack of compassion among Jews who had attained high position in non-Jewish society became evident in 1973. The link of Russian Jewry to national consciousness and to Israel has thus become the touchstone for dignity and decency among Jews. It is difficult to ascertain how this struggle affects the Jews of other countries under Soviet domination; in most of these countries, like Poland and Czechoslovakia, the number of the Jews is diminishing to vanishing point.

In the Western world Jews everywhere are active in parties of all shades and occupied with the problems that face the societies to which they feel allegiance. At the same time their ties with other Jews, and in particular with the State of Israel, are strong. The tense atmosphere in the Diaspora during the weeks preceding the Six-Day War showed their devotion at a time of crisis. On the other hand, Jews in the United States are facing, as many Jewish societies have done in modern times, an imponderable problem from without in the emergence of "black" anti-Semitism among Negro society. The horror and dialectics of this developing situation have lately been expressed forcefully in Bernard Malamud's novel *The Tenants*. The tension becomes even more dynamic when the Negro image in this work is compared with the Negro image in Malamud's earlier *The Magic Barrel*. Within the confines of their own camp as well Jews are facing hostility in the form of strong manifestations of Jewish "self-hate," in particular among intellectuals of the New Left, often in the guise of anti-Zionism, so that there now exists not only "left-wing anti-Semitism" − an old phenomenon dating from the times of Marx and Bakunin − but also "Jewish anti-Semitism." Conversely, many Jews now contribute to general culture with a conscious and articulate stress on and expression of their Jewishness, as they understand it (like Arnold Wesker in England, or Bernard Malamud and Saul Bellow among many in

The people gather around its liberated holy place — at the Western Wall on Shavuot, 1967.

the United States). Some have even elevated Jewish existence in exile to the status of a paradigm and symbol of the alienation of modern man.

In many respects the Jewish nation stands at present in a similar situation to that at the time of the Second Temple. It has its independent and creative center in Erez Israel. It has great and creative centers in the Diaspora, especially in the United States which has been compared in this connection with those of Hellenistic Alexandria or ancient Babylonia with their roles in the development of Jewish culture. Cultural hostility toward Jews, and certainly vulgar anti-Semitism, is far from disappearing. Despite Pope John XXIII's great humanist attempt to sever the old Christian attitude to the Jews, this has not disintegrated. The phrases used by Arnold Toynbee designating the Jew and his culture as a "fossil of the Syriac civilization" making the Arab refugees "the new

Jews" form but one striking instance of modern *"Salonantisemitismus."* Jews are economically active in many specific spheres; while in Jewish society the trend to megalopolization and intellectualization continues and even sharpens, this activity has established in the State of Israel a flourishing modern agriculture and a full range of modern social stratification. The number of Jews in the professions is constantly rising. With the present importance of science, sociology, and psychology for immediate military, industrial, and social needs the service of Jews to society in these fields has become of increasing importance, and their standing is becoming more assured and rewarding, socially and spiritually, both in regard to the society of the environment and in their own estimation.

The problems facing Jews have not disappeared. Many of the old dangers, opportunities, tasks, and ideals remain under a change of guise.

"Each and every chapter in the long history of our people and each and every real point of our historical reality embodies the mystery of old periods, past and future ... They are planted in the heart of every man, through them the place of Israel amongst the nations will be marked in the future" (Y. Baer, *Yisrael ba-Amim* (1955), 117).

Part Two

ASPECTS OF
JEWISH HISTORY

1

MEDIEVAL GERMANY
A PROVINCE OF JEWISH SOCIETY AND CULTURE IN THE MIDDLE AGES

The first Jews to reach Germany were merchants who went there in the wake of the Roman legions and settled in the Roman-founded Rhine towns. The earliest detailed record of a Jewish community in Germany, referring to Cologne, is found in imperial decrees issued in 321 and 331 C.E. There is, however, no evidence of continuous Jewish settlement in Germany, although the Jews' Street in Cologne remained inside the Roman town in the early days of the German Empire, indicating continuity of settlement there.

Jews entered Central Europe in this period from the west and the southwest; Jewish merchants from southern Italy and France were welcomed in Germany, and settled in the towns along the great rivers and trade routes. The Kalonymos family from Lucca established itself in Mainz in the tenth century. Like the Jews of France, German Jewry in its early stages drew its inspiration in matters of religion and religious practice straight from the centers of Jewish creative activity in Ereẓ Israel: a 12-century Jewish scholar speaks of a letter he saw in Worms, which Rhine Jews had sent to Ereẓ Israel in 960, asking for verification of the rumor that the Messiah had come (*Revue des Etudes Juives,* 44 (1902), 238). Until the end of the 11th century the Jews of Germany engaged in international trade, especially with the East, and were a respected element of the urban population. They were concentrated along the west bank of the Rhine, in Lorraine, and in ancient episcopal seats and trade centers, such as Cologne, Mainz, Speyer, Worms, and Trier, as well as religious and political centers situated more eastward, such as Regensburg and Prague. The extant reports of Jewish settlement in Germany are of a haphazard nature, and the dating of such records does not necessarily establish the sequence of settlement. The first mention of Jewish settlement in Mainz dates from c. 990, of Worms from 960, and of Regensburg from 981. Jewish communities in south central Germany (Bamberg, Wuerzburg) and Thuringia (Erfurt) are mentioned in documents from the 11th century.

The persecutions to which the Jews had been exposed from the 12th to the 14th centuries forced them to move from the south to the east and north of Germany, and they were drawn in the same direction by opportunities for trade and moneylending. Thus, although this coincided with the general migratory trend within Germany, the Jews joined the move for independent reasons. In Breslau and Munich Jews are mentioned at the beginning of the 13th century, in Vienna in the middle of that century, and in Berlin (and other places) at its end. German Jews maintained close ties with France. At the end of the tenth century (or the beginning of the 11th), the rabbinic authority Gershom b. Judah (known as *"Me'or ha-Golah"*) moved from Metz to Mainz and that city became noted for Torah learning; the *yeshivot* of Mainz and Worms became spiritual centers for all the Jews in Central Europe and even attracted students from France, among them the famous Rashi. For the Jews, the Carolingian Empire, although no longer a political entity, still remained a single social and cultural unit. In Christian Germany, which had retained many of the concepts of a tribal society, the Jews figured as aliens as well as infidels. Their social and legal status was distinct from that of the general population, and, as people who had no country and were not Christians, they required special protection to safeguard their existence.

The first known reports of persecution of Jews in Germany date from the 11th century (the expulsion of the Jews of Mainz in 1012), and the first written guarantees of rights, granted to them by emperors and bishops, also date from that century. In 1084 the archbishop of Speyer invited them to settle in his enlarged city "in order to enhance a thousandfold the respect accorded to our town," and granted the Jews far-reaching trading rights and permission to put up a protective wall around their quarters. This evidence of the high value attached to Jews for settlement of a new town and the expansion of its trade precedes by only 12 years the *"gezerot tatnav"* (the 1096 massacres; see below). In 1090 Emperor Henry IV issued charters of rights to the Jews of Speyer and Worms, and succeeding emperors followed his example. All these writs acknowledged the right of the Jews to be judged "by their peers and no others ... according to their law" (from a charter of 1090). In another such document, granted to the Jews of Worms in 1157, the emperor reserves for himself the exclusive right of judging the Jews "for they belong to our treasury." The guarantees of rights were given to the community leaders, who were also the spiritual leaders of the community, and were well-to-do men belonging to respected families. Communities that were accorded guarantees already possessed a synagogue (the Worms synagogue was founded in 1034) and public institutions. No reliable figures on the size of these Jewish communities are available; to judge by figures mentioned in the narratives of their martyrdom, there were communities of 2,000 persons (Mainz), but in general they consisted of several hundred, or several dozen. The community regulations enacted by the Jewish communities in Germany, and the commentaries and liturgical poems written by their scholars reveal a strong and simple faith, and readiness to die for it.

Their faith was put to the supreme test during the first Crusade, from April to June 1096. The brutal massacres that then took place are remembered in Jewish annuals as the *gezerot tatnav* (i.e., the massacres of 4856 = 1096). The first waves of crusaders turned upon the Jews of the Rhine valley. Although the emperor, the bishops, and Christian neighbors were reluctant to take part in this onslaught and tried to protect the Jews, this defense had small success. It was then that the Jews of Germany revealed their indomitable courage and religious devotion and chose a martyr's death *(Kiddush ha-Shem)*. In Mainz, it is related in a contemporary description of these acts of heroism that "in a single day one thousand and one hundred martyrs were slaughtered and died". The martyrdom of Mainz Jewry was preceded by negotiations with the emperor by Kalonymos ben Meshullam; in response, Henry IV published an order in defense of the Jews, but this was of little help. The Jews offered armed resistance and it was only in the final stage that they committed suicide. Similar events took place in many communities on the Rhine and along the crusaders' route; many Jews chose martyrdom; others managed to save their lives by going into hiding (Speyer, Cologne, Worms, Xanten, Metz). Some accepted temporary conversion, as in Regensburg, where "all were coerced." Later the emperor permitted their return to Judaism. The beginning of the Crusades inaugurated far-reaching changes in the social and economic structure of the Christian peoples in Western Europe and in their general outlook, and as a result also marks a turning point in the history of German Jewry. Henceforth the mob came to regard physical attacks on Jews as permissible, especially in periods of social or religious ferment. The city guilds forced the Jews out of the trades and the regular channels of commerce; this coincided with the stricter appliance of the church ban on usury in the 12th to 13th centuries. The combination of circumstances made moneylending and pawnbroking the main occupation of Jews in Germany. They also continued in ordinary trade; as late as the 13th century they dealt in wool, attended the Cologne fairs, and traded with Russia and Hungary; during most of the Middle Ages there were even Jewish craftsmen and Jews had some contact with agriculture.

However moneylending, conceived by the Church as usury, became the hallmark of Jewish life in Germany. About 100 to 150 years after usury became the main occupation of Jews in England and France, it became central to the livelihood of Jews in Germany also. Jew hatred and the evil image of the Jew as conceived in the popular imagination were nourished by this economic pattern. Owing to the scarcity of money and lack of firm securities the rate of interest was extremely high. In 1244 the Jews of Austria were given a bill of rights by Duke Frederick II based on the assumption that interest was the Jews' main source of income; the bill contained detailed regulations on moneylending, and the rate of interest was fixed at 173 1/3%. This kind of charter for Jews became typical of those granted in central and eastern Germany (and Poland) in the 13th and 14th centuries. Borrowing money from Jews against pawns became usual among the nobility and the townspeople, and enabled rabble-rousers to accuse the Jews of "sucking Christian blood" and of associating with gentile thieves who pawned their loot with the Jewish moneylenders. The Jews insisted on their right to refuse to return pawns unless reimbursed, a right confirmed as early as 1090. After the end of the 11th century the social status of the Jews steadily deteriorated. The *Landesfrieden* ("peace of the land") issued in 1103 includes the Jews among persons who bear no arms and are therefore to be spared violence and defended. The concepts which had determined the status of the Jews from the beginning of their settlement in Germany were now applied with increasing cruelty and vigor. The German political view was molded by a combination of tribal and state concepts which could not regard those who were alien in blood and faith as citizens of the state, while the Church had always claimed that the sins of the Jews condemned them to perpetual serfdom and degradation. The need of the Jews for refuge and protection was now utilized by the urge to oppress and exploit them. A long-drawn-out process of legal and social development was finally summed up in 1236 by Emperor Frederick II, when he declared all the Jews of Germany *Servi camerae nostrae* ("servants of our treasury"). This meant that from the legal point of view the Jews and their property were possessions of the emperor and hence entirely at his mercy. However they never fully experienced the severity of this concept as it was never fully applied to them; in a way, their status as servants of the imperial treasury was even welcomed for it assured them of imperial protection, protection which no other German authority was able or willing to afford them. Long after the concept of the servitude of the Jews had been applied in Germany, the rabbinical authority Meir of Rothenburg conceived that "the Jews are not *glebae adscripti* [= bound] to any particular place as gentiles are; for they are regarded as impoverished freemen who have not been sold into slavery; the government attitude is according to this" (Responsa, ed. Prague, no. 1001). The concepts that Jewish lives were not inviolable and that the Jews were in servitude to the country's rulers led to renewed outbursts of anti-Jewish violence whenever a critical situation arose. The second Crusade (1146), which was again accompanied by widespread anti-Jewish agitation, was also a living nightmare for the Jews. However the experience of 1096 had taught a lesson both to the Jews and to the authorities; the Jews took refuge in the castles of the nobility, whenever possible having the entire citadel to themselves until the danger passed. The preaching of Bernard of Clairvaux against doing the Jews physical harm also helped to restrain the masses. Thus a repetition of the earlier terrorization and slaughter did not take place. Between the second Crusade and the beginning of the 13th century the Jews were subjected to numerous attacks and libels but relatively few lost their lives as a result.

The events of 1096 had shaken German Jewry to the core; its response came in the form of tremendous spiritual and social creativity. Succeeding generations glorified the deeds of the martyrs and created a whole doctrine around the sanctification of God through martyrdom (*Kiddush ha-Shem,* see below, chap. 6). The ideas of self-sacrifice of choosing to meet "the Great Light" rather than apostasy, and of standing up to the attacker, were now formulated and transmitted as permanent principles. A special blessing was inserted into the prayer book to be recited by those who were about to be slain. The martyrs of Xanten had their own prayer: "May the Almighty avenge the blood of His servants which has been shed, and will be shed after us, in the days of those who survive us and before their very eyes: may the Almighty save us from men of evil, from destruction and idolatry and from the impurity of the gentiles." This prayer expresses the general mood of the German Jews in this period and of the "leaders in martyrdom" in particular. In the 12th and 13th centuries a group known as *Ḥasidim* (pious men) came into being, distinguished by their piety in thought and deed (see below, chap 7). The way of life to which this group adhered was established, in the main, by the members of a single family. These formulated the principles of perfect piety: observance of "Heavenly Law" *(din shamayim)* which is above and beyond the "Law of the Torah," for the latter was given to man taking into account his *yezer ha-ra* ("evil urge"). They taught that one should regard property as being held on trust (from God) only, and that one should abstain from lust without retiring from family and public life. *Sefer Ḥasidim* and *Sefer ha-Roke'aḥ,* two works written by these men, express the feelings and ideas of the *Ḥasidim* of Germany on the greatness of God, on man's conduct in life, on ghosts and spirits, on sexual temptation and how to withstand it, on the true observance of commandments, and on love of learning as a foremost religious value.

During this period further consolidation of the Jewish communal leadership in Germany took place. Jews increasingly restricted themselves to the Jewish quarter in the town, which gave them a greater feeling of security and made possible the development of an intense social life. The *meliores* (leading families) accepted the authority of the most eminent scholars. Torah learning was not interrupted in times of trouble and danger. It even received additional impetus from the need to provide leadership for the Jewish public and guidance to the individual, while the number of outstanding scholars also increased. Even the source of livelihood that was forced upon the Jews — lending money against interest — came to be appreciated as an advantage since it left time to spare for Torah study. Moneylending also determined the artificial structure of Jewish life; the Jews derived their income mainly from non-Jews, and there was hardly any economic exploitation of one Jew by another. As a result, there was a large measure of social cohesion in the German communities. The average community maintained a synagogue, a cemetery (or, if it was too small, obtained burial rights in a neighboring town), a bathhouse, and a place for weddings and other public festivities. A scholar attracted groups of students who lived in his home and were cared for by the scholar's wife. Meir of Rothenburg attests that his house was spacious and included "a *bet midrash* . . . a winter house [i.e., the main living quarters] . . . a courtyard for public use . . . a cool upper room where I eat in summer and . . . a room . . . for each student" (Responsa, ed. Cremona, no., 108). Community institutions developed. The community leaders and scholars — in gatherings on fair-days — issued *takkanot* regulating many spheres of life which were binding upon individual communities or groups of several communities.

In the 13th century, the scholar Eliezer b. Joel ha-Levi of Bonn established principle that a majority decision also obligated the opposing minority, and unanimity was not required (contradicting the 12th-century French scholar Jacob b. Meir Tam). Beginning from 1220, the *"Takkanot Shum,"* regulations issued by three of the great communities on the Rhine — Speyer, Worms, and Mainz — have been preserved; joint meetings of the leaders of these three communities had a decisive influence on all the Jewish communities in Germany. German Jewry developed an independent leadership with a series of honors and degrees of rank. The intimacy of the small community enabled a person who felt wronged to turn to the public by means of interruption of prayer in synagogue until he received redress. Families experienced the usual sorrows and joys, and also had their share of frivolities: "wild young men . . . who liked gambling" and practical jokes at festivities. The main purpose of the *takkanot* was to strengthen religious life and especially to provide for increased study of the Torah, the observance of sexual purity laws, of the Sabbath, etc. They also introduced innovations designed to strengthen community life: the obligation on the part of each individual to pay his tax assessment and to refrain from false declarations, and the right of the community officers to transfer funds from one purpose to another, when the common good required it. Considerable emphasis was put on strengthening the authority of the community leadership: members of the community were not permitted to accept appointments by the authorities or to ask the authorities for exemption from community taxes; every dispute between Jews had to be brought before Jewish judges, and Jews were not allowed to apply to non-Jewish courts. Excommunication of an individual required the consent of the community, as did the divorce of a wife. Gambling was outlawed and regulations were issued for the preservation of order in the synagogues and law courts and at public celebrations. Lending money to Jews against the payment of interest, and insulting anyone in public were also prohibited.

In the 12th century the Jews still took part in defending towns in which they lived. Eleazer b. Judah tells of "the siege of Worms by a great host on the Sabbath, when we permitted all the Jews to take up arms . . . for if they had not helped the townspeople they would have been killed . . . therefore we permitted it" (*Sefer ha-Roke'ah* (Cremona, 1557), 23a, *Hilkhot Eruvin,* no. 197). In this period, Jews also moved with the eastward trend of the population, and new Jewish communities were established in the east and southeast. Those who joined in the movement of the urban population eastward encountered the terrors and problems of new colonists: "When you build houses in the forest you find the inhabitants stricken with plague since the place is haunted by spirits . . . They asked the sage what they should do; he answered: Take the Ten Commandments and a Torah Scroll and stretch· out a cord the length of the ground, and bring the Torah Scroll to the cord . . . and then at the end say: 'Before God, before the Torah, and before Israel its guardians, may no demon nor she-demon come to this place from today and for ever' " (*Sefer Ḥasidim* (ed. Wistinetzki), no. 371).

The 13th century brought new troubles upon the Jews. The Fourth Lateran Council (1215) decreed that the clergy were to restrict business relations between Christians and Jews, that Jews had to wear signs distinguishing them from the Christians, and that they were not to hold any public office. In 1235 the first case of blood libel occurred in Germany (in Fulda) and in the second half of the 13th century the libel of Host desecration began to spread in the country. These accusations were to cost many Jewish lives, to cause Jews much anxiety and anguish, and to bring about further deterioration of their image in the eyes of their Christian neighbors, who now came to regard them as corrupt beings, capable of the most abominable crimes. The acceptance of such views of the Jews by the masses occurred at a time when imperial rule was weakening, and the right to the Jews' "servitude to the treasury" was passed on or transferred in different ways and for differing reasons to various local competencies. Religious fanaticism was rising and caused a social ferment in the cities, where the mob vented their anger on the Jews. In 1241, when the Jews of Frankfort on the Main tried to prevent one of their people from converting to Christianity, a *Judenschlacht* (Jews' slaughter) took place, in which the entire community was butchered by the Christian mob. In 1259 a synod of the Mainz archdiocese ordered that Jews within its borders should wear the yellow badge. In 1285 the entire Jewish community of Munich — some 180 persons — was burned to death, victims of a libel that had been spread against them. The Jews also had a heavy tax burden. A partial list of imperial revenue, dating from 1241, reveals that in 25 Jewish communities the Jews paid 857 marks, amounting to 12% of the entire imperial tax revenue for the year (7, 127.5 marks) and 20% of the total raised in the German cities. In addition to the regular taxes the Jews also had to make payments in the form of "presents" and bribes, or money was simply extorted from them. In this period – the second half of the 13th century – German Jewry produced great spiritual leaders. Foremost was Meir b. Baruch of Rothenburg, whose responsa and instructions guided several generations of Jews. He attacked manifestations of injustice or high-handedness in communal affairs, and in his threnodies and other writings gave expression to the sufferings of his people. In the end, his own fate symbolized the distress of the Jews: trying to escape overseas, like other persecuted Jews in Germany, he was arrested, handed over to the emperor, and died in jail in 1293.

At the end of the 13th century and the first half of the 14th, anti-Jewish excesses by the mob increased in vehemence and frequency, and the authorities were also increasingly oppressive. In 1342 Louis IV of Bavaria decreed that "every male Jew and every Jewish widow, of 12 years and above, is obliged to pay a yearly tax of one gulden." This poll tax was designed to increase the income that the emperor derived from the Jews, which had declined as the result of their "transfer" to lower authorities, and came in addition to the other taxes exacted from the Jews. In 1356 Emperor Charles IV transferred his claim over the Jews to the Imperial Electors. Within a period of 50 years the Jews of Germany suffered three devastating blows. In 1298–99, when civil war had broken out in southwest Germany, the Jews were accused of Host desecration, and the Jew-baiter, Rindfleisch, gathered a mob around him which fell upon the Jews of Franconia, Bavaria, and the surrounding area destroying no less than 140 communities (including Rothenburg, Wuerzburg, Nuremberg, and Bamberg). Many Jews chose a martyr's death and in many places also offered armed resistance. The period 1336–37 was marked by the catastrophe of the Armleder massacres, in the course of which 110 communities, from Bavaria to Alsace, were destroyed by rioting peasants. Finally, in the massacres during the Black Death, in 1348–50, 300 Jewish communities were destroyed in all parts of the country, and the Jews either killed, or driven out as "poisoners of wells." The greatest Jewish scholar of the time, Alexander Suslin ha-Kohen, was among those slain in Erfurt, in 1349. As a result of these three onslaughts, the structure of Jewish life in Germany suffered a severe blow. Nevertheless, only a short while later, Jews were again permitted to take up residence in German cities, where there was no one else to fulfill their function in society of moneylenders. Only a few weeks after the slaughter of the Jews of

Augsburg the bishop permitted some to return to the city; between 1352 and 1355 Jews reappeared in Erfurt, Nuremberg, Ulm, Speyer, Worms, and Trier. Their residence was now based on contracts which contained severe restrictions and imposed numerous payments on them. There was also increased exploitation of the Jews by the emperor; a moratorium on debts, declared by Wenceslaus in 1385 and again in 1390, dealt a severe blow to the economic situation of the Jews. Jewish vitality, however, was able to assert itself even in the adverse conditions that prevailed after the Black Death massacres. The scholars assured the continuity of Jewish creativity. In 1365, Meir b. Baruch ha-Levi established a new school in Vienna, based upon the customs and traditions of the Rhine communities, and his disciples – the "Sages of Austria" – became the spiritual leaders of German Jewry. In east and south Germany, with fewer towns and a relatively backward economy, Jews found it easier to earn their livelihood. This was also the route to Poland, which gradually turned into a refuge for the Jews. Until the Reformation there was no change in the precarious situation of the Jews of Germany. On the one hand, the disintegration of the Empire prevented large-scale countrywide expulsions: when the Jews were driven out of one locality they were able to bide their time in a neighboring place, and after a short while return to their previous homes; on the other hand, the lack of a central authority put the Jews at the mercy of local rulers. In general, the emperor, the princes, and the leading classes in the towns gave their protection to the Jews; yet a single fanatic anti-Jewish preacher, John of Capistrano, found it possible to inflame the masses against the Jews and to initiate a new wave of persecutions (1450–59) which culminated in the expulsion of the Jews from Breslau.

The 15th century was generally marked by libels against Jews and their expulsion from certain areas: in 1400 the Jews were expelled from Prague; in 1420, 1438, 1462, and 1473 there were successive expulsions from Mainz; in 1420–21 from Austria; in 1424 from Cologne; in 1440 from Augsburg; in 1475 the blood libel was raised in Trent, resulting in anti-Jewish agitation and riots all over Germany, and the expulsion of the Jews from Tyrol; in 1492 it was the turn of the Host desecration libel in Mecklenburg, and the expulsion of the Jews from there; in 1493 they were driven out of Magdeburg, and in the period 1450–1500, out of many towns in Bavaria, Franconia, and Swabia; in 1499 from Nuremberg; in 1510 there was another Host desecration libel and expulsion from Brandenburg; in the same year expulsion from Alsace; and in 1519 from Regensburg.

Nevertheless, throughout the course of the 15th century, amid these tribulations, Jews were also able to branch out into occupations other than moneylending. In the south German communities, there were Jewish wine

An idealized Jewish family group at its table. The dress and plates, and the presence of servants reflect festivity and sumptuousness. Of interest is the headgear worn by the women and by the man at the head of the table. Full-page miniature from the *Erna Michael Haggadah*, Fol. 45, Middle Rhine, c. 1400. Compare with illustration on facing page.

An Ashkenazi room, reflecting the Ashkenazi lifestyle, including details of furniture, and vessels in which a learned discourse (note the gestures) is being conducted at the table (presumably a *Seder* table). In the top part of the picture the exterior of a rich "patrician" house is represented. Full-page miniature from the *Erna Michael Haggadah*, fol. 40, Middle Rhine, c. 1400.

merchants and petty traders. Jews also began to play a role in the expanding commercial life, acting as intermediaries between the large agricultural producer (such as the monasteries) and the rising city merchant; expelled from the cities and forced to live in the small towns and villages, the Jews bought wool, flax, etc., from the large storehouses and sold these commodities to the wholesale merchant. This was the beginning of a process which culminated in Poland in the 16th and 17th centuries with the Jews entering the service of the nobility as managers of their estates. Jewish life in the small communities of Germany was frequently marked by great material and spiritual hardship. Yet the Jews did all in their power to fulfill the commandments of their faith. Israel Isserlein's *Pesakim u-Khetavim* (Venice, 1545), para. 52, records a "curious event" in south Germany, when several communities had only a single *etrog* (citron) to share among them on the Festival of Tabernacles; they cut the fruit up and sent a piece to each community, and although shriveled by the time it reached its destination, the Jews made the prescribed blessing over their slice of *etrog* on the first day of the festival. Despite their poverty and sufferings, Jews held on the normal joys of life. Jacob Moses Moellin permitted "placing tree branches in water on the Sabbath . . . in order to provide a source of joy for the house" (Jacob b. Moses Moellin, *Maharil* (Cremona, 1558), 38b); when asked about celebrating a wedding in a community where a local ordinance forbade the participation of musicians, the same rabbi advised that the wedding be moved to another community, where music could be made, rather than have the bride and bridegroom forego the pleasure (*ibid.,* 41b). Even at a time when persecutions were actually taking place, the Jews persisted in their way of life and in study of the Torah. Thus Moses Mintz, while writing a halakhic decision, records that "the time limit given us by the bishop [of Bamberg] for leaving the town has been reached, for he would not allow us a single additional day or even hour" (Responsa Maharam Mintz, para. 48). The rabbis' position became widely acknowledged in this period, and they were regarded as "the leaders."

It may be assumed that it was the school of Meir b. Baruch ha-Levi that established the custom of *semikhah* (rabbinical ordination) and of awarding the title of *Morenu* ("our teacher") to a graduate rabbi, a custom which Ashkenazi Jews still retain. At the same time the rabbis often engaged in bitter quarrels over the question of jurisdiction, and the position of the rabbi. These quarrels largely resulted from the difficulties facing the Jewish spiritual leaders, who tried, in a permanent state of insecurity, to rebuild communities that had been destroyed. The rabbinical leaders of this period were dedicated men who did all in their power to establish new *yeshivot* and spread the study of Torah, but they did not achieve the degree of leadership displayed by their predecessors. An extreme example of a scholar devoted to his *yeshivah* was that of Jacob b. Moses Moellin "who would live in a house alone with his students, next to the house of his wife, while her sons were with her in her house; nor did he enjoy a mite of his wife's property during her lifetime or eat with her. Only the communal leaders supplied him with sufficient means to support the students of his *yeshivah*, while he himself earned a livelihood as a marriage broker" (*Maharil* 76a). His *yeshivah* was attended not only by poor scholars, but by "those rich and pampered youths who had tables made for them — when they sat down in their seats they could turn the table in any direction they pleased, and kept many books on them" (*Leket Yosher*, ed. by J. Freimann (1903), *Yoreh De'ah* 39). The debate with Christianity did not die down in this period, and Yom Tov Lipmann Muelhausen raised it to new heights of sharp polemical argument in his *Sefer ha-Nizzahon*.

Emperors resorted to the most extreme measures in order to extort money from the Jews. The most extortionate was Sigismund who demanded one-third of their property. Their desire to increase the income extracted from the Jews induced the emperors to utilize the high prestige enjoyed by the rabbis by attempting to appoint one of them "chief rabbi" *(Hochmeister)*. In 1407, Rupert of Wittelsbach appointed Israel b. Isaac of Nuremberg to this office, and sought to give him sole powers of sequestering Jewish property. The communities, however, refused to acknowledge the authority of a Jew appointed by gentiles and eventually the king abandoned his attempt. Sigismund named several "chief rabbis" for the purpose of improving the collection of the oppressive taxes that he imposed upon the Jews, including well-known rabbinical leaders. It is not clear, however, to what extent these appointments were recognized by the communities, and the responsa literature of the period contains no specific references to such appointments. At any rate, a proposal made by Seligmann Oppenheim Bing to convene a conference which would create a chief rabbinate was rejected by most of his rabbinical colleagues.

In sum, the last few centuries of the Middle Ages were a period of severe and difficult changes for the Jews of Germany. The center of gravity, both in population and intellectual activity, shifted steadily eastward. From their position as desirable traders the Jews were driven by the religious and social forces which gained ascendancy in the 12th and 13th centuries into the despised occupation of usury. The 50 years from 1298 to 1348 took a tragic toll in both life and property. Throughout the trials and tribulations of the Middle Ages the Jews of Germany succeeded in preserving their human dignity and ancestral heritage. They displayed their own creative powers in halakhic literature and religious poetry, and in the establishment of communal institutions. Although they did not disdain the innocent joys of life, they were exacting in the

לדמא עטרה אל אבן ד
אבלין במאות

application of the Law and were imbued with the spirit of ascetic piety. *Kiddush ha-Shem* — martyrdom for the sanctification of God — and their particular pietism *(Ḥasidut Ashkenaz)*, in both theory and practice, were authentic contributions of German Jewry to the realm of supreme Jewish values. When the age of the Reformation set in, German Jewry, although of lesser stature than their ancestors on the Rhine in organization, learning, and religious spirit, was strong enough to stand up to the challenge of a changing world.

Maẓẓah as a frame and setting for a gallery of gentile faces by Joel ben Simeon of Cologne, 1454.

2

POLAND-LITHUANIA
A PROVINCE OF JEWISH SOCIETY AND CULTURE IN LATE MEDIEVAL AND EARLY MODERN TIMES

While Jews had visited the kingdom of Poland and been economically active there at an early stage of the country's consolidation, from the tenth century approximately, they had no contact with the grand duchy of Lithuania until King Gedimin conquered the regions of Volhynia and Galicia (as it was later called) in 1321.

Jews came to Poland mainly from the west and southwest and from the very beginning were of Ashkenazi culture. Those in the regions conquered by Gedimin had come there from the south and the southeast, chiefly from Kiev, and were thus influenced to a large degree by Byzantine Jewish culture patterns; some think that they could have had traces of Khazar ethnic descent and culture patterns. Jews in the region of Lvov and its environs were of the same provenance to a large extent. In the end the western Ashkenazi culture became dominant.

Polish-Jewish legendary tradition tells about a Jewish merchant, Abraham Prochownik (probably meaning "the dust-covered," an epithet found in the early Middle Ages in relation to merchants), who was offered the Polish crown around the middle of the ninth century, before Piast, the first, legendary, Polish king, ascended to the throne. According to another legend, at the end of the ninth century a Jewish delegation in Germany appealed to Prince Leszek to admit them to Poland. The request was granted after prolonged questioning, and later on privileges were granted to the immigrants. Although almost certainly formulated in their present version in the 16th–17th centuries – at a time of fierce struggle between Jewish and Christian townsmen – the legends do transmit meaningful historic elements. Jews did first come to Poland as transient, dust-covered merchants, and they did come there to escape the suffering and pressure brought to bear on them in the lands of the German Empire. The theories of some historians, that place-names like Żydowo, Żydatycze, Żydowska Wola, and Kozarzów indicate the presence of Jewish villages and peasants and even the presence of Khazar settlements in the regions where they are found, have been thoroughly disproved. The first Jews that the

144

Poles encountered must certainly have been traders, probably slave traders, of the type called in 12th-century Jewish sources *Holekhei Rusyah* (travelers to Russia). Some of them may have stayed for years in Poland, giving rise to the legends and fixing their dates. The chronicler Cosmas of Prague relates that the persecutions of the First Crusade caused Jews to move from Bohemia to Poland in 1098. From this point undisputed and datable information on Jews in Poland begins to appear. According to the chronicler Vincent Kadlubek, under Boleslav III heavy penalties were laid on those who harmed Jews bodily.

The first sizable groups and fixed communities of Jews settled and established themselves in the region of Silesia, then part of Polish society and culture but later Germanized. A large part of Jewish settlement in what was later consolidated as the kingdom of Poland came from Silesia, and a great proportion of the immigration from further west and from the southwest passed through it. As late as the 15th century Silesian Jewry kept its ties with Poland. Jewish settlement grew steadily, though at first slowly, in Polish principalities to the east of Silesia. Excavations in Great Poland and near Wloclawek have unearthed coins with Hebrew inscriptions issued under the princes Mieczyslaw III (1173–1209), Casimir II the Just (1177–94), Boleslav the Curly (1201), and Leszek the White (1205). Some inscriptions directly concern the ruler, like the Hebrew legend "Mieszko King of Poland" (משקא קרל פולסקי) or "Mieszko Duke" (משקא דוכוס); others include the names and titles of the Jewish mintmasters, one of them even with the honorific title of *nagid;* "of the [coining] house of Abraham the son of Isaac Nagid" (דבי אברהם בר יצחק נגיד); another showing that the Jewish mintmaster was settled in Poland: "Joseph [of] Kalisz (יוסף   קאליש). Minting

Polish coins engraved in Hebrew, 13th century.

money was an important social and economic function, and as some of the inscriptions indicate, these finds are evidence of a circle of rich and enterprising Jewish merchants in the principalities of Great Poland and Mazovia in the 12th century, some of them in close contact with the princely courts, some priding themselves on their descent from old Jewish families or on their own role in Jewish leadership. Rulers were quick to realize what they could gain from such immigrants: in 1262 Prince Boleslav the Shy forbade a monastery in Lesser Poland to take Jews under its sovereignty.

By that time, however, a new era had already begun in the history of the colonization of Poland in general and of the settlement of Jews in it in particular. From 1241 onward the Mongol invasions caused heavy losses in life and destruction to property in Poland. Subsequently, the princes of Poland eagerly sought immigrants from the west, mainly from Germany, and gave them energetic assistance to settle in the villages and towns. Various organized groups settled in the cities that were granted the privilege of living according to German Magdeburg Law; thus Polish towns became prevailingly German in origin and way of life. Though the children of the immigrants became gradually Polonized, the traditions and social attitudes of the German town remained an active force and basic framework of town life in Poland of the 15th to 17th centuries. From the Jewish point of view the most important, and harmful, result of this basic attitude of the Polish towns was the tradition of the guilds against competition and against new initiative in individual commercial enterprise and the activities of craftsmen. The townsmen also inherited a direct and bitter legacy of hatred of the Jews and the baleful and deeply rooted German image of the Jew.

Jews did not only come to Poland in the wake of the German *Drang nach Osten,* traces of which are found in the 13th-century *Sefer Ḥasidim,* for instance, in the description of the creation of a new settlement in a primeval forest (*Sefer Ḥasidim,* ed. Wistinetzki (1924), no. 371; see p. 135). For them the move was a continuation of and linking with earlier Jewish settlement in Poland. They also had compelling reasons stemming from the circumstances of their life in Western and Central Europe to leave their homes there and go to Poland-Lithuania. Their insecure position in this region was a compound of the atmosphere of fear and danger generated by the Crusades, the insecurity of settlement caused by the expulsions, the wave of massacres in Germany in particular between 1298 and 1348, the insecurity and popular hatred in Germany and German-Bohemian-Moravian towns in the second half of the 14th century and the first half of the 15th, the tensions and dangers created by the Hussite revolution and wars in Bohemia-Moravia and southern Germany in the early 15th century, and the worsening situation of Jews in the kingdoms of Christian Spain after the massacres of 1391. All these factors, combined with the success of the settlers in Poland-Lithuania, induced large and variegated groups of Jewish immigrants from various countries — Bohemia-Moravia, Germany, Italy, Spain, from colonies in the Crimea — to go to Poland-Lithuania long after the original German drive had died out. As Moses Isserles put it in the 16th century, "it is preferable to live on dry bread and in peace in Poland" than to remain in better conditions in lands more dangerous for Jews (Responsa, no. 73). He even coined a pun on the Hebrew form of Poland (Polin), explaining it as deriving from two Hebrew words, *poh lin* ("here he shall rest").

The results of this immigration were evident almost immediately. In 1237 Jews are mentioned in Plock. The Jewish community of Kalisz bought a cemetery in 1283, so it must have been organized some time before, as the fact that the first writ of privileges for Jews was issued in 1264 by the prince of Kalisz also tends to show. A *Judengasse* (Jewish Quarter) is mentioned in Cracow in 1304, lying between the town market and the town walls, but there must have been a community in Cracow long before then, for about 1234 "Rabbi Jacob Savra of Cracow that sits in Poland, a great scholar and fluent in the entire Talmud" put forward his own opinion against that of the greatest contemporary scholars of Germany and Bohemia. In 1356 there is a record of the Jewish community at Lvov; in 1367 at Sandomierz; in 1379 at Poznań; in 1387 at Pyzdry; and about 1382 at Lyuboml. In the grand duchy of Lithuania Jewish communities are found in the 14th century at Brest-Litovsk (1388), Grodno (1389), and Troki (1398). The volume of immigration grew continuously. By the end of the 15th century more than 60 Jewish communities are known of in united Poland-Lithuania. They were dispersed from Wroclaw (Breslau) and Gdansk in the west to Kiev and Kamenets Podolski in the east. The number of Jews living in Poland by that date is greatly disputed: at the end of the 15th century there were between 20,000 and 30,000.

The foundations of the legal position of the Jews in Poland were laid down in the 13th to 15th centuries. The basic "general charters" of Jews in Poland have their origin in the writ issued by Prince Boleslav V the Pious of Kalisz in 1264. This "statute of Kalisz" — as it is called in literature — was also an "immigrant" from the countries which Jews left to come to Poland, being based on the statute of Duke Frederick II of Austria and on derivative statutes issued in Bohemia and Hungary. The Jews are seen, accepted, and defended as a group whose main business is moneylending against pledges. With the unification of Poland into a kingdom, King Casimir III the Great strongly favored the Jewish element in the cities of Poland, the German element having proved untrustworthy under his father, the unifier of Poland, Ladislaus I Lokietek. Casimir broadened the statute of Kalisz while ratifying it for the Jews of his kingdom (in 1334, 1364, and 1367). Yet basically the same conception of the

Jews as *servi camerae regis* and as protected moneylenders remains throughout.[1] The legal status of the Jews changed considerably in Poland, but not through any central reinterpretation of their rights and standing, which remained in theory based on and conceived of in terms of the Boleslavian-Casimirian statutes, codified and ratified by King Casimir IV Jagello in 1453. Throughout the 14th century, there was opposition to Jews accepting landed property as security for loans; while throughout the 15th century town and church tried to insist that Jews should wear the distinctive badge.

On several occasions these undercurrents broke out in sharp and violent decisions and action. During the Black Death "All Jews . . . almost throughout Poland were massacred"[2] (Stanislas of Olivia in his *Chronica Olivska,* for the year 1349). The martyrs were defined by German Jews as "the communities and kingdom of Cracow, its scholars and population"[3]. By that time hatred of the Jews was also widespread among the nobility. In the statute of Lesser Poland of 1347, paragraph 26 claims that "the aim of the perfidious Jews is not so much to take their faith away from the Christians as to take away their wealth and property." In 1407 the Cracow populace was diverted by the spectacle of a Jewish moneylender being led through the streets adorned with a crown set with forged coins — he was accused of forging currency — to be horribly tortured and burned in public. The citizens of Cracow claimed as early as 1369 that the Jews were "dominating" the town and complained of their cruelty and perfidy. In the main King Ladislaus II Jagello was hostile to Jews, though some of them were numbered among his financial and business agents, like Volchko, whom the king hoped in vain to bring over to Christianity.

Church circles were very active in their opposition to the Jews. Many priests and directors of monasteries, who had originally come from Germany, brought to Poland the hostile traditions concerning the city-dwelling accursed Jew. As early as 1267 the Polish Church Council of Wroclaw (Breslau) outlined its anti-Jewish policy; its main aim was to isolate the Jews as far as possible from the Christians, not only from the communion of friendship and table but also to separate them in quarters surrounded by a wall or a ditch: "for as up to now the land of Poland is newly grafted on to the Christian body, it is to be feared that the Christian people will more easily be misled by the superstitions and evil habits of the Jews that live among them".[4] With various modifications, this was

---

[1]   This shows the tenacity of the concept through the centuries. See page 33.

[2]   *Omnes judaei . . . fere in tota Polonia deleti sunt.*

[3]   S. Salfeld, *Das Martyrologium des Nuernberger Memorbuches* (1898), 82.

[4]   *Quum adhuc Terra Polonica sit in corpore christiani tatis nova plantatio, ne forte eo facilius populus christianus a cohabitantium Iudeorum superstitionibus et pravis*

restated in subsequent Church councils. In the 15th century this ecclesiastical attitude found new and influential expression. Cardinal Zbigniew Oleśnicki and the chronicler Jan Dlugosz were the main leaders of the anti-Jewish faction. When Jewish representatives came to King Casimir IV Jagello to obtain the ratification of their charters, Oleśnicki opposed it vehemently. He invited to Poland "the scourge of the Jews," John of Capistrano, fresh from his "success" in engineering a Host desecration libel which resulted in the burning of many Jews and expulsion of the community of Wroclaw. In vain Capistrano tried to influence the king not to ratify the Jewish charters. Oleśnicki himself wrote to the king in support of his effort: "Do not imagine that in matters touching the Christian religion you are at liberty to pass any law you please. No one is great and strong enough to put down all opposition to himself when the interests of the faith are at stake. I therefore beseech and implore your royal majesty to revoke the aforementioned privileges and liberties. Prove that you are a Catholic sovereign, and remove all occasion for disgracing your name and for worse offenses that are likely to follow".[5] As a result of this pressure the Nieszawa statute of 1454 decreed the repeal of all Jewish charters, but the repeal was short-lived. Perhaps central to the definition of the status of the Jews was the decision of King Sigismund I in 1534 that the Jews need not carry any distinguishing mark on their clothing. Despite the contrary resolution of the Sejm (Diet) of Piotrkow in 1538, the king's decision remained.

Major changes in the status of the Jews occurred throughout the 16th and 17th centuries, but they came about either through the issuance of particular writs of rights by kings for towns and communities — both in favor of Jews as well as to their detriment (e.g., the *privilegia de non tolerandis judaeis* given to many towns in Poland) — or through the action of various magnates, whose power was continuously growing in Poland in these centuries. Some of the latter, nicknamed *Krolewieta* ("kinglets"), granted Jews many and costly rights in the new municipal settlements they were erecting on their expansive estates — the "private townships" of Poland, so-called in distinction to the old "royal townships." To a slight degree, change resulted from the new economic activity of the Jews, mainly in the east and southeast of Poland-Lithuania, and their move toward colonization there.

The foundations of the legal status of the Jews in the grand duchy of Lithuania were laid by Grand Duke Vitold in writs of law granted to the Jews of Brest-Litovsk in 1388 and to the Jews of Grodno in 1389. Though formally

---

moribus infaciatur, I. Aronius, *Regesten zur Geschichte der Juden im fraenkischen und deutschen Reiche bis zum Jahre 1273* (1902), 302 no. 724.

5 *Monumenta Mediaevi,* ed. Szugski, Codex Epistolaris s. XV, T. II past posterior p. 147.

based on the rights of the Jews of Lvov in Poland, in letter and spirit these charters reveal an entirely different conception of the place of Jews in society. The writ for the Grodno community states that "from the above-mentioned cemetery — in its present location as well as on ground that might be bought later — and also from the ground of their Jewish synagogue, no taxes whatsoever will have to be given to our treasury." Not only are the Jewish place of worship and cemetery tax free — a concession that indicates interest in having Jewish settlers in the town — but also "what is more, we permit them to hold whatever views they please in their homes and to prepare at their homes any kind of drink and to serve drinks brought from elsewhere on the condition that they pay to our treasury a yearly tax. They may trade and buy at the market, in shops and on the streets in full equality with the citizens; they may engage in any kind of craft." Thus, in granting the Jews complete freedom to trade and engage in any craft, the grand duke gave them economic equality with the Christian citizens. He also envisaged their having agricultural or partially agricultural occupations: "As to the arable lands as well as grazing lands, those that they have now, as well as those that they will buy later, they may use in full equality with the townspeople, paying like them to our treasury." The Jews are here considered as merchants, craftsmen, and desirable settlers in the developing city.

As the grand duchy merged with Poland to an ever increasing degree, in particular in the formal, legal, and social spheres, the basic concepts of the *servi camerae* also influenced the status of Lithuanian Jews (as was already hinted at in the formal reference to the rights and status of the Jews of Lvov). In spite of this, the general trend in Lithuanian towns and townships remained the same as that expressed in the late 16th-century charters. In 1495 the Jews were expelled from Lithuania. They were brought back in 1503: all their property was returned and opportunities for economic activity were restored.

Thus, on the threshold of the 16th century, the gradually merging grand duchy of Lithuania and kingdom of Poland had both a fully worked out legal concept of the status of the Jews. In Poland, the whole conception was medieval to the core: legally and formally the attitude to the Jews remained unchanged from their first arrival from the west and southwest. In Lithuania, on the other hand, from the start the formal expressions reveal a conception of a Jewish "third estate," equal in economic opportunity to the Christian townspeople. Particular legal enactments in Poland took cognizance of the change in the economic role of the Jews in Polish society. In Lithuania the formal enactments were always suited to their economic role, and to a large extent the dynamics of 16th- and 17th-century development could be accommodated in the old legal framework.

From the very first the Jews of Poland developed their economic activities through moneylending toward a greater variety of occupations and economic structures. Thus, by the very dynamics of its economic and social development, Polish Jewry constitutes a flat existential denial and factual contradiction of the anti-Semitic myth of "the Jewish spirit of usury." On the extreme west of their settlement in Poland, in Silesia, although they were mainly engaged in moneylending, Jews were also employed in agriculture. When the Kalisz community in 1287 bought a cemetery it undertook to pay for it in pepper and other oriental wares, indicating an old connection with the trade in spices. As noted above, the Jewish mintmasters of the 12th century must undoubtedly have been large-scale traders. In 1327 Jews were an important element among the participants at the Nowy Sacz fair. Throughout the 14th and 15th centuries Jews were occupied to a growing degree in almost every branch of trade pursued at that time. Jews from both the grand duchy of Lithuania and Poland traded in cloth, dyes, horses, and cattle (and on a fairly large scale). At the end of the 15th century they engaged in trade with Venice, Italy, with Kaffa (Feodosiya), and with other Genoese colonies in the Crimea, and with Constantinople. Lvov Jews played a central role in this trade, which in the late 15th and early 16th centuries developed into a large-scale land-transit trade between the Ottoman Empire and Christian Europe. Through their participation in this trade and their contacts with their brethren in the Ottoman Empire, many Jewish communities became vital links in a trade chain that was important to both the various Christian kingdoms and the Ottoman Empire. Lithuanian Jews participated to the full and on a considerable scale in all these activities, basing themselves both on their above-mentioned recognized role in Lithuanian civic society and on their particular opportunities for trade with the grand principality of Moscow and their evident specialization in dyes and dyeing. Obviously, in all these activities, all links with Jewish communities in Central and Western Europe were beneficial.

During all this period Jews were engaged in moneylending, some of them (e.g., Lewko Jordanis, his son Canaan, and Volchko) on a large scale. They made loans not only to private citizens but also to magnates, kings, and cities, on several occasions beyond the borders of Poland. The scope of their monetary operations at their peak may be judged by the fact that in 1428 King Ladislaus II Jagello accused one of the Cracow city counsellors of appropriating the fabulous sum of 500,000 zlotys which the Jews had supplied to the royal treasury.

To an increasing extent many of the Jewish moneylenders became involved in trade. They were considered by their lords as specialists in economic administration. In 1425 King Ladislaus II Jagello charged Volchko — who by this time already held the Lvov customs lease — with the colonization of a large tract of land: "As we have great confidence in the wisdom, carefulness, and foresight of our Lvov customs-holder, the Jew Volchko ... after the above-mentioned Jew Volchko has turned the above-mentioned wilderness into a human settlement in the village, it shall remain in his hands till his death." King Casimir Jagello entrusted to the Jew Natko both the salt mines of Drohobycz and the customs stations of Grejdek, stating in 1452 that he granted it to him on account of his "industry and wisdom so that thanks to his ability and industry we shall bring in more income to our treasury." The same phenomenon is found in Lithuania. By the end of the 15th century, at both ends of the economic scale Jews in Poland were becoming increasingly what they had been from the beginning in Lithuania: a "third estate" in the cities. The German-Polish citizenry quickly became aware of this. By the end of the 15th century, accusations against the Jews centered around unfair competition in trade and crafts more than around harsh usury. Not only merchants but also Jewish craftsmen are mentioned in Polish cities from 1460 onward. In 1485 tension in Cracow was so high that the Jewish community was compelled to renounce formally its rights to most trades and crafts. Though this was done "voluntarily," Jews continued to pursue their living in every decent way possible. This was one of the reasons for their expulsion from Cracow to Kazimierz in 1495. However, the end of Jewish settlement in Cracow was far from the end of Jewish trade there; it continued to flourish and aggravate the Christian townspeople, as was the case with many cities (like Lublin and Warsaw) which had exercised their right *de non tolerandis Judaeis* and yet had to see Jewish economic activity flourishing at their fairs and in their streets.

In Poland and Lithuania from the 13th century onward Jewish culture and society was much richer and more variegated than has been commonly accepted. Even before that, the inscriptions on the bracteate coins of the 12th century indicate talmudic culture and leadership traditions by the expressions used (*rabbi*, רַבִּי, *nagid*, נָגִיד). About 1234, as mentioned, Jacob Savra of Cracow was able to contradict the greatest talmudic authorities of his day in Germany and Bohemia. In defense of his case he "sent responsa to the far ends of the west and the south" (E.E. Urbach (ed.), in *Sefer Arugat ha-Bosem*, 4 (1963), 120–1). The author of *Sefer Arugat ha-Bosem* also quotes an interpretation and emendation that "I have heard in the name of Rabbi Jacob from Poland" (*ibid.*, 3 (1962), 126). Moses Zaltman, the son of Judah b. Samuel he-Ḥasid, states: "Thus I have been told by R. Isaac from Poland in the name of my father . . . thus I have been told by R. Isaac from Russia . . . R. Mordecai from Poland told me that my father said" (Ms. Cambridge 669. 2, fol. 69 and 74). This manuscript evidence proves that men from Poland and from southern Russia (which in the 13th century was part of the grand duchy of Lithuania) were close disciples of the

A Polish Jew, 1703.

leader of the Ḥasidei Ashkenaz. The names of Polish Jews in the 14th century show curious traces of cultural influence; besides ordinary Hebrew names and names taken from the German and French — brought by the immigrants from the countries of their origin — there are clearly Slavonic names like Lewko, Jeleń, and Pychacz and women's names like Czarnula, Krasa, and even Witoslawa. Even more remarkable are the names of Lewko's father, Jordan, and Lewko's son, Canaan or Chanaan, which indicate a special devotion to Erez Israel.

By the 15th century, relatively numerous traces of social and cultural life in the Polish communities can be found. In a document from April 4, 1435, that perhaps preserves the early Yiddish of the Polish Jews, the writer, a Jew of Breslau, addresses "the Lord King of Poland my Lord." The closing phrases of the letter indicate his Jewish culture: "To certify this, have I, the above mentioned Jekuthiel, appended my Jewish seal to this letter with full knowledge. Given in Breslau, on the first Monday of the month Nisan, in Jewish reckoning five thousand years and a hundred years and to that hundred the ninety-fifth year after the beginning and creation of all creatures except God Himself."[6]

6   M. Brann, *Geschichte der Juden in Schlesien,* 3(1901), Anhang 4, p. lviii.

Though Israel Bruna said of the Jews of Cracow, "they are not well versed in Torah" (Responsa, no. 55, fol. 23b), giving this as his reason for not adducing lengthy talmudic arguments in his correspondence with them, he was writing to one of his pupils who claimed sole rabbinical authority and income in the community of Poznań (*ibid.,* no. 254, fol. 103b). Israel Isserlein of Austria writes, "my beloved, the holy community of Poznań." Two parties in this community – the leadership, whom Isserlein calls "you, the holy community," and an individual – were quarreling about taxation and Isserlein records that both sides submitted legal arguments in support of their cases (*Terumat ha-Deshen, Pesakim u-Khetavim,* no. 144). Great scholars like Yom Tov Lipmann Muelhausen, who came to Cracow at the end of the 14th century, and Moses b. Isaac Segal Mintz, who lived at Poznań in 1475, must certainly have left traces of their cultural influence there. Some of the responsa literature contains graphic descriptions of social life. "A rich man from Russia" – either the environs of Lvov in Poland or of Kiev in Ukraine – asked Israel Bruna, "If it is permissible to have a prayer shawl of silk in red or green color for Sabbath and the holidays" (Responsa, no. 73, fol. 32b), a desire fitting a personality like Volchko's. Something of the way of life of "the holy community of Lvov" can be seen from the fact that their problem was the murder of one Jew by another in the Ukrainian city of Pereyaslav-Khmelnitski. As the victim lay wounded on the ground, a third Jew, Naḥman, called out to the murderer, Simḥah: "Hit Nisan till death" and so he was killed by being beaten on his head as he lay there wounded. The victim was a totally ignorant man, "he couldn't recognize a single [Hebrew] letter and had never in his life put on *tefillin.*" The murderer was drunk at the time and the victim had started the quarrel; they were all in a large company of Jews (*ibid.,* no. 265, fol. 110a-b). The rough social and cultural climate of Jewish traders in the Ukraine in the middle of the 15th century is here in evidence. Moses Mintz describes from his own experience divorce customs in the region of Poznań (Responsa (Salonika, 1802), no. 113, fol. 129b). He also describes interesting wedding customs in Poland which differed in many details from those of Germany: "when they accompany the bride and bridegroom to the *ḥuppah* they sing on the way . . . they give the bridegroom the cup and he throws it down, puts his foot on it and breaks it, but they pour out the wine from the cup before they give it to the bridegroom. They have also the custom of throwing a cock and also a hen over the head of the bride and bridegroom above the canopy after the pronouncing of the wedding blessings" (*ibid.,* no. 109, fol. 127a). Thus, in the western and central parts of Poland there is evidence of an established and well developed culture and some learning, contrasting sharply with the rough and haphazard existence of Jews living southwards from Lvov to Pereyaslav-Khmelnitski.

Jewish culture in Poland and in Lithuania seems to have had a certain rationalist, "Sephardi" tinge, as evidenced both by outside reports and by certain tensions appearing in the second half of the 16th century. At the beginning of the 16th century the Polish chronicler Maciej Miechowicz relates that in Lithuania, "the Jews use Hebrew books and study sciences and arts, astronomy and medicine." The cardinal legate Lemendone also notes that Lithuanian Jews of the 16th century devote time to the study of "literature and science, in particular astronomy and medicine." At the end of the 15th century, Lithuanian Jews took part in the movement of the Judaizers in Muscovite Russia, whose literature shows a marked influence of rationalistic Jewish works and anti-Christian arguments. The Jewish community of Kiev — in the 15th and early 16th centuries within the grand duchy of Lithuania — was praised by a Crimean Karaite in 1481 for its culture and learning. In about 1484 another Karaite, Joseph b. Mordecai of Troki, wrote a letter to Elijah b. Moses Bashyazi (J. Mann, *Texts and Studies*, 2 (1935), 1149—59) telling about a disputation on calendar problems between him and "the Rabbanites who live here in Troki, Jacob Suchy of Kaffa (Feodosiya) and Ozer the physician of Cracow" (*ibid.*, 1150). He closes his letter with ideas showing a decided rationalist tendency: "The quality of the sermon will be through the quality of the subject, therefore as we have none such more important than the Torah, for in it there is this teaching that brings man straight to his scientific and social success and the chief of its considerations is that man should achieve his utmost perfection, which is spiritual success; and this will happen when he attains such rational concepts as the soul, the active reason, can attain, for the relation between a phenomenon and its causes is a necessary relation, i.e., the relation of the separate reason to the material reason is like the relation of light to sight" (*ibid.*, 1159).

In Poland a dispute between two great scholars of the 16th century — Solomon Luria and Moses Isserles — brings to the surface elements of an earlier rationalist culture. Luria accuses *yeshivah* students of using "the prayer of Aristotle" and accuses Isserles of "mixing him with words of the living God ... [considering] that the words of this unclean one are precious and perfume to Jewish sages" (Isserles, Responsa, no. 6). Isserles replies: "All this is still a poisonous root in existence, the legacy from their parents from those that tended to follow the philosophers and tread in their steps. But I myself have never seen nor heard up till now such a thing, and, but for your evidence, I could not have believed that there was still a trace of these conceptions among us" (*ibid.*, no. 7). Writing around the middle of the 16th century, Isserles tells unwittingly of a philosophizing trend prevalent in Poland many years before. A remarkable case of how extreme rationalist conceptions gave way to more mystic ones can be seen in Isserles' pupil, Abraham b. Shabbetai Horowitz.

Around 1539 he sharply rebuked the rabbi of Poznań, who believed in demons and opposed Maimonides: "As to what this ass said, that it is permissible to study Torah only, this is truly against what the Torah says, 'Ye shall keep and do for it is your wisdom and understanding in the eyes of the gentiles.' For even if we shall be well versed in all the arcana of the Talmud, the gentiles will still not consider us scholars; on the contrary, all the ideas of the Talmud, its methods and sermons, are funny and derisible in the eyes of the gentiles. If we know no more than the Talmud we shall not be able to explain the ideas and exegetical methods of the Talmud in a way that the gentiles will like — this stands to reason" (See *Monatsschrift fuer Geschichte und Wissenschaft des Judentums,* 47 (1903), 263). Yet this same man rewrote his rationalistic commentary on a work by Maimonides to make it more amenable to traditionalistic and mystic thought, declaring in the second version, "The first uproots, the last roots." Later trends and struggles in Jewish culture in Poland and Lithuania are partly traceable to this early and obliterated rationalistic layer.

Polish victories over the Teutonic Order in the west and against Muscovite and Ottoman armies in the east and southeast led to a great expansion of Poland-Lithuania from the second half of the 16th century. In this way Poland-Lithuania gained a vast steppeland in the southeast, in the Ukraine, fertile but unpacified and unreclaimed, and great stretches of arable land and virgin forest in the east, in Belorussia. The agricultural resources in the east were linked to the center through the river and canal systems and to the sea outlet in the west through land routes. These successes forged a stronger link between the various strata of the nobility (Pol. *szlachta*) as well as between the Polish and Lithuanian nobility. In 1569 the Union of Lublin cemented and formalized the unity of Poland-Lithuania, although the crown of Poland and the grand duchy of Lithuania kept a certain distinctness of character and law, which was also apparent in the Councils of the Lands and in the culture of the Jews. With the union, Volhynia and the Ukraine passed from the grand duchy to the crown. The combined might of Poland-Lithuania brought about a growing pacification of these southeastern districts, offering a possibility of their colonization which was eagerly seized upon by both nobility and peasants.

The Polish nobility, which became the dominant element in the state, was at that time a civilized and civilizing factor. Fermenting with religious thought and unrest which embraced even the most extreme anti-trinitarians; warlike and at the same time giving rise to small groups of extreme anarchists and pacifists; more and more attracted by luxury, yet for most of the period developing rational — even if often harsh — methods of land and peasant exploitation; despising merchandise yet very knowledgeable about money and gain — this was the nobility that, taking over the helm of state and society, developed its own estates in the old lands of Poland-Lithuania and the vast new lands in the east and southeast. Jews soon became the active and valued partners of this nobility in many enterprises. In the old "royal cities" — even in central places like Cracow, which expelled the Jews in 1495, and Warsaw, which had possessed a *privilegium de non tolerandis Judaeis* since 1527 — Jews were among the great merchants of clothing, dyes, and luxury products, in short, everything the nobility desired. Complaints from Christian merchants as early as the beginning of the 16th century, attacks by urban anti-Semites like Sebastian Miczyński[7] and Przeclaw Mojecki[8] in the 17th century, and above all internal Jewish evidence all point to the success of the Jewish merchant. The Jew prospered in trade even in places where he could not settle, thanks to his initiative, unfettered by guilds, conventions, and preconceived notions. The *kesherim,* the council of former office holders in the Poznań community, complain about the excessive activity of Jewish intermediaries, "who cannot stay quiet; they wait at every corner, in every place, at every shop where silk and cloth is sold, and they cause competition through influencing the buyers by their speech and leading them to other shops and other merchants." The same council complains about "those unemployed" people who sit all day long from morning till evening before the shops of gentiles — of spice merchants, clothes merchants, and various other shops — "and the Christian merchants complain and threaten." There was even a technical term for such men, *tsuvayzer,* those who point the way to a prospective seller.[9] Miczyński gives a bitter description of the same phenomenon in Cracow in 1618. Large-scale Jewish trade benefited greatly from the traders' connections with their brethren both in the Ottoman Empire and in Germany and Western Europe. It was also linked to a considerable extent with the arenda system[10] and its resulting great trade in the export of agricultural products.

Through the arenda system Jewish settlements spread over the country, especially in the southeast. Between 1503 and 1648 there were 114 Jewish communities in the Ukraine, some on the eastern side of the River Dnieper (see map and list by S. Ettinger, in *Zion,* 21 (1956), 114–8); many of these were tiny. The table shows the main outlines of the dynamics of Jewish settlement in these regions of colonization (*ibid.,* p. 124):

7   17th-century anti-Jewish agitator and professor of philosophy at Cracow University.
8   Polish Catholic priest and anti-Semitic author in the early 17th century.
9   *Pinkas Hekhsherim shel Kehillat Pozna,* ed. D. Avron (1966), 187–8 no. 1105, 250 no. 1473, 51 no. 1476.
10   The lease of fixed assets or prerogatives, or of special rights, widespread in the economy of Poland-Lithuania from the Middle Ages.

Growth of Jewish Settlement by Places and Numbers in the Colonization Period

Wojewódstwo	Before 1569		c. 1648	
(district)	Places	Numbers	Places	Numbers
Volhynia	13	3,000	46	15,000
Podolia	9	750	18	4,000
Kiev	—	—	33	13,500
Bratslav	2	?	18	18,825
Total	24	c. 4,000	115	51,325

The further the move east and southward, the greater the relative growth in numbers and population. The Jewish arenda holders, traders, and peddlers traveled and settled wherever space and opportunity offered.

Life in these districts was strenuous and often harsh. The manner of Jewish life in the Ukraine, which as we have already seen was uncouth, was both influenced and channeled through Jewish participation in the defense of newly pacified land. Meir of Lublin relates "what happened to a luckless man, ill, and tortured by pain and suffering from epilepsy . . . When there was an alarm in Volhynia because of the Tatars — as is usual in the towns of that district — when each one is obliged to be prepared, with weapon in hand, to go to war and battle against them at the command of the duke and the lords; and it came to pass that when the present man shot with his weapon, called in German *Buechse,* from his house through the window to a point marked for him on a rope in his courtyard to try the weapon as sharpshooters are wont to do, then a man came from the market to the above mentioned courtyard . . . and he was killed [by mistake] ." The rabbi goes on to tell that a Christian, the instructor and commander of this Jew, was standing in front of the courtyard to warn people not to enter. The Jew was "living among the gentiles in a village" with many children (Meir of Lublin, Responsa, no. 43). There is reference to an enterprising group of Jews who went to Moscow with the armies of the Polish king during war, selling liquor (one of them had two cartloads) and other merchandise to the soldiers (*ibid.,* no. 128). Among the Cossack units there was a Jew about whom his Cossack colleagues "complained to God . . . suddenly there jumped out from amongst our ranks a Jew who was called Berakhah, the son of the martyr Aaron of Cieszewiec." This Jew was not the only one in the ranks of the Cossacks, for — to allow his widow to marry — one of the witnesses says that "he knew well that in this unit there was not another Jewish fighter who was called Berakhah" (*ibid.,* no. 137). Life in general was apt to be much more violent than is usually supposed: even at Brest-Litovsk, when the *rebbe* of the community saw a litigant nearing his door, he seized a heavy box and barricaded himself in for fear of harm (*ibid.*, no. 44).

Arenda did more than give a new basis to the existence of many Jewish families; it brought the Jews into contact with village life and often combined with aspects of their internal organizational structure. Thus, the Jew Nahum b. Moses, besides renting the mills, the tavern, and the right of preparing beer and brandy, also rented for one year all milk produce of the livestock on the manors and villages. Elaborate and complicated arrangements were made for payment and collection of these milk products.[11] In contact with village life, the Jew sometimes formed a sentimental attachment to his neighbors and his surroundings. In 1602 a council of leaders of Jewish communities in Volhynia tried to convince Jewish arendars to let the peasants rest on Saturday though the Polish noblemen would certainly have given them the right to compel them to work: "If the villagers are obliged to work all the week through, he should let them rest on Sabbath and the Holy Days throughout. See, while living in exile and under the Egyptian yoke, our parents chose this Saturday for a day of rest while they were not yet commanded about it, and heaven helped them to make it a day of rest for ever. Therefore, where gentiles are under their authority they are obliged to fulfill the commandment of the Torah and the order of the sages not to come, God forbid, to be ungrateful [*livot*, לִבְעֹט] to the One who has given them plenty of good by means of the very plenty he has given them. Let God's name be sanctified by them and not defiled" (H.H. Ben-Sasson in *Zion,* 21 (1956), 205).

The interests of the Jews and Polish magnates coincided and complemented each other in one most important aspect of the economic and social activity of the Polish-Lithuanian nobility. On their huge estates the nobles began to establish and encourage the development of new townships, creating a network of "private towns." Because of the nature of their relationship with their own peasant population they were keen to attract settlers from afar, and Jews well suited their plans. The tempo and scale of expansion were great; in the grand duchy of Lithuania alone in the first half of the 17th century between 770 and 900 such townships *(miasteczki)* existed.[12] For their part, the Jews, who were hard pressed by the enmity of the populace in the old royal cities, gladly moved to places where they sometimes became the majority, in some cases even the whole, of the population. Since these were situated near the hinterland of agricultural produce and potential customers, Jewish initiative and innovation

---

11   S. Inglot, in: *Studja z historji* **spolecznej** *i gospodarczej poświecone prof. Franciszkowi Bujc'... vi* (1931), 179–82; cf. 205, 208–9.

12   S. Aleksandriwicz, in: *Roczniki dziejów* **spolecznych** *i gospodarczych,* 27, (1965) 35– 65.

found a new outlet. Through charters granted by kings and magnates to communities and settlers in these new towns, the real legal status of the Jews gradually changed very much for the better. By the second half of the 17th century everywhere in Poland Jews had become part of "the third estate" and in some places and in some respects the only one.

Jews continued to hold customs stations openly in Lithuania, in defiance of the wishes of their leaders in Poland. Many custom station ledgers were written in Hebrew script and contained Hebrew terms. Sometimes a Jew is found with a "sleeping partner," a Pole or Armenian in whose name the customs lease has been taken out. That some customs stations were in Jewish hands was also of assistance to Jewish trade.

This complex structure of large-scale export and import trade, the active and sometimes adventurous participation in the colonization of the Ukraine and in the shaping of the "private cities," in the fulfilling of what today we would call state economic functions, created for the first time in the history of Ashkenazi Jewry a broad base of population, settlement distribution, and means of livelihood, which provided changed conditions for the cultural and religious life of Jews. Even after the destruction wrought by the Chmielnicki massacres enough remained to form the nucleus of later Ashkenazi Jewry. The later style of life in the Jewish *shtetl* was based on achievements and progress made at this time.

The Councils of the Lands, the great superstructure of Jewish autonomy, were an outgrowth of such dynamics of economy and settlement. Beginning with attempts at centralized leaderships imposed from above, appointed by the king, they ended with a central elected Jewish leadership. The aims, methods, and institutitons of this leadership were intertwined with the new economic structure. Great fairs — notably those of Lublin and Jaroslaw — since they attracted the richest and most active element of the Jewish population, also served as the meeting place of the councils. Throughout its existence the Council of the Province of Lithuania cooperated with its three (later five) leading communities through a continuous correspondence with them and between each of them and the smaller communities under its authority. Here the council was adapting the organizational methods of large-scale trade to the leadership structure. The concern of the councils with the new economic phenomena, like arenda, is well known. They also concerned themselves with matters of security and morals which arose from the small number of Jewish families in Christian townships and villages. On the whole, up to 1648 a sense of achievement and creativity pervades their enterprises and thought. A preacher of that time, Jedidiah b. Israel Gottlieb, inveighed against a man's gathering up riches for his children, using the argument of the self-made man: "The land is wide open, let them be mighty in it, settle and trade in it, then they will not be sluggards, lazy workers, children relying on their father's inheritance, but they themselves will try ... to bring income to their homes, in particular because every kind of riches coming through inheritance does not stay in their hands ... easy come, easy go ... through their laziness ... they have to be admonished ... to be mighty in the land through their trading: their strength and might shall bring them riches" (*Shir Yedidut* (Cracow, 1644), *Zeidah la-Derekh,* fol. 24a).

This buoyancy was based on a continuous growth of population throughout the 16th and the first half of the 17th centuries, due both to a steady natural increase thanks to improving conditions of life and to immigration from abroad resulting from persecution and expulsions (e.g., that from Bohemia-Moravia for a short period in 1542). As noted, the growth was most intensive in the eastern and southeastern areas of Poland-Lithuania, and it was distributed through the growing dispersion of Jews in the "private cities" and in the villages. At the end of the 16th century, Great Poland and Masovia (Mazowsze) contained 52 communities, Lesser Poland 41, and the Ukraine, Volhynia, and Podolia about 80; around 1648, the latter region had 115 communities. From about 100,000 persons in 1578 the Jewish population had grown to approximately 300,000 around 1648. It is estimated that the Jews formed about 2.5–3% of the entire population of Poland, but they constituted between 10% and 15% of the urban population in Poland and 20% of the same in Lithuania.

The dynamics of Jewish economic life are evident not only in the variety and success of their activities, but also in certain specific institutions and problems that reveal the tension behind their strain for economic goals which tended to entail risks. By the end of the 16th century, Jews were borrowers rather than lenders. Seventeenth-century anti-Semites — Miczyński and Mojecki — accused Jews of borrowing beyond their means and deceiving Christian lenders. From their accusations it is clear that much of this credit was not in ready cash but in goods given to Jewish merchants on credit. Borrowing was a real problem with which the Jewish leadership was much concerned. Many ordinances of the Councils of the Lands, of the provincial councils, and of single communities are preoccupied with preventing and punishing bankruptcy. Great efforts were devoted to prevent non-payment of debts to Christians in particular. Young men who were building up a family were especially suspected of reaching beyond their means. These ordinances tell in their own way the story of a burgeoning economy which is strained to dangerous limits, inciting in particular the young and the daring. A good name for credit was then a matter of life and death for the Jewish merchant. The great halakhist Solomon Luria was prepared to waive an ancient talmudic law in favor of the lender because "now most of the living of the Jews is based on credit; whereas most of those called merchants have little of their own and what they have in their hands is really taken from gentiles on credit for a fixed period — for they take merchandise [on credit] until a certain date — it is not seemly for a judge to sequester the property of a merchant, for news of this may spread and he will lose the source of his living and all his gentile creditors will come on him together and he will be lost, God forbid, and merchants will never trust him again. I myself have seen and heard about many merchants — circumcised and uncircumcised — to whom, because people said about them that they are a risk, much harm was caused and they never again could stand at their posts" (*Yam shel Shelomo, Bava Kamma,* ch. 1, para. 20). Because of the importance of credit the practice of a Jew lending on interest to another Jew became widespread in Poland-Lithuania despite the fact that it was contrary to Jewish law. This necessitated the creation there of the legal fiction of *hetter iskah*[13] formulated by a synod of rabbis and leaders under the chairmanship of Joshua b. Alexander ha-Kohen Falk in 1607. Widespread credit also led to the use of letters of credit specific to the Jews of Poland, the so-called *mamran*: the Jew would sign on one side of the paper and write on the other side "this letter of credit obliges the signed overleaf for amount x to be paid on date y."

Jewish cultural and social life flourished hand in hand with the economic and demographic growth. In the 16th and early 17th centuries Poland-Lithuania became the main center of Ashkenazi culture. Its *yeshivot* were already famous at the beginning of the 16th century; scholars like Hayyim b. Bezalel of Germany and David Gans of Prague were the pupils of Shalom Shakhna of Lublin and Moses Isserles of Cracow, respectively. Mordecai Jaffe; Abraham, Isaiah, and Jacob Horowitz; Eliezer b. Elijah Ashkenazi; Ephraim Solomon Luntshits; and Solomon Luria were only a few of the great luminaries of talmudic scholarship and moralistic preaching in Poland-Lithuania of that time. Councils of the Lands and community ordinances show in great detail if not the reality at least the ideal of widespread Torah study supported by the people in general. This culture was fraught with great social and moral tensions. Old Ashkenazi ascetic ideas did not sit too well on the affluent and economically activist Polish-Lithuanian Jewish society. Meetings with representatives of the Polish Reformation movement, in particular with groups and representatives of the anti-trinitarian wing like Marcin Czechowic or Szymon Budny, led to disputations and reciprocal influence. Outstanding in these contacts on the Jewish side was the Karaite Isaac b. Abraham Troki, whose *Hizzuk Emunah*

13   The legal device, current in the law and finance of Jews since the 17th century, under which a loan on interest is structured as limited partnership: the lender is conceived as the passive partner, the borrower as the active one, the interest as the return from the partnership due to the passive partner.

sums up the tensions in Jewish thought in the divided Christian religious world
of Poland-Lithuania. It was Moses Isserles who formulated the Ashkenazi
modifications and additions to the code of the Sephardi Joseph Caro. Isaiah
Horowitz summed up in his *Shenei Luhot ha-Berit* the moral and mystic
teaching of the upper circles of Ashkenazi Jewry. Yet his writings, and even
more so the writings of Isserles, give expression to the tensions and compromises
between rationalism and mysticism, between rich and poor, between leadership
and individual rights. To all these tensions, Ephraim Solomon Luntshits gave
sharp voice in his eloquent sermons, standing always on the side of the poor
against the rich and warning consistently against the danger of hypocrisy and
self-righteousness. Fortified and wooden synagogues expressed the needs and
the aesthetic sense of Jewish society of that time. In the old "royal cities"
magnificent synagogue buildings were erected as early as the 16th century (e.g.,
the Rema synagogue at Cracow and the Great Synagogue of Lvov). Hebrew
manuscripts were brought from abroad and some of them illuminated in Poland.
Jewish printing developed early and many beautiful works were published.
Various sources describe carnival-like Purim celebrations, and the fun, irony, and
joy of life expressed in now lost folk songs and popular games and dramas.

The Chmielnicki revolt and massacres of 1648–49, the Tatar incursions from
Crimea, and the subsequent war with Moscow combined with the Swedish War
to bring on the Jews of Poland-Lithuania approximately 30 years of bloodshed,
destruction, and suffering. Thousands were killed, thousands forced to adopt
Christianity. At the end of these convulsions, Poland-Lithuania had lost much
territory in the east which of course was also lost for Jewish life and settlement.
Thousands of refugees thronged westward, bringing heavy pressure to bear on
charity and the very structure of Jewish society. The arrangements of the
Councils of the Lands to prevent competition for arenda had to stand the severe
test of diminished opportunities and increasing demand. Contemporary figures
like Nathan Nata Hannover saw in this catastrophe a fissure in Jewish life and
institutions, as indicated by the tenor of his chronicle, *Yeven Mezulah*. In
reality, Jewish cultural and social life in the second half of the 17th century and
in the 18th continued to a considerable extent along the lines developed in the
great era of the 16th and first half of the 17th centuries. Recent research has
shown that Pinsk, a community in the east of Lithuania, recovered from its
troubles more completely and at greater speed than had been thought before. But
the dynamism had gone out of institutions and activities; inertia set in. Much
that had been full of imminent promise of development and change before the
disasters tended now to be petrified. Tensions that had been submerged in the
buoyant pre-Chmielnicki times became more open, causing dissension and revolt.
The councils and communities were burdened with the growing debts incurred

mostly to meet unexpected demands for defense against multiplying libels and massacres, but at the same time the oligarchic structure within the community and the councils and the dominating attitude adopted by the larger communities toward the smaller ones – in Lithuania in particular – caused the lower strata of the population and the members of the smaller communities to suspect their intentions and greatly resent the increasingly heavy tax burden. Jewish economic activity continued to develop, though Jews in the "private towns" and on arenda in the villages came to feel more and more the heavy and capricious hand of the Polish nobles, who by that period had lost the vigor of earlier times and become tyrannical, petty lords.

Despite the loss of territory and the worsening of conditions, the Jewish population in Poland-Lithuania continued to grow both absolutely and, from many aspects, in its relative strength in the country. With the abolition of the Councils of the Lands in 1764, a census of the Jewish population was taken. Jews tried to evade being counted by any means available for they were certain that the purpose of the census was to impose heavier taxation on them, as they had every reason to suspect the intentions of the authorities. For this reason at least 20% should be added to the official figures. Accordingly in 1764 there were approximately 750,000 Jews over a year old in Poland-Lithuania: 550,000 of them in Poland and 200,000 in Lithuania; 16.5% of the Jewish population of Poland lived in western Poland, 23.5% in Lesser Poland, and 60% in the Ukraine and neighboring districts; in Lithuania 77% lived in the western part and only 23% in the eastern, Belorussian districts. Taking into account the overall population of Poland, it can be seen that the concentration of Jewish population had shifted eastward in the 18th century to an even greater extent than in the early and successful 17th century. The census also shows that Jews lived mostly in small communities:

Distribution of Jews According to Size of Communities

Region	Percentage of communities of less than 500	Percentage of communities of more than 500
Great Poland	91.7	8.3
Masovia	93.5	6.5
Lesser Poland	76.5	23.5
Lvov	61.7	38.3
Ukraine	85.0	15.0

As the entire Christian urban population of Poland-Lithuania was estimated at that time to be about half a million, and as the Jews were concentrated mainly in the townships and "private towns," there emerges a clear picture of a predominantly Jewish population in the smaller Polish-Lithuanian urban centers, at least 70% to 90% in many of these places.

The economic structure of the Jewish population at this time is shown in the following table:

Economic Structure of Jewish Population in Poland-Lithuania in the 18th century

Region	Arenda and Alcoholic Beverages	Trade	Trans- porta- tion	Crafts	Profes- sions	Un- spec.
Great Poland	1.8	6.1	—	41.8	12.4	38.0
Masovia	15.2	0.7	—	19.0	13.0	52.0
Lesser Poland	3.1	4.8	1.0	24.0	11.0	56.0
Lvov	2.8	3.0	3.2	20.6	12.5	58.0
Ukraine	28.0	3.6	2.0	26.5	14.5	23.5

Although the predominance of unspecified professions does indicate the impoverishment of the Jews, it is largely an aspect of the evasive attitude toward the census. As this table does not include the village Jews, among whom the occupations of arenda and the production and sale of alcoholic beverages certainly predominated, only the following economic conclusions can be drawn with certainty: a considerably proportion of the Jews were engaged in crafts; and arenda and alcoholic beverages became more important as sources of livelihood as the Jews moved eastward and into villages (according to R. Mahler, *Yidn in Amolikn Poyln in Likht fun Tsifern*, 1958).

The Jewish population of Poland-Lithuania was still seething with creativity and movement in the 18th century. The messianic claims of Shabbetai Zevi not only stirred the masses of Jews in 1665–66 but also left a deep impression on later generations. This is evident in the suspicion expressed about itinerant *maggidim* (it was also demanded that they be supervised), who were suspected of disseminating heretical and critical ideas. The personality and movement of Jacob Frank made the greatest impact on the distressed population of Podolia, in the extreme southeast. From the same region too arose Israel b. Eliezer Ba'al Shem Tov and the movement of Ḥasidism he originated. Talmudic scholarship and traditional ways of life, which continued to flourish throughout the period, found a supreme exemplar in the vigorous personality and influence of Elijah b. Solomon Zalman, the Gaon of Vilna, and in the way of life and culture originated by him and his circle in the Mitnaggedic Lithuanian *yeshivot*. At that time too the first influences of *Haskalah* and assimilation began to appear in Poland-Lithuania.

With the partitions of Poland (beginning in 1772), the history of ancient Jewish Poland-Lithuania comes to an end. During the agony of the Polish state, several of its more enlightened leaders — e.g., H. Kollantaj and T. Czacki — tried to "improve the Jews," i.e., improve their legal and social status in the spirit of western and European enlightened absolutism. With the dismemberment of Poland-Lithuania, their belated efforts remained suspended. Even when broken up and dispersed, Polish-Lithuanian Jewry was not only the majority and the cultural source of Jewish society in czarist Russia, but those elements of it which came under Prussia and Austria also served later as the reservoir of Jewish spirit and manpower which resisted the ravages of assimilation and apostasy in the German and Austrian communities in the late 18th and 19th centuries.

3

LITHUANIA
A PROVINCE OF JEWISH SOCIETY AND CULTURE CRYSTALLIZED IN MODERN TIMES

The area of Jewish Lithuania is co-extensive with the Grand Duchy of Lithuania *(magnus ducatus Lithuaniae),* as it was created by the great conquests of Lithuania to the east and southeast of its ethnic core. Until the final union with Poland, i.e. the Union of Lublin, in 1569, the Grand Duchy, and hence the Jewish social and cultural formation within it, included the regions of Volhynia and Kiev. With the cession of these two provinces to Poland in 1569, Jewish Lithuania extended to the regions of Brest-Litovsk, Augustow, Grodno, Vilna, Kovno, Novogrudok, Minsk, Vitebsk, Mogilev, and to a certain extent in terms of time and culture, Smolensk and Mstislavl.[1] From then on Jewish Lithuania remained virtually united, even after the partitions of Poland, despite their great political and social impact. Certain inroads into its territorial-cultural borders were made in the 19th century, partly as a result of the inclusion of some western districts of this territory (in particular near Grodno) into the Kingdom of Poland created by the Congress of Vienna of 1815, and its union with the Russian Empire.

From the standpoint of Jewish culture and history, Jewish Lithuania was partitioned only after World War I, between independent Poland, independent Lithuania, and Belorussian S.S.R.

From the territorial, demographic, linguistic, and cultural standpoints, ethnic Lithuania, its population, language, and culture were a relatively minor element in the grand duchy. Cultural influences from Kievan and various Russian dukedoms were considerable. Since the first union with Poland in 1385, Polish cultural influences grew steadily. During the 16th century a great part of the

---

1   For historical cartography of the grand duchy and its delineation, see *Atlas Historyczny Polski,* ed. W. Czapliński and T. Tagodórski (Warszawa, 1970), 16–17, 20–21, 23, 24–29; *Grosser Historischer Weltatlas,* dritter Teil, Neuzeit, ed. J. Engel (Munich, 1957), 139, 152–153. See also W. Ostrowski, *The Ancient Names and Early Cartography of Byelorussia* (London, 1971) (with a pronounced Belorussian nationalist basis).

nobility and burghers of Lithuania became Catholic and Polonized. Those who remained Pravoslavs maintained their contact with Russian culture. The seminal centers of Jewish Lithuania were partly in the Volhynia and Kiev regions and partly to the west, in proximity to Poland. The centers of culture and autonomy were first and foremost outside ethnic Lithuania, such as Brest-Litovsk, Grodno, and Pinsk, which were for a long time the only communities represented in the Council of Lithuania. Slutsk in Belorussia and Vilna, which was highly Polonized, joined later.

The grand duchy was estimated to number 27,000 Jews in 1578 [2]; in 1676 there were an estimated 32,000 Jews there, though the actual number was probably higher. The census of 1766, though not very reliable, gives for the entire grand duchy 157,520 Jews[3] (against 454,625 Jews in Poland). This is the demographic frame for the spread of Ḥasidism and the somewhat later rise of the Lithuanian *Mitnaggedim.*

The census of 1897 of Czarist Russia gives for the same area, which was then the poorest section of the Pale, approximately 1,573,000 Jews. This area also had the largest proportion of overseas emigrants. Thus, the "Lithuanian colony" in South Africa — mostly populated from the regions of ethnic Lithuania — came to dominate the Jewish settlement there numerically, socially, and culturally from the 1890s on.

Independent Lithuania numbered 155,126 Jews in 1923 and about 160,000 in 1937. Latvia numbered 93,406 Jews in 1935 (descended partly from German Jews and partly from Russian Jews, mainly from Lithuania). According to the 1926 census there were 407,059 Jews in Belorussian S.S.R., and according to various counts taken in 1919–21 there were about 400,000 Jews in the districts of Jewish Lithuania included in independent Poland. All in all, there were at least a million Jews in Jewish Lithuania when it was partitioned in the 1920s.

To sum up, grand duchy Jewry represented about 25% of the total number of Jews in Poland-Lithuania. At the beginning of the 20th century the percentage dropped to about 20% of the number within the Pale as a result of the large waves of emigration from poorer Lithuania in the early 19th century to

2   According to the *History of the Jewish People* (Russian) 11, p. 11, Poland numbered at that time 75,000 Jews. The Jews of the grand duchy represented approximately a third of those in Poland and a quarter of the entire Jewish population of Poland-Lithuania. This proportion remained constant until the 19th century.

3   *Ibid.,* summary of Table 5, p. 121. The breakdown into the administrative units of the grand duchy gives the following figures: Brześć, Wojewodztwo, 21,994 Jews; Vilna, 26,997; Troki (including both Kaunas and Grodno), 33,738; Żmudź, 15,759; Novo-grudok, 21,101; Minsk, 13,422; Vitebsk, 11,959; Polotsk, 6,689; Mstislavl, 2,615; Inflaty (in modern times Latvia and the bordering regions), 2,996.

the Ukraine and the southeast and later to Poland, as well as overseas emigration.

Lithuanian Jews were conscious from the outset of the vast extent of their territory. The Council of Lithuania of 1623 — the first to leave records — literally meted out punishment to an over-hasty plaintiff by the yardstick; if he was "a poor man, unable to pay for the damage, he is to be excommunicated or imprisoned for as many days as the versts the defendant had to travel to attend the hearing." (*Pinkas Medinat Lita,* ed. Dubnow). This august body was accustomed to looking far afield as it carved out vast districts to be ruled by its constituent communities. Brest-Litovsk, one of the leading communities, carved out for itself a large share of Belorussia, extending as far as Minsk and Orsha in the east. The great distances and room for colonization did not prevent the Council of Lithuania from insisting on territorial rights and closing its borders to "aliens," as was characteristic of most autonomous medieval entities. This exclusiveness does not seem to have had cultural connotations. Jewish Lithuania insisted on its economic and settlement prerogatives within the grand duchy. We find it even fighting against any compulsory link in action and finances to the Councils of Poland. But this is not to say that Lithuania insisted on its rights more than any other similar entity of those times. Rabbis, teachers, preachers, and even many colonists came to settle within the domain of Lithuania. Whatever may have been said against them we do not find the complaint that they were lacking in Lithuanian-styled Jewishness or learning. Nor is there evidence of any reaction in Poland or elsewhere to specific Lithuanian modes of thought or conduct. In fact it is not until the end of the 18th century that there is mention of any distinctly Lithuanian style, though individual communities did have their sense of local pride.

Nevertheless, we do find specific Lithuanian-Jewish social policies and attitudes. The very structure of the Council of Lithuania favored leadership by a few distant communities and little representation for the others, a situation which created a great deal of friction, characterized by the high-handed attitude of the oligarchy on one side and the rebelliousness of the unrepresented communities on the other. This conflict spilled over into relations between the community and its members as well, and recourse to the state authorities was frequent. Thus, all the Lithuanian communities without exception rose in revolt against the "big five" leading constituent communities of the Council in 1720 and appealed to the state. In 1791 the common people of Shavli appealed to the secular authorities against both their rabbi and the lay leaders of the community, referring to them as "our harm and loss." The contrast with neighboring Poland in these respects is unmistakable.

The Council of Lithuania had consciously and openly adopted a policy diametrically opposed to that of Poland in the matter of farming out customs houses to Jews. Anti-Jewish agitation was at that time more intense in Poland than in the grand duchy, and it also seems that there were greater opportunities for controlling customs houses in Lithuania than in Poland. Thus the Councils of Poland ruled out such farming because of the dangers involved, while the Council of Lithuania encouraged it as a means of gaining power, which indicates that the views of the rich, who stood to benefit the most from such a policy, prevailed in the leadership of the Council. In addition, caution dominated the Councils of Polish Jewry, whereas Jewish Lithuanian leadership was more daring.

It hardly seems accidental that a rabbi who served for a long time in Lithuania, Joel Sirkes, proposed measures and policies to curb the power and initiative of the Council heads. He cited strict Torah Law in opposition to community ordinances, and though he addressed himself to the Councils of Poland, his proposals are better understood as a reaction to the more aggressive ways of the Council of Lithuania.

There is an aspect of Jewish culture in Lithuania that reveals a physiognomy of its own, etched by contact with a turbulent and variegated environment and filled out by the rationalism of both transmitted and original ideas and writings.

The Russian and Polish cultural influences, linked to religious differences between Catholic and Pravoslav and to ties with Poland and Muscovy, respectively, have been pointed out. In the 15th century Jews from Kiev, then an influential part of Jewish Lithuania, were accused, it seems with considerable justice, of promoting the heresy of "Judaization" in Muscovy. What is more important from our point of view is that they introduced translations from Hebrew rationalist writings, thus showing, through an alien mirror, that such works were owned and used by them. Nor are these the only translations from Hebrew writings made then in Lithuania and left to posterity in archives.

At the beginning of the 16th century the Polish chronicler, Maciej Miechowita, noted that in Lithuania "the Jews use Hebrew books and study the sciences and arts, astronomy and medicine." Rationalist study was paralleled by rationalist usages to the extent of "an Aristotelian prayer" instituted by young students; it was also remembered in the second half of the 16th century that there had been a deeply rooted "philosophical" trend and tradition in certain places as Moses Isserles of Cracow reminded the rabbi who brought up the matter of that prayer. Lithuania thus shared in this scholarly rationalist culture with other regions in Poland and, it seems, pioneered to a certain extent in this cultural field.

In the 16th century the grand duchy became even more variegated and turbulent than before in its culture and religion. This general development was paralleled in Poland, though to a lesser extent, particularly from the standpoint of Jewish involvement.

Heterodoxy in Lithuania in the 16th and early 17th centuries was not only represented by the Lutheran and Calvinist churches. Anti-trinitarian trends developed there too, as in Poland, also attracting leading nobles. In Lithuania there came into existence an influential group of "Judaizers," whose most prominent teacher was Szymon Budny.

Historians tend to believe that "specifically it was a Judaizing trend within certain sections of Russian Orthodoxy . . . that operated in Lithuania" to help radicalize, together with other elements of Orthodox tradition, sections of the Reformation camp in Lithuania (G.H. Williams, *The Radical Reformation,* 1962). This mosaic of nations, of languages (Russian, Polish, German in the towns, and Lithuanian in ethnic Lithuania), of churches, and of sects included for the great majority of Jews (the Rabbanites) still another element – the Karaites, in Troki and elsewhere, with whom contacts were sometimes friendly and sometimes less so.

As an outgrowth of the traditions and culture that continued to develop in the 16th century through the influence and challenge of the volatile environment, we find at the end of the 16th and the beginning of the 17th century in Lithuania works characterized by a rationalistic approach which serve to synthesize and unify the various elements of Jewish culture while at the same time constituting a sharp polemical response – again in a decidedly rationalistic manner – to challenges from without. Both the inclination to synthesize – rationalistic and mystic elements in particular – and the rationalistic response to what is considered inimical to that synthesis would be found again in Jewish Lithuanian culture in later days.

In his *Ḥizzuk Emunah,* written at the end of the 16th century, the Karaite Isaac b. Abraham Troki deals with the kaleidoscope of religions, traditions, and nations that he knew in Lithuania. Greek-Orthodox, Catholic, Lutheran, and in particular Judaizing anti-trinitarian are confronted in terms of their political status historical traditions, theological polemics, and Bible translations. He makes free use of Rabbanite chroniclers and philosophical literature.

Shortly afterwards a Rabbanite in Lithuania collected in manuscript excerpts of Isaac Troki's work and the *Niẓẓaḥon* of Yom Tov Lipmann Muelhausen. The excerpts are interspersed with notes in a decidedly rationalistic vein. Most instructive is this Rabbanite's dispute with a Karaite notable in Vilna in 1589/90. He entered the lists because he feared Karaite influences on the masses, as everyday contacts were close. In his attacks on the Karaites he makes considerable use of rationalist works (Ms Bodleian Library, Oxford, op. 593).

An even richer content of learning and a rationalist mode of thought that turned to active philosophizing are found in *Givat ha-Moreh,* 1611. It is the treatise of an influential teacher which comments on Maimonides in a way that brings out the author's own personality clearly. He is presented to the reader as: "Divine philosopher, mature in wisdom and young in years, rabbi Joseph son of Isaac the Levite, from the lands of Lithuania". His work was published on November 7, 1611. The aged Ephraim Solomon of Luntshits, then Rabbi of Prague, writes that the fame of the author as a philosophy teacher spread in Prague through the "great scholars in our community, who have listened to him and learned from him." Prague became acquainted with him as a young man; the praise lavished on him indicates that he became a sensation there. He brought with him great knowledge and a considerable capacity to influence established and recognized scholars in an alien community. He was assertive and dogmatic.

R. Joseph's reading ranged far and wide, though dominated by rationalist literature. Aristotle is mentioned frequently and with admiration. Averroes, Avicenna, and other Arab philosophers are mentioned too: he refers to former commentators of Maimonides' *Guide* such as Moses Narboni and Samuel ibn Tibbon. Levi b. Gershom, Ḥasdai Crescas, and his pupil Joseph Albo are quoted by him, the last two frequently. His inclination toward synthesis is evident in his assertion that a true understanding of Kabbalah reveals that it is in full agreement with philosophy.

R. Joseph took care to make it clear that his criticism of Maimonides was not meant to imply agreement with Maimonides' antirationalist opponents, modern or ancient. In terms used frequently by rationalists, he describes the opponents of the *Guide* and Maimonides as: "The fool and his followers — may their bones rot — who went astray and led others astray by inflicting blemishes on sacred things, as is known. The impression of these blemishes has surely remained in the hearts of the fools, both here and now as well as those not in the present." His ardent admiration for Maimonides and rationalist philosophy expressed itself in a chapter classifying and answering the opponents. He claimed there that true kabbalists are in agreement with this philosophy. As for the talmudists, they "believe that man cannot attain eternal perfection without the Talmud, in which they were brought up from their earliest years. They do not realize that man can indeed attain the maximum perception [of wisdom] possible to him, in particular through the wisdom of the *Guide.*"

Such a meeting of minds and similar modes of thought-structure in both form and content to such a degree among three scholars in a relatively short period in the same region could hardly be accidental.

The second half of the 17th century and most of the 18th century were times of calamity for Poland and Lithuania. It was also a time of reaction and suppression. Jewish society struggled hard, often successfully, to reconstruct what had been destroyed. The works of men like the Rabbi of Minsk and Dubno, R. Joseph b. Judah, the author of the *Yesod Yosef,* written in 1685, and

Rabbi Judah Leib Pukhovitser show the continuity of culture and aims, though under much harsher conditions in an environment impoverished in most respects. The halakhic and sermonizing activity of R. Shabbetai b. Meir ha-Kohen, R. Moses Rivkes, and the members of the Koidanover family represent an "export by calamity" of Jewish Lithuanian scholars who retain their consciousness and pride, stemming from their communities and traditions in Lithuania.

But at the end of the 18th century Poland-Lithuania was in the throes of disintegration. The Councils of the Lands had been officially dissolved in 1764, leaving behind them debts and tensions. The records of the Councils as well as events in individual communities provide abundant evidence of a struggle on the part of the craftsmen's guilds for a share in leadership and of attempts by community leaders to diminish the role and rights of their rabbi. In Vilna, these disputes revolved around the personality and status of R. Samuel b. Avigdor, fomenting considerable social discord. According to the philosopher Solomon Maimon, writing in 1792, the social life of the Jews, in particular in the small communities and villages, was poor and tense. Despite these tales of woe a remarkable degree of knowledge and devotion to study is found in all camps. One of the accusations leveled against R. Samuel in Vilna was that no light was seen from his study late at night. A poor Lithuanian scholar's library in rural surroundings included the *Josippon*, David Gans' chronicle *Żemaḥ David*, and what Maimon remembered as "a history of the persecution of the Jews in Spain" (Maimon, *Autobiography*).

The social and cultural scene was both enriched and complicated by the growing influence of German culture in Eastern Europe generally and in the western regions of the Russian empire in particular. Actual contacts with Germany, particularly East Prussia, added to the variety. Jewish-German culture held some attractions for Lithuanian Jews of the Vilna Gaon's circle, as the hagiographic biography of one of his pupils, R. Zalman of Volozhin, clearly shows. This influence would of course become stronger in later days with the *Haskalah* and socialist and Zionist trends. The re-entry of the Russians on the social and cultural scene carried with it the seeds of future influence and tensions.

In modern times, with the spread of Ḥasidism, Lithuania evolved a distinct shade of culture which was derived from the old ways made to look new as they emerged in a changing world. Yet it did not constitute a fossil standing out among new forms. Old forms evolved into new, specifically Lithuanian ones, out of the dialectics of an active, vital conservatism, developing to meet new problems and needs through old-new formulations and institutions. As historical fate would have it, the old was represented and defended in Lithuania by a brilliant, spirited circle under the guidance of a dynamic individualist, the Gaon of Vilna (Elijah b. Solomon Zalman). Thus did the clash between the previously irresistible Ḥasidism and the immovable center of the Gaon's circle forge modern Lithuania out of its old culture and values.

The Vilna Gaon represents — though personally in a way both many-faceted and disciplined — a synthesis between total immersion in the talmudic world, living absorption in mysticism, and considerable interest in certain fields of secular knowledge, to all of which he brought an ardently believing heart, a keenly analytical and critical mind, and an iron will and self-discipline. It was not only his immediate circle which strove to perpetuate this spiritual amalgam. As one reads the work of what may be termed a distant admirer of his, the *Sefer ha-Berit* (Bruenn, 1797), one is struck by a similar synthesis, though on a lower, popularizing level.

The Vilna Gaon and his circle faced what they considered the spiritual malaise and dangers of their time on a positive, necessarily innovating platform. As they turned from excommunication to polemics, old rationalist traits reasserted themselves, often against their own will.

In the face of charismatic ḥasidic leadership, the circle of the Vilna Gaon asserted that the charisma resides only in virtues, not in individuals, in learning and devotion to it. R. Ḥayyim Volozhiner relates an "anti-charismatic" miracle-tale: "It has been said of our master David, the author of the *Turei Zahav*, that a woman cried out to him: 'O master, my son in dying,' and he answered her: 'Am I God?' and she answered: 'I am calling out to the Torah which is in my master, for the Holy One blessed be He and the Torah are one.' And he said to her: 'Then this I will do for you. I will give you the words of the Torah in which I am now occupied with my disciples. Perhaps by virtue thereof he will live'" (*Ruaḥ Ḥayyim*, 1859). Personal charisma and supernatural powers as reflected in ḥasidic tales are here rejected, and this remained the attitude of Lithuania. It caused some difficulty with regard to great men adored in Lithuania. Toward Ḥasidism, its miracle-tales, the ways and sincerity of its *zaddikim* (leaders), who claimed personal charisma, this attitude bred biting irony, distrust, and disparagement. An aristocratic attitude found popular expression. It created such phenomena as an attitude to them similar to the attitude of *Haskalah*. On the other hand it had an erosive effect on admired and fideistic traditions, causing dialects within an orthodoxy given to ridicule of the charismatic, which was both disruptive as well as creative in Lithuanian culture.

The Vilna Gaon taught the supreme value of hard-working intellectuality which refuses any gift received through vision and rejects haste in study even with the talented. Vision and quick perception were to be mastered by the "slow grinding" of the critical and watchful mind that earns "in the sweat of its learning" its worth before God. In his life and in the tenets of his teaching he shaped the *matmid,* the young man whose life is study as engulfing holiness.

The Vilna Gaon taught that intellectual saturation is not egotism: when the vessel is full to the brim it overflows into those around it. Thus saturation in learning breeds saturation in spirit. This theory of a saturating force and saturated periphery was made more egalitarian, dynamic, and cosmic in the teaching of his pupil R. Ḥayyim. There the ḥasidic image of the *zaddik* as "the ladder standing on earth, its head reaching heaven" is turned around to mean that each man has part of his soul in heaven; each individual soul is this ladder, rooted in the body, its upper rung in heaven " . . . which is the living soul of the universe and of the powers, and of the angels on high . . . for the main task of man is first to cause the world to ascend from below to on high, and only thereafter the lights are attracted from on high to below." The dynamism of each man in the cosmos forbids the adoration of individuals: "And even to be enslaved and devoted to some worship, from the aspect of the holy spirit which is in a man, a prophet and possessed of the holy spirit, is also actual idolatry." Man moves all, heaven and earth through works, first and foremost among them Torah study. Fear of God is only the "container," learning the content. All commandments are but candles, learning is the fire and light (*Nefesh Ḥayyim,* 1859).

This concept was the motive behind the foundation of a new type of *yeshivah* in Volozhin (in 1802). Though telling much of his and others' talmudic education, Solomon Maimon knew nothing of such an institution. R. Ḥayyim summed up succinctly the basic creed of the *yeshivah* to give reality to the cosmic potentiality of Torah study through the social life of Lithuanian Jewry: "The people of the Land . . . some desire solely Talmud and no more, and they lack even a spoonful of food. And there are others who have the desire to study, but they have no teacher to teach them the ways of proper understanding . . . the Holy Torah gives life to our souls, and the world is based upon the utterance of our lips and our contemplation of it . . . who are they who will volunteer to teach the pupils? And who are they who will volunteer to support the Torah with all that they possess? I am the first to volunteer with my heart and soul as one of the teachers, and by the grace of God . . . I am confident . . . that there will be provision for the pupils in abundance, according to their needs." (From R. Ḥayyim's first appeal, published many times.)

Volozhin was to provide for these sublime goals as well as for the maintenance of the students though in principle all-Jewish and in reality all-Lithuanian care and support. Opposition to the establishment of a central institution in a tiny locality was likely to be strong. A scholar who taught at Volozhin at the side of R. Ḥayyim remembered the sermon "which I preached and expounded in public in my youth when I began to establish a *yeshivah* in the town of my birth . . . Nesvizh . . . to rebut the question which the ordinary people ask: What need is there for a general *yeshivah*? Are there not teachers of Torah in every town, so that he who wishes to study can do so in his own city?" (Y.M. Hirsch, *Le-Zekher Yisrael,* 1833.) R. Ḥayyim solved the problem by creating an all-Lithuanian network of societies, emissaries, and contributions. This made the *yeshivah* a boon to the townlet instead of a burden. It converted the student from a dependent on local charity to a recipient of impersonal support. His status and self-image were thus changed radically for the better. The *yeshivot* that soon spread over Lithuania were generally based on the same financial organization and assured their students the same standing.

The structure and life of the Lithuanian *yeshivah* can be seen in a description of one of the earliest offshoots of Volozhin: " . . . I am fully occupied in teaching in the *yeshivah,* which has over sixty students . . . and we have five courses in Talmud for all the students together. Codes, however, I teach them in groups, all four sections of the *Shulḥan Arukh* [standard code of Jewish law] with the *aḥaronim* [later rabbinic authorities], because I do not possess a sufficient number of copies of the Codes to teach all of them the same *posek* [decisor in halakhic disputes] " *(Le-Zekher Yisrael).*

The *yeshivah* was based on the social and economic life of the Pale; it was also based on the traditional admiration of the Jew for the scholar; if he had a gifted son he would send him to the *yeshivah*; if he had a daughter he wanted a scholar for a son-in-law. Almost immediately after the creation of Volozhin, R. Jacob Kranz[4] described its social integration with economic and social life and the feeling of independence it gave its students. He tells of "a rich man who came to the site of a great *yeshivah,* the group of young men who study Torah with great devotion. He saw and liked a young man, great in learning, and decided to marry him to his daughter" (*Kol Ya'akov,* 1804). When the youngster's father makes exorbitant demands for himself, the son asserts himself. This integration continued until the Holocaust.

The *yeshivot* spread first along the Minsk-Vilna axis; by the middle of the 19th century they were central to life everywhere in Lithuania. With the advent of the *Musar* Movement the *yeshivot* established later on in ethnic Lithuania, which were for that very reason more open to innovation, grew in importance.

The *yeshivot* varied from place to place and with the changing personalities of their heads, though within the Volozhin pattern. Some changes became general and almost unnoticed. Both the Vilna Gaon and R. Ḥayyim comment a great

---

4   Jacob Kranz, of the inner circle of the pupils of Elijah, the *Gaon* of Vilna; his mode of preaching, in particular his parables and stories, pioneered traditional preaching in Lithuanian Jewry in the 19th and 20th centuries. Also known as the *Maggid* of Dubno.

deal on mystic literature, its symbolism and conceptions being the core of their Torah ideology. Yet, we find no teaching or group reading of mystic literature in the *yeshivot*: there are not even elite circles for its study. After R. Ḥayyim it is rare to find any preoccupation in Lithuania with what were the main sources of quotations and imagery for the shapers of its cultural institutions. Even when *Musar* decided that it was high time to pay heed to "the container," fear of God, and not only "the content," study, in direct opposition to R. Ḥayyim's views, it did not turn to mystic literature. Although some of its works like those of Cordovero or Luzzatto were used, the basic elements of mysticism remained beyond the *yeshivah* pale (see below, chap. 8).

The *yeshivot* had at first a pronounced interest in preparing for halakhic decisions. Soon this was "forgotten" in most, though not all, Lithuanian *yeshivot,* nor were examinations normally held. *Yeshivah* life centered ideally on what might be termed the continuation of devotion to study as a mystic call and duty, in the tradition of the Vilna Gaon and R. Ḥayyim.

The *matmid* was adored. Study extended through the night. For most, *yeshivah* life was a less intense and very human experience: it was an existence in a commonwealth of the young, who listened daily to discursive talmudic lectures by the head, and were immersed in thought and learning. The *yeshivah* thus became if not "the molder of the soul of the people" as the poet Bialik wrote, then certainly the institution that shaped the elite of Jewish Lithuania during most of the 19th century. The young men who came to the *yeshivah* from village, town, or city, rich or poor, met at the *yeshivah* on equal terms and imbibed *yeshivah* manners, ideals, and modes of thought, which they transmitted wherever they later settled. Rabbi, preacher, merchant, or shopkeeper, the *yeshivah* graduate remained at heart a proud and orthodox intellectual, influencing by word and deed the lower strata and imbuing them with *yeshivah* values. These values became all-pervading, and as a result both variegated and changeable.

The preaching of *maggidim* (popular, often itinerant, preachers) was an integral element in the shaping of this culture. They came from the *yeshivot,* preaching by metaphor, exhortation, and pun. They continued to use irony, often heavy-handed, against both *Ḥasidim* and *Haskalah* and later against socialism. On the other hand they were biting and insistent social critics, liked by the masses and sometimes persecuted by the rich. They popularized the theory of the centrality of study, lowering its demands to the level of Jewish workers and businessmen. Their sing-song melody was for the masses the parallel to the *yeshivah* melodies at study.

The *Musar* Movement was initially intended to serve as a framework for the elite who were active in social and economic life and for the masses. Only with its failure in the towns did it turn to the *yeshivot* and meet with success. Its mentor, R. Israel Lipkin (Salanter), was a man much drawn to German-Jewish life, frequenting the reading rooms of the Koenigsberg University Library when he was in Germany. Again, it was a dominating personality and a synthesis of various elements which combined to resolve a crisis. The melody of the *maggid* was introduced into the *yeshivah.* Looking into moralist books became essentially an occasion for spiritual exercises to create a mood and fashion an attitude. Although in diametrical opposition to the cardinal tenets of the Vilna Gaon and R. Ḥayyim in regard to intellectuality and emotionality, *Musar* retained enough of their spirit to produce a kind of emotional intellectuality. The elite coming to Lithuanian society from the *Musar yeshivot* was to pit its sense of dedication of heart and mind against the new dedication to Zion and to the *Bund* [5].

Not every Jew in Lithuania prayed like the grandfather of the historian Simon Dubnow: "Standing straight, his face to the wall, pronouncing slowly and with concentration every word of the prayers, from time to time he would incline his head slightly and raise it again. But heartfelt inner ecstasy permeated his whole personality." Everyone in Lithuania agreed that this was the only appropriate way to pray. They would agree with the grandson's negative praise: "Grandfather's prayer had nothing to do with ḥasidic ecstasy. He would have considered all their jumping and movement and crying out in prayer as frivolity before God" (*Sefer ha-Ḥayyim* p. 24). The dominant elite and the influential preaching caused the Lithuanian town and village to admire intellectuality, knowledge, and learning. This ancient Jewish attitude was reinforced and took on a fighting edge. Memoirists of the 19th century present a picture of a society in which everyone tried to learn something. One studied Talmud, another joined a group that studied Mishnah, and, if not Midrash, at least Psalms. There developed in Lithuania a "learning among ignoramuses," who picked up something from preachers or teachers and used it in a peculiar way, becoming the butt of upper-class irony.

Ḥabad Ḥasidism had in it much of the old "Lithuanian" traits and the synthesis of rationistic and mystic elements to which it added new ingredients from *Ḥasidism*. It was intellectual and scholarly in bent, and inclined to moderation in behavior. How much of this represented the Lithuanian legacy and how much the pressure and challenge of the Vilna Gaon and his disciples is hard to determine. From one point of view *Ḥabad* could boast of possessing much of the Lithuanian conservatism, while untainted by its rejection of the

---

5   Jewish socialist party, founded in Russia in 1897, associated with devotion to Yiddish, autonomism, secular Jewish nationalism, and anti-Zionism.

miraculous and free from the dangers of erosion immanent in it. It is no accident that every leader in the mainstream of Lithuanian culture who emphasized conservatism for the sake of self-preservation turned naturally to an alliance with *Ḥabad*.

Vilna was in the 19th century a storm-center of the cultural and national struggle of the Pole against Russian influences. Both sides tried to win the Jews to their cause, each in his own way and according to the means available. To a lesser extent this was true of a considerable part of Lithuania. All Lithuania faced constantly and in growing strength the challenges of Russification on the one hand and of *Haskalah* influence coming mainly from across the German border on the other. The Vilna Gaon was revolted by the first harbingers of this entirely different attempt at synthesis. His disciples, however, were in part less able to resist for the above-mentioned reasons.

The *Haskalah* movement and literature in Lithuania took on to a considerable extent a more internalized and in some cases even a more conservative view than it did in other countries as it faced the elite of the *yeshivot*, and, later, was recruited from amongst its ranks. Abraham Mapu, Mordecai Aaron Guenzburg, Abraham Dov Lebensohn, Judah Leib Gordon, Kalman Schulman, and Isaac Meir Dick, all pioneers in Hebrew and Yiddish literature, each in his own way shaped an internalized and to a considerable degree "Litvak" response to the challenges of the Enlightenment and Jewish society of their times.

The rabbinical seminary in Vilna (1847–1873) attracted many of the young intelligentsia. But from the beginning of the 1870s many of this intelligentsia began to turn to revolutionary socialism. Yet, even so, men like Aaron Lieberman and Morris Vinchevsky turned inward to Jewish society and its problems.

Ḥevra Shas (Talmud study group), 1918 – painting by Lazar Krestin.

Ideological autonomism was formulated by S. Dubnow with an eye to both the national and secular realities in Jewish Lithuania of *Haskalah*, intelligentsia, *yeshivah* students in crisis, and above all the changing − yet changing as Jewish − reality and spirit of the Jewish masses in this cultural climate of Lithuania. Life pulsated in a rhythm that gave reason to believe that revolution may be Jewish: Yiddish began to be cherished and written. From modest beginnings in the 19th century it was to become the matrix and model in the 20th century for a movement and trend that penetrated European and American Jewry. Not by accident was Vilna the seat of the Yiddish scientific institute, YIVO, and its scientific activity.

The *Bund* as a rising phenomenon is to be understood against the background of this Lithuanian reality and mentality. It arose in the region that saw the rise of the *yeshivot* along the Vilna-Minsk axis. Poverty was not its only parent. There was much poverty elsewhere. Enraged and thinking young Jews in other regions turned in their wrath away from not only the establishment but from their people. Most of the *Bund's* early leaders, fighters, ideologists, and propagators came from Jewish Lithuania. Research has already shown this regional character of the *Bund*. Attention has not been paid to the fact that the tensions immanent in Lithuanian culture and society compelled and enabled critics not to see themselves as totally alienated from other Jews by reason of their criticism and rationalism. Preaching provided a means of communicating with the masses in an old idiom for a new cause. The assimilated socialist Julius Martov was amazed and fascinated by the love of learning and knowledge for their own sake and the affirmation of intellectual enrichment as the true human achievement displayed by Jewish laborers in Vilna. This is a Lithuanian culture trait that nurtured the Jewish consciousness and pride of workers in Lithuania and helped shape the *Bund*.

From the beginning *Bund* propaganda used the style of the *maggidim* to influence workers. The Lithuanian origin of the *Bund* caused the movement to embrace the Yiddish Lithuanian dialect as the literary one, out of admiration for the speech of the leaders, despite the fact that the majority of Jews in Russia used another dialect and the first great writers of Yiddish did not come from Lithuania.

Parallel with the *Bund* arose Zionist labor thought and movements, again in the same region; as one reads Chaim Zhitlowsky, a sense of the middle-class home as a matrix for revolutionary and national movements crystallizes. In Minsk and Dvinsk there arose especially intense national Jewish labor movement cells. The Vitebsk-born Berl Katznelson became the ideologist of the Zionist labor movement, and the first Po'alei Zion (Zionist-socialist movement) came from Jewish Lithuania. All this was in earnest competition with the assimilationist revolutionary movements that produced from these regions men like G.A. Gershuni and Eliezer Zuckermann.

When the poet Bialik wrote:

> "The wind has carried them all away,
> The light has swept them off,
> A new song gladdens the morning of their lives,
> And I, a young fledgling, have been forgotten from the heart,
> Under the wings of the divine presence lone and solitary have I remained,"

he was again exaggerating wildly. There was a crisis in the *yeshivot* and in Jewish Lithuania, yet it did not destroy the core of the Orthodox elite or popular attitudes. This Orthodox active core was differentiated according to the response of various groups and personalities within it. The mainstream of the Jewish Lithuanian cultural trend that commenced with the Vilna Gaon, R. Hayyim, and the *Maggid* of Dubno, parted in the early 20th century in reaction to the crisis, into four groups, all of them in their own view consciously following the old path though at the same time they were aware of the great differences between them. Two of these four trends were in one way or another linked together and interrelated with the involvement in common activity with non-Orthodox Jews here described.

There was a trend in the Orthodox mainstream that developed in a somewhat tortuous way toward a new synthesis. Out of an inherited attitude to the synthesis of elements that seemed to them capable of being synthesized as well as out of the degree of openness immanent in Jewish Lithuania, many of its foremost teachers became active for the settlement of the Land of Israel in its modern sense, among them the head of the Volozhin *yeshivah,* Rabbi Naphtali Zevi Judah Berlin, and Rabbi David Friedman of Karlin. With Rabbi Samuel Mohilever the involvement became even deeper and more conscious. Gradually, the participation in common Jewish and in modern work made such leaders of the Lithuanian mainstream open to innovation in practice, though their theory would not allow them the compromises they reached. With the crisis in the *yeshivot,* the Zionist rabbi of Lida, Isaac Jacob Reines — on the main axis of the "*yeshivot* land" — attempted, though unsuccessfully, to introduce secular education into the *yeshivah.* With the advent of Zionism the Mizrachi developed out of this trend. There were many who remained together though affected by the crisis in faith, ideals, and life style — when Bialik thought that they were lonely and forlorn.

Many came more and more to stress Orthodoxy as a beleaguered fortress and to see what had developed since the Gaon of Vilna as the building of a line of defense. This trend, the most widespread (though from the nature of such societies, there are no certain statistical data), is represented on the eve of the

Holocaust by R. Ḥayyim Ozer Grodzinski. In 1922 he prefaced his responsa with a moving commendation of the Torah as continuity and of the *yeshivah* as a "strong fortress for Judaism" ranged against misleaders and assimilation. In 1939, he prefaced another volume of his responsa with an attack against the Jewish West and secular education, the source of all misfortune, and a detailed writ of accusation against the sins of the Jewish people at that juncture of time and fate. "Even now, the *yeshivot* in Poland and Lithuania are a spiritual center and a bastion of light to the Jewish people. The outstanding students who selflessly devote themselves to the Torah are the pioneers of the nation and the heroes of the spirit, and the channel through which light is disseminated over all. Through them will Israel be reconstituted." When it reached his ears in 1934 that the Rabbiner-Seminar fuer das Orthodoxe Judentum intended to save itself by moving from Berlin to Tel Aviv, he wrote to its head, then already in Erez Israel, forbidding it in the strongest possible terms, mixed with scathing irony at the type of education and rabbi at this seminar.

The final development of this trend can be seen clearly in an exegetical remark of the last rabbi of Brest-Litovsk, R. Isaac Ze'ev Soloveichik (1886–1960); "On a certain occasion a *Ḥasid* asked me, what is the reason that you *Mitnaggedim* always raise for yourselves dialectic problems? If it is written thus in the Torah, it is so, and what point is there in raising all those difficulties? If the truth be told there is a certain amount of justification in this accusation, but there are certain limits which are clarified in the *baraita* of R. Ishmael with regard to the principle of 'two passages which are contradictory but a third passage resolves the contradiction.' As long as we do not find this third resolving verse we are not permitted to raise the difficulty of the two contradictory verses ... but if we find such a third verse, then, on the contrary, we are commanded by the Torah to search and to examine the two verses and decide" *(Ḥiddushei Rabbenu Z. Soloveichik)*. Dialectics have with him become a formulation of a foregone conclusion. Though relating to the Bible it expresses the bent of his own mind.

A diametrically different trend is expressed by R. Meir Simḥah ha-Kohen (1843–1926). He stresses again and again rationality, humanity, living Jewish national unity and national reality in a way that makes him an ideologist of the living and creative tensions and dialectics of Lithuanian culture. The horizon is wide; the theory of R. Ḥayyim that "Torah is light and each individual commandment a candle" has come to mean for him that commandments and holy places are legitimately the expressions of emotions and national roots, important to Israel as to the gentiles. In Israel they are subservient to the philosophic religion, and their transitoriness is properly symbolized. To this way of thinking belongs the school of Rabbi Abraham Isaac Kook, which though mystic in

Typical marketplace of a Jewish *shtetl* in the Pale of Settlement as it remained until the Holocaust — in Pilviskis, in the Vilkaviskis district, Lithuania.

formulation (a return to the Vilna Gaon and R. Ḥayyim) and even more open to national and political values, accepts the modern as a call to be open and receptive: the beleaguered fortress mentality is explicitly — even more so implicitly — combated by it.

The most radical individualization and openness to modern challenge is found with a few ideologists like R. Aaron Samuel Tamares (1869–1931). He remolds the old line in an ultra-modern way: "For indeed, occupation with the Torah is a valuable source for the sustenance of the soul! How great is the spiritual wealth which it provides to our people: 1) in the sphere of national ethics; 2) in the sphere of our national pride; 3) in the sphere of our national consolation."("*Yad Aharon,* containing Torah novellae, by me, Aaron Samuel Tamares (Piotrkow, 1923), 'A treatise on the excellency of the Torah' as a substitute for a preface.") He came out as a radical pacifist during World War I and against Zionist policy after 1929, for sacrificing human life to wood and stone — the Western Wall.

As Hitler's hordes descended to destroy Lithuania and all of Jewish Europe, its culture was as variegated and dialectical in its mainstream as it had been at the end of the 16th century with its synthesizing rationalist spirit that crystallized through the Vilna Gaon and his disciples at the end of the 18th. *Yeshivot, maggidim,* widespread culture, autonomism, Mizrachi, *Bund,* and Yiddish are the products of its integration as well as of its dialectical tensions and processes of reintegration from the days of the Vilna Gaon to the dark night of 1939.

4

THE COUNCILS OF THE LANDS
A STUDY IN JEWISH AUTONOMY

The central institutions of Jewish self-government in Poland and Lithuania from the middle of the 16th century until 1764 were the Council of the Four Lands (וַעַד אַרְבַּע אֲרָצוֹת) or Council of the Lands (וַעַד הָאֲרָצוֹת), the controlling body for the Jewish provinces ("Lands") of Poland, while the Council of the Land of Lithuania (וַעַד מְדִינַת ליטא or וַעַד הַמְּדִינָה) was the similar organization for the Lithuanian grand duchy, which was associated with the Polish crown. The two bodies were similar in structure and function. They were not constituted in either case as perpetual organizations, but were theoretically to the end *ad hoc* assemblies representing the permanent administrative entities, the local communities associated in their respective provinces or "Lands." The councils represent the highest form of Jewish autonomy within a regional or national framework attained by European Jewry, both in terms of territorial extent or of duration.

Before the councils were established, the Polish government had made attempts to set up a centralized Jewish leadership. This official appointment was unpopular with the Jews. The beginnings of regional council leadership were seen in Great Poland in about 1519. The Council of the Lands of the Polish Crown originated from the rabbinical court at the fairs held in Lublin. It acquired the status of a central *bet din* because of its activity during the meetings of merchants and heads of the communities and because famous rabbis participated in its deliberations.

After 1533 documents refer to assemblies acting in the name of all the Jews of Lithuania. From the 1560s the tax administration of Lithuanian Jewry was centralized. In 1567 two delegates dealt with taxation matters "in the name of all Jewish communities in . . . the duchy of Lithuania." Ordinances originating before 1569 issued from "the elected from all Lithuania" acting on behalf "of all the communities of Lithuania whose authority is vested in us." They enjoined

Main Jewish communities in Poland and Lithuania under the jurisdiction of the autonomous Jewish organization of the Council of Four Lands and the Council of Lithuania.

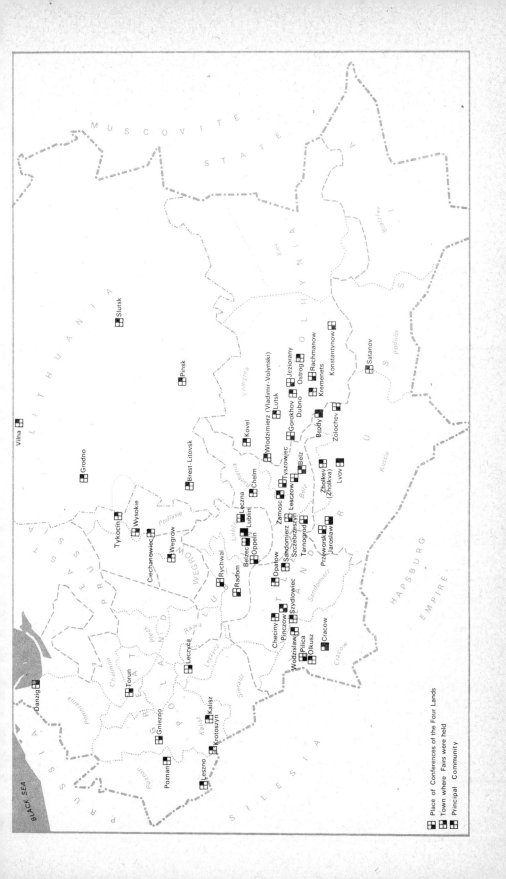

M U S C O V I T E

S T A T E

B l a c k   S e a

BLACK SEA

DANZIG

Danzig

Torun

Poznan

Gniezno

Krotoszyn

Kalisz

Leszno

Leczyca

Rychwal

Radom

Opatow

Checiny

Pinczow

Wodzislaw

Szydlowiec

Olkusz

Pilica

Cracow

Sandomierz

Szczebrzeszyn

Tarnogrod

Przeworsk

Jaroslaw

Lvov

Zholkev
(Zholkva)

Zolochev

Brody

Belz

Leszczow

Zamosc

Bełzec

Oppeln

Lublin

Leczna

Chelm

Tyszowiec

Gorokhov

Dubno

Lutsk

Ostrog

Jeziorany

Rachmanow

Kremenets

Konstantynow

Satanov

Wlodzimierz (Vladimir - Volynski)

Kovel

Brest-Litovsk

Pinsk

Slutsk

Vilna

Grodno

Wysokie

Tykocin

Ciechanowiec

Wegrow

Vila

L I T H U A N I A

P R U S S I A

P O L A N D

SILESIA

HAPSBURG EMPIRE

V O L H Y N I A

R E D   R U S S I A

Podolia

Russia

Pomerania

Chelmno

Rawa

Sieradz

Kalisz

Posen

Piock

Podlasie

Lublin

Chelm

Bug

Styr

Sandomierz

Brisk

Kiev

Bratslav

WEGROW

LUBLIN

Place of Conferences of the Four Lands
Town where Fairs were held
Principal Community

the holding of assemblies every three years and the election of "nine heads of the Lands and three rabbis."

Even at the zenith of the activities of the councils, the autonomy of the individual community, which had its own dependent boroughs *(sevivot),* was undiminished. The older, firmly established communities were known in Poland as *kehillot rashiyyot* ("principal communities"), and in Lithuania as *kehillot rashei bet din* ("communities of heads of the courts"), the only constituents of this council. Later, growing communities contended for the status of "principal community." Among those which succeeded after strenuous effort were Tiktin, in Poland, and Vilna and Slutsk in Lithuania.

The provincial council of the *galil* ("circuit") closely resembled the Polish regional Sejmik. The relationship of the provincial council to the Council of the Lands was paralleled by that of the Sejmik to the Sejm or national diet. The Council of the Lands of the Polish Crown comprised two distinct bodies: the assembly of the *rashei ha-medinot,* elders of the provinces, and the assembly of the *dayyanei ha-araẓot* ("the judges of the Lands" or "*bet din* of the Four Lands"), composed of the rabbis representing the principal communities and provinces. The *bet din* was competent to adjudge disputes among the constituents of the council, or between the council and its constituents. The two bodies frequently functioned in conjunction. These two sections of the council also cooperated frequently in Lithuania.

The constituents of the council were, first, the principal communities, acting either as a recognized part of the delegation for "their province" or as an independent delegation, and, second, the provinces. The accepted designation of "Council of the Four Lands" generally denoted its principal constitutents: the provinces of Great Poland (principal community: Poznań) and Little (Lesser) Poland (principal community: Cracow); "the Lvov Land"; and the province of Volhynia. Reference is occasionally made to Three Lands, Five Lands, or even more. In 1717 the council comprised 18 entities, nine communities which acted in their own name and nine provinces. "The Council of the Land of Lithuania" had in 1623 three "communities of the heads of the courts": Brest-Litovsk, Grodno, and Pinsk, each heading a wide area. However, even in Lithuania representatives of smaller communities were occasionally present at sessions of the council, with the right to petition on tax matters and other questions. In the regular sessions of the Council of the Lands between 20 and 30 delegates participated, in plenary sessions between 50 and 70. For the Lithuanian council a standing composition of 15 delegates was established in 1700 comprising the two heads and *av bet din* of each principal community (five at this date). The officials of the council included: (1) The "*parnas* of the House of Israel for the Four Lands," head of the council in both internal and external matters, who presided at the assemblies. He was elected from among the "heads of the Lands," not from the rabbinical delegates. (2) Second in the hierarchy was the "ne'eman" ("trustee") of the House of Israel for the Four Lands," i.e., the treasurer and chief secretary. The position was salaried and open to rabbinical candidates. (3) The *shtadlan,* who received a high salary and was obliged to be on hand at court or at the place of the assembly of the royal Sejm to represent Jewish interests before the government. (4) There was also a *kotev* ("clerk") to the council, later joined by other clerks. (5) The function of the *shammayim* or assessors, was also important. The leadership of the Council of the Land of Lithuania was for a long time assumed by the *av bet din* of Brest-Litovsk. The other offices were generally similar to those of the Council of the Lands.

Both councils maintained an official minute book, a *pinkas,* which invested the record of resolutions and budgets with legal authority. Of the original *pinkas* of the Council of the Lands only a few remnants are extant (published by I. Halpern, 1945). The first detailed ordinance recorded there dates from 1580. The *pinkas* of the Council of the Land of Lithuania from 1623 until its end in 1764 is extant (ed. S. Dubnow, 1925).

The Council of the Four Lands met twice yearly at the fairs of Lublin and Jaroslaw. During the 18th century the meetings were less regular. The venue and time of meeting of the Lithuanian council were determined as circumstances required. Between 1623 and 1764 the Lithuanian council held 37 meetings in different places; of these 15 were held in its first 30 years of existence.

The principal communities in the Council of the Lands elected their delegates under varying systems and at different intervals. The proportion of electors among the householders in the community varied with its size and the number of its dependent boroughs. The residents of the boroughs, comprising about one-quarter, or even one-third of Polish Jewry, did not have the right of election. It has been estimated that in the latter period of the council's existence approximately 1,000 householders in only 35 communities participated in the elections, i.e., about 1% of the total 92,000 adult Jewish householders. In Lithuania the percentage of electors toward the end of the council's existence for all its five principal communities was 11.3% of the total of adult householders; for Vilna — 7%; for Grodno — 10%; and for Pinsk — 20%. In relation to the total Jewish population of Lithuania the percentage of electors was only 0.7%.

In 1697 responsibility for implementation of the council's decisions rested with the "heads of the Lands, who, within their borders, will ensure that all ordinances shall be implemented." In 1666–67 the heads of the Cracow community ceased to attend meetings of the council. The council was forced to resort to persuasion and threats in order to bring them back. The Lithuanian council in 1628 decided that "all the ordinances from the beginning of the *pinkas* until its end are entrusted to the care of the heads of the Lands of each community." The means of enforcement and persuasion was excommunication *(herem),* which was decreed at the fairs, and by announcements in the synagogues (in Yiddish, with an admixture of Hebrew words). R. Joel Sirkes[1] sharply condemned imposition of the *herem* by the council and recommended a general prohibition on all such decrees to be replaced by a code of sanctions, including fines, expulsion, and handing over the accused to the non-Jewish authorities. He even suggested the establishment of a central supervisory administration under the council. The heads of the communities ignored his recommendations.

In 1596 the Council of the Lands constituted itself as the supreme court for hearing appeals and sentencing serious offenders. The Lithuanian council defined its jurisdiction and authority in 1626. Each congress would henceforward introduce ordinances on its own initiative without being bound by the proceedings of earlier congresses. Unanimous agreement to the introduction of new ordinances was demanded because of the federal nature of the council.

Relations between the Council of the Lands and the Council of the Land of Lithuania were occasionally strained. The Lithuanian council was dependent on the Council of the Lands for representation before the central government, while the Council of the Lands expected Lithuania to share in its "burdens," including gifts to magnates and the sovereign, which the heads of the Lithuanian communities often thought excessive. The two bodies also disagreed over the jurisdiction of the border communities and their boroughs, and over rights of commerce.

The competence of the council lay principally in relations with the Crown and central governmental institutions, in the representation of general Jewish interests, and in formulating legislation for the communities.

The government of Poland-Lithuania was aware of the existence of the councils as independent administrative bodies and accorded them tacit recognition. Formally, the councils were only bodies administering the collection of the Jewish tax from the generality of the Jewry of the kingdom. The councils conducted negotiations, often complicated, with the authorities on the amount of the taxation to be levied. A noteworthy achievement of the Polish council was that after 1717 the amount of taxes paid by the Jews was not increased despite depreciation of the currency. This was one of the main causes of the abolition of the council by the government.

The councils divided the total of taxes due into *sympla,* units of payment of

---

1   Talmudic scholar and rabbi in many **major** communities of Poland-Lithuania in the 17th century.

equal amount. It then directed a certain community or province to pay annually a certain number of *sympla.* The council based assessment and collection on tax lists and estimates. In principle, taxes were allocated according to the means of the individual. The difficulties of raising the taxes forced the councils to try different methods. The social tension entailed by tax collection increased as the debts incurred by the councils and individual communities accumulated. Especially large amounts were expended on maintaining the Jewish representation before the government, defraying the cost of bribes, and physical protection necessitating swift and unobtrusive action. Such demands gradually swallowed the greater part of the budget at the councils' disposal. They were forced to raise loans at high interest rates to meet their obligations.

At the same time the communities themselves developed a new system of taxation, the *korobka,* or basket tax. This was first a commodity tax, mainly levied on ritual slaughter and afterward extended to business transactions. In 1700 the Lithuanian council was forced to take over the basket tax. In the 18th century growing insolvency compelled the council to increase its demands while, on the other hand, the communities showed increasing independence. In 1721 it became known that a number of communities and provinces in Lithuania had united "to reject the assessment of the poll tax" which the previous council had imposed. The council issued a *herem* against them. In fact, the dissidents had gone so far as to complain to the Lithuanian fiscal tribunal about the "oppressive practices" employed by the council in levying taxes. The principal communities tended to shift the burden from themselves onto the shoulders of the smaller communities and new settlements. The revolt of the latter against the council's "acts of oppression" and the aspersion on the fairness of its apportionment expressed the accumulated bitterness of opposition to the councils. The individual community became more determined to retain the revenues under its jurisdiction. The administration of tax collection may be seen as the criterion of the councils' ability to fulfill their functions.

The councils considered themselves empowered to direct the manifold social, ethical, and legal aspects of Jewish life, and to frame ordinances regulating the affairs of the communities and the conduct of its leaders. They regarded themselves as the guardians of Jewish autonomy. The councils seldom attempted to meddle in affairs between the community and its members; they tended to uphold the authority of the leaders of the communities and the federal character of the council organization. In Lithuania the principal communities sometimes intervened between the individual member and his community. A plaintiff first had to lodge a deposit. The councils arbitrated in disputes between communities or Lands. The majority of such cases were laid before the rabbinic judges *(dayyanim)* of the "Land."

The oligarchic character of the community leadership was reflected in the councils, especially in that of Lithuania. In 1628 the Lithuanian council instructed its three constituents to ensure that "no communal adminstrative board shall . . . divulge the deliberations and confidences of the board; and shall refrain from involving individual members of the community with matters concerning the board; and shall impose severe punishment in such cases." Heads of the communities were warned against attempting to rally their own factions in opposition to their colleagues.

The council supported the leaders of the community in countering attempts at rebellion or the organization of internal opposition against the community boards. In 1623 they reaffirmed the former *herem* prohibiting such actions. Severe measures were to be taken against those suspected of these attempts. Any independent organization was prohibited: a plaintiff was instructed to appear before the community board "alone, or with one other, but not more."

The councils were vehement in their censures of the "common people," the "rabble in the streets and markets" who "make light of the acts of the town optimates." It was "the duty of the leaders of every community to deter these offenders with the severest sentences, reaching even to the gates of death." This was in reaction to the continual opposition which arose because the great majority of householders in the large towns, and all Jewish residents of the boroughs, were deprived of any influence or share in the leadership. The council repeatedly issued ordinances to enforce more severe sentences for "sedition" and "scorn." Concomitantly, the problem reflected the revolt of the ascendant against the old-established communities, and in the course of time it reflected the attitude of communities where lower social classes had attained leadership. In 1650 the ordinance against intrigues was extended to "communities, settlements, and boroughs" intriguing against the principal Lithuanian communities, members of the council. In 1687 "sedition" among the communities was also denounced. Opposition to the councils intensified and became more broadly based toward the end of their existence. Artisans apparently formed a major opposition group as in 1761 the Council of Lithuania felt constrained to forbid expressly their participation in the main activities and institutions of the more important communities.

The councils undertook to provide guidance in the economic sphere, in particular on occupational problems originating in the 16th and 17th centuries from the leasing and management of farm estates and related branches. Consequently their legislative activity extended to both the socioeconomic aspects and the related socioreligious problems. In regard to the first, the council instituted the *hezkat orenda* (חֶזְקַת אוֹרֶנְדָא), its sanction of preemptive leaseholding; the Jewish lessee of a farm property or related enterprise from a

Polish noble for a term of three years was henceforward upheld in possession against Jewish competitors for the lease, which might even devolve on his heirs. Similarly, it became possible to acquire preemption on houses rented from non-Jews and to establish a right after three years' undisturbed possession of market shops. As long as economic and social factors encouraged Jewish development, and the councils retained their influence, such regulations generally worked efficiently and prevented Jews from undercutting one another in dealings with the Polish nobility.

The councils also tried to ensure that Jewish religious precepts were strictly observed on rented properties — that Jews observed the Sabbath, refrained from employing Christian serfs on the Sabbath, from raising pigs, or gelding animals. The councils forbade isolated families to settle in the villages. In 1607, in an endeavor to reconcile economic realities with Jewish religious precepts, the council designated the rabbinical authorities to evolve a detailed code of ordinances regulating the permissibility of charging interest.

On one socioeconomic question the two councils adopted divergent approaches. The Council of the Lands prohibited Jewish contracting of customs duties, salt mining, and the like, since the Polish nobility themselves coveted such revenues and in pressing their own claims Jewish merchants could harm the whole community. This prohibition, however, was never obeyed to the letter, even within the limits of the Lands Council's jurisdiction, while the province of Great Poland evidently felt otherwise. The Lithuanian council several times expressed its opinion that the Jewish community would benefit if the customs revenues were in Jewish hands; the council promised its support to a group of Jewish contractors and accepted money from them. Nevertheless, the Lithuanian council agreed that it could be dangerous to contract for the mint and related operations.

Both councils applied strict safeguards to Jewish credit operations to inspire faith in Jewish business integrity. Special forms of credit instruments *(mamranot)* were authorized for the use of Jewish merchants. Numerous regulations dealt with the problems of absconding bankrupts, minors, or irresponsible persons who frivolously embarked on trade or contracted debts.

The Lithuanian council issued numerous ordinances against newcomers to protect the rights of community residence and membership *(ḥezkat yishuv)*, domicile in the towns *(ḥezkat ironut)*, and business operations within the communities. A similar trend is also discernible in ordinances introduced by the Council of the Lands. The foundations of Jewish solidarity became seriously undermined in the wake of the Chmielnicki massacres (1648), when fugitives were deprived of rights in their places of asylum.

The councils maintained an effectual system of representation before the government and self-defense to prevent the withholding of Jewish rights or to seek their renewal. They also tried to ensure that the murderer or assailant of a Jew should be brought to trial; similarly, they defrayed the cost for defense against anti-Jewish libels. On the other hand, the Lithuanian council warned, "Whosoever out of the violence of his heart shall go to provoke or assault a non-Jew . . . shall not be helped by a single penny, even if as a result he should be executed." The councils actively rebutted blood libels and charges of desecration of the Host. Toward the end of their existence, they sent a representative to Rome to obtain papal declarations against the blood libel and undertook their publication.

Study had a prominent place in the councils' concerns. They attended to the supply of teachers and the fundamentals of Torah education. Similarly, by giving their approval to the publication of books, the rabbis participating in the council could exercise control over publications intended for the Jewish public. Great care was devoted to the *yeshivot.* In 1652 the Lithuanian council ruled that "every congregation having a rabbi shall maintain a *yeshivah* for adults and youths according to their capacity, as formerly laid down: all existent agreements with the rabbi to diminish the numbers of the *yeshivah* shall be null and void." This instruction was endorsed in later assemblies. Scholars were exempted from paying tax. Yet the attitude toward scholars fluctuated, pointing to a certain tension; there were also changes in the definition of "scholar."

Social problems dealt with by the councils included assisting poor girls to marry and regulating matchmaking. Communities were directed to care for the fugitives driven from the west in the Thirty Years' War, and from the east of Poland-Lithuania after the 1648 Chmielnicki massacres. A nascent class-consciousness broke through sometimes in the ordinances relating to charitable matters: the poor bride was to be provided for – after doing service in a Jewish home. Jews were instructed to preserve modesty in dress and feasting so as to prevent dangerous excess of show. The councils arranged for the collection and dispatch of "money for Erez Israel," and notables who went there were given assistance.

The authority of the councils was also recognized to some extent in Jewish communities outside Poland and Lithuania. The councils were consulted in the Eybeschuetz-Emden controversy, while the old established community of Frankfort sought the advice of the Council of the Four Lands.

The councils' assemblies were brought to an end by a resolution of the Polish Sejm in 1764, which established a different system for collecting the Jewish poll tax. The resolution concluded: "Whereas comprehensive Jewish poll tax, established by statute in 1717, is abrogated . . . henceforward there shall be no assemblies, apportionments or other kinds of injunctions, levies or compulsions relating to the Jews as customary hitherto . . . from Jan. 2, 1765 . . we abolish them in perpetuity." The councils did not convene again. A committee authorized by the Sejm met in Warsaw for two years to wind up the commitments of the Council of the Four Lands. A similar committee was appointed for the Lithuanian council. The provincial councils continued to convene *ad hoc,* but no longer functioned regularly.

The Jews of Poland and Lithuania saw the councils as an expression and symbol of social majesty and political power. After the Chmielnicki massacres the chronicler Nathan Nata Hannover depicted them as "the pillar of justice in the Land of Poland, as in the days before the destruction of the Temple in Jerusalem"; "the *parnasim* of the Four Lands were like the Sanhedrin of the Chamber of Hewn Stone and they had authority to dispense justice to all Israel in the kingdom of Poland, to safeguard the law, to frame ordinances, and to inflict punishment as they saw fit." Idealization though it was, this still reflected the Jewish attitude. When the councils were terminated in 1764, a burning shame was felt that their "captains, the heads of the Lands, have been dispossessed of their mite of greatness, and even this small honor has been taken from Israel." In later generations the councils served as a paradigmatic ideal, and were invested with exemplary qualities, especially by the advocates of Jewish Autonomism, Simon Dubnow and his followers, at the end of the 19th and in the 20th centuries. Exponents of this ideology represented the councils as the pilot institution for national organizations of central Jewish autonomy in the Diaspora.

5

THE MOTIVE FORCE
OF MESSIANISM

The pattern on which Jewish messianic movements were based crystallized in the late Second Temple period, and furnished Jews in following generations with certain basic elements. These, when confronted by certain typical challenges, culminated in messianic movements of varying scope. The term "messianic movement" in Jewish history applies to a movement centered around or expressing the yearning for a king or leader of the house of David and for a new ideal political existence for the Jewish people that would serve as a reassertion of independence and cause their return to Erez Israel, as well as acting as a model and focus for a united and better mankind. Experiencing the miracle of Jewish redemption, mankind would attain an ideal world where true faith and real harmony would prevail. Jewish prayers for redemption, while seeking the advent of the king and the kingdom, also ask "may they all blend into one brotherhood to do Thy will with a perfect heart," and express the hope that with this change of heart, "Thou shalt reign over all whom Thou hast made, Thou alone" (in evening service for *Rosh Ha-Shanah*). This formulates the abiding hope of the Jew while in the *galut*. The basis of the movements is intense longing for the messianic era. Up to the 18th century it was both an article of faith and an emotional necessity among Jews to hope constantly for the immediate advent of the Messiah. Yet this persistent element did not of itself necessarily lead to the emergence of such movements. Jewish messianic history includes periods and religious trends in which people experienced intense and wholehearted hopes for the Messiah while being lukewarm toward active messianic movements. Thus the Karaites throughout the Middle Ages had a deep-seated feeling of being in exile; Karaite settlers in Jerusalem in the tenth century called themselves *Avelei Zion* ("Mourners for Zion"), organizing their life and patterning their thought on the basis of this attachment to Zion. Yet only one Karaite messianic movement is known for certain. The Rabbanite *Ḥasidei Ashkenaz* longed for the Messiah, yet only rarely is any active striving for a Messiah mentioned in their relatively extensive writings. Indeed, some of the expressions they use appear to satirize computations of the date of the coming of the Messiah (J. Wistinetzki (ed.), *Sefer Ḥasidim* (1924), 461, no. 1706). They even warned their readers: "If you see that a man has prophesied the advent of the Messiah, know that he is engaged either in sorcery or in dealings with devils; or that he uses the power of the Divine Name ... One has to say to such a man: 'Do not talk in this manner' ..., eventually he will be the laughingstock of the whole world ... they teach him calculations and secrets to bring shame on him and on those who believe him" (*ibid.*, 76–77, no. 212).

This attitude displayed by mystics and ascetics in opposing activist messianism finds even sharper expression in the views of the 13th-century talmudic scholar and mystic, Naḥmanides. In his disputations with the representatives of Christianity, Naḥmanides told the Spanish king at Barcelona in 1263:

"Our Law and Truth and Justice are not dependent upon a Messiah. Indeed, you yourself are more important to me than a Messiah. You are a king and he is a king. You are a gentile sovereign and he is a king of Israel. The Messiah is but a king of flesh and blood like yourself. When I serve my Creator under your jurisdiction, in exile, torment, and subjection, exposed constantly to universal contempt, I merit great reward; for I offer of my own flesh a sacrifice to God, and my reward in afterlife will be so much the greater" (*Kitvei Rabbenu Moshe ben Naḥman* ed. by H.D. Chavel, I (1963), 310).

The basic consideration put forward here is that the greatness of the individual suffering under a foreign rule can be as rewarding as redemption. In a work addressed to Jews Naḥmanides wrote:

"Even if we thought that it is the will and purpose of God to afflict us with political enslavement on this earth [forever], this would in no way weaken our adherence to the precepts of the Torah, for the sole rewards which we anticipate are those of the world to come – the beatitude of the soul which, having escaped hell's torments, enjoys the bliss of paradise."

He continues that he believes in the Messiah and redemption because it is true and because it gives him comfort to face the adversities suffered by the Jewish people; but this is not a necessary or sustaining element of his Jewish faith (*Sefer ha-Ge'ullah*, pt. 2; *ibid.*, 279–80).

The extreme wing of modern Orthodoxy in Judaism and most of the adherents of Neo-Orthodoxy – in particular Agudat Israel[1] in the period before

---

1   Political party, founded in 1912, seeking to preserve Orthodoxy by adherence to *halakhah* as the principle governing Jewish life and society.

the Holocaust and, later, Neturei Karta[2] — continued, under changed and secularized conditions, old attitudes of messianism which were halfhearted toward a messianic movement. Messianic-prompted efforts have been made toward an ingathering of the Jews without an express connection with either Erez Israel or political independence.[3] Jacob Frank[4] in the 18th century had a savage desire for armed Jewish power and a Jewish settlement on the land — but all this was to be achieved on the soil of Poland. Thus, the modern movement of territorialists[5] can claim some ancient though rare precedents in traditional Jewish messianic trends.

Within this ideological framework and set of attitudes, the emergence of an active messianic movement required a challenge that would break through the tranquility of the regular messianic hope to turn it into fervent and directed effort. and create a revolutionary constellation. There were elements in Jewish historical consciousness encouraging such active responses to various and widely differing challenges. One element basic to Jewish messianism is anticipation of the "birth pangs of the Messiah" *(hevlei Mashi'ah)* — the time of troubles and turbulence that precedes his coming. Hence, periods in which terrible massacres of Jews occurred (e.g. during the Crusades or the Chmielnicki massacres) have also been periods of fervent messianic expectations and movements. Jewish historical conception — and for that matter Christian also — interpreted Daniel's apocalyptic vision of the four evil beasts (7:2ff.) as denoting four successive evil empires. The fourth will be succeeded by the everlasting dominion of "one like unto a son of man." He will be given "dominion and glory and a kingdom that all the peoples, nations, and languages should serve Him." This conception enabled Jews to view great historical and political transformations — the fall and rise of empires and kingdoms, or revolutions and counterrevolutions — as the death throes of the fourth and last beast-kingdom and the harbingers of the messianic eternal kingdom.

The person to lead the messianic movement — the Messiah himself — was viewed from two different angles. Jews — in particular since the parting of the ways with Christianity — saw the Messiah as a man and not God; in the first place, as a national king. But here the agreement ends. Some, like Maimonides in

---

2   Ultrareligious extremists mainly in Jerusalem who, regarding the establishment of a secular state in Erez Israel as a sin, do no recognize the State of Israel.
3   See Anan b. David, *Sefer ha-Mitzvot,* ed. by A. Harkavy (1903), 6–7.
4   Pseudo-messiah and founder of the Frankist sect in the 18th century which comprised the last stage in the development of the Shabbatean Movement.
5   Movement which aimed to establish an autonomous settlement of Jews in a sufficiently large territory "in which the predominant majority of the population shall be Jewish," not necessarily Erez Israel.

the 12th century, stressed that the Messiah will himself die even though his life will be a long one. He will first be tested as the successful warrior-king of Israel and proved its lawful ruler by devotion to Torah. Mankind will follow this new exemplary Jewish state. Nature will not change its laws, though society will become perfect (*Yad Ḥazakah, Hilkhot Melakhim* (1962), 417). Along with this rationalistic conception of the Messiah, there is also a miraculous one, in which the person of the Messiah sometimes attains semi-divine heights. The 17th-century pseudo-Messiah, Shabbetai Ẓevi, concluded a letter:

"I will have to give full reward to all those who believe truly, men, women, and children — from the Lord of Peace and from me, Israel your Father, the bridegroom coming out from under the marriage canopy, the husband of the dear and virtuous Torah, this beautiful and virtuous matron, the man set on high, the Messiah of God, the lion of the upper regions and the deer of the high regions, Shabbetai Ẓevi" (his letter to Venice, in: J. Sasportas, *Ẓiẓat Novel Ẓevi,* ed. by I. Tishby (1954), 129).

The rationalistic attitude sometimes reached the extreme of conceiving a Messiah-like political leader. The 14th-century rationalist, Joseph b. Abba Mari ibn Kaspi, theorizes about

"the imminent actual possibility of our coming out from this *galut,* becoming free to rule ourselves, without a Lord. Thus, while being confined as slaves in Egypt. God took us out from there with a high hand. Now why should not this be even easier for Him in these days? Is there no longer any material available with which this Creator may create a man like Moses, or even of smaller stature, who shall come before the kings and they will give in to him, as Pharaoh gave in the end, though in the beginning Pharaoh hardened his heart to him" (*Tam ha-Kesef,* ed. by Last (1913), 44ff., sermon 8).

The miraculous conception of the Messiah evolved a complex of superhuman traits, anticipated actions, and achievements; the Messiah is to take the crown from the head of the alien sovereign by his virtue of appearance alone and redeem and avenge the Jews by miraculous means.

According to the rationalistic image of the Messiah, he should be "a very eminent prophet, more illustrious than all the prophets after Moses" (Maimonides, *Iggeret Teiman,* ed. A. S. Halkin (1952), 87). In Maimonides' view prophecy necessitated the highest intellectuality. These criteria were not accepted by most of the messianic movements, whose leadership was largely charismatic. It is related of a pseudo-Messiah who appeared around the end of the seventh century, Abu 'Isā (Isaac b. Jacob al-Isfanī), that, "the most wonderful thing about him in the opinion of his followers is the fact that although he was, as they say, an illiterate tailor and could neither read nor write, he produced books and pamphlets without having been instruced by anyone" (Jacob al-Kirkisanī's account of the Jewish sects, ed. by L. Nemoy, in: HUCA, 7 (1930), 328). Not many of the messianic claimants had such humble intellectual beginnings, but practically none of them was regarded by his contemporaries as preeminent among scholars of his day, though some were known as considerable scholars. The most widespread of the messianic movements, that of Shabbetai Zevi, had for its leader a man of less than 40 years old, while its great prophet, Nathan of Gaza, was 21 when he announced the Messiah and died at the age of 36. It is hardly surprising that men of rationalistic bent rarely saw the embodiment of their ideal in the actual messianic claimants who arose, whereas those inclined to follow a Messiah seldom found a man to rouse them in the Maimonidean ideal. This generally created a situation in which the supporters and opponents of the movement were driven into two opposing camps.

The messianic movements envisioned the coming of the Messiah as an historic breakthrough, a new lease of divine grace, and, according to some theories, as a basic change in the cosmos and divine relationships. Hence a phenomenon accompanying many messianic movements was some proposed change in the way of life of Jews. This ranged from the extreme innovations introduced by the New Testament of early Christianity, through minor variations in the law introduced by early medieval messianic movements, up to the orgiastic tendencies and activities of the Shabbatean movement and even more of the Frankists.

Some consider the events surrounding Zerubbabel of the house of David and his mysterious disappearance (c. 519/518 B.C.E.) as the first messianic movement. The charismatic leadership of the first Hasmoneans and the devotion they inspired is by rights part of the messianic movement cycle, but for the open question of the claims of this house as opposed to the claims of the house of David. The political and moral ferment created with the rise of Herod and his house, and even more so with the advent of undisguised Roman rule in Judea, led to the emergence of many messianic leaders and influenced new concepts concerning their aims and leadership. Jesus of Nazareth was one of many Jews who in this turbulent period claimed to be bringing redemption to the people and who were eventually crucified for announcing their message. Judah the Galilean told Jews about ten years before the birth of Jesus that it was shameful for them to be "consenting to pay tribute to the Romans and tolerating mortal masters after having God for their Lord" (Josephus, *The Jewish Wars*, 2:118). In the

view of the hostile Josephus, Judah and "the Pharisee Saddok" were the founders of the Zealots and had "a passion for liberty that is almost unconquerable since
they are convinced that God alone is their leader and master" (Josephus,
Antiquities of the Jews, 1823). With these men there began a heroic and tragic
line of shortlived kings, martyred leaders, and brave fighters for freedom.
Combating both the Romans and the Herodians, they developed the concept of
inaugurating the reign of the "kingdom of Heaven" for God's elected people
here and now. There were many such leaders; it is almost certain that not all of
them are mentioned in the extant sources. It is difficult to be certain about their
ideas and types of leadership, for the accounts of their activities are subject to
distortion either by uncritical admirers or by tendentious enemies. In the case of
some of them, including Jesus, miraculous elements enter the conduct of their
leadership. Of Theudas[6] it is related that he influenced "the majority of the
masses to take up their possessions and to follow him to the Jordan River."
He stated that he was a prophet and that at his command the river would be
parted and would provide them an easy passage (Josephus, *Antiquities*, 20:97ff.;
see also *Acts of the Apostles* 5:35–39). For this, he and many of his
followers paid with their lives, about 45 C.E. Also mentioned is a Jew from
Egypt "who had gained for himself the reputation of a prophet"; followed by
"about thirty thousand" Jews, he went to "the Mount of Olives. From there he
proposed to force an entrance into Jerusalem" and to free it from the Romans.
Many of his followers were killed in battle (Josephus, *Wars*, 2:261ff.). How he
was regarded by the Romans appears clearly from the fact that the Christian
apostle Paul was mistaken for him (*Acts* 21:37–38). It is almost certain that
Menahem b. Judah [7] was considered a Messiah by the Zealots, as possibly was
Simeon Bar Giora.[8]

The unflinching heroism displayed by the warriors in the great revolt against
the Romans (66–70/73 C.E.) is comprehensible only in the context of a
messianic movement. Some consider that the reason why the Jews did not
despair when their messianic leaders had fallen in battle was because of their
belief in the Messiah in the person of the son of Joseph, who is destined to fight
and die before the coming of the Messiah in the person of the son of David. Even
Josephus — who tried to conceal the messianic motives of the great revolt —
once had to reveal that "what more than all else incited them to the war was an
ambiguous oracle, likewise found in the sacred Scriptures, to the effect that at

6   His Greek name shows the degree of religious feeling awakening even in circles that
     were influenced by Hellenism.
7   Patriot leader at the outset of the Roman War (66–70 C.E.).
8   Jewish military leader in the Roman War.

that time one from their country would become ruler of the world" (*Wars,* 6:312; cf. Tacitus, *Historiae,* 5:13, and Suetonius, *Lives of the Caesars,* Vespasian, 4). The Dead Sea Scrolls also point to messianic hopes and suffering as activating factors in the life and thoughts of this sect, though lacking the Davidic element.

As the great revolt, the precedent of many types of messianic leadership and activity, lay crushed, many new concepts of messianic challenge and response entered the Jewish mind and imagination as the legacy of this period. One trend of Jewish messianism which left the national fold was destined "to conquer the conquerors" – by the gradual Christianization of the masses throughout the Roman Empire. Through Christianity, Jewish messianism became an institution and an article of faith of many nations. Within the Jewish fold, the memory of glorious resistance, of the fight for freedom, of martyred messiahs, prophets, and miracle workers remained to nourish future messianic movements.

Jewish messianic revolt against the Roman Empire did not cease with the severe defeat of 70 C.E. The Jewish revolt against Emperor Trajan in 115–17, which spread like wildfire through Egypt, Cyrenaica, and Libya, had a messianic king-figure at its head. Simeon Bar Kokhba was at first only one of several messianic figures, though he became the dominating one in the uprising of 132–35 C.E. It is related that the great *tanna*, Akiva, "when he saw [him] would say: 'This is the king Messiah'." It was only after the death of this semi-legendary figure that the messianic movements had to aim at redeeming the Jews and carrying them back to both homeland and kingdom. Symptomatic of this change is the story about the Jew who appeared in 448, approximately, in Crete and "said that he is Moses and promised the many Jews on this island to bring them through the sea without ships to Judea." He fixed a certain date for this miracle, and ordered them to jump into the sea; several of them drowned (Socrates Scholasticus, *Historia Ecclesiae,* 12:33).

The challenge of the appearance of the victorious Arabs and the Muslim caliphate on the world scene gave rise to a new upsurge of Jewish messianic movements. They again assumed a warlike temper, while utilizing social tensions within the Jewish community and some of the military tactics used among Muslims to attain their aims. About 645 there is mention of a Jew who "asserted that the Messiah had come. He gathered around him weavers, carpet makers, and launderers, some 400 men. They burned down three [Christian] sanctuaries and killed the chief of that locality." The leader of these craftsmen was crucified, after his followers and their families had been massacred (Nestorian Chronicle, as quoted in S.W. Baron's *Social and Economic History of the Jews,* 5 (1957), 184). Similar movements relying on miracles are recorded in Muslim Spain and its vicinity in the eighth to ninth centuries.

Much more significant was the movement led by the above-mentioned Abu 'Isā. His teachings include many significant halakhic variations. According to the Karaite sources, he followed the Rabbanite rite and laws in many matters for tactical reasons so that the Rabbanites did not persecute his followers. Abu 'Isā acknowledged the prophecy of Jesus and Muhammad, regarding them as prophets for their own followers only. This practical motivation and tendency to temporize was belied by the direction his movments took: Abu 'Isā led a battle and fell in the fighting, though some of his followers later believed "that he was not killed, but entered a hole in a mountain and was never heard of [again]" (Kirkisānī, ed. by L. Nemoy, in: *Hebrew Union College Annual,* 7 (1930), 328, 382–3). Those who followed him in the Islamic lands in the eighth to ninth centuries, like Yudghan and Mushka, resembled him in inaugurating changes in aspects of religion and in their warlike spirit.

With the Crusades, certain new features in messianism appeared. In the Balkans a general movement of repentance was induced by crusader violence. At Salonika, in 1096, Jews and Christians reported "that Elijah . . . had revealed himself openly, and not in a dream, to certain men of standing." People saw "many signs and miracles." There was widespread excited anticipation. It was reported that, under the impression that the redemption was at hand, "the Jews were idly neglecting their work." They sent letters to Constantinople to appraise them of the good news. Other communities sent to inquire about it. There was also a rumor "that all the Byzantine congregations were together in Salonika, and would leave from there" for Ereẓ Israel (J. Starr, *The Jews in the Byzantine Empire 641–1204* (1939), 203–6 no. 153). This was apparently a messianic movement without a Messiah. Jews were united by general feelings of excitation, rumors, and indeterminate tidings.

Maimonides heard that a miracle-working Messiah had appeared – at Lyons in France or Leon in Spain – about 1060. He also heard a tradition that in approximately 1100 a man had been influenced by a dream to proclaim himself Messiah. The man, Ibn Aryeh, was flogged and excommunicated by the community leaders, and with this the affair ended. In the first half of the 12th century messianic ferment was strong in Jewish communities everywhere. About 1121, Obadiah, the Norman proselyte, met a Karaite *kohen,* Solomon, who prophesied that within two-and-a-half months all the Jews would be gathered together in Jerusalem, "for I am the man whom Israel is waiting for." The proselyte was amazed that a man of Aaronide descent should claim messiahship: "It is 19 years since I entered the Covenant and I never heard that Israel is looking for redemption at the hands of a son of the tribe of Levi – only at the hands of the prophet Elijah and the King Messiah of the seed of King David" (J. Mann, in: *Ha-Tekufah,* 24 (1928), 336–7). This encounter in the Near East reveals how deep-rooted, even in the case of a proselyte, was the concept that the Messiah should be of Davidic descent, whereas in sectarian circles the ancient sectarian concept of an Aaronide Messiah (as shown in the Dead Sea Scrolls) still persisted.

More or less about the same time, in 1120/21, there was messianic excitation in Baghdad centered around a young prophetess (see S.D. Goitein, in: *Jewish Quarterly Review*, 43 (1952/53), 57–76). In 1127 approximately the same occurred in Fez, Morocco, where the man, Moses Al-Dar'i, a great scholar – and admired by Maimonides even after he proclaimed his messiahship – announced the coming of the Messiah.

"He told them that the Messiah was about to appear on the first night of Passover. He advised them to sell all their property and to become indebted as much as possible to the Muslims, to buy from them a thing worth a dinar for ten dinars, and thus to fulfill the words of the Torah [Exodus 12:36], for after Passover they would never see them. As Passover came and went and nothing happened, these people perished for they had sold all their property and their debts overwhelmed them" (*Iggeret Teiman*, 103).

Nevertheless, Maimonides expressed satisfaction that this Moses managed to escape to Erez Israel:

"There he died, may his memory be blessed. As had been told to me by those who have seen him when he left, he prophesied all that happened later on to the Maghreb Jews, the main outlines as well as the details" (*ibid.*, 103).

The story is not only remarkable in demonstrating the influence wielded by the Messiah on large groups of Jews, and their obedience to his instructions, but also instructive since this movement occurred soon after the visit to Fez of Muhammad ibn Tumar, the founder of the Almohads, and the public discussions he held there with the leaders of the Muslim establishment. Maimonides' attitude to Moses. his blessing him after his death, and his statement that his prophecies were true, reveal that even such a consistent rationalist could be inconsistent with regard to messianic movements.

The first half of the 12th century also saw the remarkable messianic movement led by David Alroy. Though the dates and personalities are very confused in the sources mentioning this event, they all indicate that it occurred in the first half of the 12th century, and in the remote eastern districts of the Muslim Empire. Most traditions indicate his great and widespread influence and an extensive campaign of written and oral propaganda. All of them agree about the military character of the movement. The apostate to Islam, Samuel al-Maghribi, relates that Alroy attempted to take the fortress of Amadiyah, in the mountains Azerbaijan, by the stratagem of having masses of his believers enter the fortress with hidden weapons (tactics resembling those used by the earlier Muslim founder of the Assassins, Ḥasan ibn al-Sabbah, with regard to the fortress of Alamut). The apostate adds:

"When the report about him reached Baghdad two Jewish tricksters, cunning elders, decided to forge letters by Menahem to the Jews of Baghdad bringing them the good tidings which they had been expecting since of yore; that he would appoint for them a certain night in which all of them would fly to Jerusalem. The Jews of Baghdad, their claim to sagacity and pride in craftiness notwithstanding, were all led to believe it. Their women brought their moneys and jewels in order that it all might be distributed on their behalf, as charity to those whom the two elders considered deserving. In this manner the Jews spend the bulk of their wealth. They donned green garments and on the night gathered on the roofs expecting, he asserted, to fly to Jerusalem on the wings of angels. Women began to weep over their nursing infants; what if the mothers should fly before their children or the children before their mothers? The children might suffer because of the delay in feeding" (*Ifḥām al-Yahūd: Silencing the Jews*, ed. and trans. by M. Perlmann (1964), 73).

Despite its obvious intention to ridicule, this tale cannot be dismissed out of hand, for this readiness among Jews to believe in miracles is also found in Maimonides' story about the movement in North Africa.

About 1172 a Messiah appeared in the Yemen. Maimonides' hostile reaction to him shows that he had a clear and proclaimed revolutionary social aim, incomprehensible to Maimonides:

"He told them that each man shall distribute all his money and give to the poor. All those who obey him are fools and he is a sinner; for he acts against the Torah. For according to our Torah a man should give as charity only part of his money and not all of it . . . No doubt his heart and mind that have misled him to say that he is a Messiah have also brought him to tell the people to leave all their property and give it to the poor. Thus they will become poor and the poor rich, and according to his law they [the former poor] will have to return to them [the now impoverished rich] their money. In this fashion money will go back and forth between rich and poor unceasingly" (*Iggeret Teiman*, 89).

Maimonides advised the communities to proclaim him a madman or put him to death (*ibid.,* 93, 95). Later on, in a letter to the scholar of Marseilles, Maimonides related further details about the movement and its end. By this time he knew that the man in the Yemen was only

> "saying that he is a messenger to smooth the path for the King Messiah. He told them that the Messiah [is] in the Yemen. Many people gathered [around him] Jews and Arabs and he was wandering in the mountains . . . He gave them new prayers . . . After a year he was caught and all who were with him fled. Asked by his Arab captor for proof of the divine source of his message, the Yemen Messiah answered him: 'Cut off my head and I will come back to life immediately,' and so he was killed. Maimonides heard that there were still many foolish people in the Yemen who believed that he would arise and lead them yet" (A. Marx, in: *Hebrew Union College Annual,* 3 (1926), 356).

In the 1240s a new source of messianic excitation accompanied the rumors and hopes centering around the news of the Mongol advance into European countries. Meshullam Da Piera in a poem was certain that

> "in our days the kingdom shall be renewed for the lost nation and the scattered communities. Tribute will be brought to the son of David, and gifts to my counts and dukes. My Temple will be rebuilt . . . There are tribes that have been exiled and now they have left the land of the living. Proof that God has sent them is that many rulers have come to harm . . . Babylonia, Aleppo, and Damascus were taken [by the Mongols in 1260] . . . My Savior has broken through the mountainous wall."

To about the same time should be ascribed the information that "women in the land of Canaan [i.e., Bohemia] were reciting the entire Book of Isaiah by heart and ignorant people knew by heart all the prophecies of consolation" (J. Wistinetzki (ed.), *Sefer Ḥasidim* (1924), 77 no. 212).

At the end of the 13th century the Spanish kabbalist Abraham b. Samuel Abulafia saw himself as the Messiah or the harbinger of the Messiah and tried to spread the word through apocalyptic writings. The Spanish rabbinical authority Solomon b. Abraham Adret had to oppose the "prophet of Avila" who prophesied the coming of the Messiah in 1295 and had a large following in Avila. There is some information that there was an upsurge of messianic excitation around 1350. The catastrophe of the persecutions of 1391 in Christian Spain led to widespread messianic ferment. In the vicinity of Burgos there appeared a prophet who foretold the imminent coming of the Messiah. At the Disputation of Tortosa in 1613–14 the Christian protagonist claimed that "in our day R. Ḥasdai Crescas has announced a report and preached to congregations in the synagogues that the Messiah had been born in Cisneros, in the kingdom of Castile." Crescas entertained, it would seem, even more earthly hopes. He imagined the realities of the Second Temple period "as if the king of Egypt, who now reigns over the land of Israel, were to grant permission to Jews living elsewhere in his empire to go and rebuild the sanctuary, on the condition that they submit to his rule" (in his *Or Adonai*). In a letter of that time from which all proper names have been carefully deleted, it is related that a certain teacher taught that the calamities of the period should be seen as the birth pangs of the Messiah; there was a proliferation of confused messianic tidings:

> "This one writes about the Lord's Messiah, that he shall surely come by Passover time, and that one says: 'Behold, he stands already at our walls . . . ' Another declares that if the Feast of Tabernacles should arrive and there is yet no Messiah, then surely it is God's will to have us die and to harden our hearts from his fear. But before he has done talking, yet another comes and says: 'It is rumored that a prophet has arisen in Israel who has seen a vision of the Almighty . . . The Lord revealed himself in a dream at night and assured him of great amelioration: misery and grief shall flee the years wherein we have seen evil shall be no more; lo, this presages good, this proclaims salvation' " Y. Baer (*History of the Jews in Christian Spain,* 2 (1966), 158–62).

As the position of the Jews in Christian Spain steadily deteriorated, messianic hopes were kept alive. The fall of Constantinople in 1453 awakened great messianic hopes and speculations both in the communities of Spain and among Ashkenazi Jewry. Among the forced converts *(anusim)* men and women prophesied the coming of the Messiah. Letters from the Constantinople community related tales about the birth of the Messiah, the place of his activity, and mode of living. A mother and daughter told their Converso friends: "The gentiles do not see us [do not understand us], for they are blind and know not that the Lord our God hath decreed that for a time we should be subject to them, but that we shall now surpass them [have the upper hand], for God hath promised us that after we go to those lands [overseas], we shall ride on horses and pass them by" (*ibid.,* 292–5). Even on the eve of the expulsion of the Jews from Spain, both Jews and *anusim* actively harbored these hopes. About 1481 a Converso told a Jew, when at his request the latter read the messianic prophecies to him: "Have no fear! Until the appearance of the Messiah, whom all of us wait for, you must disperse in the mountains. And I — I swear it by my life — when I hear that you are banished to separate quarters or endure some other hardship, I rejoice; for as soon as the measure of your torments and oppression is full, the Messiah, whom we all await, will speedily appear. Happy the man who will see him!" One Marrano was certain that the Messiah would possess the philosopher's stone and be able to turn iron into silver. He also hoped that "in 1489 there will be only one religion" in the world. Even after the expulsion many Marranos expressed these hopes and were punished for them by the Inquisition (*ibid.*, 350ff.).

In the 16th century there were numerous expressions of messianic expectation. In 1500–02 Asher Lemlein (Lammlin) preached repentance and the imminent coming of the Messiah. He had great influence. The grandfather of the 16th-century chronicler David Gans "broke up the oven that he had for baking unleavened bread, being sure that next year he would be baking it in the Holy Land" *(Zemah David)*. From the end of the 15th century tales originating in and letters from Jerusalem show messianic hopes centering around the Ten Lost Tribes of Israel. Joseph Ḥayyun[9] commenting on the verse "In his days Judah shall be redeemed and Israel will live secure" (Jer. 23:6) wrote:

"He [Jeremiah] said that Judah shall be redeemed and not that Israel shall be redeemed, for Israel need no redemption for they are not in *Galut*. I mean the Ten Tribes, for they are a great people and they have kings — according to what has been told about them — but Judah needs redemption, whereas [the people of] Israel will then live secure in Ereẓ Israel, for now they are not living so secure as they are abroad. What is more, they fight continuously with the gentiles around them" (his commentary to Jeremiah, British Museum, Add. Ms. v 27, 560, fol. 106).

The great Mishnah commentator Obadiah of Bertinoro wrote in 1489 from Jerusalem to his brother in Italy:

"Jews have told us that it is well known, as related by reliable Muslim merchants, that far away, a journey of 50 days through the desert, there lies the famous Sambatyon River[10]; it surrounds the whole country where the Children of Israel live like a thread. It throws up stones and sand, resting only on the Sabbath. The reason why no Jew goes to this country is because they avoid desecrating the Sabbath. According to their tradition

9   Last rabbi of Lisbon before the expulsion.
10   A legendary river across which part of the ten tribes were exiled.

all of them — the descendants of Moses — are saintly and pure like angels; there are no sinners among them. On the outer side of the Sambatyon River there are Children of Israel as numerous as the sands of the seashore, kings and lords, but they are not as saintly and pure as those living on the inner side of the river" (A. Yaari, *Iggerot Ereẓ Yisrael* (1943), 140).

Obadiah believed in the existence of a Jewish realm beyond and around the miraculous river which was not only independent and strong but also consisted of two circles of life — an inner, more holy one, and an open, less holy one. Messianic expectations in this period centered actively around these images and fantasies as shown, for example, in the writings of Abraham b. Eliezer ha-Levi from Jerusalem.

With the advent of David Reuveni[11] and Solomon Molcho[12] many Jews were convinced that they were seeing and hearing a prince of those tribes and one of his devoted companions. About the same time many Jews pinned their hopes on Martin Luther as a man who had come to pave the way for the Messiah through gradually educating the Christians away from their idolatrous customs and beliefs. In Safed, messianic hopes were strong in the circles around the mystics Isaac b. Solomon Ashkenazi Luria and Ḥayyim b. Joseph Vital. The latter once dreamed:

"I stood on the peak of the great mountain to the west of Safed ... over the Meron village; I heard a voice announcing and saying, 'The Messiah is coming and the Messiah stands before me.' He blew the horn and thousands and tens of thousands from Israel were gathering to him. He said to us, 'Come with me and you shall see the avenging of the destruction of the Temple.' We went there; he fought there and defeated all the Christians there. He entered the Temple and slew also those who were in it. He commanded all the Jews and told them, 'Brethren, cleanse yourselves and our Temple of the defilement of the blood of the corpses of these uncircumcised ones and of the defilement of the idolatry that was in it.' We cleansed the Temple and reconstructed it as it was, the daily burnt offering was brought by the arch-priest who looked exactly like my neighbor Rabbi Israel" (his *Sefer ha-Ḥezyonot* (1954), pt. 2, no. 2, p. 41).

This blend of the Safed reality and messianic visions of war and glory expresses the intensity of messianic hopes in kabbalistic circles that found expres-

---

11   Adventurer who aroused messianic hopes in the first half of the 16th century.
12   16th-century Marrano kabbalist and pseudo-messiah.

sion in Shabbetai Zevi in the 17th century. Most communities became involved with Shabbetai Zevi and the messianic movement he led in the 1660s. In it many aspects of the messianic movements reached their highest expression, to be faced by crisis: his followers fervently believed that the Messiah would achieve a miraculous victory and were cruelly disappointed when Shabbetai Zevi collapsed before the terror of punishment; the masses of his followers repented, but repentance proved of no avail. The movement stimulated Jews to feelings of liberation, but they remained subjugated; orgiastic aspects developed which discredited the movement. The movement led by Jacob Frank in the 18th century introduced the elements of nihilism, licentiousness, and severance of the connection between messianism and Erez Israel.

Scholars are divided as to whether in its origins Hasidism bore traits of a messianic movement or whether it was on the contrary a kind of sublimation of messianism.

In modern times the *Haskalah* and Reform wings of Judaism increasingly tended to regard their activity in spreading pure and rational monotheism as a kind of collective movement of messianic "mission." In his letters Leopold Zunz referred many times to the European revolution of 1848 as "the Messiah." Even many Jews who left the faith tended to invest secular liberation movements with a messianic glow. Martin Buber expressed the opinion that the widespread Jewish activity in modern revolutionary movements stemmed both from the involvement of the Jew with the state and his criticism of it through his messianic legacy.

Zionism and the creation of the State of Israel are to a large extent secularized phenomena of the messianic movements. The ideology of the Zionist religious parties, Mizrachi and Ha-Po'el ha-Mizrachi, tends to regard them – in particular the achievements of the State of Israel – as an *athalta di-ge'ulla* ("anticipation and beginning of redemption"), thus retaining the traditional concepts held by messianic movements in conjunction with the new secularized aspects of the State and its achievements.

Jewish messianism, though appearing in many shapes and permutations, has been and continues to be an activist element in world culture. For Jews it has retained, through the leaders and movements to which it has given rise, the life-force of charisma, and the binding spell of Jewish statehood and kingship to be realized immediately through God's will, through the passion and devotion of His people. Some have spoken of "the price" that Jews and Judaism have had to pay for disappointment and disenchantment after every failure of the messianic movements. Against these are to be set the benefits that these visionary movements gave to a suppressed people – in inspiring them to activity, revitalization, and a sense of sacrifice.

6

KIDDUSH HA-SHEM
TO DIE FOR THE GLORY
OF GOD AND HIS PEOPLE

Kiddush ha-Shem means literally "the sanctification of God's name" and is generally applied to martyrdom. This concept has always been implicit in the Judaic faith and view of life. Its first explicit expression occurred during the confrontation of Judaism with Hellenism, the first pagan culture with "missionary" and synthesizing tendencies. The Book of Daniel tells about the three "Jewish men" — Shadrach, Meshach, and Abed-Nego — who disobeyed a royal command to worship an idol and endangered their lives. Under Antiochus Epiphanes Hellenization employed violent and coercive methods in regard to Jews. After the victorious revolt of the Hasmoneans, a Jew in the Hellenistic Diaspora recorded the martyrdom of an old man, little children, and their mother who had died for their faith:

"Eleazar, one of the principal scribes, ... of a noble countenance, was compelled to eat swine's flesh ... Now those in charge of that forbidden sacrificial feast took the man aside, for the sake of old acquaintance, and privately urged him to bring some flesh of his own providing, such as he was lawfully allowed to use, and to pretend he was really eating of the sacrifice which the king had ordered, so that in this way he might escape death and be kindly treated for the sake of their old friendship. But he with a high resolve, worthy of his years and of the dignity of his descent ... and, still more, of the holy laws divinely ordained, spoke his mind accordingly: ... 'It ill becomes our years to dissemble,' said he, 'and thus lead many younger persons to imagine that Eleazar in his ninetieth year has gone over to a heathenish religion ... for the mere sake of enjoying this brief and momentary life ... Even were I for the moment to evade the punishment of men, I should not escape the hands of the Almighty in life or in death ... I will ... leave behind me a noble example to the young how to die willingly and nobly on behalf of our reverend and holy laws.' With these words he stepped forward at once to the instrument of torture, while those who a moment before had been friendly turned against him, deeming his language to be that of a sheer madman

... Under the strokes of torture, he groaned out: 'The Lord who has holy knowledge understandeth that, although I might have been freed from death, I endure cruel pains in my body from scourging and suffer this gladly in my soul, because I fear Him' "(II Maccabees 6:18–30; Charles, *Apocrypha*, 140).

The basic ideals motivating *kiddush ha-Shem* are thus set out at this early stage: personal nobility and courage, a categorical refusal to employ any form of dissimulation or live an undercover existence, and readiness to undergo bodily and spiritual torture in the full knowledge that this behavior may appear sheer madness to those who inflict it. Hannah, "the mother of the Maccabees" according to Christian tradition, exhorts her seven sons in a similar way not to be afraid of either hangmen or death. These figures became the prototypes for and symbols of martyrdom and martyrs in both Judaism and Christianity. The Fourth Book of Maccabees is almost entirely a philosophical sermon on the meaning and glory of *kiddush ha-Shem* in Hellenistic times.

Whereas in the Christian and Muslim interpretation the Jewish *kiddush ha-Shem* became an act of mainly individual martyrdom, the lot of saints chosen by God for their individual path of suffering — and (in Christianity) their participation in the mystery of Crucifixion, the martyred saints following Christ on the cross — in Judaism *kiddush ha-Shem* remained a task set for each and every Jew to fulfill if the appropriate moment came. It found logical expression in the readiness to die as a son of the Chosen People. In the war against Rome of 66–70/73, whole communities committed suicide as a culmination of their fight against alien power. Thus, in the many trials of revolt and war in which Jews were tested, from the wars of liberation of the Maccabees up to the failure of the revolts against the Romans both in Erez Israel and the Diaspora, *kiddush ha-Shem* acted as a motivating force giving meaning to the struggle of the Jewish warriors, strength of endurance under cruel torture by victors, and offering suicide as a way out of submission and slavery. The famous mass suicide at Masada was inspired more by the conception of *kiddush ha-Shem* as a commandment, and a proud refusal to submit to the Roman enemy, than by the philosophical argumentations that Josephus, an arch enemy of the self-sacrificing Zealots, put in the mouths of the defenders of Masada.

As if referring to an everyday, ordinary incident, one of the *tannaim* describes "those who dwell in the land of Israel and risk their lives for the sake of the commandments: 'Why are you being led out to be decapitated?' 'Because I circumcised my son to be an Israelite.' 'Why are you being led out to be burned?' 'Because I read the Torah.' 'Why are you being led out to be crucified?' 'Because I ate the unleavened bread.' 'Why are you getting a hundred lashes?'

'Because I performed the ceremony of the *lulav*.' These wounds caused me to be beloved of my Father in heaven" (*Mekhilta, Ba-Hodesh,* 6). They knew that this behavior appeared strange to the gentiles who asked the Jews: What is the nature of your God that "you are so ready to die for Him, and so ready to let yourselves be killed for Him ... you are handsome, you are mighty, come and intermingle with us" (*Mekhilta, Shirata,* 3). Samaritans also chose the Jewish path of *kiddush ha-Shem* in the course of their revolts and sufferings for the Torah and its truth as they conceived it.

The ideology of *kiddush ha-Shem* and devotion to it as crystallized in antiquity continued and strengthened in the Middle Ages. Christian persecution and the humiliation meted out to Jews intensified the underlying wish to safeguard individuality, and fortified the ethic of *kiddush ha-Shem* in the struggle to preserve their national identity and freedom to profess their faith. For Jews living in the lands of their enemies *kiddush ha-Shem* became the only convincing way of asserting when faced with Christian missionary coercion that if they were not to be permitted to live openly as Jews they chose not to live at all. Surrounded by feudal warriors and the feudal mode of fighting, torn from their country and appearing as aliens everywhere, for Jews suicide as *kiddush ha-Shem* was in many cases the only way in which they could exemplify and give expression to human courage. When confronted by brute force, Jews tried to defend themselves wherever and however they could; however, since they often failed, as was inevitable in the case of a small minority, readiness to die was the only way of maintaining a lofty exemplar for Jewish existence. Where Christian knights ruled through their warrior techniques and conformed to their specific knightly scale of values, Jews, influenced involuntarily by this spirit, could hold their own — both in point of physical survival and more importantly from the spiritual and psychological aspect — only through ultimate readiness to face the supreme sacrifice.

In the 11th century the conception of holy war became predominant in Western Christian thought. Popular religious feeling in the West became more fanatical and was often connected with social unrest. Even before the beginning of the crusades, cases of suicide to avoid forced conversion to Christianity are recorded. The suicide of Jews in the tenth century in southern Italy for the sake of their faith is described by contemporaries as "pure total burnt offering." In the spring of 1096 many of the participants in the First Crusade conceived that their armed pilgrimage to free the sepulcher of Jesus logically demanded either the extinction of the Jewish religion in Christian countries or the annihilation of those Jews who would not accept Christianity. In the atmosphere of holy war many Jews believed that the glory of the Lord and the honor of their Law would be debased if they did not bear witness for them by open and public proclamation of their abiding truth in a chivalrous manner. Thus, through the curious workings of historic irony the Christian crusading venture and Jewish martyrdom by *kiddush ha-Shem* each became in its own particular way expressions of a holy war waged for the glory of God.

During the crusading onslaught on them in 1096 the communities of the Rhine district sacrificed themselves for their faith in this spirit. Those who remained alive related the sacrifices of the martyrs in the same spirit. Thousands of Jews lost their lives in the course of those terrible months; a few of the victims fell in direct battle, and the majority perished through suicides of whole families. In the chronicles of the massacres of the First Crusade and the threnodies composed on the martyrs the ideology of *kiddush ha-Shem* is reformulated. A mother in Mainz is related as having said that she killed her children as sacrifices to God to fulfill His commandment to be "whole with him" (A.M. Habermann (ed.), *Sefer Gezerot Ashkenaz ve-Zarefat* (1945), 34), thus tacitly framing a condemnation of forced converts leading a halfhearted underground existence as *anusim*. The writings about these acts employ the ancient symbols of aggadic literature – the binding of Isaac *(Akedah)*, Abraham's bosom, and the divine light which will be vouchsafed to the martyrs – and stress the open challenge offered to the crusaders by the Jews who proclaimed the superiority of their faith over Christianity. The silence of the sources sometimes bears eloquent testimony to the conception of *kiddush ha-Shem* as the Jewish way of waging the holy war: the pillage and robbery, loss of property and homes that accompanied the attacks are only hinted at, while the motives of the crusaders are formulated in a way that conveys their Christian religious determinants only (see *ibid.*, pp. 24, 26, 27, 72, 93, 94). Wherever possible, in these attacks Jews tried to fight off their assailants at the gates and at the entrances to houses (*ibid.*, pp. 30–31a, 33, 97, 99–100), but when their endeavors at defense failed they killed themselves and took special care to slay their children first to prevent them from being carried off and brought up as Christians. Such sources describe these events for future generations not as acts committed out of desperation but from the feeling that these Jews had chosen to die in this way so that the remnant of the nation should be able to continue its existence with pride. The community of Xanten is remembered for having added to their last communal benediction after food, just before the mass suicide, the following prayer: "The merciful One will avenge in the days of those who will remain after us, before their eyes the blood shed by your servants and the blood that is to be shed" (*ibid.*, p. 49).

After the wholesale burning of Jews at the stake in Blois in 1171 a Jewish sage signing his name "Obadiah" summed up something like a set of rules for Jewish behavior under enemy sovereignty, speaking as if from the mouths of the martyred: "For the saints have proclaimed . . . if the rulers decree . . . as to taxation . . . it is permissible . . . to plead to ease the burden . . . but . . . when they take it into their evil hearts . . . to blandish, to terrorize, to make them impure [through apostasy] . . . the chosen ones shall answer . . . we shall pay no heed to your lies . . . we shall remain true [to the Jewish faith] " (see S. Spiegel, in: *Sefer ha-Yovel . . . Mordekhai Menaḥem Kaplan* (1953), 286). This same steadfastness continued to fortify Jews throughout the tribulations, libels, and massacres to which they were subjected in these centuries. When the Nordhausen community was led to be burned on the pyre during the Black Death massacres in 1349 they obtained permission to hire musicians, and went singing and dancing to their deaths. Medieval Jewish prayer books include, in addition to the benedictions for bread and drink, a benediction to be recited by a Jew before killing himself and his children. Special memorial lists were compiled to preserve the memory of those who had sacrificed themselves for *kiddush ha-Shem*. As the victims of the blood libel, Host desecration libel, and other calumnies were subjected to continuous torture intended to extort "confessions," endurance under excruciating pain or suicide to avoid making a false confession came to be considered a true manifestation of *kiddush ha-Shem*.

Among the Jews of Christian Spain *kiddush ha-Shem* was recognized both as a phenomenon distinguishing Ashkenazi Jewry and a problem to be reckoned with in their own existence, as the writings of Judah Halevi and Naḥmanides show for the 12th and 13th centuries. From the end of the 14th century *kiddush ha-Shem* became part of the fate and sufferings of Spanish Jewry, whether upheld through massacres, persecutions, or libels as Jews openly professing their faith, or under the fire and torture of the Inquisition chambers and tribunals as *anusim*. Abraham b. Eliezer ha-Levi applied the ancient Maccabean tradition and theory of *kiddush ha-Shem* to the victim of the torture chambers and at the auto-da-fé:

"Whoever firmly resolves to devote himself to the honor of His name . . . such a man, being exposed to cruel tortures and sorely tormented, as was the case with the holy martyrs in the Land, those marvelous young men, the sons of saintly Hannah, in the days when the priests could come near the Presence of God; they were the heroes who fought God's battles — if such a man will but concentrate and put between his eyes the 'awe-inspiring and great Name,' resolve to undergo martyrdom, and his eyes will incline toward the Holy One of Israel . . . then he may be sure that he will withstand the test . . . nor feel any pain, blows or torments . . . And these things are worthy to be made known to His people Israel for the generation is one of religious persecution, and no Israelite

שֵׁת לְשָׁאֵיָה גְרַע וְכִלָּה בְּשַׂר נ...

תּוּשִׁיָה גְבִירוֹת שְׁתַּיִם בְּיוֹם גָלָה

גָלַל כֵּן בְּשָׂרֵיהֶם נָתְלוּ גוֹרִים וְאַבְיוֹנִים

בְּמִגְדָל הַפִּלָּה ..... רִימוֹי לְטַנָּה

בְּזִבְחֵיהֶם אֶלְעָזָר דִּתוֹ שָׁבִיר וְעֻזַּי נָאֳ...

רְהוּבֵז דָּבְרִי וְאָבְזָה רִיכֵב רַאֲבַתִי :

עַל נִמְסַר דְּחוּשׁ אֲדִירוֹשׁ קָרְשֵׁד דּוֹב

כִּבּוֹ הָאָבְיַצְטַוְ וְאַנְטְשִׁיר דִּילָה מֵן ה

תִּשְׁעִים שָׁנָה אָבִי דְּהוֹל אֱלֹהֵי בְּמִרְיָה

תַּבְלִיכֵי דְמִיד בַּלֵּה וְצַהֲוַת מִלְהָחֵב

הַלָּזֶה יָאֱחַז יָצֵרְק דִּיכוֹ הַבְּהָרִי

יוֹסֵיהָ אוֹמֵץ בְּרַכִּי הַיָּשִׁישׁ בְּשׂוֹרִי נְהָרַג

בְּעֶרְכּוֹ הַעַל אֵלֶּה לֹא הַפְּסוֹר הַיַּצְפִּיר וּ...

וְהַשָּׂעִיר בַּחֶרְדַּר לִיקוּי הַרְאַשְׁתַּרְהַגָל

וְהַזָּקֵן יַהֲקֹר־קֹר הַבֵּט וּזְכוֹר אֶת בֵּל קָתְלָא

הַדִּישׁ צַחָעֵרַת יָצְלִיחָה וְנָה אֵלָה הָעוֹלָם

תָּמֹצֶה בְּרַבַּת הַלָּאָה ..... וְאָבִיָה עוֹד בִּיקְרָה שׁ

שָׁנָה וַתִּקַחֵם אַהֲרֹן הַבְּמַעֲנִי הָיְשָׁה וְכֹלֵב בְּאֵשׁ בֵּן

כְּשַׁוְא נְגַעָה וַגֵיל לֹא אָחֵלִי מִזְבֵּחוֹ

וַיִדְבְּקוּ בְּעוֹשֵׂה הַבֵּל בִּכְבֹדוֹ וְשָׁכַב .

גְּבַל בְּאַבְזַרְיָה דְּוְרוּ וּבְיְהוּרַם

נְדַשְׁתְּ כְּאוּר רִיפָתוֹ וְיַטְשָׁה

should go in ignorance of this principle . . . And it may well be that it was to such a saintly person, who, albeit his soul is given over completely to God and rejoices in His love, is yet buried together with the wicked and consumed by fire, the wise Solomon alluded when he said [Song of Songs 8:5], 'Who is that coming up from the wilderness, leaning upon her beloved?' For the promise of the Lord proves true: she [the soul] leans and falls, limb by limb and piece by piece; but of such a saintly soul the righteous who dwell in the innermost mansion of the King, where joy resides, expound· Who is that coming up from the terrestrial world, which is like unto a wilderness? . . . Out of love for her beloved her body falls part by part; because of the trials she undergoes, her flesh pierced by tongs or cut to pieces by the sword; and the King, to Whom all peace belongs, for Whose love she suffers so, looks down from His abode and proclaims as she ascends to Him: 'Behold thou are upright and pure, today have I begotten thee' [Psalms 2:7] and 'under the apple tree I awaken thee [Song of Songs 8:5]' " (as quoted in Y. Baer, *History of the Jews in Christian Spain,* 2 (1966), 430–1).

In this early 16th-century summation the wheel has turned full circle: the motives which inspired individuals to choose the path of *kiddush ha-Shem* at the time of the clash with Hellenism merge with the sufferings of the tortured body of the individual Jew in his pain and fire-wracked isolation looking from his physical breakdown to his meeting with the loving God in heaven.

In early modern times the general trends of enlightenment and abatement of medieval religious pressures were accompanied by growing secularization in Jewish life and thought, leanings toward assimilation, and the striving for emancipation, all factors which both separately and in combination conduced to disintegration in Jewish society and abandonment of specifically Jewish values.

Part of a section of a manuscript containing *piyyutim* relating to Hanukkah, based on II Maccabees, showing the martyrdom of the Jews during the reign of Antiochus IV Epiphanes. Right: the aged scribe Eleazar scorning the advice to save his life by pretending to eat the forbidden sacrificial meat (6:18ff.); center left: the killing of Eleazar; bottom left: the seven sons of Hannah being burned to death (7). The picture at top left, showing the mothers being hanged by their breasts and the babies being thrown from a high tower, is a misreading by the artist of a passage in the *piyyut* which describes babies hanging from their mothers' breasts (i.e., being suckled). The underlying intention of these illustrations was to present ancient martyrdom as a model for actual sacrifice during the Middle Ages. From the *Hamburg Miscellany,* c. 1427.

Thus, while the necessity to uphold *kiddush ha-Shem* diminished in fact, the concept also lost actuality and significance.

With the awakening of Jewish national feeling in later modern times, as expressed by the formation of political parties like the *Bund,* the organization of self-defense against pogroms, and Zionism, the principle of *kiddush ha-Shem* reasserted its influence, consciously or sub-consciously, manifested in new ideological frames for the defense of Jewish dignity and in modes of response by Jews to social and spiritual challenge. Jewish revolutionary attitudes bear its imprint in the courage and readiness to struggle and self-sacrifice for the sake of humanity even when there is no immediate prospect of victory on the horizon. In the same way, the fight and death of the rebels in the Nazi ghettos was ultimately inspired by this ancient Jewish tradition.

Kiddush ha-Shem is an original contribution by the Jewish faith and culture to the whole monotheistic world. Through it was expressed for the first time in human history the readiness of simple people to die for their faith and opinions. It is an ultimate prop of individual expression when all other physical supports have been withdrawn.

Kiddush ha-Shem has played a central and formative role in Jewish history both through the reality of the sacrifices made to uphold it as well as through the spiritual images and attitudes by which it has been activated. It is a powerful and valid expression of human courage and readiness for supreme sacrifice. In large measure due to the principle of *kiddush ha-Shem* Jews have escaped spiritual degradation throughout the long *galut* ("Diaspora"), thus failing to justify the hopes and views of their enemies and detractors. Through it courage and the spirit to resist have been continuously kept alive in Jewish hearts and transmitted to posterity from the days of Daniel to the present. Individual exemplary behavior and collective enthusiasm have sustained it in changing situations and forms.

The valor and heroism shown in defense of the State of Israel in the 20th century can be seen as the direct inheritance of chivalrous courage which Jews from generation to generation have transmitted in upholding the principle of *kiddush ha-Shem.*

7

ḤASIDEI ASHKENAZ
AN ELITE MOVEMENT AND IDEOLOGY
OF THE MIDDLE AGES

The term *Ḥasidei Ashkenaz* means "the pious men of Ashkenaz." The movement denoted was given this name long after its main force had been spent, by people for whom the word Ashkenaz, as a concept in the vocabulary of Jewish cultural geography, connoted Germany and France. Thus from the 15th century, the *Ḥasidei Ashkenaz* were part of the glorified past of the Jews but not an element of their life experience.

When these pious men were active and creative, in the 12th and 13th centuries, they called themselves "the good" *(tovim),* "the just and righteous" *(zaddikim),* and "the pious" *(Ḥasidim);* in their exemplary tales, the man who guides and teaches is called the *ḥakham* — the sage. They saw themselves as both of the people and above them, the latter by choice and by virtue of their spiritual qualities. The first centers of the movement were Regensburg in southern Germany, and the communities of Speyer, Worms, and Mainz on the Rhine. They were led from the outset by a narrow and venerated inner circle of several teachers, who were largely members of a single family. Thus the movement had the character of a self-conscious elite group. The leading family, Kalonymos, originated from southern Italy, and mystic and magic traditions of that region contributed to their theory and practice.

Although part of the ḥasidic literature is still in manuscript, enough has been published to show the form of their literary creativity and the main trends of their thought. A considerable part of their writings is composed of exempla, tales carrying a moral. This is the structure of the greatest part of the *Sefer Ḥasidim* — the Book of the *Ḥasidim* — traditionally attributed to Judah he-Ḥasid (c. 1150—1217), but in fact a collective work of the earliest and most active generations of the movement, embodying considerable elements of Judah's teachings. Also extant are more or less systematic exegetical, mystic, and legal-moralistic treatises, the most important being those of Eleazar of Worms (c. 1165—c. 1230).

The *Ḥasidei Ashkenaz* were much concerned with the purity of monotheism, and opposed any contamination by corporeality or hint of plurality. In this they were influenced by popularizations of the teachings of the tenth-century Jewish

leader and philosopher, Saadiah Gaon, and they stressed his concept of Divine Glory — the *Kavod* — to which they ascribed all expressions of the Bible and Talmud that seemed to imply corporeality.

In writings which from the point of view of their form followed the traditional structure of the Jewish Law — as, e.g., the *Rokeah* of R. Eleazar of Worms — the *Ḥasid* touched on all aspects of the law, though with his own emphasis. Where he used his own structure, the exemplum or short, pithy, exegesis, he was often innovative, even revolutionary to a degree, not only in what was said, but also in what was left unsaid. The thousands of tales about the *hasidim* cover certain aspects of life, law, and morals, and pass in silence over others; thus it is possible to "map out" the areas of intensity and concern of the *Ḥasidei Ashkenaz.*

Their religious climate was suffused with the passionate desire for a love of God that would elevate their relation to Him. This love was achieved through thought and will, but it was also a gift of Grace. "If [one] prays and suddenly there has descended into his heart the joy and love of God, let him know that God desires to receive his prayer ... One should pray thus: May it be Thy Will, that this love will be forever implanted and attached in my heart and the hearts of my progeny ... Day and night, even when not praying, while one's heart is joyful and one's soul is glad with God, one should not talk to anyone until it [this feeling of joy and love] passes from his heart" (*Sefer Ḥasidim*, ed. Wistinetzki (1924), par. 425, p. 126). We have here the elements of their conception of the desired attitude to God; it may be a gift that is prayed for; it may come suddenly; it will leave with time, one has to struggle for it perpetually; it may come and go at any time. While it is in one's heart, spiritual joy is granted. Their sincerity in introspection is evident here too, and is a constant element in all their teaching.

The followers of *Ḥasidut Ashkenaz* regarded themselves as bearers of a religious consciousness deeper than that generally prevailing and subject to religious duties severer than the accepted ones. The maximum was asked of the person able and willing to take upon himself the "restrictions of *Ḥasidut* (piety)" while a lesser standard sufficed for those who had not entered its circle. From the *tovim* (the "good"), the *Ḥasidim* (the "pious"), and the *zaddikim* (the "righteous"), a maximum of emotional fervor and utmost purification of soul and thought were demanded, together with exact attention to the details of both major and minor precepts. The other members of the community at large were divided into the *ra'im* ("evil ones") and the despotic ones — whom the *Ḥasidim*

Nature and men merging in the acceptance of revealed Torah. Vision of *Ḥasidei Ashkenaz* in the *Regensburg Pentateuch,* 1300, fol. 154v.

fought against — and the *peshutim* ("simple ones") — whom the *Hasidim* guided inasmuch as they were capable of observing and feeling. In its relations with the community and its institutions, the *Hasidut Ashkenaz* therefore fluctuated between two contrasting attitudes: between the desire for leadership and service, and the tendency among its members to seclude themselves in order to live their exalted individual lives.

The array of symbols of *Hasidei Ashkenaz* is based to a considerable extent on faith in the strength of the Holy Names and the mystic power of the letters of the Holy Language (Hebrew) and their combinations; these are the channels of man's communication with the celestial worlds, through study and prayer: "every blessing and prayer . . . everything . . . according to its measure and its weight, its letters and its words; if it were not so, then our prayers would, God forbid, be comparable to the song of the uncircumcised nations." Love of the Creator played a dominant role in the doctrine of the *Hasidei Ashkenaz* and among the duties of the *Hasid;* this love must saturate all his senses and resources; its strength must lead him toward joy so that no void remained in his instincts through which sin or the thought of it might penetrate. In the writings of the *Hasidim* the fervor of their emotional love and joy is expressed in symbols and parables drawn from the experiences and emotions of sexual relationships.

"Prayer is called a service like the service on the altar; when the Temple existed, the angels rose heavenward in the flame of the sacrifices . . . and today . . . they rise in the prayer which issues from the heart; for prayer is like a ladder. If there is no devotion behind the words of any blessing, the ladder stops there." The perfection of the "ladder" is so conceived that "the pronunciation of every word must be prolonged, so that there is devotion in a man's heart for every word that issues from his mouth" (*Sefer Hasidim,* no. 11). Inner devotion is achieved through external methods: the letters should be counted. Melodies should be appropriate: "For supplications and demands, a melody which causes the heart to weep; for words of praise, a melody which causes the heart to rejoice." However, he who is not a *Hasid* may be content with general devotion; simple men and women may be exempted from reciting the prayers in Hebrew, and in certain cases even exempted from saying them in their established form, as long as they devote their hearts to their Father in Heaven.

The supreme manifestation of love for God is *kiddush ha-Shem* ("the sanctification of the Holy Name," i.e., martyrdom; see chapter 6), a glory for which the *Hasid* yearns. In this act, he wages the war of the people of God against Christian heresy and serves the Creator by sacrificing his body. The *Hasidim* were among "the first of the martyrs" during periods of persecution. Their courage, their service of the *Kavod* and the Lord, and their self-sacrifice became an example for others.

Jewish faith and Western European iconography combine to render a view of heavenly bliss. Detail from the *Birds' Head Haggadah,* S. Germany, c. 1300. fol. 33v.

In hasidic doctrine concerning the world and man, there are numerous occult elements. The Jew lives in a world and in a community in which, to a certain extent, the dead continue their association with the living; demons and spirits also encompass man from all sides and Judah he-Hasid even used to say, that "the demons believe in the Torah and do everything commanded by the [Talmudic] sages" (as quoted by the 13th-century Isaac b. Moses, in his *Or Zar'ua,* Laws of Eruvin, no. 147). Sorcery is a concrete factor and a common occurrence in people's lives, and the teachings of the *hasidim* contain many instructions and rules of conduct which serve as a protection against these powers. In these conceptions can be discerned the imprint of Christian superstitions current in their surroundings.

The *hasidim* make no reference to two inclinations in man – toward the "good" and the "evil" – and it appears that man is regarded as having only "one inclination"; the way in which this is used determines whether a deed is good or evil. The *hasidim* therefore taught that the instincts, desires, and longings of the heart were to be turned toward the good side. According to them, mortification of the body was a method of repentance. They taught "commensurate repentance," that is, the acceptance, measure for measure, of affliction and degradation in return for the pleasure and the reward gained from sin; in some details these ideas show the influence of the notions and practices of repentance current among Christian monks. Mortification, however, had a merit of its own: the sufferings of the righteous vindicate the masses: "the Messiah bears the sins" of the nation and it is incumbent upon the *Hasidim* to adhere to this principle. In this approach there is undoubted evidence of Christian influence.

In relations between man and man, they demanded of themselves a mode of behavior according to "the law of Heaven," the application of absolute justice in the fullest sense of its spiritual significance and content; the "law of the Torah" was sufficient only for the man who was not a *Hasid*. There were some *Hasidim* who decided: "When two people come before the rabbi for him to dispense justice, if these two are of a quarrelsome disposition, the rabbi will apply the law of the Torah, even though a contrary decision would be reached according to the law of Heaven; if, however, these two are good and God-fearing men and heedful of the words of the rabbi, he must apply the law of Heaven, even if the law of the Torah requires the opposite." A practical example of this was their willingness to admit the testimony of "honest women." In their statements of the "two laws" lie occasional criticisms of the *halakhah* because of their demand for perfection of the soul. Some said that the punishments detailed in the Torah "corresponded to man's conception of what is unlawful" – that is, in respect of social codes of behavior, but "do not correspond to instinctive awareness" – that is, they do not accord with the standard by which the *Hasid* assesses sin, which gives due consideration to temptations and the difficulty of overcoming them.

From the words of the *Hasidim* there emerges a kind of cynical indifference toward those who mock them; to bear insult in this fashion they regarded as a pious virtue. In this they reveal the reaction of a minority which is resolute in its opinion and convinced of its uniqueness in the face of possible attacks from the majority and a clash with accepted habits. Their place in society can thus be deduced from this aspect of their doctrine. In the eyes of the *Hasidim* "humility for the sake of Heaven" is a virtue which elevates the soul of the individual, and through this the public attains stability and unity. Their extreme candor and their belief in the single uniform instinct in man brought them to realize the dialectic tension which is entailed when the way of life of the minority becomes known and honored by the many. They describe how "others honor themselves with their humility . . . they are greater than us and yet do not want to take precedence over anyone, as if to say, we are humble."

The social doctrine of the *Ḥasidim* assumes that the original and desirable situation is complete equality in respect of property and social status; inequality is the result of sin. However, they attributed moral significance to the unequal distribution of riches: wealth is given to the rich so that they may sustain the poor. In accordance with this, they were accustomed to give a tenth of their money to charity. Because of this outlook, the *Ḥasidim* were troubled by the problem of the criterion of uniformity – which does not draw any distinction between rich and poor – in the imposition of taxes and public obligations on individuals. They justified the prevalence of this system in public life through the fear that if individual considerations were taken into account, the "evil ones" would attempt to evade their responsibilities. However, they required that "good ones" judge for themselves, after the general imposition, their ability and duty to see whether they were capable of making restitution to the poor for that which had unjustly been taken from them. R. Judah b. Samuel he-Ḥasid and his colleagues even advised a man to forgo the public honor of a *mitzvah* purchased in the synagogue if someone was prepared to acquire it for a higher price; the reward for this *mitzvah* would belong to him who had relinquished it if he secretly gave to the poor the sum he had previously paid in public for the *mitzvah*.

This outlook resulted in some tension between the circle of the *Ḥasidim* and the community leaders on several occasions. The writings of the *Ḥasidim* contain a critical account of these leaders and their deeds; clashes between the leaders of the *Ḥasidim* and the community are also mentioned. It is evident that the *Ḥasidim* disapproved of several principles of the leadership, while many others in the community objected to the attempt at practical application of the doctrines of the *Ḥasidim* within the communities.

To the *Ḥasidim* family life is the basis and framework of piety. Love between man and woman is legitimate as long as it does not lead to sin; they also considered that this love had a definite spiritual content. A man fasts and prays in order to win the woman he loves. In their writings, they gave considerable thought to matchmaking, believing that love and family descent were commendable and desirable factors and considerations. Family descent was also regarded as a basic element in the preservation of the proper way of life of the community. However, they considered money as a negative factor and consideration in matchmaking, although they did not ignore its importance in practice.

Along with their emotional depth and mysticism, the *Ḥasidim* also preserved the tradition of meditation and study. Their respect for books is profound: in the *Sefer Ḥasidim,* the "righteous" bewail the fact that their libraries are scattered after their deaths. They believed that it was commendable not to haggle over the price of a book.

The attitude of the *Ḥasidim* to the non-Jewish world is imbued with the bitterness of those who battle against a successful foe and suffer cruel oppression. But even here, in several instances, it is possible to recognize the influence of the spiritual environment of Christianity and current ideas.

The *Ḥasidei Ashkenaz* became influential in the Jewish world, while at the same time they adopted many and profound elements foreign to that world. They were marked by a refinement of feeling and simplicity of thought, and were woven together by bonds of personal honesty and responsibility before the Creator. Even at its height, the movement comprised only a small group within German Jewry, but as a result of the example of its leading personalities and its growth from the spiritual climate of the time, it succeeded in leaving its imprint. The testaments and customs of the leading *Ḥasidim* greatly influenced the general way of life, as well as specific details, conceptions of *halakhah,* and the versions of prayers. From the second half of the 13th century onward they even exerted some influence over Spanish Jewry. The Jews of Poland-Lithuania of the late Middle Ages also pointed out with pride that "we are of the lineage of the *Ḥasidei Ashkenaz,*" although the atmosphere of their social and religious life had undergone many changes since the time of the *Ḥasidim.*

THE MUSAR MOVEMENT
AN ELITE MOVEMENT AND IDEOLOGY OF MODERN TIMES

The *Musar* Movement for the education of the individual toward strict ethical behavior in the spirit of *halakhah* arose in the 19th century, continuing into the 20th, in the Jewish culture of the *Mitnaggedim* in Lithuania, in particular becoming a trend in its *yeshivot*. Originally inspired by the teachings and example of the life of Joseph Sundel b. Benjamin Benish Salant[1], it began as a movement for influencing members within the community. Circumstances, however, caused a radical change in its character at an early stage and turned it from the ideal of creating a pattern for leading and exemplary members of the community to forming the personality of the young students in the *yeshivot*.

Israel Lipkin (Salanter)[2] had primarily intended to establish the movement for members of the community through their activities. About the middle of the 19th century the mitnaggedic Jewish culture was facing a severe crisis, as a result of its vulnerability to the corroding influence of *Haskalah* ideology. The growing poverty and congestion in the *shtetl* in the Pale of Settlement were causing severe tension and bitterness within Jewish society. The world of the leading circles of Lithuanian Jewry was breaking up. The pupil and co-worker of Israel Lipkin, Isaac Blaser (1837–1907), complained in the second half of the 19th century about the moral degeneration: "The fear of God has terribly deteriorated . . . sins are proliferating whereas formerly Torah and the fear of God went together among Jews . . . now, because of our many sins, this unity has broken up; the bonds have gone and the connection joining them has been severed. In the end, without the fear of God, the knowledge of Torah will disappear too, God forbid" (his introduction to Lipkin's *Or Yisrael* (1900)). This expressed a typical complaint of the *Mitnaggedim* of the period. Blaser was alarmed by the new phenomenon presented by the graduates of the *yeshivah*, who, though learned, were no longer devoted to the rigorous pattern of *halakhah*. Confronted by Ḥasidism on the one hand, and on the other by the trends in German Jewry of *Haskalah*, Reform, and Neo-Orthodoxy, mitnaggedic

---

[1] Lived 1786–1866.
[2] Lived 1810–1883.

225

Jewry was faced with the problem of how to sustain a rigorous traditional Jewish life, based mainly on learning and intellectuality. Israel Salanter at first intended to tackle the problem directly in the communities. In his first letter to the Vilna community in 1849, proposing the creation of a *Musar shtibl* ("a room for moral deliberation"), he wrote: "The busy man does evil wherever he turns. His business doing badly, his mind and strength become confounded and subject to the fetters of care and confusion. Therefore appoint a time on the Holy Sabbath to gather together at a fixed hour ... the notables of the city, whom many will follow, for the study of morals. Speak quietly and deliberately without joking or irony, estimate the good traits of man and his faults, how he should be castigated to turn away from the latter and strengthen the former. Do not decide matters at a single glance; divide the good work among you – not taking up much time, not putting on too heavy a burden. Little by little, much will be gathered ... In the quiet of reflection, in reasonable deliberation, each will strengthen his fellow and cure the foolishness of his heart and eliminate his lazy habits." His program, meant to meet the needs of busy traders, proposed their meeting for moral reflection and self improvement on the day of rest. In his third letter to the Vilna community he proposed that women join in this concern with and study of morals. In his *Iggeret ha-Musar,* Salanter particularly stressed the sin of financial fraud.

However the movement failed to attract the settled members of the community; their "laziness of habit" was too deeply ingrained. Blaser, and not Salanter, had estimated correctly: the trouble lay not so much in the area of individual morality as in the dichotomy between Torah learning and the fear of God. It may be surmised that Israel Salanter's personality – which was both admired and criticized by Orthodox and *Haskalah* circles – was also one of the reasons for the failure of the movement among the upper circles of mitnaggedic society.

In the later years of Israel Salanter, through the energetic drive of his devoted pupils Isaac Blaser and Simḥah Zissel Broida (1824–98), the supporters of the *Musar* Movement turned to the education of the young, and in particular to influencing the students of the *yeshivot* to form early in life the alertness of moral habit which had proved so difficult to instill at a later age. Blaser founded a *kolel* (advanced talmudical academy) at Lubcz. In 1872 Simḥah Zissel founded a *musar shtibl*[3] at Kelme. He also founded a school for youngsters at Grobina, Courland, obtaining some financial support from Orthodox circles in Germany. As the *Musar* Movement began to penetrate the *yeshivot,* both through the indirect influence of its own institutions and through the direct introduction of

3   A tentative effort was thus made towards establishing a unit for the propagation of the new movement.

musar study and methods (see below) into the *yeshivot,* sharp opposition arose from the traditional *yeshivah* leadership. Rabbis and leaders such as Isaac Elhanan Spektor[4] of Kovno openly opposed the new educational system, but without success. Subsequently some of its opponents explicitly renounced their objection, while others ceased to speak openly against it. By the beginning of the 20th century, *musar* had become the prevailing trend in the Lithuanian *yeshivot.*

After its adoption by the *yeshivot,* and the earlier establishment of *musar shtibl* and educational institutions, the *Musar* Movement developed an individual institutional and educational pattern. The reading of ethical works, of isolated sayings from the Midrash and Talmud, and of verses from the Bible, served as vehicles for creating a certain mood and for implanting certain feelings. The principal activity was to recite passages from these works, or a saying or verse, to a melody — taken from the repertoire of the *maggidim* — suitable for evoking a pensive atmosphere of isolation and mood of emotional receptivity toward God and His commandments, preferably in twilight or subdued lighting (from a certain aspect this resembles the "spiritual exercises" recommended by Ignatius of Loyola for the Jesuits). The reading of the intellectual matter in the text served to stimulate an emotional response, which was intended to help the student both in forming moral personality and in devotion to Talmud study.

Formally, the *Musar* Movement was based on the study of ethical literature, although its conception of this was highly eclectic, and its libraries included works by authors as diverse as Jonah b. Abraham Gerondi (13th century author of ethical works), Moses b. Jacob Cordovero (16th century Kabbalist), Moses Hayyim Luzzatto (18th century kabbalist who had been excommunicated in his time), and Naphtali Hirz Wessely (one of the leaders of Enlightenment). However, several generations of study of this variegated literature by many brilliant young men did not produce for the movement, as far as known, a single systematic commentary, either on the literature as a whole or on an individual work.

In the "minimalistic" *musar yeshivot* students devoted at least half an hour daily to studying one of these texts in unison, intoning them in the same plaintive melody. Unity was demanded only in the melody used, each student being allowed to read the book of his own choice. In these *yeshivot,* the *mashgi'ah* ("supervisor") became a second spiritual mentor of the students, equal to the *yeshivah* head; in the case of some personalities such as Jeroham Lebovitch at the Mir yeshivah, he was even superior. The *mashgi'ah* held a *shmues* ("talk") with all the yeshivah students at least weekly, on either a general

---

4   Lived 1817–1896; rabbinical authority and communal leader.

moral topic — a kind of a special *yeshivah* sermon — or some specific incident
that had occurred in *yeshivah* life. Devout *musar* students often combined into a
va'ad, several youngsters gathering together for a period to chant some *musar*
saying and achieve the proper *musar* mood. Larger groups would create a *musar
berzhe* (lit. *"musar* stock exchange") in which they would act collectively and
enter collectively through a more protracted way into the same mood. In these
yeshivot, commonly called "Slobodka-style" *yeshivot,* the student's mind was
molded through this activity, through his comradeship in emotivity with fellow
students, and through the influence of the *mashgi'aḥ.* In this highly charged
emotional life intellectual Talmud study became encapsulated by the
atmosphere created by *musar.*

The crisis in the *yeshivot* brought about by secularizing influences, such as
the *Bund,* general socialist revolutionary trends, Zionism, and *Haskalah,* was
counteracted to a large extent by the influence of the *Musar* Movement. Israel
Salanter's original aim was also largely achieved, though indirectly, as the
"muserniks" who entered the life of the upper circles of the *shtetl* were now
imbued with the new proud and rigoristic spirit engendered by *musar* and the
collective sense of identity.

There also developed a second, "maximalist," trend of *musar yeshivot,* in the
so-called "Novaredok style." Its proponent, Joseph Josel Hurwitz, the "old man
of Novaredok" (Novogrudok), who founded a *yeshivah* and *kolel* there in 1896,
applied a deeper psychological approach. This not only included many hours
devoted to the study of the *musar* texts, employing if possible a more plaintive
melody, with less light, but the student would also be taught to discipline
himself by a series of *peules af . . .* ("actions to . . . "). Such actions were
calculated to subdue his natural instincts of vanity, economic calculation, or love
of material goods. A student, for example, might be ordered to go to a drug
store and ask for something inappropriate, such as nails, to mingle with
well-dressed people in rags, or to enter a train without a coin in his purse. By the
Novaredok method, a man not only trained himself to subdue his animal and
social nature, but also to check if he did so in complete emotional depth. The
Yiddish author Chaim (Ḥayyim) Grade described it:

"When you ask the *Nawardoker,* 'How do you do?' the meaning is 'How is
Jewishness with you? Have you advanced in spirituality?' . . . He who has
studied *musar* will never enjoy his life further. Ḥayyim, you will remain a
cripple your whole life. You write heresy . . . but is there any one of you
really so strong that he does not desire public approval for himself? Which
one of you is prepared to publish his book anonymously? . . . Our spiritual
calm you have exchanged for passions which you will never attain, for

doubts which, even after much self-torture, you will not be able to explain away. Your writing will not improve a single person, and it will make you worse" ("My Quarrel with Hersh Rasseyner," in: I. Howe and E. Greenberg (eds.), *Treasury of Yiddish Stories* (1954), 579–606).

The *Musar* Movement is thus a civic trend which, deflected from its original aim, gradually developed an entire educational system, based on, and aiming toward, integration and subjection of the youthful emotions to a deeply instilled emotional defense system of a rigoristic Jewish life according to *halakhah.* It promoted unity through pride in this fraternity of feelings and intentions and thus served as a social bond among those who emerged from the *musar* hothouse in the *yeshivot.* The Slobodka and Novaredok approaches differed in their degree of extremism and the emphasis on spiritual exercise, but were based on the same principle. By the 1970s the main yeshivot of the Lithuanian type were *musar* orientated, the majority of Slobodka style, and a small minority Novaredok style. Despite the system, or to some extent because of it, many left the *musar yeshivot* for more secular trends of education.

9

THE MAIMONIDEAN CONTROVERSY
THE CONTEST AROUND RATIONALISM IN RELIGION AND CULTURE

The Maimonidean controversy is a vast complex of disputed cultural, religious, and social problems, focusing around several central themes. Some elements of this controversy considerably antedate Maimonides (1135–1204); and of the questions brought into sharp relief by his ideas and writings, some have remained topical in many Jewish circles. Vast fields of human experience and thought are encompassed by it: reason and philosophy in their relation to faith and tradition; what components are permitted and what prohibited in the education of a man following the Torah; the proper understanding of anthropomorphism as expressed in the Bible and Talmud; central theological concepts such as the resurrection of the body; and the very form of Maimonides' legal code *Mishneh Torah* and its attitude toward talmudic discussion. The question of hierarchical leadership versus intellectual, personal leadership was one of the early causes of this controversy. In the Middle Ages the controversy had three climaxes: around 1180 (in the lifetime of Maimonides); around 1230–32 (involving David Kimḥi, Solomon b. Abraham of Montpellier, Naḥmanides, and others, and centering in Provence); and around 1300–06 (in connection with Abba Mari b. Moses Astruc, Solomon b. Abraham Adret, Asher b. Jehiel, Jedaiah b. Abraham Bedersi (ha-Penini), and Menahem b. Solomon Meiri, and centering in Christian Spain and Provence). In between these moments when the conflict flared up anew, tensions and disputes continued. The crisis of Spanish Jewry in the 15th century accentuated the main educational and social themes of the old controversy. In Renaissance Italy and in the diversified and flourishing Jewish center of Poland-Lithuania the old quarrel again became topical, though in a milder form. With the enlightenment *(Haskalah)* of the 18th century the "Maimonidean side" of the controversy was given a new, greatly secularized, and radical expression by Moses Mendelssohn and his followers — an expression that could scarcely have been imagined by the former protagonists. In German neo-Orthodoxy, the "Maimonidean side" — particularly in its striving for a synthesis of Jewish faith and "general culture," as well as in certain of its social tendencies — found a new, conservative expression.

In Yemen in the 19th century and well into the 20th, there was a distinct "Maimonidean camp" and a struggle against it.

Through the charisma of his personality and the trend of his thought and leadership Maimonides himself initiated this. An exile from Muslim Spain, he met in the Near East the hierarchical traditions of the exilarchate and the *geonim.* Maimonides was willing and ready to respect the exilarch as scion of the royal house of David and as the proper authority, from the halakhic point of view, to appoint and ordain judges.

His mind and heart vehemently opposed the claims of the *geonim,* criticized sharply the way they

> "fixed for themselves monetary demands from individuals and communities and caused people to think, in utter foolishness, that it is obligatory and proper that they should help sages and scholars and people studying Torah . . . all this is wrong. There is not a single word, either in the Torah or in the sayings of the [talmudic] sages, to lend credence to it . . . for as we look into the sayings of the talmudic sages, we do not find that they ask people for money, nor did they collect money for the honorable and cherished academies" (Commentary to *Avot* 4:5).

This attempt to undermine the economic and social foundations of leadership of the Babylonian *geonim* went hand in hand with Maimonides' opposition to their program of studies and his contempt for their very office. The *gaon* at Baghdad at this time was Samuel b. Ali, a strong and authoritarian personality. In an ironic "apology" for Samuel b. Ali's attacks on the *Mishneh Torah.* Maimonides explains to one of his pupils:

> "Why, my son, should you take offense that a man whom people accustom from his youth to believe that there is none like him in his generation; when age, high office, aristocratic descent, the lack of people of discernment in that town, and his relationship with individuals, all have combined to produce this execrable consequence that each and every individual hangs expectantly on each word pronounced from the academy in anticipation of an honorific title from there . . . — why do you wonder that he has acquired such [evil] traits? How, my son, could you imagine that he should love truth enough to acknowledge his weakness? . . . This is a thing that a man like him will never do, as it was not done by better men who preceded him" (letter to Joseph b. Judah in: D.H. Baneth (ed.) *Iggerot ha-Rambam* (1946), 54f.).

The gaonate is represented as corrupt, and typical academy study as being of questionable value. Concerning Zechariah, the son-in-law of the *gaon,* Maimonides writes:

"He is a very foolish man. He studies very hard at this talmudic discussion and its commentaries, and thinks that he is the greatest of his generation, having already attained the peak of perfection. My esteemed son knows that my appreciation of the greatest of the sages of Israel is such that I evaluate their worth according to their own criteria. They themselves have defined 'the argumentations *[havayot]* of Abbaye and Rava[1] [as] a small matter.' If this is a small matter, why should I pay attention to an old man who is really miserable, an ignoramus in every respect? To my eyes he is like a newborn baby; one has to defend him, according to the measure of his [Zechariah's] foolishness" (*ibid.,* 56ff.; the bulk of this passage has been erased in most manuscripts).

This vehement revolt against the authority of the *geonim* came at a time when Samuel b. Ali was attempting to minimize the authority of the exilarch on the grounds that what the people needed then was no more than the leadership of the *geonim* and the guidance of their study in the academy. Small wonder that such a revolt aroused reciprocal anger, coming, as it did, in defense of Maimonides' *Mishneh Torah* which claimed expressly (in the introduction) to supersede the Talmud in popular usage, replacing its deliberations – the very core and substance of the life of academies and *geonim* – by his systematic code. The claim of the intellectual to replace an aristocratic hierarchy seemed to be combined with an attempt to impose Greek systematic modes of codification in place of the traditional many-voiced flow of talmudic discussion. It is hardly surprising that Samuel b. Ali, Zechariah, and Daniel b. Saadiah ha-Bavli (Babylonian talmudist) all sought and found halakhic flaws in this code. Some of their arguments have philosophical and theological overtones, but these were to come to the forefront only in the second stage of the controversy. In the main, in this phase, it was Maimonides' creativity which was found provocative, as well as his attitude to Talmud study and to the leadership of established institutions, all of which were being defended against him.

Maimonides' works reached Europe, chiefly in the southwest – Spain and Provence – entering a cultural and social climate very different from the one in which they had been created in Egypt. His authority in *Mishneh Torah* was impugned halakhically by Abraham b. David of Posquières and Moses ha-Kohen,

---

1   Babylonian scholars in talmudic times.

among others. The Christian Reconquest was proceeding apace in the Iberian peninsula. Mystical tendencies and visionary approaches began to find explicit and strong expression in the developing Kabbalah of Provence and Spain. Jews everywhere were suffering from the impact of the Crusades, with martyrdom *(kiddush ha-Shem)* in their wake. Maimonides' grandiose attempt at a synthesis between the Jewish faith and Greek-Arabic Aristotelian philosophy was received with enthusiasm in some circles, mainly of the upper strata of Jewish society, and with horror and dismay in others, imbued with mysticism and dreading the effects of Greek thought on Jewish beliefs. The old and continuously smoldering issue of "Athens versus Jerusalem" now burst into flames. Essentially the problem is one of the possible synthesis or the absolute antithesis between monotheistic revealed faith and intellectually formulated philosophy. This problem is interwoven in the great monotheistic religions with the clash between rationalistic religious belief, inclining in the main toward synthesis, and mystic belief, which is largely opposed to it.

The problem was not new in Judaism. In Islamic countries in the tenth century it was in the main decided in favor of rationalism and synthesis. Maimonides was not the only one in the 12th century who expressly sought a synthesis between Greek philosophy and Judaism: a philosophic approach was attempted by Abraham ibn Daud (c. 1110–80), and he was preceded by Saadiah Gaon and Samuel b. Hophni, who denied, in the name of rational exegesis, the historical veracity of the incident of Samuel and the Witch of Endor.

Yet in that same century changes were taking place. The influence of the Christian environment became more pervasive. Increasingly Christianity was involved in similar problems, as the conflict between Peter Abelard and Bernard of Clairvaux clearly shows. Social upheavals in Jewish society during the 12th and 13th centuries added communal tension to the spiritual strife. When Maimonides was still young, most of his work as yet unwritten, Judah Halevi warned: "Turn aside from mines and pitfalls. Let not Greek wisdom tempt you, for it bears flowers only and no fruit . . . Listen to the confused words of her sages built on the void . . . Why should I search for bypaths, and complicated ones at that, and leave the main road?" (from his poem beginning *"Devarekha be-Mor Over Rekuhim"*).

This opposition hardened and developed with the passage of time. Against it stood the rationalistic attitude of the upper circles. Meir b. Todros ha-Levi Abulafia, in many respects a sincere admirer of Maimonides, was shocked at the implication that Maimonides did not affirm the resurrection of the body as a halakhic principle. In an angry letter sent to the scholars of Lunel he not only sought to prove by copious quotations the dogmatic truth of bodily resurrection, but also added passionately that if there is no such resurrection, "to what end did the bodies stand watch for their God, did they go in darkness for the sake of their God? If the bodies are not resurrected, where is their hope and where are they to look for it?" (*Kitāb al-Risā'il* (1871), 14). Abulafia also attacked Maimonides on other halakhic points. While some of his correspondents agreed with him, others tried to convince him that he had misunderstood the purport of Maimonides' teaching on resurrection, and this latter view was accepted wholehearedly by the *nasi* Sheshet b. Isaac of Saragossa, who in a very radical sense gave expression to Maimonides' rationalism and philosophic synthesis. Writing about 1200, he attacked sharply and derisively what he regarded as the simplicism and materialism of Abulafia's view (A. Marx, in: *Jewish Quarterly Review,* 25, 1934/35), 406–28). To speak about bodily resurrection is "to bring down our saintly fathers from the highest level — the status of the angels who enjoy divine glory and live forever — to the status of man, through their returning to the impure body which cannot exist except through food and drink, and must end in dust and worms . . . but the life of Wisdom is greater than foolishness, as light is greater than darkness. These notions seem to me like the words of one confused" (*ibid.,* 418). The only correct conception of resurrection, he thought, is the one also accepted by the pagan philosophers. Resurrection means the eternal life of the soul of the sage-philosopher. "If the soul — while still in the body — was yearning for its Creator, subordinating its passion to its reason, [then] when it leaves the body, [it] will attain the highest status, for which it yearned while still in the body; and over it God will emanate of His spirit. This, in the view of the sages, is the resurrection of the dead and the reward of the just at the end of days" (*ibid.,* 421ff.). All pronouncements in the Bible and the Talmud about bodily resurrection are only for the simple men who constitute the majority of mankind and who understand only material rewards, and the same holds true for the Muslim paradise (*ibid.,* 424).

> "I ask this fool who maintains that the souls will return to the dead corpses and that they are destined to return to the soil of Israel. Into which body will the soul return? If it is to the body from which it has departed, [then this will] already have returned to its elements thousands of years earlier; [it is now] earth, dust, and worms. Where it has been buried, a house has been built, a vineyard planted, or some other plants have taken root and you cannot find the earth or the dust or the worms into which the body has turned. If, however, this soul is to return to another body, which God will create, then it is another man who will be created in his own time, and has not been dead; how, then can you say that he is being resurrected and that God rewards him, as he has not as yet achieved anything?" (*ibid.,* 426).

Sheshet records opposition to the *Mishneh Torah* by reporting the opinion of one of the judges who quarreled with him and refused to judge according to Maimonides: "As he does not adduce proofs from the sayings of the talmudic sages for his decisions, who is going to follow his opinion? It is far better to study Talmud. We will have nothing to do with his books and his writings." In Sheshet's view this opposition stems from the fact that until the *Mishneh Torah* the whole matter of legal decision was so confused that the vast majority of Jews, being ignorant of the Talmud, had to obey their judges, whereas now people had before them a clear and open code and were not dependent on judges alone (*ibid.*, 427).

Despite common admiration for Maimonides and his all-embracing devotion to Torah and the Jewish faith, there was in reality no common language between the two radical positions. Gradually the opponents of Maimonides began to attack his very conception of a synthesis between Greek philosophy and Jewish faith. When David Kimḥi (c. 1160–1235) traveled about the communities of Provence to rally the supporters of Maimonides, he was greatly surprised to be answered by the physician and courtier, Judah ibn Alfakhar, with a bitter attack on Maimonides' very attempt to rationalize and explain away miracles and wondrous tales. Ibn Alfakhar was against half acceptance; logical proofs were not so important, "for each true proof needs great checking, since sometimes it may include misleading elements of that false wisdom called sophistry in Greek, and when a proof is joined to this it misleads even sages." Maimonides' "erroneous" intention was to explain matters according to the laws of philosophy and nature "so as to put the Torah and Greek wisdom together, to make out of them one whole. He imagined that the one would live with the other like two loving twin deers. In reality this has resulted in sorrow and dissension, for they cannot live together on the earth and be like two sisters, for the Hebrew women are not like the Egyptian ones. To this our Torah says: 'No, my son is the living one, and yours is the dead' (I Kings 3:22) and her rival angers her. I want peace; if I start to talk to them, they go to war" (letter to Kimḥi, *Iggerot Kena'ot,* in: *Koveẓ Teshuvot ha-Rambam* (1859), 2a). Thus, through radical rationalistic argumentation, this physician and courtier in Spain rejects the synthesis of the physician and courtier in Egypt and the logical compromise it involves.

The demand for logical consistency was also answered from the Maimonidean camp. Increasingly they inclined toward extreme allegoristic explanations of talmudic and even biblical expressions and tales. Their opponents accused them of even inclining to explain away as no more than symbols certain practical commandments, which need be fulfilled only by simple men, but not by educated people. The rationalists denied this. Social overtones became stronger.

The anti-Maimonideans berated their upper-class opponents for their hedonistic, luxurious, and sinful way of life. The Maimonideans countered by accusing their adversaries with anarchy, harshness, ignorance, simplicity of mind, and of being under Christian influence.

The anti-Maimonidean camp turned to the great sages of northern France. Never having been acquainted with Aristotelian philosophy, they never felt the need for synthesis with it; therefore, they unhesitatingly pronounced a *herem* on Maimonides' philosophical works. Some report that they excommunicated even parts of his halakhic code. In Provence and Spain the anti-Maimonidean camp was led by Solomon b. Abraham of Montpellier, Jonah b. Abraham Gerondi, the poet Meshullam da Piera, and above all Nahmanides. The position of Nahmanides is remarkable for its simultaneous flexibility in expression and rigidity of mental attitude. Seeing that the extreme anti-Maimonidean stance taken by the rabbis of northern France and by Solomon of Montpellier had no chance of finding support among the leading circles of Jewish society in Provence and Spain, he therefore advised the anti-Maimonidean camp to adopt a moderate stand in order to achieve at least what was possible. Writing to the north French rabbis (printed in: *Monatsschrift fuer Geschichte und Wissenschaft des Judentums*, 9 (1860), 184–95) he expresses his devotion and admiration, but he humbly submits that they "are nourished in the bosom of [true] faith, planted in the courts of tradition," and therefore had to understand Maimonides in his peculiar cultural and social circumstances. The situation he describes is actually that of Spanish and Provençal Jewish upper society in the early 13th century:

"They have filled their belly with the foolishness of the Greeks . . . . . . make fun . . . of the trusting souls . . . They did not enter profoundly into the ways of our Torah; the ways of alien children suffice for them. But for the words of [Maimonides], but for the fact that they live out of the mouth of his works . . . they would have slipped almost entirely."

It is not only a matter of false spiritual pride and alien culture; it is also a case born of social necessity:

"God save and guard us, my teachers, from such a fate. Look about and see: is there a pain like our pain? For the sons have been exiled from their fathers' tables; they have defiled themselves with the food of gentiles and the wine of their feasts. They have mixed with them and become used to their deeds . . . courtiers have been permitted to study Greek wisdom, to become acquainted with medicine, to learn mathematics and geometry, other knowledge and tricks, so that they make a living in royal courts and palaces."

This intrinsically hostile description of the life of the upper classes of Jewish society in Provence and Spain is given in order to put Maimonides in the light of a great talmudic sage who — argues Nahmanides — would certainly and gladly have written and lived as the northern French rabbis did. Alas, it was not granted him: "Did he trouble himself for your sake, you geniuses of the Talmud? He saw himself compelled and constrained to structure a work which would offer refuge from the Greek philosophers . . . Have you ever listened to their words, have you ever been misled by their proofs?" He goes on to explain that extremism would bring about an irreparable split. It is far better to educate gradually this misled society and bring it back to the right way of northern France, by partial prohibitions only. The region most afflicted is Provence; Spain he considers to be in far better order.

Nahmanides was merely temporizing in his writings to the northern French rabbis. His true temper and the temper of the entire anti-Maimonidean camp is revealed in his commentary on the Pentateuch, which is basically a mystical work against Maimonides and Abraham ibn Ezra. The very concept of a system of laws of nature ordained by God in His wisdom to be admired by man through his reason, as expressed by Maimonides (see e.g., *Mishneh Torah, Sefer ha-Madda*), he and his colleagues believe to be sheer heresy. The workings of nature are to be conceived of only and always as "hidden miracles." God performs extraordinary miracles in order that we should understand the miraculous nature of all existence and life:

"Through the great and obvious miracles man recognizes the hidden miracles, which are the foundation of the entire Torah. For no man has a share in the Torah of Moses until we believe that all our matters and accidents are miracles, the product neither of nature nor of the way of the world, whether for the multitude or for the individual; but if a man fulfills the commandments his reward will bring him success, if he transgresses them his punishment will strike him — all by divine decree" (Commentary to Exodus 13:16).

Though their tactics might thus vary, dogmatics were radical and clearly defined on both sides. *Herem* was hurled against *herem*, as the authority of northern France was met by the authority of local scholars and communal leaders in Provence and Spain. Emissaries of both camps traveled about, rallying their supporters. A profusion of letters and counter-letters, sermons and counter-sermons, commentaries and counter-commentaries poured out. The weapons in the campaign were polemics, original and translations, and the Ibn Tibbon and Anatoli families made their name in both. In the work of men like Jonah Gerondi the struggle against Maimonides was merged with a general reforming spirit in morals and community leadership. This battle was ended by a terrible shock when Maimonides' books were burned by the Dominicans in 1232. Jonah Gerondi relented in his views and many adherents of the anti-Maimonidean camp followed suit.

    The controversy returned to the Muslim countries in the East. Maimonides' son, Abraham b. Moses b. Maimon, was outraged at what had happened in the West. He attacked "many overseas [scholars who are] mistaken. They cling to the literalistic sense of biblical verses, Midrashim, and *aggadot.* This pains our heart; at the sight of this our eyes have darkened, and our fathers are dumbfounded: How could such an impurity, so like the impurity of idol worship, come to be in Israel? They worship idols, deny God's teaching, and worship other gods beside Him." Flinging these accusations against Maimonides' opponents in Europe, Abraham holds that through their exegetical explanations they are guilty of pagan-like anthropomorphism (*Milḥamot ha-Shem,* ed. by R. Margalioth (1953), 52). He compares their faith to that of the Christians (*ibid.,* 50). Continuing his father's line of thought, he attacks the European antirationalistic scholars for their exclusive devotion to talmudic studies only, while neglecting the philosophical and philological foundations of the faith (*ibid.,* 49). They are among "those that walk in the darkness of their understanding and in the paucity of their wisdom" (*ibid.,* 50). He expressly prefers Islamic surroundings and influence – conducive to a rationalistic-monotheistic faith – to a Christian environment, which influences men in the direction of antirationalism and anthropomorphism (*ibid.,* 51). Abraham restates the basic rationalistic principle of faith and exegesis:

> "Know ye God's people and His heritage, that God differentiated men from animals and beasts through the reason, wisdom, and understanding which He granted them. He also differentiated Israel from the gentiles through the Torah He gave them and the precepts He commanded them. Hence reason preceded Torah, both in creation of the world, and in each and every one living in it. Reason has been given to a man since the six days of creation; Torah was given to man 4,448 years after creation. Should someone say to you, 'But the sages have explained that the Torah was created two thousand years before the world,' you should reply that this Midrash needs many commentaries to justify it. It is impossible to take it in its simple sense . . . Reason was implanted in each and every one of the seed of Israel before his knowledge of Torah. Know and understand

that it is because the child's reason is not yet ripe, that God did not oblige him to fulfill commandments" (*ibid.*, 57–58).

While this blast was going forth from the East, extremists from the West caused the desecration of Maimonides' tomb at Tiberias, which shocked not only the Maimonidean camp but also the majority of the anti-Maimonideans. When in the early 1240s the Disputation of Paris and the burning of the Talmud added shock to shock, public quarrels among Jews were set aside for several decades. It remains a much disputed point whether the Dominicans set fire to Maimonides' writings on their own initiative, scenting heresy wherever they could find it, or whether their action resulted from a denunciation by Jews, as contemporary Maimonideans believed. Neither the social nor the cultural motivating forces of the controversy disappeared with the cessation of polemics. The rise of kabbalistic circles and literature on the one hand, and the continuing philosophical activity and way of life of the upper and "professional" circles of Jewish society on the other implied a continuation and an intensification of the struggle between the rationalists and antirationalists.

When the controversy flared up again at the end of the 13th and beginning of the 14th century, the immediate catalyst was the extreme allegorical exegesis of certain rationalists. However, it came to encompass the whole range of the content of Jewish education and the question of the possibility or impossibility of synthesis between "Greek wisdom" and the Torah of Moses. Abba Mari Astruc of Lunel turned to Solomon b. Abraham Adret for guidance on these allegorical interpretations, to his mind heretical ones. After much hesitation, and spurred on by the influence of Asher b. Jehiel, Solomon b. Abraham Adret and the Barcelona community issued a *ḥerem* on July 26, 1305, against "any member of the community who, being under the age of 25 years, shall study the works of the Greeks on natural science or metaphysics, whether in the original language or in translation."

Works by Jewish philosophers were excepted, as was the study of medicine. The ban was intended to prevent young men from being influenced by Greek philosophy to turn away "from the Torah of Israel which is above these sciences. How can any man dare to judge between human wisdom based on analogy, proof, and thought, and the wisdom of God, between whom and us there is no relation nor similarity? Will man, who is embodied in a vessel of clay, judge . . . God his creator to say, God forbid, what is possible and what he cannot do? Truly this, sometimes leads to utter heresy" (Response of Rashba, pt. 1, no. 415). A ban was also pronounced against all who "say about Abraham and Sarah that in reality they symbolize matter and form; that the 12 tribes of Israel are [an allegory] for the 12 planets . . . [and] that the Urim and Thummim are to be understood as the astrolabe instrument . . . Some of them say that everything in the Torah, from Genesis to the giving of the law, is entirely allegorical" (*ibid.*, no. 416).

The condemnation of extreme allegory did not arouse opposition, but the prohibition on the study of "Greek wisdom" until the age of 25 was sharply opposed on grounds of principle, though to Adret and his group this formula was certainly in many respects a compromise. Among the many communities and individual sages in Provence and Spain who opposed the ban, the great talmudic scholar Menaḥem b. Solomon Meiri was one of the most eloquent voices. In his counter-*ḥerem* (printed in excerpts in *Jubelschrift . . . L. Zunz* (1884), Heb. pt. 153–72) he reminded Adret of the failure of the early 13th-century attacks against Maimonides. Rejecting insinuations that the study of philosophy causes heresy, he pointed to many talmudic scholars who were students of philosophy. Meiri stressed that sciences such as mathematics were necessary for the understanding of many passages in the Talmud. He regarded the prohibition against certain types of study as self-defeating: "Each individual [nature] will search for what suits him according to his natural inclination." This trait of human intellect and nature, he maintains, will even cause the second generation of the excommunicating community to seek ways out of this prohibition. Meiri was well aware that there was a more radical wing among the rationalists, which he opposed (see his commentary to Psalms, ed. by J. Cohn (1936), e.g., ch. 36, p. 78f., and many passages in his commentary to Proverbs and to Mishnah *Avot*).

Finally, Jedaiah b. Abraham Bedersi (ha-Penini) wrote Adret a "letter of apology" – actually a sharp attack against the antirationalists – basing himself on spiritual greatness of Provençal Jews and praising rationalism and philosophy. He daringly proclaims:

"My rabbis, please look into the mighty pattern of the benefits of philosophy to all of us, even to those who despise it. For it is extremely well-known that in ancient times anthropomorphism was widespread, one may say almost in the entire Diaspora of Israel . . . but in every generation there arose *geonim* and sages – in Spain, in Babylonia, and in the cities of Andalusia – who, thanks to their familiarity with the Arabic language, had the great opportunity to smell the perfume of the sciences, some much, some a little, for they are translated into this language. It is thanks to this that they began to elaborate and clarify many of their opinions on the Torah, above all as to the unity of God and the abolition of anthropomorphism, especially by the philosophical proofs taken from scientific works."

He goes on to list this rationalistic literature, from the days of Saadiah Gaon onward (Responsa of Rashba, pt. 1., no. 418). This long epistle concludes:

"Relinquish your *herem* for the heart of this people will not turn away from philosophy and its books as long as there is breath in their frame and soul in their bodies, especially as together with it [i.e., with devotion to philosophy], they are true to Torah and commandments. Even if they had heard it from the mouth of Joshua bin Nun they would never have accepted it, for they intend to do battle for the honor of the great teacher [i.e., Maimonides] and his works; and for the holiness of his teaching they will sacrifice fortune, family, and soul as long as there is a breath in their bodies. And thus they will teach and command their children in generations to come" *(ibid.).*

On this sharp though inconclusive note, the great controversy of the early 14th century petered out.

The tension between rationalists and antirationalists never abated throughout the Middle Ages. Among the beleaguered Jews of 15th-century Christian Spain, Maimonidean rationalism was seen by many as the root cause of the misfortunes and the reason for apostasy. On the other hand a man like the Spanish philosopher Abraham Bibago, throughout his *Derekh Emunah,* defended rationalism, not only as being justified but as the very essence of Judaism. Proudly calling himself "a pupil of Maimonides," he believed that the Jewish people is the bearer of reason — weak in this world as reason is weak against the unreasonable passions. Generalizing the traditional rationalistic view, he stated:

"The reasonable creature having reason has to study the sciences; and being a believer, he will study Torah and acquire faith and its roots and dogmas. The first study will be a kind of carrier and vessel to bear the second study. In the same way that life is an assumption and carrier by which humanity and speech are carried, so through the form of reason — by whose accomplishment one studies and acquires the sciences — Torah study will be assumed and carried. This faith will be complete and without doubt, and the one attitude [faith] will not conflict with the other [philosophy]. Therefore did the sage say, 'Reason and faith are two lights.' To solve all doubts we must explain that 'Greek wisdom' cannot be the above-mentioned wisdom of reason belonging to man insofar as he is a man. Hence it is a human wisdom and not a Greek one. The wisdom called [by talmudic sages] 'Greek wisdom,' must be something peculiar to the Greeks and not to another nation."

That views like this were acceptable also among 16th-century Ashkenazi Jewry is proved by the fact that the *Sefer ha-Miknah* by Joseph b. Gershon of Rosheim (prominent German Jewish leader) is in reality a kind of synopsis of Bibago's *Derekh Emunah.* In Renaissance Italy Jehiel b. Samuel of Pisa wrote a detailed treatise *(Minḥat Kena'ot)* against rationalism, while the life and works of many of his contemporaries and countrymen constituted a clear espousal of it. In Poland-Lithuania in the 16th-17th centuries the tension between Maimonideans and anti-Maimonideans likewise continued, as evidenced, for example, by the dispute between Moses Isserles and Solomon b. Jehiel Luria.

The problems of the synthesis between Judaism and other cultures, of the proper content of Jewish education, and of the right way to God — through reason or through mystic union — has remained, though formulations and expressions have changed considerably. The old hierarchial basis of Jewish leadership, wholeheartedly hated by Maimonides, has disappeared, but the leadership of the individual scholar, even after Maimonides, retained many hierarchical and sacral elements. The *Mishneh Torah* did not supersede the Talmud, and Maimonides' aristocratic opposition to monetary support for Torah study failed completely. So strong was his personality, however, that most of his opponents made great efforts to say that they opposed not Maimonides himself but some element of his teaching or, better still, some misguided interpretation or citation of his work. The Maimonidean controversy is both very specifically at the heart of Jewish culture and, at the same time, part of a set of problems central to Judaism, Islam, and Christianity alike.

10

ELEMENTS OF THE EVIL
IMAGE OF THE JEW

THE BLOOD LIBEL

The allegation, called the "Blood Libel," that Jews murder non-Jews, especially Christians, in order to obtain blood for the Passover or other rituals is a complex of deliberate lies, trumped-up accusations, and popular beliefs about the murder-lust of the Jews and their bloodthirstiness, based on the conception that Jews hate Christianity and mankind in general. It is combined with the delusion that Jews are in some way not human and must have recourse to special remedies and subterfuges in order to appear, at least outwardly, like other men. The blood libel led to trials and massacres of Jews in the Middle Ages and early modern times; it was revived by the Nazis. Its origin is rooted in ancient, almost primordial, concepts concerning the potency and energies of blood.

Blood sacrifices were practiced by many pagan religions. They are expressly forbidden by the Torah. The law of meat-salting *(meliḥah)* is designed to prevent the least drop of avoidable blood remaining in food. Yet pagan incomprehension of the Jewish monotheist cult, lacking the customary images and statues, led to charges of ritual killing. At a time of tension between Hellenism and Judaism, it was alleged that the Jews would kidnap a Greek foreigner, fatten him up for a year, and then convey him to a wood, where they slew him, sacrificed his body with the customary ritual, partook of his flesh, and while immolating the Greek swore an oath of hostility to the Greeks. This was told, according to the 1st-century Alexandrian anti-Semite Apion, to King Antiochus Epiphanes by an intended Greek victim who had been found in the Jewish Temple being fattened by the Jews for this sacrifice and was saved by the king (Josephus, *Contra Apion,* 2:89–102). Some suspect that stories like this were spread intentionally as propaganda for Antiochus Epiphanes to justify his profanation of the Temple. Whatever the immediate cause, the tale is the outcome of hatred of the Jews and incomprehension of their religion.

To be victims of this accusation was also the fate of other misunderstood religious minorities. In the second century C.E. the Church Father Tertullian complained: "We are said to be the most criminal of men, on the score of our sacramental baby-killing, and the baby-eating that goes with it." He complains that judicial torture was applied to Christians because of this accusation, for "it

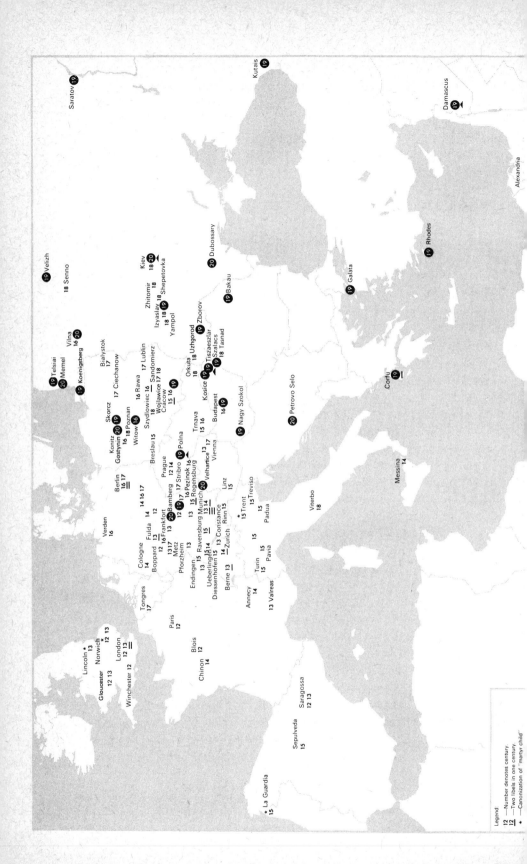

Legend:
12 —Number denotes century.
12 —Two libels in one century.
✝ —Canonization of "martyr child".

ought . . . to be wrung out of us [whenever that false charge is made] how many murdered babies each of us has tasted . . . Oh! the glory of that magistrate who had brought to light some Christian who had eaten up to date a hundred babies!" (*Apologeticus,* 7:1 and 1:12, Loeb edition (1931), 10, 36).

During the Middle Ages some heretical Christian sects were afflicted by similar accusations. The general attitude of Christians toward the holy bread of the Communion created an emotional atmosphere in which it was felt that the divine child was mysteriously hidden in the partaken bread. The popular preacher, Friar Berthold of Regensburg (13th century), felt obligated to explain why communicants do not actually see the holy child by asking the rhetorical question, "Who would like to bite off a baby's head or hand or foot?" Popular beliefs and imaginings of the time, either of classical origin or rooted in Germanic superstitions, held that blood, even the blood of executed malefactors or from corpses, possesses the property of healing or causing injury. Thus, combined with the general hatred of Jews then prevailing, a charge of clandestine cruel practices and blood-hunting, which had evolved among the pagans and was used against the Christians, was deflected by Christian society to the most visible and persistent minority in opposition to its tenets.

As Christianity spread in Western Europe and penetrated the popular consciousness, influencing the emotions and imagination even more than thought and dogma, various story elements began to evolve around the alleged inhumanity and sadism of the Jews. In the first distinct case of blood libel against Jews in the Middle Ages, that of Norwich in 1144, it was alleged that the Jews had "bought a Christian child [the 'boy-martyr' William] before Easter and tortured him with all the tortures wherewith our Lord was tortured, and on Long Friday hanged him on a rood in hatred of our Lord." The motif of torture and murder of Christian children in imitation of Jesus' Passion persisted with slight variations throughout the 12th century (Gloucester, England, 1168; Blois, France, 1171; Saragossa, Spain, 1182), and was repeated in many libels of the 13th century. In the case of Little Saint Hugh of Lincoln, 1255, it would seem that an element taken directly from Apion's libel (see above) was interwoven into the Passion motif, for the chronicler Matthew Paris relates, "that the Child was first fattened for ten days with white bread and milk and then . . . almost all the Jews of England were invited to the crucifixion." The crucifixion motif was generalized in the *Siete Partidas* law code of Spain, 1263: "We have heard it said that in certain places on Good Friday the Jews do steal children and set them on the cross in a mocking manner." Even when other motifs eventually

Map showing sites and periods of blood libels. Gray numbers denote 12th and 13th centuries, circled numbers 19th and 20th centuries.

predominated in the libel, the crucifixion motif did not disappear altogether. On the eve of the expulsion of the Jews from Spain, there occurred the blood-libel case of "the Holy Child of La Guardia" (1490–91). There Conversos were made to confess under torture that with the knowledge of the chief rabbi of the Jews they had assembled in a cave, crucified the child, and abused him and cursed him to his face, as was done to Jesus in ancient times. The crucifixion motif explains why the blood libels occurred at the time of Passover.

The Jews were well aware of the implications of sheer sadism involved in the libel. In a dirge lamenting the Jews massacred at Munich because of a blood libel in 1286, the anonymous poet supposedly quotes the words of the Christian killers: "These unhappy Jews are sinning, they kill Christian children, they torture them in all their limbs, they take the blood cruelly to drink" (A.M. Habermann (ed.), *Sefer Gezerot Ashkenaz ve-Ẓarefat* (1946), 199). This ironical "quotation" contains an added motif in the libels, the thirst of the Jew for blood, out of his hatred for the good and true. This is combined in 13th-century Germany with the conception that the Jew cannot endure purity: he hates the innocence of the Christian child, its joyous song and appearance. This motif, found in the legendary tales of the monk Caesarius of Heisterbach in Germany, underwent various transmutations. In the source from which Caesarius took his story the child killed by the Jews sings *erubescat judaeus* ("let the Jew be shamed"). In Caesarius' version, the child sings the *Salve Regina*. The Jews cannot endure this pure laudatory song and try to frighten him and stop him from singing it. When he refuses they cut off his tongue and hack him to pieces. About a century after the expulsion of the Jews from England the cultural motif only became the basis of Geoffrey Chaucer's "Prioress' Tale." Here the widow's little child sings the *Alma Redemptoris Mater* while "the serpent Sathanas, That hath in Jews herte his waspes nest" awakens indignation in the cruel Jewish heart: "O Hebraik peple, allas! /Is this to yow a thing that is honest, /That swich a boy shal waeken as him lest/In your despyt, and singe of swich sentence/Which is agayn your lawes reverence?" The Jews obey the promptings of their Satanic master and kill the child; a miracle brings about their deserved punishment. Though the scene of this tale is laid in Asia, at the end of the story Chaucer takes care to connect Asia explicitly with bygone libels in England, and the motif of hatred of the innocent with the motif of mockery of the crucifixion: "O yonge Hugh of Lincoln, slayn also/With cursed Jewes, as it is notable,/For it nis but a litel whyle ago;/Prere eek for us."

In the blood libel of Fulda (1235) another motif comes to the fore: the Jews taking blood for medicinal remedies (here of five young Christian boys). The strange medley of ideas about the use of blood by the Jews is summed up by the end of the Middle Ages, in 1494, by the citizens of Tyrnau. The Jews need blood because "firstly, they were convinced by the judgment of their ancestors, that the blood of a Christian was a good remedy for the alleviation of the wound of circumcision. Secondly, they were of opinion that this blood, put into food, is very efficacious for the awakening of mutual love. Thirdly, they had discovered, as men and women among them suffered equally from menstruation, that the blood of a Christian is a specific medicine for it, when drunk. Fourthly, they had an ancient but secret ordinance by which they are under obligation to shed Christian blood in honor of God, in daily sacrifices, in some spot or other . . . the lot for the present year had fallen on the Tyrnau Jews." To the motifs of crucifixion, sadism, hatred of the innocent and of Christianity, and the unnaturalness of the Jews and its cure by the use of good Christian blood, there were added, from time to time, the ingredients of sorcery, perversity, and a kind of "blind obedience to a cruel tradition." Generation after generation of Jews in Europe was tortured, and Jewish communities were massacred or dispersed and broken up because of this libel (see map). It was spread by various agents. Popular preachers ingrained it in the minds of the common people. It became embedded through miracle tales, in their imagination and beliefs. This caused in Moravia, in about 1343, "a woman of ill fame to come with the help of another woman and propose to an old Jew of Brno, named Osel, her child for sale for six marks, because the child was red in hair and in face. The Jew simulated gladness, immediately gave three marks to the woman, and invited them to come with the child to a cellar the next day, early in the morning, under the pretext that he had to consult about the buying of the child with the bishop of the Jews and the elders." The Jew invited Christian officials, who imprisoned the women and punished them horribly (B. Bretholz, *Zuellen zur Geschichte der Juden in Maehren* (1935), 27—28).

The majority of the heads of state and the church opposed the circulation of the libel. Emperor Frederick II of Hohenstaufen decided, after the Fulda libel, to clear up the matter definitively, and have all the Jews in the empire killed if the accusation proved to be true, or exonerate them publicly if false, using this as an occasion to arbitrate in a matter affecting the whole of Christendom. The enquiry into the blood libel was thus turned into an all-Christian problem. The emperor, who first consulted the recognized church authorities, later had to turn to a device of his own. In the words of his summing-up of the enquiry (see *Zeitschrift fuer die Geschichte der Juden in Deutschland,* 1 (1887), 142—4), the usual church authorities "expressed various opinions about the case, and as they have been proved incapable of coming to a conclusive decision . . . we found it necessary . . . to turn to such people that were once Jews and have converted to the worship of the Christian faith; for they, as opponents, will not be silent about anything that they may know in this matter against the Jews." The emperor adds that he himself was already convinced, through his knowledge and wisdom, that the Jews were innocent. He sent to the kings of the West, asking them to send him decent and learned converts to Christianity to consult in the matter. The synod of converts took place and came to the conclusion, which the emperor published: "There is not to be found, either in the Old or the New Testament, that the Jews are desirous of human blood. On the contrary, they avoid contamination with any kind of blood." The document quotes from various Jewish texts in support, adding, "There is also a strong likelihood that those to whom even the blood of permitted animals is forbidden, cannot have a hankering after human blood. Against this accusation stand its cruelty, its unnaturalness, and the sound human emotions which the Jews have also in relation to the Christians. It is also unlikely that they would risk [through such a dangerous action] their life and property." A few years later, in 1247, Pope Innocent IV wrote that "Christians charge falsely . . . that [the Jews] hold a communion rite . . . with the heart of a murdered child; and should the cadaver of a dead man happen to be found anywhere they maliciously lay it to their charge." Neither emperor nor pope were heeded.

Jewish scholars in the Middle Ages bitterly rejected this inhuman accusation. They quoted the Law and instanced the Jewish way of life in order to refute it. The general opinion of the Jews is summed up thus: "You are libeling us for you want to find a reason to permit the shedding of our blood" (the 12th-13th centuries *Sefer Nizzahon Yashan – Liber Nizzachon Vetus*, p. 159 in *Tela Ignaea Satanae*, ed. J. Ch. Wagenseil, 1681). However, the Jewish denials, like the opinion of enlightened Christian leaders, did not succeed in preventing the blood libels from shaping to a large extent the image of the Jew transmitted from the Middle Ages to modern times. (It was only in 1965 that the church officially repudiated the blood libel of Trent by canceling the beatification of Simon and the celebrations in his honor.)

From the 17th century, blood-libel cases increasingly spread to Eastern Europe (Poland-Lithuania). The atmosphere at such trials is conveyed by the protocols of the investigation of two Jews and a Jewess who were put to torture in a blood-libel case at Lublin in 1636: "The Jew Baruch answers: 'I haven't seen the child.' Second torture: 'I am innocent and other Jews are innocent.' Third torture: 'I am innocent and other Jews are innocent, and everything that Joseph [the accuser] said is a lie. Jews need no Christian blood.' " Fegele the Jewess struggled courageously to defend the truth, as evident in the cross-examination: "Judge: 'Are you acquainted with sorcery?' Fegele: 'I never dabble in this. I am a poor widow who sells vodka and *kwas*'; Judge: 'For what purpose do Jews need Christian blood?: Fegele: 'Jews need no Christian blood, either of adults or of children'; Judge: 'Where have you hidden

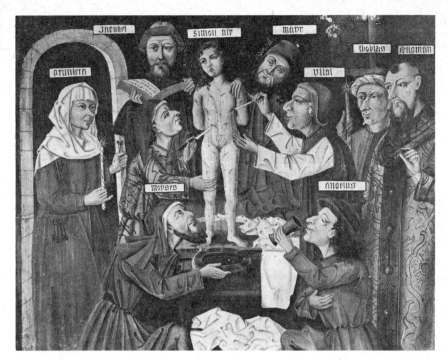

Simon of Trent tortured ritually by Jews, both male and female — an oil painting depicting the famous blood libel, artist unknown, South Tyrol, c. 1475.

the child's blood?: Fegele: 'The use of blood is forbidden to Jews, even of animal blood?' Judge: 'For what purpose do Jews need Christian blood?' Fegele: 'Jews use no Christian blood.' Judge: 'And are you a sorceress?' Fegele: 'No. I have nothing to do with this.' " She remained unbroken under torture, and even the threat of torture with a red-hot iron. Hugo Grotius, the Protestant legal philosopher, when told about the case expressed the opinion that the blood accusation was simply a libel generated by hatred of the Jews, and recalled that the early Christians and later Christian sectarians were accused in a similar way (Balaban, in *Festschrift S. Dubnow* (1930), 87–112).

In Eastern Europe, as late as the 17th century, the blood libel is identified with Jewish sorcery in the minds of the accusers, while the motif of the use of Christian blood for Passover unleavened bread increasingly comes to the fore. As conditions in Poland deteriorated, blood-libel cases multiplied. Through the Councils of the Lands the Jews sent an emissary to the Holy See who succeeded in having an investigation ordered and carried out by Cardinal Lorenzo Ganganelli, later Pope Clement XIV. In a detailed report submitted in 1759

Ganganelli examined the veracity of the blood libel in general and of the recent cases in Poland-Lithuania in particular, quoting *in extenso* from former church authorities against the libel. His main conclusion was: "It may be realized with what lively faith we ought to ask God with the Psalmist, 'deliver me from the calumnies of men.' For it cannot be denied that 'Calumny maketh the wise man mad and destroyeth the strength of his heart.' . . . I therefore hope that the Holy See will take some measure to protect the Jews of Poland as Saint Bernard, Gregory IX, and Innocent IV did for the Jews of Germany and France, 'that the name of Christ be not blasphemed' by the Jews" (see C. Roth, *Ritual Murder Libel and the Jews* (1935) 94).

In the 19th century the ringleaders of Jew-hatred in its modern form of anti-Semitism made conspicuous use of the blood libel for incitement against Jews in various countries. It was also used as a weapon to arouse the uneducated masses for specific political reasons, as occurred, for instance, in the Damascus Affair (1840) in the struggle among the Western powers for influence in the Near East. Anti-Semitic "experts" wrote treatises which set out to prove the truth of the libel from the records of past accusations and Jewish sources. Two such were Konstantin Cholewa de Pawlikowski (*Talmud in der Theorie und Praxis,* Regensburg, 1866) and H. Desportes (*Le mystère du sang chez les Juifs de tous les temps,* Paris, 1859, with a preface by the notorious anti-Semite E. Drumont). In the blood-libel trials held in the second half of the 19th and early 20th century, such as the Tiszaeszlar[1] and Beilis[2] cases, "experts" such as August Rohling appeared to testify in court; all were irrefutably answered by Jewish and pro-Jewish scholars (J.S. Block, H.L. Strack, J. Mazeh). Another weapon developed in the arsenal of anti-Semitism was an insidious way of implying the truth of the blood-libel charge by stating it as a fact without denying it. A notorious example is found in the article *Blut* (in *Handwoerterbuch des deutschen Aberglaubens,* 1 (1927), cols. 1434–42) where it is remarked (col. 1436): *"Moses verbot umsonst das Bluttrinken"* ("Moses in vain prohibited the drinking of blood"), and *"Dass die Frage der juedischen Ritualmorde immer noch nicht verschwunden ist, lehren Prozesse neuerer Zeit"* ("Trials in modern times show the problem of ritual murder has still not disappeared"; col. 1439).

The Nazis unashamedly used the blood libel in full force for anti-Jewish propaganda. They revived old allegations and instituted reinvestigations and trials in territories under their rule or influence: at Memel in 1936; at Bamberg in 1937 (a revival); and at Velhartice, Bohemia, in 1940. On May 1, 1934, the Nazi daily, *Der Stuermer,* devoted a special horrifyingly illustrated number to

---

1   Town in N.E. Hungary where the Jews were accused of murdering a young girl.
2   Mendel Beilis, accused in Kiev in 1911 of murdering a young boy.

the blood libel, in which German scientists openly served the Nazi aims. The above-mentioned *Handwoerterbuch* (vol. 7 (1935–36), cols. 727–39) printed an article entitled *Ritualmord* written by Peuckert, a man who remained active and respected in German science, which is throughout simply an affirmation and propagation of the blood libel, although using some cautious phrasing. The epitome appears in the remarkable enquiry: *"Es mag im Anschluss an dieses erschuetternde Register nur noch die Frage Behandelt werden: zu welchem Zweck verwendeten die Juden das Blut"* ("In conclusion to this shocking list, there remains only one question: for what purpose did the Jews use the blood?"; col. 734).

The blood libel, in the various forms it assumed and the tales with which it was associated, is one of the most terrible expressions of the combination of human cruelty and credulity. No psychological or sociological research can convey the depths to which the numerous intentional instigators of such libels, and the more numerous propagators of this phantasmagoria, sank. It resulted in the torture, murder, and expulsion, of countless Jews, and the misery of insults. However, the dark specters it raised were even more harmful in their effects on the minds of Christians. The Jew had only to refer to himself, his upbringing, laws, way of life, and attitude to other people and to cruelty, to perceive the falsity and baselessness of these allegations. In modern times the Zionist thinker Aḥad Ha-Am found "some consolation" in the existence of the blood libel, for it could serve as a spiritual defense against the influence on Jewish self-evaluation of the consensus of hostile opinion. "This accusation is the solitary case in which the general acceptance of an idea about ourselves does not make us doubt whether all the world can be wrong, and we right, because it is based on an absolute lie, and is not even supported by any false inference from particular to universal. Every Jew who has been brought up among Jews knows as an indisputable fact that throughout the length and breadth of Jewry there is not a single individual who drinks human blood for religious purposes ... Let the world say what it will about our moral inferiority: we know that its ideas rest on popular logic, and have no real scientific basis ... 'But' − you ask − 'is it possible that everybody can be wrong, and the Jews right?' Yes, it is possible: the blood accusation proves it possible. Here, you see the Jews are right and perfectly innocent" (*Selected Essays* (1962), 203–4).

THE BLACK DEATH HORROR

The epidemic of various contagious diseases, bubonic, septicemic, and pneumonic, all caused by the same bacillus, *Pasteurella pestis,* a combination of which raged throughout Europe between 1348 and 1350, usually called "the

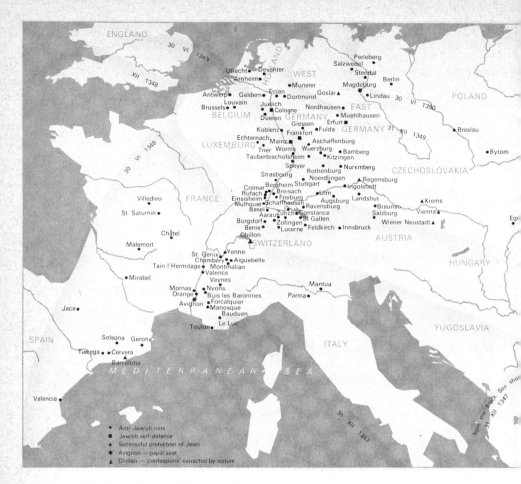

The Black Death. The map shows, in progressive shades of gray, the spread of the plague across Europe in six-month periods from Dec. 31, 1347, to June 30, 1350. (Background: modern countries.)

Black Death", was the worst plague experienced since the sixth century. Between one-quarter and one-half of the total population perished. In centers with denser populations, such as the monasteries, the proportion of victims was much higher. As the bacteria of this disease live in certain temperatures only, the peak periods of sickness and mortality usually occurred at certain months in the year, according to the local climate.

The impact of this unprecedented catastrophe had a profound effect on the behavior of the population. People reacted by extremes, either seeking recourse to religion through repentance and supplication to God, or reverting to licentiousness, lawbreaking, and savagery. These two types of reaction often combined, in particular where they concerned the attitude of the non-Jewish population to the Jews. Toward the end of 1348 and in early 1349 countless numbers of Jews lost their lives in a wave of massacres which spread throughout Europe as a result of the accusation that the Jews had caused the death of Christians by poisoning the wells and other water sources. According to L.F. Hirst, a leading authority in this field, the Black Death "in all probability . . . originated somewhere in the central Asiatic hinterland, where a permanent reservoir of infection is maintained among the wild rodents of the steppes. Rumors of a great mortality among Asiatics, especially Chinese, reached Europe in 1346, and by the spring of that year bubonic plague had reached the shores of the Black Sea . . . From ports on the shores of the Crimea besieged by Tatars, who perished in vast numbers from the epidemic . . . the infection was carried on shipboard to Constantinople, Genoa, Venice, and other European ports. The disease spread as rapidly as the transport of those days permitted . . . to the Mainland." At the time of the Black Death no one was aware of this connection and the existence of contagion was only vaguely perceived. By some persons the catastrophe was ascribed to astrological conjunctions; others regarded it as a divine visitation. Pope Clement VI, in his bull defending the Jews from these accusations, saw it as "the pestilence with which God is afflicting the Christian people." The vast majority of the population, however, was inclined to view it as a *pestis manufacta* (an artificially induced malady), the simplest explanation to the unsophisticated mind, and therefore sought the human agents thought to be spreading the disease. Initially, the Jews were not the only persons accused; strangers of every type were suspected. An Avignonese physician relates: "Many hesitated, in some countries they expelled paupers suffering from deformity; and in yet others, the nobles." Sometimes itinerant monks were suspected of placing the poison and spreading the disease, and they were attacked instead.

Soon, however, the feelings of inability to stem the plague, and the fierce urge to react against the death and destruction it caused, concentrated the force of the populace on the age-old target of popular Christian hostility, the Jews. Anti-Jewish violence was particularly rabid in Germany, where it had been preceded by a dark half century of anti-Jewish persecution in conjunction with a succession of blood libels and accusations of host desecration. This had added to the sinister traits already attributed to the hateful image of the Jew. In France, also, the way had been paved for this accusation by a similar charge leveled during the Pastoureaux persecutions of 1321. Amid the general atmosphere of hostility, and the cruelty of the persecutions to which the Jews had been subjected, it was almost logical that Christians could imagine that the Jews might seek revenge. Thus, a Jew who was tortured in Freiburg im Breisgau in 1349, "was then asked . . . 'why did they do it . . . ?' Then he answered: 'because you

Christians have destroyed so many Jews; because of what king Armleder[1] did; and also because we too want to be lords; for you have lorded long enough.' "

The first occasion on which Jews were tortured to confess complicity in spreading the Black Death was in September 1348, in the Castle of Chillon on Lake Geneva. The "confessions" thus extracted indicate that their accusers wished to prove that the Jews had set out to poison the wells and food "so as to kill and destroy the whole of Christianity." The disease was allegedly spread by a Jew of Savoy on the instructions of a rabbi who told him: "See, I give you a little package, half a span in size, which contains a preparation of poison and venom in a narrow, stitched leathern bag. This you are to distribute among the wells, the cisterns, and the springs about Venice and the other places where you go, in order to poison the people who use the water ... " This indictment, therefore, shows that his accusers recognized that the plague had spread from the south northward. As the case dragged on, details were extracted telling of further consultations held among the Jews, about messengers from Toledo, and other wild allegations. On Oct. 3, 1348, during the summing up, an allegation providing a motive for the total destruction of Jewry was made; it was asserted that "before their end they said on their Law that it is true that all Jews, from the age of seven, cannot excuse themselves of this [crime], since all of them in their totality were cognizant and are guilty of the above actions".

These "confessions" were sent to various cities in Germany. The accusation that the Jews had poisoned the wells spread there like wildfire, fanned by the general atmosphere of terror. The patricians of Strasbourg attempted to defend the Jews at a meeting of representatives of the Alsatian towns at Benfeld, but the majority rejected their plea, arguing: "If you are not afraid of poisoning, why have you yourselves covered and guarded your wells?" Correspondence on the subject between the authorities in the various cities has been preserved. In general, it reveals a decision to expel the Jews from the locality concerned for good, and to launch an immediate attack to kill them while they still remained. At Basle the patricians also unsuccessfully attempted to protect the Jews. In various cities Jews were tortured to confess their part in the conspiracy. The defamation, killings, and expulsions spread through the kingdoms of Christian Spain, France, and Germany, to Poland-Lithuania, affecting about 300 Jewish communities. On Sept. 26, 1348, Pope Clement VI issued a bull in Avignon denouncing this allegation, stating that "certain Christians, seduced by that liar, the devil, are imputing the pestilence to poisoning by Jews." This imputation and the massacre of Jews in consequence were defined by the pope as "a

---

[1] Title assumed by bands of German marauders who massacred thousands of Jews in Franconia and Alsace, 1336–39.

horrible thing." He tried to convince Christians that "since this pestilence is all but universal everywhere, and by a mysterious decree of God has afflicted, and continues to afflict, both Jews and many other nations throughout the diverse regions of the earth to whom a common existence with Jews is unknown [the charge] that the Jews have provided the cause or the occasion for such a crime is without plausibility." Both the emperors Charles IV and Peter IV of Aragon also tried to protect the Jews from the results of the accusation. The arguments generally put forward by the rulers were expressed by the physician Konrad of Megenberg in his *Buch der Natur* arrived at in the light of his own experience: "But I know that there were more Jews in Vienna than in any other German city familiar to me, and so many of them died of the plague that they were obliged to enlarge their cemetery. To have brought this on themselves would have been folly on their part." However, all these appeals to reason were ineffective. The massacres of the Jews continued, and Jewish property was confiscated. Despite his policy of protecting the Jews, in 1350 the emperor Charles IV formally absolved the burghers of Cheb (Eger) in Bohemia for the killings and robbery they had committed among the Jewish population. In doing so, he stated: "Forgiveness is [granted] for every transgression involving the slaying and destruction of Jews which has been committed without the positive knowledge of the leading citizens, or in their ignorance, or in any other fashion whatsoever." By this time it was well known that the accusation that Jews had spread the plague was false. In many places Jews were killed even before the plague had visited the locality. Further outbreaks of plague continued later in the 14th century but Jews were no longer accused of being the cause.

It was recognized by the Jews that the Christians "have opened wide their mouths about me: they have put and spread poison on the water, so they say, in order to libel and attack us," to quote a contemporary dirge. Faced with this overwhelming antagonism, the Jews tried to defend themselves wherever possible and in whatever way they could. In many localities fierce conflicts took place between the Jewish population and their attackers. At Mainz the Jews set fire to their homes and to the Jewish street: according to some sources, 6,000 Jews perished in the flames. This also occurred at Frankfort on the Main. In Strasbourg, 2,000 Jews were burnt on a wooden scaffold in the Jewish cemetery. The manner in which the martyrs met their deaths is described in a contemporary Hebrew source concerning "the holy community of Nordhausen . . . They asked the burghers to permit them to prepare themselves for martyrdom: permission having been given . . . they joyfully arrayed themselves in their prayer shawls and shrouds, both men and women. They [the Christians] dug a grave at the cemetery and covered it with wooden scaffolding . . . The pious ones [among the Jews] asked that a musician be hired to play dancing tunes so that they should enter the presence of God with singing. They took each other by the hand, both men and women, and danced and leapt with their whole strength before God. Their teacher, R. Jacob, went before them; his son, R. Meir, brought up the rear to see that none should lag behind. Singing and dancing they entered the grave, and when all had entered, R. Meir jumped out and walked around to make certain that none had stayed outside. When the burghers saw him they asked him to save his life [by apostasy]. He answered: 'This now is the end of our troubles, you see me only for a while, and then I shall be no more.' He returned to the grave; they set fire to the scaffolding; they died all of them together and not a cry was heard" (*Sefer Minhagim* of Worms). This was the spirit that enabled European Jewry to emerge spiritually unscathed from the avalanche of hatred and cruelty released on the Jews by the Christians in Europe.

The Black Death not only resulted in the immediate destruction of thousands of Jewish lives and the loss of Jewish homes and property in hundreds of communities, but had more far-reaching consequences. Popular imagination invested the already odious image of the Jew with even more horrible characteristics. It was this image that helped to shape the stereotype of the Jew represented by anti-Semitism and racism in modern times. After the Black Death the legal status of the Jews deteriorated almost everywhere in Europe. Although Jews were frequently received back into the cities where many had been killed or driven out, sometimes within a year of the decision to expel them for good, they usually only gained permission to resettle on worse terms and in greater isolation than before. The position of the Jews in Aragon and Castile deteriorated sharply after 1348–49. The only countries in Europe where the events of the Black Death did not leave a permanent scar on the Jewish communities were Poland-Lithuania. The reconstruction of the Jewish communities and of Jewish life and cultural activity in the second half of the 14th and the beginning of the 15th century clearly evidence the social and spiritual vitality of the Jewish people in Europe in the period.

11

JUDEO-CHRISTIAN
DISPUTATIONS
AND POLEMICS

Up to early modern times dialogue between members of different faiths attempted either to prove the superiority and absolute validity of one faith over the other, or to defend the totality of one faith and its Holy Scriptures, or elements in them, against questioning and criticism by believers in another faith. In some cases the representative of one side has been put on a quasi-legal trial to justify his convictions, as often happened to Jews in the Middle Ages. Disputations and polemics between believers of the three monotheistic faiths — Judaism, Christianity, and Islam — inevitably start from and return to the common ground of the Hebrew Bible and certain religious concepts held by all three, but always in order to confute the opposing view and prove the validity of the proponent's argument.

In recording the most open public disputation to take place in the Middle Ages, that of Barcelona in 1263, the Christian account stresses that the object of the disputation was not to question the validity of Christianity, "which because of its certainty cannot be subjected to debate." This was to remain the ultimate standpoint of disputants throughout the centuries. As late as 1933, a representative of Protestant Christianity, Karl Ludwig Schmidt, declared to his Jewish partner, as representative of German Jewry, the Zionist and philosopher Martin Buber, in a Christian-Jewish dialogue before a gathering of Jews: "The evangelical theologian who has to talk to you, must talk to you as a member of the Church of Jesus Christ, must endeavor to talk in a manner that will convey the message of the Church to Jewry. He must do this even if you would not have invited him to do so. The assertion of a mission to you may have a somewhat bitter taste as if intending an attack; but such an attack precisely involves caring about you as Jews — so that you may live with us as our brethren in our German fatherland as throughout the world" (*Theologische Blaetter,* 12 (1933), 258). This liberal German theologian found it necessary to declare at the outset of the debate the missionary character of Jewish-Christian disputation.

Despite the self-assurance and aggressiveness implicit in this attitude, both sides were inevitably influenced to a certain degree by the dialectics of their opponents. At a very early stage of the Jewish-Christian debate this challenge was perceived in a Midrash which relates that "the *minim* [i.e., early Christians] were continuously disputing with Rabbi Judah, the son of Nakosa: they would ask him and he would answer them . . . When he was called [to Heaven] his pupils said to him: Rabbi, you were helped from on High and were victorious. He said to them: . . . Go and pray for this . . . basket that was full of diamonds and pearls and now is full of burnt-out charcoal" (*Ecclesiastes Rabbah* 1:8, no. 4).

Disputations sometimes started from a casual encounter, sparked off by an actual problem or object noticed. Sometimes, in particular from the 13th century in Europe, they were formally conducted in public. Authors of polemical literature like Judah Halevi employed the artifical framework of the disputation to set forth their arguments. Alternatively, the dialectic climate of an actual dispuation led to systematic theological formulations such as the *Sefer Ikkarim* ("Book of Principles") of Joseph Albo (see below) or *Cur Deus homo* . . . of Anselm of Canterbury. The reports and impressions of the actual disputations that have been preserved are conflicting. The same motifs tend to recur time after time, any variation reflecting the spirit of the times, personal interests, or particular circumstances.

The history of disputations and their content, while concomitantly a record of constant tension and deliberate animosity, is also a process of continuous mutual interpenetration of ideas and influence stimulated by this tension.

In biblical times, the pagan polytheism of the period precluded the holding of any discursive dialogue of this nature. Claims are made asserting the might of one deity or deities above that of others, usually uttered in the heat of war after victory. Jewish monotheistic prophecy makes frequent use of scathing and ironical polemics to denounce polytheism and idolatry.

However, in the cultural milieu of the Hellenistic-Roman world, Jewish monotheism was challenged by missionary Hellenistic philosophy and beliefs. Thus the Mishnah records that pagans asked the elders (in Rome): "If God does not desire idolatry why does He not destroy it? They answered: If men had been worshiping objects unnecessary for the cosmos He would have destroyed them, but they worship the sun and moon and the stars and the planets. Should He destroy His world because of fools? They [the pagan questioners] said to them: Then let Him destroy those objects [of pagan worship] of which the cosmos has no need, and leave only those necessary for the cosmos. They answered: Then the arguments of the worshipers of those [necessary objects] would have been strengthened, for they would say: these are divinities, for they have not been destroyed" (*Avodah Zarah* 4:7).

The exculsiveness and superiority claimed for Jewish monotheism against idolatry are developed in the following disputation: "A *philosophus* asked Rabban Gamaliel: Your Bible states 'for I the Lord thy God am a jealous God.'

Is there any merit in idolatry to give rise to jealousy? A hero is jealous of a hero, a sage of a sage, a rich man of a rich man; hence there must be merit in idolatry since it provokes jealousy. He answered him: If a man called his dog by the name of his father, and wanting to take an oath takes it on the life of the dog, of whom would the father be jealous, of the son or of the dog?" (*Mekhilta, Ba-Hodesh,* 9). Details of Jewish worship also enter the disputation, as when "a gentile asked Rabban Johanan b. Zakkai: Those things that you perform resemble a kind of magic — you take a cow, slaughter it and burn it, and keep its ashes; and when one of you has become defiled by contact with the dead they sprinkle him two or three times [with water mixed with the ashes] and say, You have been purified." In replying to the gentile R. Johanan drew a comparison with similar rituals employed in exorcism. To his own pupils, however, he explained it as an act of faith: "The dead does not defile nor does water purify; it is just a decree of the King of Kings. The Almighty, Blessed be His Name, said: This is my order, this is my rule, and no man may transgress it" (*Pirkei de-Rav Kahana* 40 a–b).

Gradually the motif of Jewish weakness and dispersion was introduced into the argument against Judaism. When a certain "heretic" stressed that although the Jews were at the mercy of Rome, the gentiles refrained from destroying them, he was answered by R. Hoshaiah: "This is because you do not know how to carry this out. If you [seek to] destroy us all, we are not all to be found within your borders. [If you seek to destroy] only those within your borders you would be reputed a maimed empire. [The heretic] answered: By the body of Rome, we are engaged constantly with this problem" (*Pesahim* 87b). This last motif, in stressing the enmity of the Romans and the dispersion of the Jews in both the Roman and Persian empires, seems to sound the note of the emerging predominance of Christianity.

The Talmud sometimes ascribes legendary disputations to biblical figures, for instance between Abraham and Nimrod. There are also accounts of litigations, supposed to have taken place before courts of law and kings, between representatives of the Jewish people and other claimants to the Land of Israel. Josephus tells about litigation that took place between the Jews of Alexandria and the Samaritans "in the presence of Ptolemy himself, the Jews asserting that it was the Temple at Jerusalem which had been built in accordance with the laws of Moses, and the Samaritans that it was the Temple on Mount Gerizim. And they requested the king to sit in council with his friends and hear their arguments on these matters" (Josephus, *Antiquities,* 13:74–75; and see the argumentation, 75–79).

Some sages appear in talmudic literature as having engaged in disputations that not only concern the Jewish faith and way of life but also show to advantage the breadth of knowledge and acuity of Jewish scholarship, for instance, Joshua b. Hananiah (see *Ḥagigah* 5b; *Ḥullin* 59b–60b; *Bekhorot* 8b–91a).

The developing cleavage between Christianity and Judaism, until the final parting of the ways in the second century, led to increasing disputation between Christians and Jews. The lists of *testimonia* from the Hebrew Bible prepared by early Christian teachers consist of biblical quotations to be used not only to convince pagans but also, in most cases, to persuade Jews to accept the Christianity clauses. With the growing distance between Christian and Jewish theological concepts and ways of life, the disputations became more formal and were noted down. The early disputations in the form of independent treatises are written down by the Christian side although fragments and impressions of such disputations are on record in talmudic literature.[1] The challenges and pressures of these disputations in the world of the *amoraim* (third to fourth centuries) are projected in the explanation given by Abbahu, the celebrated disputant with the Christians at Caesarea, to Christians who questioned the learning of a scholar from Babylonia: "We [i.e., the scholars of Erez Israel] who are living with you regard it as our task to study [Scripture] thoroughly. They [the scholars of Babylonia] are not so well versed" in it (*Avodah Zarah* 4a).

Representing the Christian view is a work well-known by around 500, the *Altercatio Simonis Judaei et Theophili Christiani* (ed. by A. v. Harnack, Leipzig, 1883). Although the text was subsequently lost for centuries the form of the *Altercatio* and the arguments put forward there influenced later Christian presentations of disputations with Jews.

Of fundamental importance both for the authority it carries and the arguments met there is Justin Martyr's Dialogue with Tryphon held about the time of the Bar Kokhba revolt (132–135 C.E.) and written down between 156 and 161. While the argument of general issues and detailed points is sharp and bitter in this early discussion between Christians and Jews, the relationship between the disputants is represented as one of mutual courtesy. They part with an acknowledgment by the Jewish debater that he has "been extraordinarily

---

1   *Mekhilta* Shira, 7; Ba-Ḥodesh, 5; Kaspa, 3; *Mekhilta de-R. Simeon bar Yoḥai* to Shemot, p. 2; *Sifrei Deuteronomy* 87–91, 306; Jerusalem Talmud (TJ), *Berakhot* 9:1, 12d–13b; TJ, *Ta'anit* 2:1, 65b; TJ, *Sanhedrin* 1:1, 18a; TJ (Venice, 1523), *Sanhedrin* 13:9, 23c–d; TJ, *Sanhedrin* 10:1, 27d–28a; *Berakhot* 7a, 10a, 12a–b; *Shabbat* 88a–b, 116a–b; *Pesaḥim* 56a; *Eruvin* 22a; *Sukkah* 48b; *Ta'anit* 27b; *Ḥagigah* 5b; *Yevamot* 102b; *Sotah* 47a; *Gittin* 57a; *Sanhedrin* 38b–39a, 43b (in *Ḥesronot ha-Shas*, in "El ha-Mekorot" ed. of the Talmud, 1963), 98b–99a, 106a–b; *Avodah Zarah* 4a, 6a–b, 17a; Tosefa *Ḥullin* 2:2, *Ecclesiastes Rabbah* 1:8, no. 4; 2:1, nos. 1,2; 4:8, no. 1; *Song of Songs Rabbah* 7:3.

charmed with our intercourse," with Justin stating that the Jews "departed, finally praying for my deliverance both from the dangers of the sea, and from all ill. And I prayed also for them, saying: I can make no greater prayer for you, Gentlemen, than this, that . . . you may do in all respects the same as we, acknowledging that the object of our worship is the Christ of God" (Justin Martyr, *Dialogue*, 142:1–3, Eng. trans. by A.L. Williams (1930), 289).

Even so, politeness does not hinder Justin from hurling at the Jews their harsh fate, at a time of life and death struggle with Rome, which he saw as the punishment designated by their Law: "The circumcision according to the flesh, that was from Abraham, was given for a sign, that ye should be separated from the other nations and us, and that ye alone should suffer the things that ye are rightly suffering now, and that your lands should be desolate and your cities burned with fire, and that foreigners should eat up the fruits before your face, and none of you go up unto Jerusalem. For by nothing else are ye to be known from other men, save by the circumcision that is in your flesh . . . All this has happened to you rightly and well. For ye slew the Just One and His prophets before Him, and now ye reject, and, as far as in you lies, dishonor those that set their hope on Him . . . , cursing in your synagogues them that believe in Christ" (*ibid.*, 16:2–4, pp. 32–33). He also frequently explains other precepts as having been given to the Jews to their detriment: "Now because of your sins and those of your fathers God charged you to keep the Sabbath as a sign . . . and has also given you His other ordinances" (*ibid.*, 21:1, p. 42). The true meaning of the Torah and commandments enjoined in the Prophets is to be found in the Christological, spiritual-figurative sense. Physical rest could not really be enjoined on Saturday, for "you see that Nature does not idle nor keep Sabbath. Abide as ye have been born" (*ibid.*, 23:3, pp. 47–48). The stubborn and sinful Jewish people continue in existence only because God "has not yet brought the Judgment, nor has begun to bring it, because He knows that every day some [of the Jews] are becoming disciples unto the name of His Christ, and are leaving the way of error" (*ibid.*, 39:2, pp. 77). Justin categorically rejects any form of Judeo-Christianity (*ibid.*, 46:1–2, p. 90; 47:1–2, pp. 93–95). A large part of Justin's argumentation consists of *testimonia* from the Prophets adduced in evidence of the validity of Christianity. His methods of dialectic and manner of presentation became the prototype of later Christian argumentation against Jewry and Judaism.

Tryphon objects in principle to the method of adducing Christological *testimonia* from the Hebrew Bible: "Why do you select for citation only such parts as you choose out of the sayings of the Prophets, and make no mention of those [that do not fit the Christian view]," and brings examples to prove his point (*ibid.*, 27:1, p. 53). Justin was fully aware that the main concern of responsible Jews at this critical period was not discussion of Greek beliefs or philosophical debate. Thus he describes how "Tryphon's companions sat down opposite, and after one of them had made a remark about the war in Judea, they conversed about it" (*ibid.*, 9:3, p. 20). However, the Jew regards philosophical paganism as preferable to superstititious Christianity: "It were better for you to continue to hold the philosophy of Plato or of some other learned man, . . . than to have been completely led away by false speeches, and to follow men of no account. For while you remained in that mode of philosophy and lived a blameless life, a hope was left you of a better fate, but when you forsook God, and placed your hope on a man, what kind of salvation yet remains for you?" (*ibid.*, 8:3, p. 17). The Christians suffer persecution for their credulity: "You people, by receiving a worthless rumor, shape a kind of messiah for yourselves, and for His sake are now blindly perishing" (*ibid.*, 8:4, p. 19). The true hope of salvation lies in strict fulfillment of the Law: "First be circumcised, then . . . keep the Sabbath and the Feasts and God's New Moons, and, in short, do all the things that are written in the Law, and then perchance you will find mercy from God" (*ibid.,* 8:4, p. 17).

Not only is the Christian method of citation and evidence seen as falsifying the words of the Hebrew Bible by removing them from their context and failing to have regard for the spirit of the Hebrew language, but many of the events related by Christians and the interpretations they give are regarded as blasphemous and foolish. When Justin insulted the Jew by quoting the words of the Bible according to the version of Paul, which stigmatizes the Jews as prophet-killers, and added the remark referred to above that the Jews are still permitted to exist because of those among them who convert to Christianity, Tryphon interjected: "I would have you know that you are out of your mind when you say all this" (*ibid.*, 39:1−3, p. 77). To the long list of *testimonia* cited by Justin on the prophecies relating to Jesus and his primordial divinity, the Jew reacts: "You say many blasphemous things, thinking to persuade us that this man who was crucified, has been with Moses and Aaron, and has spoken to them in a pillar of cloud, that he then became man and was crucified and has ascended into Heaven, and comes again on earth, and is to be worshiped" (*ibid.*, 38:1, p. 75).

Belief in incarnation and crucifixion in relation to the preexistent Divinity is rejected as irrational: "For your assertion that this Christ existed, and was God, before all ages, then that He is not man by origin, seems to me to be not only strange but even foolish" (*ibid.*, 48:1, p. 95). The Christian claims for Jesus amount to an attempt to "prove to us that the existence of another God besides the Maker of the universe is recognized by the spirit of the Prophets" (*ibid.,* 55:1, p. 108; and see also 50:1, p. 100). The interpretation given by Justin to *"ha-almah"* in Isaiah 7:14 to mean "the Virgin" (*Dialogue*, 66, pp. 138–139) is corrected by Tryphon who states that its actual meaning is "the young woman" and places the prophecy in its historical context in the reign of King Hezekiah. He adds that the Christian concept of a virgin birth is pagan in origin and character: "Among the tales of those whom we call Greeks it is said that Perseus had been born of Danae, still a virgin, by him that they entitle Zeus flowing down upon her in the form of gold. And in fact you ought to be ashamed of saying the same sort of things as they, and should rather say that this Jesus was a man of human origin, and, if you prove from the Scriptures that He is the Christ, [say] that because of his perfect life under the Law he was deemed worthy to be chosen to be Christ. And do not dare to assert marvels, that you be not convicted of talking folly like the Greeks" (*ibid.,* 67, pp. 139–140). Hence it would seem, according to Justin's rendering, that Tryphon would have found some satisfaction in a Christianity which recognized Jesus as the human redeemer of the gentiles alone. Tryphon tries at some length to elicit Justin's attitude regarding whether Judeo-Christians should observe the Law (*ibid.,* 46:1, p. 90; 47:1–2, p. 93; and see above Justin's rejection of the Judeo-Christians).

According to Justin's account, Tryphon expressly proposed: "Let Him be recognized of you who are of the Gentiles as Lord and Christ and God, as the Scriptures signify, seeing also that you have all acquired the name of Christians from Him. But as for us, who are worshipers of God who made even Him [Jesus], we do not need to confess Him or worship Him." Anger at this proposition provoked Justin into a rare outburst of personal invective against his Jewish opponent (*ibid.,* 64:1–2, p. 133). Tryphon pointed out that the Messiah awaited by the Jews was a king-savior, not a redeeming God: "For all of us Jews expect that the Christ will be a man of merely human origin, and that Elijah will come and anoint Him" (*ibid.,* 49:1, p. 97). The King will come to his people, the descendants of Abraham. When Justin quotes to him from *testimonia* that the Messiah will come to Israel, Tryphon asks what that implies: "Are you Israel, and does He say all this about you?" (*ibid.,* 123:7, p. 256).

This relatively early encounter between a separated Christianity and Judaism established the main themes and groundwork of future Jewish-Christian *testimonia*, the polemical statements by Tertullian against the Jews in the same century, and the fragments of Jewish-Christian disputation found in tannaitic and amoraitic literature mentioned above. Constantly recurring subjects in disputation from the end of the second century, therefore, are the significance of *"Bereshit"* ("In the beginning") and of *"ad ki yavo Shiloh"* (Genesis 49:10). Are the Just Men and Patriarchs who lived before the giving of the Torah to be regarded as observers of the Law or not? Why was the Law given to the Jews? For their benefit, or as a punishment? Is the true meaning of the Law and the

Prophets to be elicited by a "literal" or a "spiritual" interpretation? What is the significance of the use of the plural form in referring to the Divine in the Bible? Is it intended to convey the concept of Trinity? Who is "the suffering servant of God" in Isaiah 52 and following? What is the correct translation of *"ha-almah"*?

Although variations of these questions occur, this remained the exegetical core of Jewish-Christian disputation. The fate of the Jewish people, the course of history and empires, and war and peace in the world enter and are developed in the debate at a later stage. Although as yet not clearly defined, certain attitudes are already embryonic: the Jewish objection to the concept of the Trinity as being inherently idolatrous, and to Incarnation as insulting to the divine nature of God; the insistence on the Jewish side that understanding of Scripture should be based on a comprehensive knowledge of the original language without depriving the words of their literal meaning or isolating them from their context. There also emerge the mystic-fideistic standpoint of the Christian side; the critico-rationalistic approach of the Jewish side; the universalist-individualistic claims of Church spokesmen against the Jewish concept of Israel as a national "natural-historical-cell," the "kingdom of priests and holy nation" entrusted in this social pattern to carry the Divine call to the world.

Also dating from the early period of the disputations are the somewhat dissimilar strands of anti-Christian argumentation quoted by Celsus in his anti-Christian polemic written about 178. There the Jew is reported to have said: "I could say much about what happened to Jesus which is true, and nothing like the account which has been written by the disciples of Jesus" (in Origen, *Contra Celsum*, translated and edited by H. Chadwick (1953), 2:13, p. 78). Celsus' record, which contains numerous extra-New Testamentary details and innuendoes adverse to Jesus, in some way prefigures the later polemical version of Jesus' life and death, *Toledot Yeshu*.[2] The Jew also repeats many of the anti-Christian arguments used by Tryphon and the *amoraim*. In addition, he is quoted as sharply condemning Jewish apostasy to Christianity, saying: "Why do you take your origin from our religion? And then, as if you are progressing in knowledge, despise these things although you cannot name any other origin for your doctrine excepting our Law" (*ibid.*, 2:4, p. 69; and see also 2:1, pp. 66–67). He attacks the concept of the resurrection of Jesus, in particular comparing it to similar pagan legends (2:55, p. 109), and adds: "While he was alive he did not help himself, but after death he rose again and showed the marks

---

2   Origen: *Contra Celsum,* 1:28, pp. 27–28; 1:32, pp. 31–32; 1:38, p. 37; 1:67, p. 62; 2:8, pp. 71–72; 2:9, p. 73; 2:15, p. 81; 2:16, pp. 81–82; 2:26, p. 90; 2:27, p. 90, 2:32, p. 93; 2:34, p. 94; 2:44, p. 100; 2:46, p. 101; 2:55, p. 109; 2:70, p. 121.

of his punishment and how his hand had been pierced. But who saw this? A hysterical female, as you say, and perhaps some other one of those who were deluded by the same sorcery, who either dreamt in a certain state of mind and through wishful thinking had a hallucination due to some mistaken notion (an experience which has happened to thousands), or, which is more likely, wanted to impress the others by telling this fantastic tale, and so by this cock-and-bull story to provide a chance for other beggars" *(ibid.)*. His attack on resurrection is continued by the argument: "But if he really was so great he ought, in order to display his divinity, to have disappeared suddenly from the cross" (*ibid.*, 2:68, p. 118). The Jew continues: "Where is he then, that we may see and believe?" (*ibid.*, 2:77, p. 126). He uses Jesus' rejection by the Jews as an argument against his divinity: "What God that comes among men is disbelieved, and that when he appears to those who were waiting for him? Or why ever is he not recognized by people who have been long expecting him?" (*ibid.*, 2:75, p. 123).

The problems raised here denote the type of argumentation used by Jews against Christians in the Christian-Judeo-Pagan triangle of the second half of the second century. When Judaism alone remained face to face with Christianity much argumentation of this category was omitted in the direct confrontation.

In the fourth century, the rise of Christianity to imperial dominion in the late Roman Empire, the shock of Julian "the Apostate's" revolt against this domination, and the fire and smoke of internal Christian doctrinal battles were accompanied by bitter and brutal denunciation of Judaism and the Jews, their character and way of life by John Chrysostom, Eusebius and other fathers of the Church. Not only was the concept of divine election now claimed for the Church only, as the "spiritual Israel," but it was categorically denied to the historical Jewish people, leaving the title only to those of the nation who were considered "Christians before Christ," like the Patriarchs and the Prophets. Much of the argumentation in the talmudic literature cited above was in answer to this mode of attack.

The changed atmosphere at the courts of the German Christian rulers in Europe, and the standpoint of an educated Jew there, emerge in the account of a disputation recorded by Bishop Gregory of Tours in his *Historiarum Libri decem* (6:5; ed. R. Buchner, pp. 8–13). In 581 the Jewish merchant Priscus was confronted with the bishop in the presence of King Chilperic, who initiated the disputation, in an attempt to win the Jew to Christianity. Gregory rests his argument on chapter and verse while the Jew puts questions and cites contrary biblical testimony. Priscus said to the king: "God did not enter into marriage and did not bring forth a son, neither can he have a partner to his sovereignty, as Moses says: 'See now that it is I, even I, and there is no God with Me. I put to death and I make alive; I strike and I heal' " *(ibid.)*. And again: "Can God be man, can He be born of woman? Can he suffer beatings and be sentenced to death?" *(ibid.).* At this point the bishop intervened to cite lengthy Christological *testimonia,* and the Jew asks: "What necessity was there for God to suffer in such a manner?" To the bishop's explanation that He did so in order to save mankind from sin and reconcile man with God, the Jew rejoined: "Could not God send prophets or apostles who would bring man back to the way of salvation? And had He only the means of humiliating himself in the flesh?" *(ibid.).*

With the growth of Christian power, its clash with the conquering armies of Islam, and the consequent changes in the Jewish fate, theological argument was increasingly related to the actual historical situation. The letters of Archbishop Agobard of Lyons against the Jews include fragments of disputations he had with them. The conversion of the Christian priest Bodo-Eleazar to Judaism not only provoked his own vituperative anti-Christian polemics but is also evidence of the meetings and disputations which took place between Jews and Christians at the court of Emperor Louis the Pious.

A large portion of both Jewish and Christian biblical exegetical literature and Jewish liturgical works contain polemical argument with religious, historical, and social overtones.

Under Islam, in particular in Baghdad of the tenth century where both Jews and Christians were in the position of a minority, disputations between the two, as well as between Jews and Muslims, are found taking place in a relatively open atmosphere. Saadiah Gaon's Arabic work *"The Book of Beliefs and Opinions"* incorporates and summarizes much of the argument in these disputations. His works also convey the main line adopted in the Jewish Rabbanite controversy with the Karaites. The writings of the Karaites Daniel b. Moses al-Qūmisi, Abu-Yusuf Jacob al-Kirkisānī, Sahl b. Maẓli'ah ha-Kohen, and Salmon b. Jeroham contain the Karaite attack on Rabbanite tradition. Many of the Karaite arguments against the Talmud, the anthropomorphic legends, contradictions, and immoral views found there, later became part of the Christian arsenal for attack on the Talmud.

About five years before the catastrophe brought on Jewry by the First Crusade a disputation took place in England between the abbot of Westminster, Gilbert Crispin, and a Jewish scholar. The latter, who had studied at Mainz, came there both for business and in order to meet Gilbert, who regarded the Jew as a personal acquaintance. He records: "Each time that we would meet, immediately we would have a talk in a friendly spirit about the Holy Scriptures and our faith." Gilbert noted that the answers of the Jew seemed logical and worthy to those present at the discussions to be preserved. He therefore wrote down both sides of the disputation, and sent the text to Anselm, archbishop of Canterbury

(*Gisleberti Crispini Disputatio Judei et Christiani;* ed. by B. Blumenkranz, Utrecht (1956), 27–8). It was the wish of both sides to hold the talk "in a tolerant spirit", as the Jew phrased it, while Gilbert calls for discussion "in a patient spirit" guaranteeing to dispute "for the cause of faith and out of love to thee." The atmosphere of tolerance in which the disputation was held makes it a valuable record. In addition to the discussion of former points raised in disputations between Jews and Christians, the Jew stresses the anomaly of the position accorded to Jews in Christian countries: "If the Law is to be kept [as the Jew had argued previously], why do you regard its keepers like dogs, pushing them with sticks and persecuting them everywhere?" (*ibid.*, 28). The troubled state of the world is brought as evidence against accepting Jesus as the messiah, since it contradicts the words of the prophet, "and they shall beat their swords into plowshares . . ." He states: "The iron with difficulty suffices the smiths for the preparation of weapons. All over the world, nation fights with nation, neighbor oppresses his neighbor and kills him. One king wars with the other" (*ibid.*, 34). Apparently describing paintings that he has seen in the Church the Jew points out: "God Himself you paint as the Man of Sorrows, hanging on the cross, pierced with nails — a terrible sight and yet you adore it . . . Again sometimes you paint God enthroned on high gesturing with outstretched hand, and around him — as if for greater glory — an eagle and a man, a calf and a lion; yet all this is forbidden in Exodus 20:4" (*ibid.*, 65). There is evidence of a certain interpenetration of ideals. The Christian responds to the Jew's condemnation of the warlike society of his environment by holding up monastic ideals: "There are many men of war and wrath who have left fighting and temporal riches and have turned to serve God in poverty" (*ibid.*, 38). When the Jew claimed that the Law was given to be observed the abbot pointed to Christian asceticism: "There are many of us who abstain not only from eating pork but from meat altogether" (*ibid.*, 35). On the other hand, the Jew not only insists that all the precepts of the Law should be observed but also reconciles it with the figurative understanding of the Scriptures: "Shall we condemn the letter [of the Law] because we listen to its figurative sense? And because we obeyed the letter, is there any sense in condemning the figure? We follow the letter and perceive also the figurative sense of the letter" (*ibid.*, 32). Even scholars who consider this dialogue a literary fiction would have to concede that in tone and content it expresses the spirit of arguments exchanged between Jews and Christians in a friendly atmosphere on the eve of the First Crusade.

The development of Christian religious drama in the 12th and 13th centuries permitted disputation with Jews to be presented in a popular dramatic form. In the Latin mystery play *Ordo Prophetarum*, a "reader" summons the Jews before him in the introduction to the Birth of Christ. The prophets appear one after the other, range themselves around the "reader," and quote passages considered to be Christological in content. In these debates the Jews are often led by an *archisynagogus,* while the prophets are led by the "reader" who in many plays is identified with Augustine. Later, from the middle of the 12th century, beginning with the German *Ludus de Antichristo,* the rival disputants receive personification as Ecclesia and Synagoga. Basically, all these dramas are disputations. The tone imputed to the Jews, particularly in later versions, is coarse and jeering.

Certain motifs in Jewish polemical literature which developed and changed over the centuries originated in reaction to the impressive display made by Christian religious life. The southern Italian 11th-century Chronicle of Ahimaaz b. Paltiel tells of a disputation supposed to have taken place between the Jew Shephatiah b. Amittai of Oria (ninth century) and the Byzantine emperor Basil I concerning the beauty and splendor of the Church of Hagia Sophia in Constantinople. The Jew quotes from Scripture to prove that Solomon's Temple was even greater and more magnificent: "Then did the king say: 'Rabbi Shephatiah has overcome me in his wisdom'; and Rabbi Shephatiah answered: 'My lord, Scripture has been victorious over you and not I.' " (*Megillat Aḥima'az,* ed. by B. Klar (1944), 21).

From the 12th century, apparently, chance encounters between Christians and Jews might often flare up into religious arguments. Both Jewish and Christian writers prepared manuals for the use of simple people of their faith when encountering arguments of the other side. In Christian literature this led to a long line of polemical writings against the Jews (*Adversus Judaeos,* a type that originated much earlier), intended for this purpose, some in the form of a dialogue. In Jewish literature, such manuals are generally entitled *Sefer Nizzaḥon,* being the outcome of former chance encounters and a preparation for future ones. The subject matter of these books and the methods employed by both sides largely follow traditional lines, although concrete situations and new themes may interpose themselves.

Joseph Kimḥi not only defends the Jewish way of life of the 12th century but also indicates how a Jewish patrician saw the mainly feudal Christian patterns of behavior: "You cannot claim that you are circumcised in heart, for he who . . . murders and whores and robs and molests people, ridicules them and behaves like a brigand, is uncircumcised in heart. Hence you are uncircumcised both in heart and body and Israel is circumcised both in heart and body. For ye will not find a Jew whom they [the Jews] will hang, neither will they gouge out his eyes, nor will they mutilate one of his members for any transgression that he may have committed" (*Sefer ha-Berit,* in *Milḥemet Ḥovah,* Constantinople, 1710, 26b). "You see with your own eyes that the Christian goes on the road to meet strangers, not to honor them but to seize all their provisions" (*ibid.*, 21a). "Even of your priests and bishops who do not take wives, it is well known that they whore" (*ibid.*, 21b).

In the 12th/13th-century *Sefer Nizzaḥon Yashan* there is a discussion in relation to the Cathedral of Speyer between Kalonymus and Emperor Henry II. Here the Jew again quotes chapter and verse to prove that the Temple surpassed the cathedral in greatness but the argument ended with an embittered denial of the sacredness of the cathedral precincts: "After Solomon built the Temple and finished it, it is written, 'the priests could not stand to minister by reason of the cloud; for the glory of the Lord filled the house of the Lord.' Yet if they were to load dung on a donkey and lead him through this cathedral nothing would happen to him" (J.C. Wagenseil (ed.), *Tela ignea Satanae* (1681), 41–42). Some arguments in this tract appear to be directed to Christian circles opposed to the Church establishment. The Jewish adversary is advised to cite certain verses in Isaiah to "those monks and priests that have taken into their hands the whole land ... that rise early and stay late in their church for their payment that is called praebenda" (*ibid.*, 82). The problem of saint adoration and miracles performed by saints is dealt with at length (*ibid.*, 128–32). The Jewish disputant is advised to tell his Christian adversaries that one proselyte to Judaism who accepts the Jewish way of life and the Jewish fate of humiliation and suffering achieves greater glory for Judaism than many apostates to Christianity who gain materially and socially by their apostasy (*ibid.*, 242–3).

With the rise of the Dominican order and the development of scholasticism, disputation became the principal method of learned disquisition and was frequently used to combat the Albigenses in the south of France.

The disputations held in the countries of Islam were, as mentioned above, much more diversified than those taking place in Christian countries. The *dhimmī* (protected minorities) numbered many sects and creeds. Philosophical schools also took part in such disputations. While the argument was predicated on almost complete agreement between Muslims and Jews concerning monotheism, and opposition to Christian concepts such as incarnation, the Trinity, and icon worship, a consistently held principle of Muslim argumentation was that the Jews had falsified the original text of the Bible, having added to or subtracted from it. Samuel b. Moses al-Maghribī, an apostate to Islam, fastened the major responsibility on Ezra the Scribe, arguing that the Torah given to Moses, which originally had been in the possession of the levites only, and known orally to the priests, had been destroyed: "When Ezra saw that the Temple of the people was destroyed by fire, that their state had disappeared, their masses dispersed and their Book vanished, he collected some of his own remembrances and some still retained by the priests, and from this he concocted the Torah that the Jews now possess. That is why they hold Ezra in such high esteem and claim that a light appears over his tomb . . . for he produced a book that preserves their religion. Now this Torah that they have is in truth a book by Ezra, and not a book of God. This shows that the person who collected the sections now in their possession was an empty man, ignorant of divine attributes. That is why he attributed anthropomorphism to God — regret over His past actions and the promise of abstention from similar acts in the future" (Samuel al-Maghribī, *Ifḥām al-Yahūd* — "Silencing the Jews," ed. and tr. by M. Perlmann, in: *Proceedings of the American Academy for Jewish Research, 32* (1964), 5). This attitude caused Maimonides to forbid all religious disputation with Muslims "according to what is known to you about their belief that this Torah was not given from Heaven" (J. Blau (ed.), *Teshuvot Rambam* (1958), no. 149).

Apart from this problem of the authenticity of the text, and the anthropomorphisms the Torah was said to contain in its present state, Muslim-Jewish disputation mainly centered around charges of anthropomorphism in the Talmud and attacks on the Jewish way of life, as for example made by the Muslim theologian Ibn Ḥazm. On their side the Jews attacked Muhammad as "a madman" and described the Koran as a book full of follies fit only for simpletons. Muslim pride and their oppression of the Jews were also bitterly castigated, in particular after the shock of the Almohad atrocities in the 12th century.

By the 13th century the arguments used in ancient Christian, Karaite, and Muslim debate and current trends of dialectic, culminated in a series of public disputations between Jews and apostates arranged with ceremonial splendor before royalty and high dignitaries of the clergy. The first great debate of this type to be held was the disputation of Paris (1240) between the apostate Nicholas Donin and the talmudic scholar Jehiel b. Joseph of Paris, which centered on the Talmud. The arguments of the apostate were to a large extent a continuation and development of the anti-talmudic arguments of the Karaites. The Christian side regarded and conducted the disputation as a trial in which the Jews were called upon to defend their errors. It resulted in the burning of the Talmud. In 1263 there took place in Aragon the disputation of Barcelona. The apostate Pablo Christiani led the Christian side. The Jewish side was represented by R. Moses b. Naḥman (Naḥmanides). This disputation centered on the problem of the nature and coming of the Messiah. A version of the disputation was recorded by Naḥmanides (published in various editions), who obtained the right to express himself freely in the debates. The apostate "said that he will prove from our Talmud that the Messiah prophesied by the Prophets has already come." The nature and authority of *aggadah* were also a prominent issue.

Nahmanides, like the Jewish opponent of Gilbert Crispin and other Jewish disputants, not only stressed the warlike aspect of the world after the advent of Jesus but also added that war had become integral to feudal society: "And how difficult would it be for you, my lord the king, and for these your knights, if war was no longer learned." The Jew fearlessly questioned the nature of Christian authority and teaching: "The core of the contention and quarrel between the Jews and the Christians lies in that what you state concerning the dogma of the Divinity is a very bitter thing. And you, my lord king, are a Christian, the son of a Christian father and mother. You have listened all your life to what priests, Franciscans, and Dominicans tell about the birth of Jesus, and they have filled your mind, yea, your very bones, with this matter; and it has thus become ingrained in you through habit. Yet that which you believe — and it is the heart of your faith — reason cannot agree to, nature opposes, and the Prophets never said such a thing. Miracle also cannot extend to this . . . that the Creator of Heaven and Earth and all that is in them shall become an embryo in the womb of a Jewess, shall grow there for seven months, shall be born a tiny creature, shall then grow up and later be given over to his enemies, and that they will sentence him to death and kill him. And you say that later he has risen from death and returned to his first place. Such beliefs cannot convince either a Jew or any other human being. Thus your speeches are made in vain and emptiness, for that belief lies at the heart of our quarrel. But let us also talk about the Messiah, if you want it so" (*Kitvei R. Moshe b. Nahman,* ed. by H.D. Chavel, 1 (1963), 310–1).

The last of these great spectacles was the long drawn-out disputation of Tortosa (1413–14). The many representatives of Judaism, who were compelled by official command to come to Tortosa and stay there during the disputation, defended themselves with acumen, and, in the difficult circumstances following the massacres in Spain of 1391, acquitted themselves with considerable courage against the attacks and calumnies of the apostate Maestro Hieronymus de Sancta Fide (Joshua Lorki), a former champion of Judaism in discussion and writing. The *Sefer Ikkarim* of Joseph Albo (see above), who participated in this disputation, is largely a summing up of the Jewish position taken there. In 15th-century Spain, when the Jews were subjected to the pressure of constant persecution and missionary persuasion, an impassioned polemical exchange developed. The sermons and writings of Vicente Ferrer represent the most influential and penetrating presentation of the Christian side. Jewish writings attest that the breakdown of Jewish existence in Christian Spain seemingly contributed historical testimony in support of Christian supremacy, in addition to the traditional Christological argumentation. The persuasiveness of this line of thinking had already been strikingly demonstrated in the 14th century with the conversion of Abner of Burgos. In the 15th century a series of Jews crossed over to Christianity to wage a bitter war on Judaism. In addition to Joshua Lorki, one of the most prominent was the former Rabbi Solomon ha-Levi, who as Pablo de Santa Maria became archbishop of Burgos. His writings, and the sermons and argumentation of others like him, ultimately sealed the fate of Spanish Jewry. The exchange of views between estranged brethren introduced the genre of letter exchange into the area of disputation from the 14th century.

On the Jewish behalf arose a witty and penetrating polemicist and satirist Profiat Duran. In his *Kelimat ha-Goyim* ("Confusion of the Gentiles") he makes a systematic attempt to show that early Christianity was a conglomeration of mistaken conceptions held by naive persons, exploited by, and supplemented with, the tales and ideas of later-day Christian "deceivers" who had shaped the present form of Christianity. His satirical *Al Tehi ka-Avotekha* ("Be not Like Your Fathers"), addressed to an apostate, presents apostasy as a process of tiredness and reaction from Jewish rationalistic, intellectual inquiry, coupled with attraction to the mystic doctrines of Christianity. These views are voiced here by the apostate who attacks the Jews: "Your fathers have inherited falsehood and were following foolishness; through overmuch inquiry their intellect has become disturbed . . . it appears to me [the Jew] that the Holy Spirit hovers over you [the apostate] in nightly vision and talks with you while awake . . . Human reason does not draw you to its dwelling, the abode of darkness . . . You regard it as alien, cruel as the serpent, the eternal enemy who injures faith . . . It was a reprobate who said that reason and religion are two lights. Reason has no part with us . . . it does not know the way toward light . . . Faith alone soars upward" (*Al Tehi ka-Avotekha*, in: *Koveẓ Vikkuḥim*, ed. by Isaac b. Abraham Akrish, Breslau, 1844, 6b–7a.).

The physician Ḥayyim ibn Mūsā around 1460 wrote a systematic manual for Jewish disputation, directed formally against the writings of Nicholas de Lyre and the works of the persecuting apostates and influenced by similar earlier works of Ḥasdai Crescas and others. He was faced with the weight of Christian cultural achievement and theological literature in Spain in a disputation with a Christian scholar in the presence of the grandee on whom he attended as physician: "It happened that we three were sitting together and suddenly the above-mentioned scholar said as an opening: 'Sir, surely you know that the Jews have one theological work only, called *Guide of the Perplexed*, whereas we have so many books on theology that even a palace as great as this would not contain them, if they were stacked from earth to heaven.' To this I remained silent. The lord ordered that I should answer him. Then I said, 'Jews have no need of such books; they need only a single page.' " Ḥayyim then briefly enumerates what he considers are the self-evident doctrines of Judaism, and continues: "In these doctrines all believe [i.e., Christians also]. Only concerning two or three dogmas is there some doubt. There is total difference in unity that you have made three . . . as to incorporeity, you say that the son became incarnate, but after his death everything returned to one Divinity . . . As to the changing of the Law, you say that he came to add and not to diminish, and our Torah says 'Ye shall not add to it neither diminish from it.' There is no quarrel between us that the Messiah means salvation. Our dispute concerns only whether 'he has come' or 'he will come.' But to believe that God could not eradicate the Original Sin of Adam except through his own death, that He became incarnate in the womb of a woman, that His wisdom could not find a way to atone for this sin except through His death, that He suffered so much abuse and pain until He died — and that after all this and despite all this men still die and go to Hell, both Christians and the sinners, all the books in the world will not convince intelligent people, and in particular those who have grown up in the way of the Torah . . . therefore the Jew requires only a single page for theology, for its plain meaning agrees entirely with reason . . . Then both of us fell silent and the lord was amazed at this speech and ordered that we should not talk before him lest we should lead him to doubt; and we remained silent" (his *Magen va-Romah,* Ms. Heb. Univ. Lib. Heb. 8° 787, pp. 67–68).

The 15th century was also a period of controversialist debate in troubled and divided Germany. The apostate monk Petrus Nigri (Schwarz) preached to the Jews in Nuremberg and tried to dispute with them. Aroung 1410 Yomtov Lipmann Muelhausen wrote his *Sefer Nizzahon* (Nuremberg and Altdorf, 1644), which sums up the traditional Jewish line of defense in disputation and also puts forward systematically the arguments for attacking Christian views. Written in a rationalistic vein, it evidences signs of the strains present in the Christian Church at this time. As often occurred, some of his argumentation shows the impress of Christian molds of thought. He writes: "The Christian mocked saying, females who are uncircumcised have no Jewish character. They [the Christian mockers] do not know that faith does not depend on circumcision but is in the heart; circumcision does not make a Jew of one who does not believe correctly, and one who believes correctly is a Jew even if he is not circumcised, although he is guilty of one transgression. And circumcision is not possible with women" (*Sefer Nizzahon* p. 19).

Later in the 15th century, Johanan Luria represented the Jewish side in occasional disputations with courage and skill. Traces of Christian impressions of disputations with Jews are found in the writings of Hans Folz. John of Capistrano complains that "the Jews say [apparently in disputations] that everyone can be saved in his own faith."

At the Renaissance courts of Italy, in the atmosphere of excitement generated by Humanism on the eve of the Reformation, Jewish-Christian encounters often resulted in religious argumentation; sometimes such disputations were formally arranged. Abraham Farissol tells that "our Lord Ercole, the duke of Ferrara, and his wife and brother . . . ordered me many times to come before their majesties to speak and dispute with two celebrated scholars of that time and place, of the Dominican and Minorite orders. I was compelled, on their order and with their permission, to step out publicly and speak before them many times, politely and temperately . . . Against my will I obeyed the above-mentioned friars and the demand of certain other scholars, such as the sage bishop of Trani who compelled me to write down in detail, in a book in their language, the questions and answers during the disputation, exactly as they had asked and I had answered them. They said that they wished to see in writing whether there could be any substance in my answers so that they would be able to answer all of them, also in writing, and sum up in a book the evidence and strength of their point of view and prove their assumptions" (cf. *Ha-Zofeh le-Hokhmat Yisrael,*, 12 (1928), 286). The Hebrew version of his disputations, *Magen Avraham* (largely in manuscript), touches on a variety of subjects. It can be seen that Farissol was in close touch with both heretical "Judeo-Christian" circles among Jews, in particular among the exiles from Spain and Portugal, and heretical Christian "Judaizing," or anticlerical and anti-traditional, circles of Christian society. He quotes the opinions of such circles and sometimes gives information about their leaders. Farissol indicates that leadership is necessary for man's salvation, secular or spiritual (cr. *Revue des Etudes Juives,* 105 (1940), 37). In this context, for the sake of argument, under the heading "That the True Messiah to Israel has not yet come," he expresses the view: "I regard it a plausible possibility that they [i.e., the Christians] may call him [Jesus] their messiah and savior. For they as well as he say that after his coming and his teachings they were saved and cleansed from the stain of idolatry. And through him, and his apostles and companions, they have come very near to believing after a fashion in the unity of the First Cause, combining other assumptions and additions and innovations to believe in the Divine Law . . . coming nearer to the truth than any others for they have approached him from a very far distance, previously worshiping the dual forces that God hates" (*ibid.,* 38). Farissol proceeds to show at length that Jesus does not fulfill the conditions of the Messiah promised to Israel (*ibid.,* 38–40). He also defends Jewish moneylending, arguing that in 16th-century society there could be no social or ethical reason for differentiation between income from money and income from other sources (*Ha-Zofeh le-Hokhmat Yisrael,* 12 (1928), 290–7). He devoted a detailed chapter to criticism of the Bible translation of Jerome (*ibid.,* 287–90).

With the rise and development of the Reformation in Central Europe, Martin Luther and others among its originators made strenuous efforts to persuade the

Jews to join their new brand of Christianity. Their failure turned Luther and Martin Bucer (Butzer) into rabid enemies and persecutors of the Jews. From both the benevolent and the hostile standpoint they frequently had occasion to take issue with Judaism. An anonymous Jew, who early perceived the reliance placed on primary biblical sources in Lutheran argumentation, advised Jewish disputants as a preliminary to state that Jewish monotheism does not need support from texts: "The way of nature, through heart and through mind, obligates man to believe in pure monotheism. One has to believe it necessary that there be a Unity ruling the whole cosmos ... And so shall you speak to them in order to purify, cleanse them – if there were [no] book in the world, what could be done [to prove Christianity]? And how can you believe in it now? For their faith is founded on our Prophets and Holy Scriptures. If we have no Prophets. they have no testimony to adduce nor Scripture to expound. Whereas we have a root and foundation, even lacking every book or writing, in nature – for we believe in His unity and greatness as the Creator through His action in first place and because whatever we do each day cannot be done, except by His will" (cf. H.H. Ben-Sasson, in: *Harvard Theological Review,* 59 (1966), 388–9).

Not only do the writings of Jewish leaders and authors in the heart of Christian Europe, such as the communal leader Joseph (Joselmann) b. Gershon of Rosheim, the chronicler Joseph ha-Kohen, and the kabbalist Abraham b. Eliezer ha-Levi, contain many impressions of the Reformation movement and its ideas and actions, sometimes in a polemical vein, but there are also remoter echoes of the Christian-Jewish debate. In the first half of the 16th century, the physician Abraham ibn Migash, living in the Muslim capital of Constantinople, tells, "there came to my house an uncircumcised Spaniard, who esteemed himself wise, and he questioned me." The ensuing dispute on the initiative of the Christian, written down by the Jew, mainly includes traditional elements of "the exegetical core" of Christian-Jewish disputation. The Jew argues in principle against basing exegesis on translations of the biblical text: "Tell me, please, where do you find in any science or teaching that a word is isolated from its meaning, as understood in the language in which it is current and fixed within the frame of that language, to give it a separate meaning taken from an alien language? ... This cannot be done, for if you do so the meanings of words and concepts will change and intermingle and will not be understood immediately. Communication will cease." The Christian complains of the pride displayed by Jews in their divine election. He argues that the Law concerning the election is not eternal, and bases his argumentation on talmudic quotations. The disputations shows that the Spaniard had knowledge of Hebrew and rabbinical sources and that the Jew was well acquainted with the principles of Christianity.

He ends his written report with a prayer for the conversion of the Christian (*Kevod Elohim,* Constantinople, 1585, 128b-31b; and see also his anti-Christian remarks and tales, *ibid.,* 124b-8b).

The medieval and Reformation Jewish anti-Christian disputation is brought to perfection in the *Ḥizzuk Emunah* (ed. by D. Deutsch, 1872) of Isaac b. Abraham Troki. The criticism of the New Testament in this work profoundly influenced Voltaire, according to his own evidence. It was written to strengthen Jews in combating Christian argumentation, being the outcome of the questions that Isaac "disputed with bishops and lords . . . My speech with them was mild, to influence and not to anger . . . I said nothing for which I could not provide a true biblical quotation . . . I am not afraid of the multitude in writing down words of truth and good taste, for the truth is loved by every wise man . . . I intended to write down those arguments which are deemed by the uncircumcised to be strong as the work of a great artist, firm and true. With their refutation, the weaker arguments will fall of themselves . . . My first proposition is to explain what caused the Christian scholars, with all their great learning in the sciences known to man, to hold beliefs which are foreign to the human intellect and without authentic evidence from the words of the Prophets" (*ibid.,* 9–13). Isaac not only defends the Jewish interpretation of the Bible and points out in detail discrepancies in the Gospels but also finds much to his advantage in the controversy within the Christian camp. The anti-Trinitarian arguments of Szymon Budny and others are used by him against the Trinitarians. The innovations of Lutheranism and Calvinism, the reciprocal persecution of Catholics and Reformers, the low status of the Greek Orthodox community in Catholic Poland, and the prosperity and power achieved by Islam, all these elements perceived on Isaac's horizon are used to rebut Christian argumentation based on Jewish weakness and suffering in the Exile.

The first disputation under conditions which assume a certain equality between the opponents took place in the Netherlands in 1686 between the Jew Isaac (Balthazar) Orobio de Castro and the Christian Philipp van Limborch, written down and published as an exchange of letters by Van Limborch under the title *De veritate religionis christianae; amica collatio cum erudito Judaeo* (Gouda, 1687). While the discussion largely follows traditional lines, there is a difference in tone; thus the Jewish argument based on the prevalence of war and strife in the world becomes internalized and psychologized. Orobio states that so far as he can see the Christian messiah has not changed men by enabling them to love their neighbors more than they could before his coming (*ibid.,* Ch. 17). Van Limborch, on the other hand, claims that true Christians do not consider Jesus as God, but state only that he was the "Son of God," meaning that he was greater than Moses, being both prophet and messiah.

In 1757, at Kamenets and in 1759, at Lvov, a disputation took place between Jacob Frank and his followers and the rabbinic leaders of Polish Jewry. This essentially began as an internal quarrel within the Jewish camp, as the first phase of the debate, at Kamenets, proved conclusively. The theses of the Frankists in the second phase, at Lvov, were dictated to them by their Christian patrons and were a result of their own frustration and bitterness. Hence they included, as their seventh point in the disputation, the charge that Jews require Christian blood for ritual purposes at Passover, thus giving currency to the old blood libel. On this they were answered by the chief Jewish spokesman, Ḥayyim ha-Kohen Rapoport, who cited from Christian documents and authorities refuting the libel, supported by comparisons from outside Europe: "You adduce against us this seventh point and say that you are arguing not with evil intent or out of revenge but only through love of the truth. But this [the blood libel] is not a matter relating to the Catholic Church or its faith. Here we truly perceive your evil intent toward us and your passion for revenge . . . Can you supply thorough evidence in support of these false claims about a matter in opposition to man's habits and nature which supposed that we, the breed of Abraham, from whom we come and to whom we shall return (after death) require and use human blood? A charge that has not been heard of in Asia, in Africa, or in Europe, or in the whole world against any other nation (even the most heretical one). And this you intended to prove against us?" (M. Balaban, *Toledot ha-Tenu'ah ha-Frankit* (1935), 256).

Moses Mendelssohn (see p. 67-68) was shocked and dismayed when he was called upon by J.C. Lavater in 1769 either to refute the "evidence for the truth of Christianity" that he, Lavater, had translated into German from the French and published, or to do "what Socrates would have done if he had read this work and found it irrefutable." Mendelssohn, who rejected in principle the demand for public disputation, at first stated that his continued adherence to Judaism, in its present state of humiliation, and his well-known constant search for philosophical truth furnished self-evident proof that he had investigated Judaism and found it worthy to adhere to and suffer for, and that he had found no reason for turning to Christianity, even though he was well aware that this would give him full civil rights and a better social life. He thus uses its humiliation as an argument for Judaism and its ability to confer material advantages on apostates as an argument against Christianity. Mendelssohn claimed that to hold a public disputation would endanger the present status of this brethren in Christian society. He also stated that Judaism is not missionary; the proselyte is warned before he joins it: "he who is not born under our Laws need not live according to them." Mendelssohn regarded missionary work as ridiculous when addressed to intelligent people and pictured it as trying to convert Confucius to Judaism or Christianity.

As the storm raised by Lavater grew, Mendelssohn reluctantly abandoned his opposition to controversial debate. In the spirit of medieval Jewish argumentation he told his adversaries: "A single Christian who agrees to be circumcised proves more for Judaism than a hundred Jews who agree to be baptized prove for the truth of Christianity." In another context Mendelssohn is ironical about the Christian conception that Jesus had abolished the Law given by God, while not having done so expressly. When the Crown Prince of Brunswick-Wolfenbuettel respectfully asked Mendelssohn to explain his position, Mendelssohn answered in a clear polemical vein, listing four principles that he would have to accept as a Christian and that reason rejects: "(1) a Trinity in the Divine essence; (2) the incarnation of a God; (3) the physical sufferings of a person of the Divinity which would contravene its Divine majesty; (4) the satisfaction of the first Person in the Divinity through the suffering and the death of the humiliated second Person." These, and similar principles of Christianity, Mendelssohn states, he would not believe even if they were vouched for in the Old Testament. He was also unable to accept the concept of Original Sin. In addition to contending that Jesus did not abolish the Law expressly, he also points out that he, Mendelssohn, was well acquainted with the Hebrew of the Bible and could not find Christological evidence there (M. Mendelssohn, *Gesammelte Schriften,* 7 (1930), in particular 7–13, 63, 91, 299–304, 321; see also 16, (1929), 142, 148, 150–1).

Relationships between Christians and Jews in the modern environment were faced with the paradox of emancipation of the Jews on the one hand and modern-type anti-Semitism on the other. Trends toward assimilation were confronted with Zionism. Jews entering the environing society encountered the romantic reaction of nationalist *Volksgeist* and "Christian state" conceptions. Christian-Jewish discussion enters a new phase in the 20th century. It is held in an arena where a plethora of diverse opinions, each claiming orthodoxy for itself and heresy for the others, are argued both informally and in the public eye.

In this dynamic climate of tension there took place the friendly but trenchant disputation between an apostate devoted to Christianity, the legal historian, philosopher, and sociologist Eugen Rosenstock-Heussy, and the great Jewish philosopher, Franz Rosenzweig, then a young man. During their exchange of letters both were serving in the German army, writing almost from foxhole to foxhole. Between May and December 1916 they exchanged 21 letters, originating from a spirited conversation they had had in 1913. Although intended as a private exchange of views, the correspondence contains in a nutshell the dilemmas confronting a Jewish intellectual at that time. Later, in 1917, Rosenzweig described Rosenstock as "a persistent but inexperienced missionary" and stated in retrospect that the letters "cannot be made into a 'dialogue,' for they were not; they were simply a bombardment between two learned canons with a lyrical urge." Hence, at least in the view of the Jewish participant, this was a disputation in the subjective medieval sense.

In his letters, Rosenstock-Heussy stresses the traditional Christian arguments that the Law had been abolished and salvation lay in Christianity. Inherent in the character of Jewish Law are self-righteousness and impassivity in contrast to the true spirituality and dynamics of Christianity. Rosenstock regards as presumption the Jewish reliance on their descent and on their continued history as an argument in favor of Judaism. The Jews had crucified Him who came to fulfill the Divine promise that all the gentiles would come to Jerusalem. Christianity had liberated the individual from the bonds of family ties and national limitations. Present-day Jews live non-Jewish lives, as present-day Christians live non-Christian lives, but to the Christian the discrepancy between the ideal and its realization is part of the cross he has undertaken to carry. What, however is the sense to a Jew who lives a non-Jewish life, "plays the organ and thinks in a non-Jewish way"; to a Jew without the Temple and without the Law, who does not marry at the age of 18, does not evade army service; to a Jew who makes his girl a Jewess so that he can marry her; where then remain the metaphysics of "the children of Abraham"? Rosenzweig pointed out in his answer that many elements in this attack on modern Jewish life in Germany were derived from a picture taking the "true Jewish life," to mean that represented by the Jews from Eastern Europe, the despised *"Ost-Jude."* Rosenstock compares the binding of Isaac by Abraham, the sacrifice of a son, with the sacrifice according to the New Testament whereby he who fulfills the covenant with God sacrifices himself. This is the dividing line. The synagogue has talked for two thousand years about what she has, because she has nothing; Israel in this world assumes the pride of Lucifer. Judaism is in the age of blind senility: "I know that Judea will outlive all 'the nations,' but you have no capacity for theology, for inquiry after truth, or for beauty. Thou shalt not make any image. At this price the Eternal Jew may live because he hangs on tenaciously to the life granted to him. But he is cursed to live by the sweat of his brow, taking loans everywhere, and making loans everywhere. The Jew dies for no fatherland and for no mission. He lives because his life does not approach the margin of life. He lives in a chimerical reflection of a real life that cannot be envisaged without the sacrifice of death and the nearness of the abyss. That Judea shall live on is dependent on the success of the individual Jew, on the number of his children. He is a paragraph of the Law, *c'est tout.* You may well believe that you have your own ship, but you do not know the sea at all, otherwise you would not speak in this way, you who are never shipwrecked . . . You do not know that the world is movement and change; the Christian says there is day and there is night, but you are so moonstruck that you think that the night view is the only view that exists and you consider as the ideal conception the minimum of light, the night. You consider that this encompasses day and night" (F. Rosenzweig, *Briefe* (1935), 682). Subconsciously or consciously, Rosenstock the apostate combines medieval Jew-hatred with the images and expressions of modern social and economic anti-Semitism. He considers that "the emancipation of the Jews is a process of self destruction, for Europe," in its modern phase. He is violently opposed to Zionism. Even if Hebrew is made into a living language it cannot be saved in the metaphysical sense.

To this attack Rosenzweig answers that "the serious acceptance in reality in which the theological principle about Jewish stubbornness is being worked out is Jew-hatred. You know as well as I that all the realistic explanations of this hatred are only so many fashionable dressings to hide the only true metaphysical reason, which is, metaphysically formulated, that we refuse to take part in the fiction of the Christian dogma that has gained world acceptance because (although reality) it is fiction (and *fiat veritas, pereat realitas,* for 'Thou God art truth'), and, formulated in the manner of enlightenment (by Goethe in *Wilhelm Meister*): that we deny the basis of present culture (and *'fiat regnum Dei, pereat mundus,'* for 'a kingdom of priests shall ye be unto me, and a holy people'); to formulate it in an unenlightened way: that we have crucified Christ and, believe me, we shall do it again any time, we alone in all the world (and *fiat nomen Dei Unius, pereat homo,* for 'whom shall you make equal to me that I will be equal')" (*ibid.,* 670–1). Thus Rosenzweig points out that the Church is obliged to formulate the concept of Jewish stubbornness; it is part of her dogma. "Do whatever you want, you cannot get rid of us. We live on, 'the Eternal Jew,' out of a feeling of duty to life and not because of hunger for it." He agrees that there is a contrast between the sacrifice of Isaac and the crucifixion, but in a different sense from the apostate's conception. Abraham sacrificed "not a child but the 'only' son and what is more: the son of the promise to the God of that promise . . . the content of which is being made impossible according to human concepts through this sacrifice. We do not read this pericope on our most solemn Holy Days without reason. It is the prototypal sacrifice, not of one's own individuality (Golgotha) but of the folk existence of 'the son' and of all future sons . . . Abraham sacrificed all that he could be; Christ all that he was" (*ibid.,* 689). Jewish life is not the way of life of the Polish Jew as depicted by Rosenstock. "Alongside this life, which is amoral in the deepest sense and external, there exists a purely Jewish life, which is internal, one that serves all that has to be worked out internally, not bought from externally, for the sake of the preservation of the people, its 'life.' To this realm belong the internal-Jewish leadership activity, here Jewish theology, here the art of the Synagogue (so even 'beauty'). However much these phenomena may hold of the alien, Judaism cannot but help assimilate them to itself. It does so of itself even if not intending to . . . The extent to which the Jew takes part in the life of other nations is not determined for him by himself, but they dictate it for him" (*ibid.*, 691). Rosenzweig relates himself to the metaphor of the ship traveling eternally on high seas. He answers Rosenstock that the Jew may give up everything "except one: hope; before God's seat the Jew, so it is said, is asked only this: Have you hoped for salvation?" (*ibid.*, 693).

This dispute is marked by a deep interpenetration of problematics and symbolism. Rosenstock demands from a Jew that he live a full Jewish life both personally and in family life. He attacks Zionism as an evil manifestation of Judaism. Rosenzweig even as a young man was deeply influenced by Christian symbolism, which permeated his thought. He wrote in 1913, "I thought that I had Christianized my Judaism, in reality I have Judaized Christianity . . . I was envious of the Church scepter because I thought that the Synagogue clings to a

Statue of Synagoga, the medieval Christian personification of defeated Judaism, blindfolded with a fallen crown, overturned Tablets of the Law, and broken staff. From the Liebfrauen Church (Trier), c. 1250.

broken scepter" (*ibid.,* 72). The image of the synagogue created by Church art haunts Rosenzweig. He explains it as a kind of Jewish symbol: "The Synagogue, immortal, but with a broken staff and a scarf over her eyes, must renounce all worldly work and concentrate all her strength on keeping herself alive and pure from life . . . The Synagogue had a scarf over her eyes; she didn't see the world — how could she have seen the idols in it? She looked and saw only with the prophetic eye of the internal, and therefore only the last things and the farthest ones" (*ibid.,* 74—5).

In this exchange of views, rich in symbols and intellectual allusions, the turbulent, disintegrating world of the German-Jewish intellectual of the early 20th century — still craving some sort of integration — is mirrored through its divided souls.

The agonized, semiformal disputation between Karl Ludwig Schmidt and Martin Buber took place as the fate of German Jewry hung in the balance, at the beginning of the road to the Nuremberg laws and the Holocaust. The Christian, who was fully aware of the predicament which Jewry was already facing at the time the disputation was held (Jan. 14, 1933), dismissed the crucial issue by saying: "It would be ostrich policy to attempt to deny the racial biological and racial hygienic problems which arise with the existence of the Jews among other people" (*Theologische Blaetter,* 12 (1933), 264). He rightly considered it a courageous act to invite Jews to brotherhood with Christians, which he repeatedly urged in this disputation, although only as sons of a Germany united through the Christian conception of the Church as the spiritual Israel (*ibid.,* 258, 259, 264, 272, 273). He was sure that "the Christian message says in this context: God has willed all this; Jesus, the Messiah rejected by his people, prophesied the destruction of Jerusalem. Jerusalem has been destroyed, so that it will never again come under Jewish rule. Until the present day the Jewish diaspora has no center" (*ibid.,* 262). Not only is the ancient Christian argument about Jewish suffering and loss of political existence invoked here in the year 1933 of the Christian era, but it was made with an eye on Zionism, which Schmidt looked upon as even worse than the old simple Judaism: "The modern world reacts to Zionism, which is national or even racist, on its own side in a racist way; of course it must not be forgotten that racist anti-Semitism in the modern world is pre-Zionist" *(ibid).* Schmidt asks why the Jews participate so actively in revolutions when so much is said about their conservatism (*ibid.,* 263). He declares to the Jews, or perhaps warns them, "that the Church of Jesus Christ has again and again shown her want of this Jewry, demonstrating her patience by waiting in hope that finally the Jews also . . . will be able to perceive that only the Church of the Messiah, Jesus of Nazareth, is the people of God, chosen by God, and that the Jews should become incorporated in it, if they indeed feel themselves as Israel" (*ibid.*, 264). He assures the Jews that "if and when the Church becomes more Christian than it is today, its conflict with Judaism will also become sharper, as it can and may do now. This sharp conflict has been present from the beginning of the history of Christianity." The conflict expresses the hurt and pain of the first Christians, Jews themselves, at the rejection of the Messiah by their brethren in the flesh (*ibid.*, 272). Schmidt strongly and courageously repudiates the racist attitude against the Jews and glorification of the state. To Buber's assertion that in the present condition of the world the signs of salvation are lacking, Schmidt answers with the hope of the second coming of Jesus *(ibid.)*.

Toward the end of the disputation Buber answered the Christian, from the plane of spiritual strength and pride derived from existential and material weakness and humiliation, in the ancient tradition of Jewish disputation: "I live not far from the city of Worms, to which I am bound by tradition of my forefathers; and, from time to time, I go there. When I go, I first go to the cathedral. It is a visible harmony of members, a totality in which no part deviates from perfection. I walk about the cathedral with consummate joy, gazing at it. Then I go over to the Jewish cemetery consisting of crooked, cracked, shapeless, random stones. I station myself there, gaze upward from the jumble of a cemetery to that glorious harmony, and seem to be looking up from Israel to the Church. Below, there is no jot of form; there are only the stones and the dust lying beneath the stones. The dust is there, no matter how thinly scattered. There lies the corporeality of man, which has turned to this. There it is. There it is for me. There it is for me, not as corporeality within the space of this planet, but as corporeality in my own memory, far into the depths of history, as far back as Sinai.

"I have stood there, have been united with the dust, and through it with the Patriarchs. That is a memory of the transaction with God which is given to all Jews. From this the perfection of the Christian house of God cannot separate me, nothing can separate me from the sacred history of Israel.

"I have stood there and have experienced everything myself; with all this death has confronted me, all the dust, all the ruin, all the wordless misery is mine; but the covenant has not been withdrawn from me. I lie on the ground, fallen like these stones. But it has not been withdrawn from me.

"The cathedral is as it is. The cemetery is as it is. But nothing has been withdrawn from us" (*ibid.*, 273).

Israel, strong and united in its national-religious continuity, cannot accept the Christian view that the world has been redeemed with the coming of Jesus. Buber in Nazi Germany declares: "We also know, as we know that there exists air that we take into our lungs, that there exists the plane on which we move;

nay, deeper, more truly we know that world history has not yet been probed to its roots, that the world is not yet redeemed. We feel the unredeemability of the world" (*ibid.*, 267). Israel is both a nation and a religion, hence it is different from all other nations and religions. Man's confrontation with God demands nationality "as the precondition of the whole human answer to God. There must be a nation in which the human answer can be fulfilled in life in its entirety, to which public life also belongs. Not the individual as an individual, but only the community as a plurality and unity, working together . . . can give God the full life-answer of man; therefore . . . there is Israel" (*ibid.*, 268). The European community of nations has agreed, by accepting emancipation, to accept Jews as individuals. It rejects Jewish participation in creative life as a nation. Hence the stress placed by Zionism on the national aspect as a counter balance to the prolonged denial of this aspect in modern times (*ibid.*, 270). To Schmidt's question, or insinuation, concerning Jewish conservatism and revolutionary activity, Buber answers that Jewish messianism calls forth both these aspects. Viewed from the standpoint of messianism, every state, however structured, is a problematical model of the divine state in the *eschaton*. But this same messianism always demands the Jew to see the other, questionable side of the state, its failure in realizations of the ideal: "Israel can never turn away its face from the state; it can never deny it; it must accept it; at the same time it must long for the perfection of the state, which is only so unsatisfactorily hinted at by every realization it achieves. Both the conservative and the revolutionary Jewish attitudes stem from the same [messianic feeling]" (*ibid.*, 271).

To the harsh and uncompromising postulate that the Jews can live in Europe only on acceptance of Christian conditions and conceptions, Buber presents his thesis of open dialogue between Israel as a nation and religion, and Christianity as a religion for other nations. He proposes personally "to accept what others believe against our existence, against our consciousness of existence, as their religious reality, as a mystery. We cannot judge its meaning because we do not know it from the inside as we know ourselves from the inside" (*ibid.*, 266). "God's gates are open to all. The Christian need not come to them through Christianity in order to arrive at God" (*ibid.*, 274). "No man that is not of Israel understands the mystery of Israel, and no man that is not of Christianity understands the mystery of Christianity; but unknowing they may acknowledge each other in mystery. How it can be possible that mysteries exist alongside each other is God's mystery" (*ibid.*, 267).

With these words Buber opened a way to divesting religious disputation of the polemical form it had assumed throughout most of its history and presenting it as an open and friendly meeting, ecumenical in the fullest sense. He had ancient Jewish ideological precedents for looking upon plurality of creeds and customs as "God's mystery" (notably the statements by various Jewish disputants in the 15th to 16th centuries and Maimonides' views on Christianity as expressed in the uncensored version of the last chapter of his *Mishneh Torah*. Buber, however, reformulated this conception in modern terms, where it assumes a validity through anguish that disregarded fear, facing danger and humiliation.

Jewish-Christian disputation thus began with the meeting of Justin and Tryphon under the shadow of the Bar Kokhba revolt. The darkness and flames of the Holocaust and the light from Zion may illumine the pilgrimage to ecumenical conversation, on equal terms, toward understanding and harmonious living, waiting for God to solve His own mystery in history.

12

FACING REFORMATION
IN CHRISTENDOM

Like most revolutions the Reformation within the Christian Church in 16th-century Europe combined ultraconservative trends with a drive for change. In his attitude toward the Jews, Martin Luther moved from a conscious attempt at a form of reconciliation, through a missionary effort, to a most extreme, abusive outlook aimed at putting an end to their very existence in Christian states. His more benevolent approach finds expression in his *Das Jesus Christus eyn geborner Jude sey* (1523); while his *Von den Jueden und jhren Luegen* (1543) exemplifies his most vehement attitude. This vacillation between extremes was typical of Luther's personal approach to many problems (e.g., toward the peasant revolt and toward toleration in general); more than that, however, it was also an expression of, on the one hand, the reform movement's feeling that their revolutionary return to a "pure" biblical Christianity would make a greater appeal to the Jews — the earlier missionary attempts having failed because they were made in the name of corrupt Christianity — and, on the other, the deeply ingrained fear and hatred of the Jews which characterized most of the Reformation leaders. As their mission to the Jews failed too, they felt deeply insulted; the deep layers of their baleful image of the Jew came to the fore in Luther's scurrilous attacks. His work is described by Joseph b. Gershon of Rosheim as "such a boorish and inhuman book, containing curses and vilification hurled at us, hapless Jews, such as by the will of God can truly never be found in our beliefs and Judaism generally" (*Zeitschrift fuer die Geschichte der Juden in Deutschland,* 5 (1892), 331). Of the legal and social measures vis-à-vis the Jews proposed by Luther toward the end of his life, Joseph b. Gershon said that the like "never has . . . been contended by any scholar, that we Jews ought to be treated with violence and great tyranny, that none was bound to honor any obligation toward us" (*ibid.,* 332).

Less abuse and violence but a similar mixture of innovation and hatred marked the attitude to the Jews of John Calvin — in his "*Ad quaestiones et objecta Judaei cuiusdam Responsio*" (*Opera quae supersunt omnia,* 9 (1900), 653–74), of Martin Bucer — in many of his writings and public appearances, and especially in the *Ratschlag ob die Christliche Oberkait gebueren muege, dass sye*

286

die Juden undter den Christen zu wonen gedulden, und wa sye zu gedulden
welche gestalt und mass of 1539 (in his *Deutsche Schriften,* 7 (1964), 319–94),
and of many of their followers and imitators. Exceptions to the rule were Wolf-
gang Fabricius Capito of Strasbourg and the Bavarian Andreas Osiander, who
dared to give the lie to one of the basic elements of popular hatred of the Jews,
the blood libel, in:

> *Ob es war vn-glaublich sey dass die Juden der Christen Kinder heymlich*
> *erwuergen, und jr blut gebrauchen, ein treffenliche schrifft, auff eines*
> *yeden urteyl gestelt. Wer menschen blut vergeusst, des blut sol auch*
> *vergossen werde*

(written in 1529; published in 1893), an eloquent and well-reasoned treatise
against this appalling accusation.

For the Jews, the Reformation brought humiliation and suffering and an
additional burden because of Catholic Counter-Reformation claims that they
were responsible for its "Judaizing" tendencies. There is also the impression
that, at a far later date, Luther's teaching of the submission of the individual to
his rulers, combined with his latter-day virulent anti-Semitism, was one of the
root causes of racist Nazism, preparing the soil for the acceptance of the
Holocaust in the German mind and society. Yet in spite of all these elements
(some certain and some arguable) in Jewish history the Reformation was not
only, nor even largely, negative and harmful. Not only were many elements of
Catholic faith changed in a way that removed the grounds for anti-Jewish
accusations – e.g., charges of desecration of the Host disappeared in Protestant
circles because of the change in beliefs about transubstantiation – but many of
the reformers' innovations removed some differences between Jews and
Christians on the Reformation environment. About 1524 Jews coming from
Europe described with joy to the kabbalist Abraham b. Eliezer ha-Levi in
Jerusalem the iconoclastic and anti-clerical tendencies of the reformers. On the
basis of this much exaggerated report the kabbalists regarded Luther as a kind of
Crypto-Jew who was trying gradually to educate Christians away from the bad
elements of their faith (Abraham's letter of 1525; see *Kirjath Sepher,* 7
(1930/31), 444–5).

Of more importance and real impact for the future relationship with
Christians – and for that matter for the relationship with Christians of other
denominations in the post-Reformation period – was the great weight the Reformation gave to the Bible in Hebrew and to Hebrew in general. Although it had
originated with the Renaissance, this tendency was given major religious sanction
in the Reformation. According to Abraham b. Eliezer ha-Levi, this was one of the

mysteries of "God's mind, who decreed this beforehand . . . when He turned the hearts of many nations in the lands of the uncircumcised toward the study of the Hebrew language and writing. And they delve into these, each according to his powers of attainment" (*ibid.*, 445). Later, in many Protestant groups and sects, this was combined with the appreciation of the law and values of ancient Jewish society which were seen as the proper basis for the life of a model sectarian society. Away from the individualistic spiritual path of the evangelists, they looked to the Hebrew Bible for the modes of justice and moral way of life appropriate to a closely knit group. Many of them — both before and after him — would have agreed with Samuel Langdon, president of Harvard, when he declared in his election sermon delivered in 1775 that "the Jewish government, according to the original constitution which was divinely established, if considered merely in a civil view was a perfect republic" (in J. Wingate Thornton, *Pulpit of the American Revolution* (1860), 239). This sums up the attitude of many settlers in New England from the time it was first expressed by John Cotton in his *Moses, His Judicials* (1641). The great debate in Reformation countries, in Cromwellian and Restoration England in particular, about the divine right of kings and regicide was conducted to a large degree on the basis of texts and ideas from the Old Testament, which were taken as valid paradigms for actual Christian society. In many such circles, from the Netherlands to the eastern boundaries of Reformation Europe, Jews and Judaic ways came to be considered respectable and exemplary. Gradually this appreciation of the Jewish past developed into an appreciation of the Jews of the day, as abundantly shown by the paintings of Rembrandt and a great deal of literary and social evidence.

Yet the main importance of the Reformation for Jewish history lies more in what it failed to achieve than in its direct attitudes and achievements. No less fervently than the pope, its leaders wanted to have one Christian, all-embracing, orthodox Church. In the clash between the various strands of the Reformation and between all of them and the Catholic Counter-Reformation, this concept of an all-inclusive orthodoxy had perforce gradually to be abandoned. Through the fire and blood of the wars of religion (at least up to 1648), toleration reluctantly dawned in European culture. The centuries-old reality of a fixed religious, legal, and social attitude toward the Jews vanished; many established attitudes were now reexamined. Toleration embraced only very reluctantly the notion of including a non-Christian, let alone a Jew, within its permissive outlook. An anonymous Jew began to urge this change in Luther's lifetime. To the demand for apostasy he advised that the Jew reply with a polite refusal based on historical continuity and loyalty. Jews will not listen: "now, in our [the Jewish] old age, after we have suffered the servitude to the kingdoms and the hand of our enemies . . . God forbid that we should relinquish what our fathers left to us,

a tradition in our hands, with proof, more than the other nations of the world."
This refusal is addressed to the "very few men of reason who ply their words
mildly" (published from Ms. by H.H. Ben-Sasson, in *Harvard Theological
Review,* 59 (1966), 388).

Yet by the very implication of the concept, and through forces inherent in the
very logic of its birth, toleration had to relate to the Jews. This move was first
made only by small splinter groups like some Puritan sectarians in the
Netherlands and England. But the attitude of the eminent lawyer and theologian
Hugo Grotius in his memorandum of 1616 (as member of a committee of two
appointed by the municipality of Amsterdam to regulate the status of the newly
admitted Jews) shows the considerable change in the thought of the Calvinist
Netherlands. He assumes the right of the Jews to basic equality, while advocating
many specific legal disabilities; thus, much of medieval practice was to remain
without the medieval frame of mind. Oliver Cromwell's readmission of Jews into
England was intended to be on a similar basis; in the end popular opposition
resulted in factual readmission without explicit legal formulation. The
pro-Jewish trend continued both in England and the Netherlands, widening to
embrace more and more sectors of the population. By 1697 the city of London
had demanded that Jews be admitted as members of the London Stock
Exchange. The writings of men like John Toland and Roger Williams give an
explicit edge to the reform attitude of toleration toward Jews, providing a
weapon for its advocates. Thus the fluid situation following on the Reformation
offered the chance of a change (both for better and worse) in the status and
image of the Jews in Europe.

As noted, Jewish reaction to the Reformation was related from the beginning
to the actions and expressions of the movement, but from the very first moment
the Jews appreciated the element of revolutionary breakthrough, as they had
done much earlier in relation to other heretical and revolutionary movements in
Christianity, as evident in their disputations and in their attitude toward the
Hussites. Old traditions and ideas looked to a change in Christianity that would
bring back its beliefs to the right Jewish way that they had erroneously departed
from. Some made an extreme evaluation of the reports of the new leader and his
acts. In a "prophecy" ascribed to "the sage and astronomer R. Abraham
Zacuto," Abraham b. Eliezer includes "what a great astrologer in Spain, named
R. Joseph, wrote in a forecast on the significance of the sun's eclipse in the year
1478. He states: 'having no desire to favor any particular religion or mores I say
that a man will arise who will be great, valiant, and mighty. He will pursue
justice and loathe butchery. He will marshal vast armies, originate a religion, and
destroy the houses of worship and clergy. In his days Jerusalem shall be rebuilt.'"
Abraham b. Eliezer adds that "at first glance we believed that the man

foreshadowed by the stars was Messiah b. Joseph. But now it is evident that he is none other than the man mentioned [by all; i.e., Luther, according to the general trend of Abraham b. Eliezer's thought at this time], who is exceedingly noble in all his undertakings and all these forecasts are realized in his person" (in H.H. Ben-Sasson, *Yehudim mul ha-Reformazyah* (1969/70), Eng. translation in bibl.).

Admiration for Luther vanished in many Jewish circles, in particular in Germany, in view of his later enmity and cruelty. To Joseph b. Gershon of Rosheim, Luther is the archenemy of the Jews, a second Haman. But some still retained their sympathy for the Reformation movement if not for Luther himself. The growing diversity within the Reformation camp encouraged the rationalist Abraham ibn Migash, physician to the sultan in the 16th century, to think that "their faith has reverted to a state of primeval flux. Where there are a thousand of them one cannot find ten men willing to rely upon a single doctrine or consent to a given line of reasoning. Thus they are in a state of formlessness, ready to take shape, since faith has departed and no longer finds expression in their utterances. But they have been made ready to assume form when they will find favor with God, after being scourged for their sins and the sins of their fathers, for all that they and their fathers have perpetrated against Israel. And when they find favor with God they will be ready to accept the faith" (*Kevod Elohim* (Constantinople, 1586), essay no. 3, ch. 3, fols. 127v.–128r.). Even from afar, the capital of the Ottoman Empire, Ibn Migash recognized that the Protestant camp was splintered because it was ardently striving for true faith; they had lost their form in the Aristotelian sense of the term. He could not understand their remaining outside of the true Jewish form except through accepting that this is a temporary withholding of grace to enable them to expiate their sins in persecuting Jews in former generations. To the Portuguese Marrano Samuel Usque the Reformation was a revolt of descendants of Jewish Conversos who had naturally taken the opportunity to avenge their forced conversion: "For since throughout Christendom Christians have forced Jews to change their religion, it seems to be divine retribution that the Jews should strike back with the weapons that were put into their hands; to punish those who compelled them to change their faith, and as a judgment upon the new faith, the Jews break out of the circle of Christian unity, and by such actions seek to reenter the road to their faith, which they abandoned so long ago" (*Consolation for the Tribulations of Israel,* trans. by M.A. Cohen (1965), 193).

Another Jewish chronicler, Joseph ha-Kohen — born in Avignon but living and writing in Italy — supported the Reformation camp and described events and personalities consistently from this point of view. To him Luther was the sage among the Christians; the Council of Trent failed because the Lutherans did not come and, left to themselves, the Catholics could only do foolish things. His sympathy goes out to the Reformation fighters of southern France in particular. He describes their plight in a way that shows that he made use of their information and sources. The death of the heads of the population of a Protestant city in the province is described as true martyrdom *(kiddush ha-Shem);* "the leaders of the populace they [the Catholic forces] took along with them, torturing them and burning them alive ... But they [the Reformation martyrs] exclaimed: 'This indeed is the day we have hoped for – our souls shall return to God while our bodily clods return to dust' " (*Divrei ha-Yamim* (Sabbioneta, 1554), pt. 2, fol. 289v.). Joseph ha-Kohen was happy to witness and describe the sack of Rome in 1527, but when a Protestant church in Metz was destroyed by the Catholics and some of the people killed, he commented that the Catholics had "polluted the land with blood" (in H.H. Ben-Sasson, *op. cit.,* 284). Perceiving the hope of toleration emerging from the wars of religion, he felt that the essential factor to emerge from a peace pact between reformers and Catholics in France was "that each man could worship his God according to his wish without fear. So all the people were exceedingly pleased" *(ibid.).* This is quite in the spirit of the middle-of-the-road party in France.

With sectarian existence under Catholic rule in Bohemia and Moravia, Hungary, and Poland-Lithuania, ties between Protestants and Jews became closer, for there was a growing similarity between their modes of existence. In the 1530s there were complaints in Poland that Jews exploited the Reformation disquiet for proselytizing. Much more clear are the contacts – both through disputations and through direct influence – between anti-trinitarians and Jews, as, e.g., in Poland between Isaac b. Abraham of Troki and Szymon Budny, and between Marcin Czechowic and Jacob of Belzyce. In the thought of Judah Loew b. Bezalel of Prague and his circle, there is much evidence of contacts with sectarians. Judah Loew's plea against censorship of books – antedating Milton's *Areopagitica* by about 50 years (Judah Loew's plea was printed in 1598) – has the marks of sectarian pleading for tolerance. Yet his brother Ḥayyim felt contrained to warn "the Jews that . . . when they slacken in their regard for the Torah and its commandments, God bestows His bounty upon the unclean cattle. So that even if Israel subsequently repents, it is difficult for God to reject that nation on their account. This is all due to the fact that we, in our manifold sinfulness, are daily drawing farther away from the truth, whereas they, on the contrary, realize day by day that they are in the grip of falsehood. A different spirit is manifesting itself to some extent in their midst, bringing them nearer to truth, since they, too, for the most part are descended from the true seed" (*Sefer ha-Ḥayyim, Sefer Ge'ullah vi-Yshu'ah,* ch. 7, fol. 46v.). Ḥayyim feared that the new and eager spirit of the Reformation was endangering the covenant between the Jewish people and the Torah.

In modern times some Reformation patterns of worship and behavior and modes of thought influenced not only the Reform trend in Judaism but also some of the Orthodox communities, in particular in English-speaking countries. The ideology of religious pluralism accepted in the U.S., and welcomed by Jews, is a direct result of Reformation development. On the other hand, Nazism reawakened in Europe all the scars and problems of the Reformation's anti-Semitic inclination. In modern Jewish historiography and thought, the 19th century may be described mainly as the pro-Reformation period, while in the 20th century some pro-Catholic and anti-Reformation historiography and ideas emerged and developed.

13

MOVING OUT OF JEWISH IDENTITY

COMPULSION

Persons compelled by overwhelming pressure, whether by physical threats, psychological stress, or economic sanctions, to abjure Judaism and adopt a different faith are known in Hebrew as *anusim* ("forced ones") in contradistinction to *meshummadim* (or voluntary apostates). Our attention here will be directed only to instances of group compulsion. An edict or systematic attempt to force Jews to convert to another faith is termed in Hebrew *gezerat shemad* ("edict of destruction"). In Jewish sources, the term *anusim* is applied not only to the forced converts themselves, but also to their descendants who clandestinely cherished their Jewish faith, attempting to observe at least vestiges of the *halakhah* — the Jewish Law and way of life — and loyalty to their Jewish identity. Both the elements of compulsion and free will enter the psychological motivation of the forced convert. The concept denoted by the term *anusim*, therefore, is fluid, bordering on that applying to apostates and even to Marranos; it has been the subject of much discussion.

The vituperation heaped on Jews by Christian ecclesiastics, and the violent methods employed by the church in the fourth century, led to many forced conversions. There is clear evidence that *anusim* existed in the Frankish kingdoms of the sixth century, for the typical pattern of mass violence combined with threat of expulsion is already present in the mass conversion of many Jews to Christianity in Clermont-Ferrand in 576. The almost inevitable result of the creation of a Jewish "underground" within the Christian society is also clearly visible. The events in Clermont were set in motion after a Jew, who had voluntarily adopted Christianity, was molested by other Jews during a religious procession. The participants in the procession then made an attack "which destroyed [the synagogue] completely, razing it to the ground." Subsequently, Bishop Avitus directed a letter to the Jews in which he disclaimed the use of compulsion to make them adopt Christianity, but announced at the end of the missive: "Therefore if ye be ready to believe as I do, be one flock with us, and I shall be your pastor; but if ye be not ready, depart from this place." The community hesitated for three days before making a decision.

Finally the majority, some 500, accepted Christianity. The Christians in Clermont greeted the event with rejoicing: "Candles were lit, the lamps shone, the whole city radiated with the light of the snow-white flock" (i.e., the forced converts). The Jews who preferred exile left for Marseilles (Gregory of Tours, *Histories*, 5:11). The poet Venantius Fortunatus composed a poem to commemorate the occasion. In 582 the Frankish king Chilperic compelled numerous Jews to adopt Christianity. Again the *anusim* were not wholehearted in their conversion, for "some of them, cleansed in body but not in heart, denied God, and returned to their ancient perfidy, so that they were seen keeping the Sabbath, as well as Sunday" (*ibid.*, 6:17).

Persistent attempts to enforce conversion were made in the seventh century by the Visigoths in Spain after they had adopted the Roman Catholic faith. Comparatively mild legal measures were followed by the harsh edict issued by King Sisebut in 616, ordering the compulsory baptism of all Jews. After conversion, however, the *anusim* evidently maintained their Jewish cohesion and religious life. It was undoubtedly this problem that continued to occupy Spanish sovereigns at the successive Councils of Toledo representing both the ecclesiastical and secular authorities; it is difficult to conceive that the term *Judaei*, employed in the texts of the canons subsequently promulgated by the councils, actually refers to professing Jews; the restrictive measures adopted against the *Judaei* only make sense if directed at the devoted underground. Thus, steps were taken to secure that the children of converts had a Christian religious education as well as to prevent the older generation from continuing to observe the Jewish rites or from failing to observe the Catholic ones. A system of strict supervision by the clergy over the way of life and movements of the *anusim* was imposed. The attitude of the victims is seen in a letter they were compelled to address to the Visigothic king Recceswinth in 654, in which they promised to live as faithful Christians but pleaded not to be compelled to eat pork against which they felt physical revulsion.

Attempts from the beginning of the eighth century to compel Jews in the Byzantine Empire to accept Christianity similarly resulted in the creation of *anusim* leading a crypto-Jewish existence. According to the chronicler Theophanes, when in 722 the Emperor Leo III "compelled the Jews and the Montanists to undergo baptism, the Jews, although unwilling, accepted baptism and then washed it off" (*Chronographia*, ed. by De Boor, 1 (1963), 401). At the end of the ninth century and in the first half of the tenth, attempts were made to convert Jews to Christianity in the Byzantine Empire by physical threats, missionary disputations, and the offer of rewards to the converts. Basil I is particularly notorious in Jewish chronicles for these attempts.

Compulsory conversions took place in the Rhineland in the tenth century, and during the Crusades amid the anti-Jewish attacks after 1096. The action of Emperor Henry IV, who later permitted the victims to return to their former faith, was violently resented by the Pope and the Christian populace, hence Henry's successors did not always follow this policy. In Spain and North Africa in the 12th century, the Muslim Almohads forced both their Jewish and their Christian subjects to convert to Islam, apparently by terrorization rather than legislative measures. The converts from Judaism and their descendants remained isolated from their environment and humiliated by society. All the evidence points to their having led a crypto-Jewish existence.

At the close of the 13th century the Jews in southern Italy were given the choice of baptism or death, and there followed a wave of forced conversions under which the Jewish population in Apulia completely disappeared. Many were driven to simulate Christianity to save their lives. The *neofiti* (neophytes), or *mercanti* as they were called because of their commercial activities, remained a recognizable and unpopular group suspected of retaining their fidelity to their ancestral faith for over two centuries. In 1453 Pope Nicholas V wrote of them: "their forefathers were Jews who adopted Christianity 150 years ago, rather from compulsion than of their own free will."

The best known and most numerous group of *anusim,* marked by a specific individuality, was found in the kingdoms of Christian Spain. These converts continued to live an underground existence there from 1391 to the 18th century or even later. The masses of Jews who were converted to Christianity were pressured by terror of the mob violence in Spain and, later, also by legal sanctions and social persecution, popular missionary preaching, and the effects of religious disputations. In the cultural and religious atmosphere of the period even the violent onslaught on Judaism was interpreted by some as being divinely inspired. The *anusim* in Spain therefore found themselves from the outset in a peculiar social and moral position. Christian society, particularly urban society, did not accept the converts favorably: the designation "New Christians" or Conversos by which they became known, was, in fact, a new label of identification officially provided for this social phenomenon. Toward the close of the 15th century the manifestations of popular animosity toward the New Christians, the probings and punishments of the Inquisition, and the prevalence of such concepts as *limpieza de sangre* ("purity of blood") in Spain combined to strengthen the allegiance of the converts to their Judaic antecedents. The inquisitional records of the period, which register the impressions of both Jewish and Christian witnesses, show that the *anusim* tried their utmost to preserve their Jewish faith and observe the religious laws. Thus, many of the converts avoided intermarriage with the "Old" Christians. They gradually developed a liturgy of their own, and sometimes even an internal communal organization.

Anusim at an Auto-de-fé held in Madrid's Plaza Mayor on June 30, 1680, in honor of Carlos II and his bride, Louise Marie d'Orleans, and lasting 14 hours; 51 people were "relaxed" (burned) and 67 penitents were "reconciled." The *anusim* seen here wear sack-like garments *(sambenito)* and tall miters *(coraza)*. Detail from a painting by François Rizi.

They also developed the rudiments of a specific ideology, centering on two beliefs: that forced conversion is part of the divine punishment of *galut* ("exile") and that Naaman and Esther were in some way prefigurations of the crypto-Jewish way of life. The *anusim* were frequently able to transmit their religious views to their children; however, the degree of their enthusiasm for the Jewish tradition is difficult to judge. A "third estate" was thus formed within the intensively religious environment of a militantly Christian state bent on religious unification which became the target of scandal among Christians and a problem to Jews and Christians alike. The expulsion of the Jews from Spain in

1492 was officially justified on the ground that it was essential to separate the converts from Jewish influence. After the expulsion a new situation arose in which the *anusim* remained isolated from their Jewish origins and increasingly exposed to external pressures.

The Jews of Portugal were made to adopt Christianity by brute force in 1496–7, when King Manuel ultimately decided to retain his Jewish subjects, who were valuable economic assets, while purging his realm of heresy. He therefore set about a systematic campaign of forced conversion unparalleled in history. This was first directed against the children, who were seized and dragged from their parents' arms in the hope that the latter would follow suit, and later against the entire population of the Jewish communities of the kingdom. By the end of 1497 not a single professing Jew was left in Portugal. The former Jewish communities were replaced by forced converts who had been baptized against their will and who were to maintain their individuality for generations to come. Converts of this category who, in due course, escaped from Portugal to reenter Judaism formed a *kahal kadosh shel ba'alei teshuvah* ("Community of the Penitent") in Salonika and elsewhere. Many also settled in Erez Israel in consequence of the popular interpretation of the verse "And his land shall atone for his people" (Deuteronomy 32:43). In rabbinical responsa, such persons are referred to as *anusim me-anusei ha-zeman* ("contemporary *anusim*"). Even in Portugal, however, the typical *anusim* existence, in the more literal sense, must have died out soon after the beginning of the 17th century.

Later instances of forced conversion occurred in Persia. From 1622 to 1629 the Jews of Isfahan were compelled to accept Islam, and in 1656 Abbas II issued a decree ordering all Persian Jewry to convert, despite open protest and petitions. The specific ceremonies attending their acceptance into Islam and the name by which they were known, *Jadid al-Islam* (New Muslims), show that a typical *anusim* existence and society was created there. In 1839 the entire Jewish community of Meshed was forced to convert in similar circumstances. Outwardly devout Muslims, they meticulously continued to observe the Jewish rites in secret, as did their descendants, who were also known as the *Jadid al-Islam*.

The lot of European Jews, particularly Jewish children, who outwardly embraced Christianity in order to save their lives during the Nazi persecution between 1939 and 1945 was in many ways similar to that of the *anusim* of former ages. It has proved impossible to assess the number of conversions among the Jewish people in this period. Research into this question has been further complicated by emotion and anger on the part of Jews against those who tried "to steal souls" during the Holocaust on the one hand, and on the other, of gratitude to those who had endangered their lives to save the children.

APOSTASY

Jews use the term "apostasy" to denote the desertion of their faith, their set of loyalties and their worship for another faith, set and worship. The conception of apostasy could not arise in the atmosphere of polytheism practiced in antiquity before the advent of Hellenism. The Bible frequently condemns those worshiping other gods, but though this is conceived as a heinous transgression it still lacks the totality of apostasy-conversion.

A product of the spread of Hellenistic culture in Ereẓ Israel was the group of *Mityavvenim* (hellenizers), who according to Jewish sources adopted Hellenistic ways of life and religious worship during the reign of Antiochus IV Epiphanes in the second century B.C.E. Some scholars take these to be the instigators of his persecution of the Jewish faith. In the Books of the Maccabees, the Jews who abetted the officials of the Seleucids or joined their armies are described as renegades and apostates. The Tosefta (Sukkot 4:28) has preserved the tale of "Miriam of the House of Bilga [a priestly house] who apostatized and married an official of one of the kings of Greece. As the Greeks entered the Temple, Miriam came and struck the top of the altar, saying . . . 'you have destroyed the property of Israel and did not come to their help in their trouble.' " The woman appears to express disillusionment with the Jewish God. Because of her apostasy, her family was disqualified from certain privileges and symbols of priestly status. Tiberius Julius Alexander, the nephew of the philosopher Philo Judaeus, went to the extreme of commanding some of the Roman units during the siege and subsequent destruction of Jerusalem and the Temple. As described in the Talmud, the figure of the second-century scholar and teacher Elisha b. Avuyah, who joined the pagan-philosophic camp, disputed with Jewish scholars, and ridiculed the Jewish religion, has a certain grandeur and is accorded a grudging respect.

After the rise of Christianity apostasy became an accompanying phenomenon of Jewish life, a problem between Jews and their neighbors, and a constant source of irritation to the various religious camps as well as to the apostates themselves. The forlorn hope of Judeo-Christians of reconciling the Law with the Cross petered out. By the latter half of the second century it had been rejected both by the vast majority of Christians and by Jews. The parting of the ways between church and synagogue had been reached. Acceptance of Christianity that had forsaken the Law was regarded by Jews as apostasy in the fullest sense. The Christian dogmas of Incarnation and Trinity gave to the acceptance of Christianity an idolatrous character *(avodah zarah)*.

The history of ferocious persecutions and systematic humiliations which the Jews subsequently endured for their religion combined to invest apostasy from

Judaism with the character of desertion from the persecuted and a crossing over to the persecuting ruling power. This attitude was enhanced by the fundamental divergence between Jewish and Christian approaches to conversion to the respective faiths, which led Jews to draw a strong moral distinction between apostasy and proselytism, regarding the two in an entirely different light. As developed in Jewish theory and practice, proselytism to Judaism was made dependent on full and deliberate acceptance of partnership in the Jewish fate and historical consciousness, as well as of belief in its faith and hopes. The attitude to apostasy, however, was conditioned by the Christian missionary approach, which, even when abstaining from the use of threats or forcible coercion, still set out to gain converts by compelling Jews to attend missionary sermons and involved automatic betterment of the social and legal status of the apostate.

This, therefore, appeared in the Jewish view as a vulgar and essentially nonspiritual attempt to harm souls through moral pressure and promise of material gain. The fear of expulsion or massacre, which always loomed in the background, very often was the root cause of apostasy. Even an apostate whose sincerity was beyond all doubt, like Abner of Burgos, stated in the 14th century that the starting point for his apostasy was the "revelation" he experienced, in which "I saw the poverty of the Jews, my people, from whom I am descended, who have been oppressed and broken and heavily burdened by taxes throughout their long captivity — this people that has lost its former honor . . . and there is none to help or sustain them . . . when I had meditated on the matter, I went to the synagogue weeping sorely and sad at heart. And I prayed . . . And in a dream, I saw the figure of a tall man who said to me, 'Why dost thou slumber? Hearken unto these words . . . for I say unto thee that the Jews have remained so long in captivity for their folly and wickedness and because they have no teacher of righteousness through whom they may recognize the truth' " (Y. Baer, *History of the Jews in Christian Spain,* 1 (1961), 328–9). To those who gloried in shouldering the burden of the Jewish fate and history, were imbued with love of Jewish culture and way of life, and continued to hope for salvation and the establishment of God's kingdom in the future, such a motivation inevitably appeared the outpourings of a weakling and the self-justification of a traitor. This attitude was strengthened in regard to many apostates who became willing and active virulent enemies of Judaism, like Abner of Burgos himself.

Naturally, apostasy was not always motivated by debased considerations, the historical situation, or meditations of this nature. The autobiography of an apostate of the first half of the 12th century (*Hermannus quondam Judaeus, opusculum de conversione sua,* ed. by G. Niemeyer, 1963) demonstrates the effect of gradual absorption of Christian ideas and acclimatization to the

Christian mode of life through everyday contacts and conversation. It brought the author, Judah ha-Levi of Cologne, to convert to Christianity and become a Premonstratensian monk.

In the Islamic environment the problems were much the same; some apostates attained prominent positions in Islamic states and society, the outer expressions of tension caused by apostasy being on a smaller scale. In the perpetual conflict and tensions that existed between Jews and Christians in medieval Europe, conversion from one faith to another, although rare, was still more frequent than either side cared to admit clearly. Thus, on the occasion of a halakhic deliberation in the 12th century, the talmudist Jacob b. Meir Tam reported: "More than 20 letters of divorce from apostates have been written in Paris and France . . . and also in Lorraine . . . I have also seen myself the letter of divorce given by the son-in-law of the late noble R. Jacob the Parnas who has apostatized" (*Sefer ha-Yashar,* ed. by S. Rosenthal (1898), 45, no. 25).

Some apostates founded influential families whose Jewish origin was well known among Christians, such as the Pierleoni family in Rome, the patrician Jud family in Cologne, and the Jozefowicz family in Poland-Lithuania. Certainly not all apostates from Judaism attempted to injure their brethren. When a number of apostates were asked in 1236 whether there was truth in the blood libel, they denied it categorically. Prominent among the apostates who deliberately set out to attack Judaism were Nicholas Donin in France, Pablo Christiani, and Hieronymus de Sancta Fide (Joshua Lorki) in Spain, and Petrus Nigri (Schwarz) in Germany. These in the 13th to 15th centuries led the attack on Judaism in the theological disputations, preached against Judaism, and proposed coercive measures to force Jews to adopt Christianity. Other converts who achieved high rank in the church, like Pablo de Santa Maria (Solomon ha-Levi), who became archbishop of Burgos, did everything in their power to combat Judaism. The most virulent representative of anti-Jewish animus was Abner of Burgos, who initiated the intensified persecution of the Jews in Christian Spain during the 14th and 15th centuries by formulating a complete theory which subsumes the necessity for, and justification of, such persecution. He advised the abolition of Jewish autonomy, arguing with vicious irony that the Messiah would not come to the Jews "until the Jews possess no authority, not even such petty authority as is exercised over them by their rabbis and communal wardens, those coarse creatures who lord it over the people like kings. They hold out vain promises to them in order to keep them under constant control. Only with the elimination of these dignitaries and judges and officers will salvation come to the masses" (polemical tract, Baer, *op. cit.,* 350). In the name of "many discerning Jews," Abner blamed the pope and Christian monarchs for failing to oppress the Jews adequately. The conditions of salvation for the Jews would come only "when many Jewish communities are massacred and the particular generation of Jews is thereby reduced in numbers, some Jews immediately convert to the dominant Christian faith out of fear, and in that way a handful are saved . . . and the pain of impoverishment will lead to an increase of shamelessness among them, that is, they will no longer be ashamed to profess the truth openly and convert to Christianity" (Baer, *op. cit.*, 353–4). By this means this apostate tried to reinforce his own experience of Jewish weakness and convert it into a terrible reality that would force many more Jews to relinguish their faith.

At the time of the expulsions from Spain and Portugal at the end of the 15th century, a sharp distinction was made by Jews between the renegade apostates, whom they considered an evil and the root cause of the wave of persecutions, and the mass of forced converts, the *anusim* or Marranos, whom they still regarded as brethren, though obliged to practice Judaism clandestinely. However, in realization, the program promoted by Abner of Burgos and others like him created a strong revulsion in Christian society against both the Marranos and genuine converts alike. Political events and social attitudes in Christian Spain in the 15th to 16th centuries fomented the concept whereby the "New Christians" were not to be equated with, and trusted as, the "Old Christians" of "pure Christian blood." Thus it could happen that the second general of the Jesuit order, Diego Lainez, had to face opposition within the order because of his Jewish blood.

In the Renaissance and Reformation environment apostasy occurred in various circumstances. One type of apostasy was the rootless intellectual like Flavius Mithridates, a translator from Hebrew and an influential expositor of Hebrew works. Others were led to convert to Christianity by their superficial contacts with Renaissance circles and the new importance attached by humanists like Johannes Reuchlin and Pico della Mirandola to learning Hebrew from Jewish teachers. The impoverished conditions of late medieval Germany gave rise to the opportunist who could change over at least three times from Judaism to Christianity and back again, and who on one occasion of reconversion quoted a proverb he had heard: *"lasse dich taufen, ich will dir vil Gulden schaffen"* ("Become baptized: I will get you plenty of money"; R. Strauss, *Urkunden und Altenstuecke zur Geschichte der Juden in Regensburg* (1960), 64–66). The basic attitude of both Jews and Christians toward apostates did not change with the Reformation. Many of the teachers of Hebrew to Christians were Jews, most of them apostates. They also cooperated in bringing out Reformation translations of the Bible. In his later days Martin Luther displayed marked distrust of apostates from Judaism. The attacks on the Talmud made by Johann

Pfefferkorn[1] on the eve of the Reformation and the denunciation poured by Anton Margarita[2] on Jewish ritual practices and way of life continued in new circumstances the tradition of virulent anti-Jewish hatemongering by apostates.

The stimulus provided by the 18th-century Enlightenment, stirrings toward assimilation on the cultural and social plane, and aspirations to attain Emancipation, inaugurated a trend toward apostasy in the upper circles of Jewish society in Central and Western Europe. A number of Jews opted for Christianity as the basis of European culture and its most sublime expression, despising their Jewish background and traditional way of life as debased and degraded. Others considered apostasy the most facile and ready way of attaining civil equality as an individual before the Jews as such had achieved emancipation. Moses Mendelssohn was publicly challenged to become converted if he did not refute the testimony advanced in proof of Christianity. David Friedlaender[3] proposed in the name of several "Jewish heads of families" to be permitted to accept Christianity without having to subscribe to its "historical dogmas." Jews also left Judaism because they did not find communal obligations or activity to their taste.

The English writer Isaac D'Israeli stated in 1813 to the board of the Bevis Marks congregation in London, as a reason for his refusal to act as warden, that he was "a person who has always lived out of the sphere of your observation; of retired habits of life; who can never unite in your public worship, because, as now conducted, it disturbs, instead of exciting, religious emotions, a circumstance of general acknowledgment; who has only tolerated some part of your ritual, willing to concede all he can in those matters which he holds to be indifferent" (see also p. 80). This indifference led him to baptize his son Benjamin in 1817 while formally remaining a Jew himself, a path taken by many others of a similar frame of mind who had their children baptized at the end of the 18th and beginning of the 19th centuries. The attitude of indifference was reinforced by the view that relegated religion to the status of an element in the universal culture or a cell in the social structure.

From the second half of the 18th century the ties linking the individual with the social unit became loosened in the upper strata of European society. Jews then increasingly absorbed the culture and adopted the language of their

---

1   Apostate from Judaism in Germany (1496–after 1521) and calumniator of Judaism and the Talmud.
2   Apostate from Judaism, born c. 1490; in writings he derides Jewish life and rites.
3   Radical Jewish Enlightenment theoretician and leader (1750–1834); was prepared at one stage to embrace Christianity in return for political rights, if he would be permitted to subscribe to its "eternal truths" only and not to its "historical truths."

environment. Baptism was submitted as the visiting card demanded by Christian society for its price of admission. Many able young Jewish intellectuals, among them men outstanding in their field like the jurist Eduard Gans, the author Ludwig Boerne, and the poet Heinrich Heine, who had first wanted to use their creative activity in the Jewish framework, left Judaism to be able to work within, and contribute to, European culture and society. In some communities, such as Berlin, more than half of the descendants of the patrician Jewish families adopted Christianity, including the Mendelssohn family. The majority of these did not claim to be drawn by an essential attraction to Christianity or act under rigorous pressure. Apostasy was regarded as a social formality performed for the sake of culture, society, or career. Many of the sensitive among them bitterly regretted their action. Much of Heinrich Heine's work is dominated by a pervasive longing for Judaism, and a biting irony against himself and his fellow apostates, their snobbery and social climbing by means of Christianity.

Karl Marx, baptized as a child, later professed contempt for and revulsion against Judaism as the representative of Mammon. In his Christian environment Benjamin Disraeli developed a kind of pride in what he considered the destiny and genius of the Jewish "race." The heroine of his novel *Tancred,* Eva, sarcastically asks Tancred: "Pray are you of those Franks who worship a Jewess; or of those others who revile her, break her images, and blaspheme her pictures?" When the Christian refers to the punishment of the Jews for crucifying Jesus, Disraeli's Jewess answers with the ancient argument used by Jews in disputations: "Suppose the Jews had not prevailed upon the Romans to crucify Jesus, what would have become of the Atonement?" When the Christian answers that the Crucifixion was preordained, " 'Ah,' said the lady, 'preordained by the creator of the World for countless ages! Where then was the inexpiable crime of those who fulfilled the beneficent intention? The holy race supplied the victim and the immolators . . . Persecute us! Why if you believed what you profess, you should kneel to us! You raise statues to the hero who saves a country. We have saved the human race, and you persecute us for doing it.' "

Benjamin Disraeli was representative of a group of apostates who considered themselves deeply Christian in a mythical and social sense and in consequence Jewish in a racial and spiritual sense. In the 19th century they were often active in missions to the Jews, like Bishop Michael Solomon Alexander in Jerusalem, while at the same time being very responsive to Zionism and its aspirations.

With the granting of emancipation to Jews in most of Western and Central Europe the brutal social pressure for the "visiting card of baptism" moderated. On the other hand, many Jewish scholars and scientists, in particular in Germany and Austria, became baptized for the sake of a university career, which was usually closed to a professing Jew. Some deeply committed apostates like the

Ratisbonne brothers in the 19th century founded special religious orders or groups for the propagation of Christianity among Jews. According to statistics available there were 21,000 apostates in Poland in the 18th century, and 204,500 throughout the world in the 19th. However these figures are exaggerated since they include the Frankists in Poland and the Cantonists in Russia.

In czarist Russia, up to 1917, there was relentless pressure for social acceptance through baptism. However, Jewish social and moral cohesion was strong and undeniable, and to a certain degree the Jewish cultural level was superior to that of the surrounding population. Here apostasy of a different type developed: people who accepted Christianity for the sake of a government or university career (a number of apostates were employed for censorship of Hebrew books) but still retained their ties with Jewish society, and a pride in their Jewish origin, like the orientalist Daniel Chwolson. Apostates like Jacob Brafman[4], however, did much to bring discredit on the institutions of Jewish self-government and to provide fuel for anti-Semitism.

In the 20th century the phenomenon of apostasy has become more complex, with deeper implications. While its effects are more subversive for Judaism, it arouses problems of Jewish nationality and culture which were less prominent previously. Boris Pasternak is representative of the type of apostate who left Judaism because he rebelled against historical and social realities and obligations. After describing the beatings and humiliations to which the Jews were subjected by the Cossacks of the Christian Russian army in his novel *Dr. Zhivago,* he states concerning the incident he has described, "that, and other incidents like it — of course none of that is worth theorizing about." Having disposed of pogroms and anti-Semitism by refusing to face them on the intellectual level, he continues that, in regard to "the Jewish question as a whole — there philosophy does enter." The philosophy he perceived — his theory was formulated when World War II was raging and the Jewish people was being systematically destroyed in the Holocaust — was that Jewish history is a self-inflicted punishment through refusal to heed that in "this new way of life and of communion, which is born of the heart and is called the Kingdom of God, there are no nations, only persons." Having denied the existence of the question of nations and nationality around the year 1941, Pasternak goes on to accuse "the ordinary run of politicians" who like to have "a nicely restricted group" so that they can deliberate and continue "settling and deciding and getting pity to pay dividends. Well now, what more perfect example can you have of the victims of the mentality than the Jews? Their national idea has forced them, century after century, to be a people and

---

4   Apostate from Judaism in Russia in the 19th century; attacked Jewish self-government.

nothing but a people — and the extraordinary thing is that they have been chained to this deadening task all through the centuries when all the rest of the world was being delivered from it by a new force which had come out of their own midst ... In whose interests is this voluntary martyrdom? ... Why don't the intellectual leaders of the Jewish people ever get beyond facile *Weltschmerz* and irony? Why don't they — even if they have to burst like a boiler with the pressure of their duty — dismiss this army which is forever fighting and being massacred, nobody knows for what? Why don't they say to them: 'That's enough, stop now. Don't hold on to your identity, don't all get together in a crowd. Disperse. Be with all the rest. You are the first and best Christians in the world. You are the very thing against which you have been turned by the worst and weakest among you' " (*Dr. Zhivago* (1958), 116–8). Facile anti-Semitic allusions to the character of the Jewish intellectual, and his looking for gain, are mingled here with a self-righteous denial of Judaism as a religion and an imputation that nationalism is the original and abiding sin of Judaism. Pasternak's resentment toward the religion and community he has abjured is expressed in his poetry on the basis of ancient Pauline symbols, rejecting the "barrenness" of Judaism and substituting another tree for the fertile olive:

> "Near by stood a fig tree,
> Fruitless, nothing but branches and leaves. He said to it:
> 'What joy have I of you?
> Of what profit are you, standing there like a post?
>
> 'I thirst and hunger and you are barren,
> And meeting you is comfortless as granite.
> How untalented you are, and how disappointing!
> Such you shall remain till the end of time!'
>
> The doomed tree trembled
> Like a lightning conductor struck by lightning,
> And was consumed to ashes.
>
> If the leaves, branches, roots, trunk,
> Had been granted a moment of freedom,
> The laws of nature would have intervened.
> But a miracle is a miracle, a miracle is God" (*ibid.*, 497–8).

Like another apostate, Eugen Rosenstock-Huessy (see above, chap. 11), a German of the generation of World War I, Pasternak expresses a categorical and hostile repudiation of Jewish nationalism as the evil archetype of all forms of nationalism. Both men are typical of the modern apostate who joins Christianity as an individual, rejecting communal solidarity as an unwonted yoke, and repudiating Jewish historical continuity, yearning for a mystic penetration of their individuum with the suffering Christian God. In his attitude to Jewish nationalism, Pasternak displays a considerably greater hostility than his German fellow apostate, logical in a man who left Eastern European Jewry in a period of revolution, distress, and annihilation of order.

Another trend in apostasy from Judaism in its modern form is represented by Oswald Rufeisen, who as Brother Daniel entered the Carmelite order in 1945. Born in Poland in 1922, and in his youth an active Zionist, he worked in the wartime underground and saved Jews during the Holocaust. He became a Christian in 1942, but continued to consider himself a Jew. After he became a monk, he wrote to the Polish authorities applying for permission to leave Poland for Erez Israel: "I base this application on the ground of my belonging to the Jewish people, to which I continue to belong although I embraced the Catholic faith in 1942 and joined a monastic order in 1945. I have made this fact clear whenever and wherever it has been raised with me officially . . . I chose an Order and Chapter in Israel in consideration of the fact that I would receive the leave of my superiors to travel to the land for which I have yearned since my childhood when I was a member of the Zionist youth organization" (*High Court Application of Oswald Rufeisen v. The Minister of the Interior* (1963), 54–55). In 1962 Brother Daniel appealed to the Israel High Court to be recognized as a Jew under the terms of the Law of Return, which grants Jews settling in Israel automatic citizenship. This application raised the problem of "Who is a Jew?" in Israel in its full modern implications. For the majority, Judge Silberg refused his petition. The judge admitted that Brother Daniel was a Jew according to *halakhah,* but in rendering judgment stated that the Law of Return is not based on *halakhah* but on the Jewish national-historical consciousness and the ordinary secular meaning of the term "Jew" as understood by Jews. After referring to the "great psychological difficulty" facing the court due to the deep sympathy and sense of obligation felt for the petitioner, the spokesman for the majority stated: "I have reached the conclusion that what Brother Daniel is asking us to do is to erase the historical and sanctified significance of the term 'Jew' and to deny all the spiritual values for which our people were killed during various periods in our long dispersion. For us to comply with his request would mean to dim the luster and darken the glory of the martyrs who sanctified the Holy Name *[kiddush ha-Shem]* in the Middle Ages to the extent of making them quite unrecognizable; it would make our history lose its unbroken continuity and our people begin counting its days from the emancipation which followed the

French Revolution. A sacrifice such as this no one is entitled to ask of us, even one so meritorious as the petitioner before this court" (*ibid.*, 1—2). The court stated that in order to be declared a Jew from the point of view of the modern Jewish secular conception of Jewish nationality, adherence to the Jewish religion is not essential. At the same time apostasy to Christianity removes that person from this nationality.

Between the two wings representing current tendencies in apostasy exemplified by Pasternak and Rufeisen stands the middle-of-the-road attitude displayed by the Anglican bishop, Hugh Montefiore. The bishop acknowledges loyalty to the memory of his fathers and maintains contact with Anglo-Jewish society without adhering to his Jewish national identity. He and others like him would seem to continue in an attenuated form the attitude of Disraeli. On the other hand one wonders if in the hostile attitude to Israel of other apostates there is not the direct continuation of the medieval Jew-hating figure of the apostate.

The issues raised by the Rufeisen decision remain very much at the heart of public deliberation in Israel. Essentially the present time marks a return to the core of the historical Jewish position on unity of faith and nation and to consideration of the apostate from this standpoint. Shortly before the expulsion of the Jews from Spain, Isaac b. Moses Arama wrote that when "one of the gentile scholars, seeing that Jews were very eager for a letter of divorce to be given by an apostate and he refused . . . asked . . . 'Why do you want it from him? As he left his religion it would be proper for them to consider him as if he did not exist. Hence his wife should be considered a widow in every respect . . . ' The answer was: 'Apostasy cannot be of the essence but only accidental, meaning only a change of name or the street where he lives. He cannot change his essence, for he is a Jew . . . . , This answer is true according to our religion. This is the meaning of the saying of our Sages, 'Even if he has sinned, he remains of Israel' " (*Akedat Yizhak* (Venice, 1573), 258b no. 97, Ki-Teze). The Jewish sage adds that the Christian will not accept this definition since for him religion is the sole criterion. Prevailing halakhic opinion throughout the ages had always considered the apostate a Jew for all purposes of obligations, ties, and possibilities given to a Jew, but denying him some specific legal rights, in particular in the economic sphere, and in the performance of certain honorary or symbolic acts. In terms of conscience and consensus of opinion Jewish society regarded the apostate up to the 18th century as "dead," as proscribed from the Jewish community, considering him as the very essence of desertion and treason.

At the present time extreme individualism or mysticism are the main paths leading some people away from Judaism. Snobbery and careerism, missionary blandishments and promises, still play some role in bringing about apostasy, but this is diminishing. The passive attitude of the majority of believing Christians at the time of the Holocaust, and even more, the conception of many of the courageous minority who risked their lives to save Jews but insisted on "saving their souls" at the same time, often souls of children in their care, threw into relief the harsh and ugly implications in apostasy. The concept of a multi-religious Jewish nation now facing the people of the State of Israel is tied up with and intersected by the problems and phenomena of historical continuity, mutual toleration, and social cohesion of the unique concept of the people of Israel as "a kingdom of priests and a holy nation," forming the cohesive religio-national entity that has united Jews and carried their specific message through the ages.

ASSIMILATION

The sociocultural process in which the sense and consciousness of association with one national and cultural group changes to identification with another such group, so that the merged individual or group may partially or totally lose its original national identity, is termed assimilation. Assimilation can occur — and not only on the unconscious level — in primitive societies. It has been shown that even these societies have sometimes developed specific mechanisms to facilitate assimilation, e.g., adoption; mobilization, and absorption into the tribal fighting force; exogamic marriage; the client relationship between the tribal protector and members of another tribe. In more developed societies, where a stronger sense of cultural and historical identification has evolved, the mechanisms, as well as the automatic media of assimilation, become more complicated. The reaction of the assimilator group to the penetration of the assimilated increasingly enters the picture.

Various factors may combine to advance or hinder the assimilation process. Those actively contributing include the position of economic strength held by a group; the political advantages to be gained from adhesion or separation; acknowledged cultural superiority; changes in religious outlook and customs; the disintegration of one group living within another more cohesive group; the development of an "open society" by either group. Added to these are external factors, such as changes in the demographic pattern (mainly migration) or those wrought by revolution and revolutionary attitudes. Sociologists have described the man in process of assimilation as "the marginal man," both attracted and repelled by the social and cultural spheres in which he lives in a state of transition.

Within its environment in antiquity, as far as known, the Jewish national and social group mainly operated as the assimilator, aided by the attraction of monotheism and exerting the power of its social cohesion and state mechanism. During the period of the conquest of Erez Israel, Jewish society gradually absorbed many of the ethnic elements living there. The process continued well into the reigns of David and Solomon. While the prophets of the time deplored the cultural influence exerted by the assimilated group, they did not not reject the end results of the process. The isolated yet striking instance of Naaman the Syrian demonstrates the element of partial assimilation into Judaism. In Judaism the very concept of proselytism involves readiness on the part of the Jews to accept and assimilate a group or an individual prepared to adopt the religion and become assimilated. The attitude of Ezra and Nehemiah, who opposed the assimilation of other ethnic elements, did not prevail. Some of the Hasmonean rulers, John Hyrcanus and Alexander Yannai, adopted a clear-cut policy of forcible proselytization; the assimilation of the Idumeans was so complete that the last dynasty to rule the Jewish commonwealth in the Second Temple period was the Idumean house of Herod, and some of the most devoted fighters in the war against Rome were Idumeans. Both Jewish and external sources yield plentiful information about groups and individuals living within the Roman Empire that had totally or partially adopted Judaism and assimilated the Jewish way of life. According to some scholars, the large number of Jews in the later period of the Roman Empire was the result of the assimilation of the Phoenician diaspora into the Jewish communities. On the other hand, sources dating from as early as the reign of Antiochus Epiphanes (175–164 B.C.E.) mention the Hellenizers, a group wishing to accept the mode of life and culture of Hellenism. To some degree the path of early Pauline Christianity is viewed from the Jewish standpoint as a process of assimilation of the early Jewish Christian apostles and groups into the gentile ethnic identity and way of life.

In the course of Jewish history, processes that began as quasi-assimilatory were later transmuted to become hallmarks of continuing Jewish consciousness and identity. This applied to the adoption of the Greek language in the ancient period and of German and Spanish in the Middle Ages. As the alien language gained acceptance, it became not only a vehicle of Jewish cultural and religious creativity, but also gradually became converted into a specifically Jewish idiom and mark of Jewish identity that even formed barriers to later assimilation. Yiddish became the idiom of East European Jewry amid a Slavic linguistic environment, and hence of Jewish emigrants from this area in the Anglo-Saxon countries. Similarly the Spanish Jews carried their language of Castile with them after the expulsion from Spain, developing it into Ladino. During the Middle Ages the strength of Jewish cohesiveness was so powerful that only apostates from Judaism became assimilated into the adopted environment, and not always even then.

Assimilation has been a major centrifugal force in Jewish life since the second half of the 18th century. It became an element of increasing magnitude in Jewish thought and society and helped to mold a new image of the Jew in literature and art, in which the problems it posed were reflected. Various factors combined to create this situation. The Court Jews, their families, and social circle gradually, sometimes imperceptibly, assimilated the mores of the Christian court. The Enlightenment *(Haskalah)* movement was accompanied by a certain readiness on the part of groups of Christian and Jewish intellectuals to create an "open society." The grant of civic emancipation apparently premised that Jews could enter the emancipating society as equals if they relinquished their Jewish national cohesion. In rejecting the medieval system of corporation, the attitude of early capitalistic society militated against a continuance of Jewish autonomy and its institutions. Similarly, the dictates of the modern state, postulating observance of a single legal code and an undifferentiated legal status for its citizens, militated against Jewish judicial autonomy while assisting Jewish emancipation. All these elements hastened the assimilatory process. As members of the upper strata of Jewish society in Central and Western Europe became assimilated, they left their positions of leadership in the autonomous Jewish body, thereby weakening it further. Other Jews in less influential positions followed their example. Jewish intellectuals who accepted the values and criteria of the Enlightenment and Christian culture and society tended to regard the Jewish counterpart as barren and primitive. Their attitude became devastatingly critical. They measured the Jewish past and culture by alien and historically inimical standards.

The first wave of assimilation carried Jews toward the ahistoric society envisioned by the 18th-century Enlightenment, a society that would not insist on national or religious definitions. For some Jews, assimilation served as a shortcut to attaining individual emancipation and advancement, hence there were many nominal apostates like Heinrich Heine. Later, their admiration for the modern national state, a growing appreciation of the mores and social structure of the dominant nations, and the idea of progress combined to create the conception that the perpetuation of a Jewish national existence was obsolete. Such Jews also felt that they were guilty of intellectual and emotional dishonesty in cherishing Jewish messianic hopes. The evaluations, way of life, writings – both in German and in Hebrew – and influence of intellectuals like Moses Mendelssohn and David Friedlaender, although in fact they formulating no clear-cut theory of assimilation, furthered the tendency. Socialite assimilation in the salons of Berlin and Vienna, fostering freedom in thought and with their romantic attractions, drew both the gifted and the wealthy away from the Jewish fold to a humanistic, cosmopolitan, and Christian allegiance. The

German socialite Rahel Varnhagen-Levin saw her life vitiated by the blemish of
her Jewish descent. Moses Mendelssohn's daughter, Dorothea Schlegel, not only
left her faith but also developed the feeling of self-hatred typical of many
modern assimilated Jews. In 1802 she wrote to Friedrich Schleiermacher:

" . . . according to my own feeling, Protestant Christianity [is] much purer
and to be preferred to the Catholic one. Catholicism has for me too much
similarity to the old Judaism, which I greatly despise. Protestantism,
though, seems to me to be the total religion of Jesus and the religion of
civilization. In my heart I am completely, as far as I can understand from
the Bible, a Protestant."

The ideology of assimilation gained momentum in the first half of the 19th
century as it developed an eschatological message. This trend was part of the new
direction which assimilation took when projected on the intense nationalistic
society and state that prevailed in Europe with the romantic movement. The
former nexus between the Jewish people and its religion and law was rejected;
attempts were made to purge the Jewish religion of its nationalistic elements in
order to relieve individual Jews in dispersion of the sense of being an alien and
an exile. Instead of looking to Erez Israel for redemption, the assimilationists
stressed their attachment was to the land in which they and their forefathers had
lived for generations. Nevertheless Jewish identity would be preserved in a
redefinition as "Germans of Mosaic faith" or "Frenchmen of Mosaic faith," and
so on.

The desire for emancipation blended with the will for religious reform and
with revolutionary fervor for change at first in the liberal, and later in the
socialist sense. The "messiah" envisaged by Leopold Zunz[1] was civic and
political revolution in Germany and Europe, bearing on its wings freedom for
mankind and equality for Jews. Derision of the former Jewish messianic hopes
was intrinsic to burning faith in the new assimilationist form of existence. Thus
in 1848, the year of the "Spring of Nations," Jews of the ancient community of
Worms formulated the following program for religious reform, motivated by the
ideal of assimilation:

" . . . We have to aspire to truth and dignity in Divine worship, coordina-
tion between faith and life, to put away empty concepts and shape new
institutions for the spirit of Judaism. We must no longer utter prayers for

---

1   Lived 1794–1886; scholar and historian; among the founders of the Wissenschaft des
Judentums ("Science of Judaism") movement.

the return to Palestine while we are wholeheartedly attached to the German fatherland whose fate is indissolubly our fate; all that is beloved and dear to us is contained in this fatherland. We must not mourn in sackcloth and ashes the destruction of the Temple when we long ago came into the possession of a fatherland that has become so dear to us. We may commemorate yearly the destruction of the Temple, but why be in heavy mourning, which no longer comes from feelings of the heart, and sing songs of mourning about an historical fact, for which we praise the loving hand of God? We should not try to enlighten our children in the religious schools with facts that the living Jewish spirit looks upon as dead ballast, to be thrown overboard; no longer teach them to pray in a language that is dead, while the word and sound of our German mother tongue is understandable and dear to us and therefore is the only one fit to be raised in praise to our Creator. It is time to put a stop to this conflict, this sin of dishonesty in our midst."

Attachment to German soil, language, culture, and statehood was the compelling reason for effecting the change in prayer and its language, and for eradicating the hope for redemption in Erez Israel. This attitude continued to persist in some circles; it led the British Liberal rabbi Israel Mattuck in 1939 to the conclusion that "the position which the Jews should seek and the world should give is one which combines separatism in religion with assimilation in all the other elements of national life, political, social, and cultural" (*What are the Jews?* (1939), 239).

Assimilation through the 19th and 20th centuries was not a unified process and was beset with a host of problems and complications. The position taken by assimilationists oscillated between the cosmopolitan and nationalist aspects of assimilation. Their theories clashed with the national spirit of exclusiveness of the assimilator group: Germans, Frenchmen, and others, resented the pollution of their race and culture by alien elements. Jews wishing to assimilate became involved in the array of conflicting assimilating nationalities and cultures within the same territorial arena. With the national awakening of the Czechs, the Jews of Prague, for instance, were confronted simultaneously by German and Czech demands for assimilation into one or the other national camp. The same conflict occurred between the demands of the Magyar and German cultures in Hungary; the Polish, German, and Russian cultures in Polish lands; the German, Polish, and Ukrainian cultures in East Galicia. In many countries the process of assimilation was deliberately assisted by social and educational measures. In Russia, Nicholas I tried to promote assimilation of the Jewish youth through the mechanism of army mobilization, the so-called Cantonists. On the other hand the complications of the assimilation process itself necessarily acted to spur Jewish nationalism, and offered it a springboard. At the same time a school of historical thought that viewed each epoch and culture as a distinct phenomenon to be judged by its own system of values was gaining ascendancy. Thus, appreciation of the Jewish culture and history, achievements, values, and criteria strengthened, while the arrogance and ridicule on which the assimilationists based their arguments lost ground.

Assimilation into modern nationalities was described by Solomon Schechter[2] in 1901 upon viewing the disappointment that was felt when the concept of assimilation intrinsic to the hopes for a humanist, non-nationalistic society was definitively superseded by assimilation into different militarist, nationalist states. Schechter saw " . . . the ancient chosen people of God going about begging for a nationality — clamoring everywhere 'We are you!'. . . Using the last crumbs of the sacred language, in which God-Shalom addressed His children, to invoke His blessing upon the *'Mitrailleuse,'* the 'Krupp gun,' 'dum-dum' and 'Long Tom,' and other anti-messianic contrivances" ("Epistles to the Jews of England," in *Jewish Chronicle,* 1901). The disappointment at these developments in European society and the reaction that Jewish assimilation had provoked did not deter assimilationists from their beliefs. Even after World War II and the experience of the Holocaust, and after his disillusionment with the Communist revolution, Boris Pasternak clung to the Christian Orthodox faith and his Russian cultural identity. He dared to call upon Jews to assimilate as salvation from the fate which their nationality imposes. In the wake of the martyred Jews, he denied that there could be any sense in retaining a separate Jewish identity: "In whose interests is this voluntary martyrdom? . . . Dismiss this army which is forever fighting and being massacred, nobody knows for what? . . . Say to them: 'That's enough. Stop now. Don't hold on to your identity. Don't all get together in a crowd. Disperse. Be with all the rest' " (*Dr. Zhivago* (1958), 117–8).

When this call for assimilation was pronounced, several years had elapsed since the suicide of a man who wrote at the beginning of Nazi rule and the end of the liberal German society of the early 20th century:

"I thought of my terrible joy when I realized that nobody would recognize me for a Jew; of the first day of the war and my passionate longing to prove that I was a real German by offering my life to my country; of my writing from the front to the authorities to say that they could strike my name from the list of the Jewish community. Had it all been for nothing?

---

2   Lived 1847–1915; Rumanian-born rabbinic scholar who headed the Jewish Theological Seminary of America.

Had it all been wrong? Didn't I love Germany with all my heart? Had I not stood in the rich beauty of the Mediterranean landscape and longed for the austere pine woods, for the beauty of the still, secret lakes of north Germany? And wasn't the German language my language, the language in which I felt and thought and spoke, a part of my very being? But wasn't I also a Jew? A member of that great race that for centuries had been persecuted, harried, martyred and slain; whose prophets had called the world to righteousness, had exalted the wretched and the oppressed, then and for all time. A race who had never bowed their heads to their persecutors, who had preferred death to dishonor. I had denied my own mother, and I was ashamed. It is an indictment of society at large that a child should have thus been driven to deception. How much of me was German, how much Jewish? Must I then join the ranks of the bigoted and glorify my Jewish blood now, not my German? Pride and love are not the same thing, and if I were asked where I belonged I should answer that a Jewish mother had borne me, that Germany nourished me, that Europe had formed me, that my home was the earth and the world my fatherland" (Ernest Toller, *I Was a German* (1934), 280–2).

This anguished cry powerfully expresses the dynamics and problems that persisted after the doctrine of assimilation had been tested for over a century and a half. The assimilationist remained torn between his ideals and rejection by the assimilator society, between the allegiance he was seeking and the pride awakened by Jewish nationalism; he oscillated between the choice of assimilation into one nation and internationalist assimilation.

More recently the ideals of assimilation have assumed a different form. This has been determined by the combined impact of the Holocaust, the creation of the State of Israel and its struggle for survival, and the emergence of a monistic nationalism in Eastern and Central Europe. But if the advocates of assimilation have sometimes changed their formula, the substance of their arguments remains. This viewpoint clearly emerges in the evaluation of Jewish assimilation made by a philosopher of history hostile to Jewish nationalism, Arnold Toynbee. Toynbee regards assimilation and intermarriage as beneficial and a natural process. By assimilating, a Jew is "deserting the Diaspora individually in order to lose himself in the ranks of a modern, Western, gentile, urban bourgeoisie. The liberal Jew [is] ... assimilating himself to a gentile social milieu that had previously gone far, on its side, to assimilate itself socially and psychologically to the Jewish Diaspora" (*Study of History*, 8 (1954), 310). Nevertheless, in volume 12 of the same study, published in 1961, Toynbee describes the solution he proposed for the Jews in 1954 as the fate of the Ten

Tribes, who "lost their national identity through being assimilated . . . The Ten Tribes' way is passive, involuntary, and inglorious, and it is natural that the Jews should be on their guard against meeting the fate of their lost kinsmen." What he proposed in 1961 was that the Jews become "denationalized" without becoming totally assimilated. As an alternative to emigration to Israel he proposes that they "incorporate Gentiles in a Jewish religious community by converting them to the religion of Deutero-Isaiah" (p. 517). Thus, ideationally, the process has turned full circle. An opponent of Zionism and the creation of the State of Israel, Toynbee proposed to the Jews of the Diaspora in 1961 that they undertake the conversion of the peoples in their environment to a non-national Jewish religion. For all practical purposes, however, the goal is the same: the abolition of Jewish national identity.

BIBLIOGRAPHY

GENERAL

S.W. Baron, *Social and Religious History of the Jews*, vols. 2–3 (1959[2]), 1–14 (1957–69).

idem., *The Jewish Community, its History and Structure to the American Revolution*, 3 vols. (1942).

Y.F. Baer, *Galut* (1947).

L. Finkelstein (ed.), *The Jews* (1970–71[4]).

S. Grayzel, *A History of the Jews* (1953[2]).

S. Dubnow, *History of the Jews* (1967).

C. Roth, *A Short History of the Jewish People* (1938).

H.M. Sacher, *The Course of Modern Jewish History* (1958).

J. Bright, *A History of Israel* (1958).

World History of the Jewish People, 4 vols. (in prog.).

H. Graetz, *History of the Jews*, 6 vols. (1891–1902).

H.H. Ben-Sasson (ed.), *Toledot Am Yisrael*, 3 vols. (1969).

B. Dinur, *Yisrael ba-Golah*, 2 vols. in 7 (1959–68).

H.H. Ben-Sasson and S. Ettinger (eds.), *Jewish Society through the Ages* (1972).

POLAND AND LITHUANIA

S. Dubnow, *History of the Jews in Russia and Poland*, 1 (1916).

H.H. Ben-Sasson, "The Personality of Elijah, Gaon of Vilna, and his Historical Influence." in: *Zion*, 31 (1966), 39–86, 197–216.

MESSIANIC MOVEMENTS

J. Klausner, *The Messianic Idea in Israel* (1955).

A.H. Silver, *A History of Messianic Speculation in Israel* (1959[2]).

G. Scholem, *Sabbatai Ṣevi* (1973).

HASIDEI ASHKENAZ

J. Dan, *Torat ha-Sod shel Ḥasidei Ashkenaz* (1967).

G. Scholem, "Hasidism in Mediaeval Germany," in: *Major Trends in Jewish Mysticism* (1955[3]).

H.H. Ben-Sasson, "The Distribution of Wealth and of Intellectual Abilities according to Ashkenazi Hasidim." in: *Zion*, 35 (1970), 61–79.

Y.F. Baer, "Theory of the Natural Equality of Early Man according to Ashkenazi Hasidim," in: *Zion*, 32 (1967), 129–36.

MUSAR MOVEMENT

Z.F. Ury, *Musar Movement* (1970).
D. Katz, *Tenu'at ha-Musar — Toledotehah, Ishehah ve-Shitotehah*, 5 vols. (1948–63³).

MAIMONIDEAN CONTROVERSY

D.J. Silver, *Maimonidean Criticism and the Maimonidean Controversy, 1180–1240* (1965).
J. Sarachek, *Faith and Reason: the Conflict over the Rationalism of Maimonides* (1935).

DISPUTATIONS

A.L. Williams, *Adversus Judaeos* (1935).
J.W. Parkes, *Conflict of the Church and the Synagogue* (1964²).
O.S. Rankin, *Jewish Religious Polemic . . .* (1956).
H.J. Schoeps, *Jewish-Christian Argument* (1963).

REFORMATION

H.H. Ben-Sasson, *The Reformation in Contemporary Jewish Eyes* (1970).

ANUSIM

C. Roth, *History of the Marranos* (repr. 1966).
C.H. Lea, *History of the Inquisition of Spain,* 4 vols. (repr. 1958).
H.A.F. Kamen, *The Spanish Inquisition* (c. 1967).

ILLUSTRATION CREDITS

New Haven, Conn., Yale University: p.4,
Jerusalem, Israel Museum: pp. 50, 138, 139, 153, 218, 221.
New York, Leo Baeck Institute: p.51.
Jerusalem, Jewish National and University Library, Schwadron Collection: p. 52.
Courtesy Association Consistorial Israélite de Paris: p. 69.
New York, Dan Friedenberg Collection: p.86.
Cecil Roth Collection: p.92.
H. Hapgood, *The Spirit of the Ghetto*, Rishin ed. Belknap Press of Harvard University Press, 1967: p. 93.
Tel Aviv, Haganah Historical Archives: p. 107.
Jerusalem, Keren Hayesod, United Israel Appeal Photo Archives: p. 113.
Jerusalem, Yad Vashem Archives: p. 116.
Photo David Harris, Jerusalem: p. 125.
New York, Jewish Theological Seminary, Ms. Mic. 8279 fol. 15 v. Photo Frank J. Darmstaedter, New York: p. 142.
Jerusalem, Central Archive for the History of the Jewish People (CAHJP): p. 145.
En Harod, Mishkan le-Omanut: p. 177.
Jerusalem, Yad Vashem Archives, Y.D. Kamson Collection: p. 183.
After I. Halperin *Pinkas Va'ad Arba Arazot* (1945): p. 185.
Hamburg, Staats- und Universitaetsbibliothek, Cod. Heb. 37: p. 214.
Cambridge, Mass., Harvard University, Houghton Library: p. 249.
Trier, Bischoefliches Museum: p. 281.
Madrid, Prado Museum: p. 296.

INDEX

Aaronsohn, Aaron, 109
Abbas II, 297
Abenaes, Solomon, 51
Abner of Burgos, 271, 299–301
Abraham ben Eliezer ha-Levi, 207, 213
    274, 287, 289–90
Abraham ben Moses ben Maimon, 238
Abraham of Béziers, 41
Abulafia, Meir ben Todros ha-Levi, 233–4
Academies, 8, 18–22, 231–2
Adret, Solomon ben Abraham, 41, 206,
    230, 239–40
Agnon, Shemuel Yosef, 103, 115
Agobard, 17, 23, 266
Agriculture, 3–6, 13–5, 79, 101, 106,
    112, 131, 150, 156
Agudat Israel, 102, 111, 195
Aḥad Ha-Am, 106, 251
Ahimaaz chronicle, 17, 22, 268
Ahl al-Dhimma, see Dhimmt
Ahl al-Kitāb, 13, 15
Albert Achill of Brandenburg, 33
Albigenses, 269
Albo, Joseph, 172, 258, 271
Alconstantini family, 36
Alexander I, 74
Alexander II, 79
Alexander, Michael Solomon, 303
Alexander Suslin ha-Kohen, 136
Alfasi, Isaac ben Jacob, 23
Algeria, 70
Al-Ḥākim bi-Amr Allah, 15–6
Alkalai, Judah, 88
Alliance Israélite Universelle, 84, 101
Al-Maghribī, Samuel, 269
Almohads, 29, 38, 202, 270, 295
Alroy, David, 202–3
Alsace-Lorraine, 65, 68–9, 76, 136–7, 254
Alterman, Nathan, 115
Ambrose of Milan, 8

American Council for Judaism, 103
American Jewish Joint Distribution
    Committee, 102
Anan ben David, 20–1
Anatoli, Jacob, 41
Anglo-Jewish Association, 84
Anti-Defamation League, 101
Antiochus IV Epiphanes, 209, 243, 298,
    309
Anti-Semitism, 5, 28–30, 32, 63, 70, 84,
    86, 91, 95–6, 98–101, 104–5, 110,
    118–20, 124–5, 130–2, 135–7, 157,
    161, 250, 255, 278, 280, 282, 287,
    292, 304–5
Anusim, 205, 212–3, 293–7, 301
Apion, 243, 245
Apostasy, 5, 10, 11, 29, 34, 39, 48, 68,
    75, 89, 131, 166, 264, 269–72, 288,
    293, 298–308
Arabia, 9
Arabs, 9, 13, 111–4, 119, 121–5, 200
Arama, Isaac, 307
Arbeter Farband, 81
Archisynagogus, 268
Arenda, 157–9, 164–5, 190
Argentina, 94, 101
Arianism, 5, 10
Armleder massacres, 136, 254
Art, 4, 5, 27, 103, 267, 281–2
Asch, Sholem, 115
Asher ben Jehiel, 41, 46, 230, 239
Ashkenaz, Ashkenazim, 22, 24–5, 38, 41,
    45–7, 53, 55, 65, 70, 78, 88, 116,
    140, 144, 160, 162–3, 205, 213,
    217–24
Ashkenazi, Eliezer, 162
Ashkenazi, Solomon, 51
Assembly of Jewish Notables, 69
Assimilation, 71, 77, 79, 80, 82–6,
    88–90, 96, 105, 124, 166, 278, 308–15

TRIAL AND ACHIEVEMENT
Currents in Jewish History

Most of the problems facing the Jews today are not new to those familiar with Jewish history. The framework is now contemporary but the basic challenges have recurred under different guises throughout the ages. Assimilation, anti-Semitism, community organization, relations of a minority to a majority culture are all examples of the centuries-old Jewish struggle for survival that at present remain very relevant.

It is in this context that one of the outstanding Jewish historians of today, Prof. Haim Hillel Ben-Sasson of the Hebrew University, Jerusalem, has written this survey of Jewish history. He has brought together the political, religious, social, and economic threads to present an overview of Jewish history over the past sixteen centuries infused with topicality and meaning for the reader today.